Welcome to

McGraw-Hill's
Praxis I and II

Congratulations! You have chosen the Praxis guide from America's leading educational publisher. You probably know us from many of the textbooks you used in school and college. Now we're ready to help you take the next step — and become a licensed teacher.

This book gives you everything you need to succeed on the Praxis test. You will get in-depth instruction and review of every topic tested, tips and strategies for every question type, and plenty of practice exams to boost your test-taking confidence. To get started, go to the following pages where you'll find:

- **How to Use This Book:** Step-by-step instructions to help you get the most out of your test-prep program.

- **50 Fast Tips for Test Day:** The most important things you need to know to get a top score.

- **The 10 Most Common Praxis Writing Topics:** a preview of the kinds of writing prompts you're most likely to encounter on test day.

- **Praxis Writing Checklist:** Handy tips to help you evaluate your practice PPST essays.

ABOUT THE AUTHOR Dr. Laurie Rozakis taught high school for more than a decade and is now a full professor of English and Humanities in the State University of New York. A master teacher, Dr. Rozakis was awarded the highly prestigious New York State Chancellor's Award for Excellence in Teaching.

ABOUT McGRAW-HILL EDUCATION

This book has been created by a unit of McGraw-Hill Education, a division of The McGraw-Hill Companies. McGraw-Hill Education is a leading global provider of instructional, assessment, and reference materials in both print and digital form. McGraw-Hill Education has offices in 33 countries and publishes in more than 65 languages. With a broad range of products and services — from traditional textbooks to the latest in online and multimedia learning — we engage, stimulate, and empower students and professionals of all ages, helping them meet the increasing challenges of the 21st century knowledge economy.

Learn more. Do more.

How to Use This Book

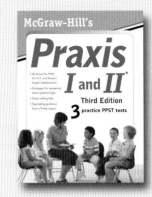

You lead a hectic life. Most likely you're in school and perhaps even working at the same time. You want to devote a lot of time to studying for the Praxis, but you just don't have the time to do so. As a result, you need to make the most of the study time that you do have. You need a book and a study plan that work for you.

There are many different ways to approach a test review book. As a result, it's not as easy as it might appear to know how to use this book to your best advantage. We've designed this book to make it as easy for you as possible to earn your highest possible score on the Praxis. Follow these guidelines to make the most of your study time.

1 Read This Section
This section gives you hands-on advice for doing your best on this all-important test. The advice in this part of the book will help you get your studying off to a great start no matter which Praxis tests you take.

2 Read *Chapter 1: The Ten-Step Power Study Plan*
Follow the suggestions described in this section. For instance, set up a personal study center, choose a test strategy, and set up a study routine. Familiarize yourself with the Praxis test, too, and boost your reading comprehension by reading high-quality novels and nonfiction for pleasure. Be especially vigilant about dealing with any special needs that you may have, as described in Step 8. By the time you finish reading this section, you'll have the tools you need to power up your studying.

3 Take the Three Diagnostic Pretests in Part 2
Take these tests under the exact test conditions you will have on the day of the Praxis. Sit in a quiet room and time yourself. Be sure to use only the amount of time you are allocated for each section. Then analyze the results to determine your strengths and weaknesses. List these so you know where to spend the most time as you study.

4 Review Parts 3 through 6
Here's where you'll fill in the gaps in your knowledge. As you read these sections, refer to the list of your strengths and weaknesses. Use this analysis to decide how to allocate your time. Spend the most time on the areas in which you are most deficient and the least time on the areas where you are proficient.

5 Complete Part 7, the Practice Tests
Take the practice tests one at a time. After each practice test, carefully analyze the questions you missed. Go back to the book and review the sections that cover these topics before you move on to another practice test. Always focus on the topics that will gain you the most points.

6 Go Over *50 Fast Tips for Test Day*
On the day of the Praxis exam, review *50 Fast Tips for Test Day*. Not only will these suggestions help boost your score, but they will also help you relax. You'll feel fully equipped to do your very best on the Praxis.

50 Fast Tips for Test Day

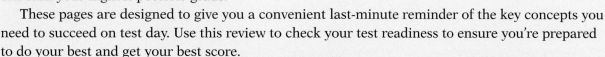

Three, two, one…The countdown is over and it is test day! You know that you are well-prepared because you have read this book, completed all the exercises, and worked through the practice tests. You have checked your answers and reviewed the most challenging concepts, too. Now is the time to put the final polish on your preparations to take Praxis I or II. The best way to do that is to study these 50 Fast Tips. They are designed to help you identify the key elements to remember as you take Praxis I or II so you can earn your highest possible grade.

These pages are designed to give you a convenient last-minute reminder of the key concepts you need to succeed on test day. Use this review to check your test readiness to ensure you're prepared to do your best and get your best score.

Overall Test-Taking Tips

Here are some useful tips to help you maximize your Praxis I or II score on test day.

USE THE TEST-TAKING SKILLS YOU HAVE LEARNED FROM THIS BOOK

1 Have a test strategy. Since you can complete the test in any order you wish, decide beforehand how you will attack the questions. As you learned in this book, you can work from the beginning of the test to the end, but you might just as well decide to complete all the easiest questions first and then return to the more difficult ones. Select the strategy that works best for you, the one that you have practiced while taking the sample tests in this book.

2 Make notes. If you are taking the paper-and-pencil version, write in your test booklet. Underline main ideas and key points, do calculations, make notes, and so on.

3 Use process of elimination. Always try to cross out incorrect choices. The more choices you can eliminate, the better your chances of choosing the right answer. This is especially important if you have to guess. Remember that there is no penalty for guessing, so don't leave any answers blank.

4 Double-check your work. If you are taking the paper-and-pencil version, be sure to bubble in the correct choices.

5 For the computerized version. Take advantage of the computer tutorial that is offered before you begin the actual test. At any point during the test, you may return to the tutorial by clicking your mouse on the "HELP" box at the bottom of the screen. Also be aware of scroll bars. Some images and text are too big to fit on your screen and require you to scroll down to view them.

PACE YOURSELF

6 Watch the time. Be sure to bring a watch. Don't count on the test room having a clock. If you take the computer version of Praxis I, there is a clock on the screen, but you should still bring a watch. You will NOT be able to use your cell phone as your watch.

7 **Stick to your plan.** Decide beforehand how much time to allot for each test question, and stick to your plan. Remember that on average, you should allow no more than 90 seconds per question.

8 **Stay on track.** Don't get stuck on any one question; if you can't answer a question, leave it and move on.

9 **Stay focused.** Ignore how quickly or slowly other test-takers are working.

10 **Check your work.** Be sure to leave time to check your answers.

STAY COOL

11 **Reread.** The questions on Praxis I and II are designed to be clear, not tricky. If a question seems confusing, read it again.

12 **Don't second-guess yourself.** Doing so can make you feel tense.

13 **Don't look for traps.** Remember that the test does not contain trick questions.

14 **Use relaxation techniques.** If you feel yourself tensing up, take a few deep breaths and visualize a peaceful scene. Then return to the test.

15 **Stay calm.** Even if you're having a hard time answering the questions, keep cool. Recall that you don't have to answer all of the questions correctly to get a good score.

Tips for the Praxis I Reading Test

16 **Read the passage first.** Read it thoroughly and carefully, all the way through.

17 **Identify the main idea and key details.** If you are taking the pencil-and-paper version of the test, underline these or mark them in some other way.

18 **Predict the answers.** Read each question in turn. Cover the answer choices and predict each answer. Then look at the choices to find which one (if any) matches. Chances are good that the answer you predicted will be correct.

19 **Refer to the passage to check your answers.**

20 **Use strategy.** If you can't find the answer, use process of elimination. Then skim the passage to find information you need to find literal details or make inferences.

21 **Categorize.** If you are having difficulty answering a question, try to identify it as a literal detail or making inference question. Then you will know whether you can find the actual fact you need or if you'll have to draw a conclusion from stated and unstated information.

22 **Use ONLY the information contained in the passage.** Do not use information that you already know.

23 **Paraphrase.** Put difficult questions and answer choices into your own words to make them easier to understand.

24 **Don't get sidetracked by unfamiliar words.** Chances are they are not critical to your understanding. If you do need to define the word, use context clues as well as roots, prefixes, and suffixes to figure out what unfamiliar words mean.

25 **Work in sections.** Try to complete every question in a reading set, even if you have to make an educated guess. You will lose a lot of time if you have to go back and reread the passage to answer one or two questions.

Tips for the Praxis I Writing Test

USAGE QUESTIONS

26 **Know the format.** These questions have four underlined parts; the fifth choice (E) is always "No error."

27 **Be thorough.** Even if you think you have identified the answer early on, read the sentence all the way through.

28 **Know which changes to make.** When you find an error in an underlined part, you can delete it, change its form (such as tense or spelling), replace it, or add a mark of punctuation.

29 **Keep it simple.** If you have to guess, keep it simple. Go for the answer that creates the most direct, least complex and convoluted sentence.

SENTENCE CORRECTION QUESTIONS

30 **Know the format.** These questions have one underlined part. The first choice (A) will always repeat the original part; the other four choices offer different revisions.

31 **Read the sentence all the way through.** Even if you think you have figured out the answer immediately, read the entire sentence.

32 **Read the sentence "aloud."** Of course, do this in your head so you don't disturb other test-takers. Often, "hearing" the sentence can help you figure out the answer.

33 **Make predictions.** Cover the answers, predict the correction, and then look for your revision among the answer choices.

34 **Avoid traps.** If you can't find your choice, use process of elimination. Length is not a good predictor of correctness: a long answer may be better than a short one, and vice-versa. As a result, have a reason for your choice. (See tip #35 for reasons.)

35 **Consider the basics.** The test-makers go for the most common sentence errors rather than esoteric writing problems. As a result, look for problems with sentence boundaries (run-ons and fragments), parallel structure, pronoun case ("who" and "whom," for instance), pronoun reference, agreement of subject and verb, agreement of pronoun and antecedent, degree of comparison, misplaced and dangling modifiers, and so on.

36 **Make predictions.** Predict the correction and then look for your revision among the answer choices.

37 **Avoid traps.** If you can't find your choice, use process of elimination. Length is not a good predictor of correctness: a long answer may be better than a short one, and vice-versa, so go for logic rather than length.

38 **Look for logic.** Your choice must be logical and fit with the rest of the sentence as well as grammatically correct.

THE ESSAY

39 **Stay on topic.** You must address the specific topic, not a topic of your own choice. No matter how well-written your essay, you will not receive any credit if it is off topic. Always choose the position that you can most strongly support.

40 **Start with a topic sentence.** State your position in the first paragraph, organize your ideas clearly, and use ample specific details and examples. Follow the rules of standard written English and be sure to leave sufficient time to proofread your essay.

Tips for the Praxis I Math Test

41 **Do a "memory dump."** Jot down key formulas when you begin working on this part of Praxis I and II. Even if you don't use these formulas, having written them down will give you confidence.

42 **Check the operation.** Make sure you do the correct operation, such as addition or subtraction. Look for key words such as *sum, more than, increased* (addition) and *minus, difference,* and *less than* (subtraction).

43 **Draw a picture on your scratch paper.** This will help you visualize the problem. Also create a number line to help you visualize and figure out "less than" and "greater than." This strategy is especially helpful for word problems.

44 **Base your response only the data given.** Do not include any outside information you may have.

45 **Make a number line.** Remember that negative numbers have less value than positive numbers.

46 **Consider working backwards.** To do so, start with the possible answers and work backward through the problem. This technique is especially helpful with algebra-based problems, where you are trying to find a variable. Use each possible answer choice in place of the variable to see which one works.

47 **Estimate the answer.** This will help you to make sure that your conclusion is reasonable.

48 **Consider charts.** Do not let a chart or graph daunt you. Figure out what the data mean before you look at the question and the answer choices.

49 **Make educated guesses.** Do so after you have used process of elimination.

50 **Check your calculations.**

The 10 Most Common Praxis Writing Topics

To earn your best possible score on the PPST: Writing Test essay, you must know what to expect. Although you can't know exactly what writing prompt will be on your exam, you *can* familiarize yourself with the kinds of prompts that have appeared on previous tests. The following list shows the ten most common types of PPST: Writing Test essay prompts, based on prior exams.

Try writing at least one multiple-paragraph essay for each of the prompts below. Organize your ideas logically and include examples and clear explanations. When you have completed each essay, use the checklist on the next page to evaluate your efforts.

1. Success and Goals

Erma Bombeck once said: "Don't confuse fame with success. Madonna is one; Helen Keller is the other." Define "success" and explain what you hope to achieve that will make you a success.

2. Values

The United States should remain an island of plenty in a sea of hunger. The future of humanity is at stake. We are not responsible for the rest of the world. Agree or disagree.

3. Government and Laws

To date, eighteen states and the District of Columbia have banned text messaging for all drivers. Texting while driving should be illegal in the entire United States. Agree or disagree.

4. Education and Educational Reform

Same-sex schools provide a better education than co-ed schools. Take a stand on this issue and argue your point with specific examples and details.

5. Personal Responsibility

Athletes have an enormous influence on children. As a result, they have a responsibility to act as positive role models. Agree or disagree.

6. Technology

Television is more interesting and educational than most people. Agree or disagree.

7. Multiculturalism

Currently, the United States does not have an "official" language, although English is generally accepted. English should be the official U.S. language. Agree or disagree.

8. Maturity

All students should be required to take a year off between high school and college, a "gap year," to work and assess their future plans. Take a stand on this issue and argue your point with specific examples and details.

9. Censorship

The Internet should be censored, its objectionable content filtered, to protect everyone, but especially children. Take a stand for or against censoring the Internet. Persuade your readers by using convincing evidence.

10. The Influence of Society on the Individual

Everyone is influenced in significant ways—both good and bad—by the area in which they grow up. Agree or disagree with this statement. Convince your audience by using specific evidence.

Praxis Writing Checklist

Use this checklist to evaluate your practice essays on the **PPST: Writing Test**.

Overall: Did I...

___ take a clear and logical side of the argument?
___ clearly state my thesis in the opening paragraph?
___ include the opposition but show that my view has more merit?
___ end with a strong conclusion that sums up my main points and makes my case?

Organization: Did I...

___ organize my ideas in a logical way?
___ present the opposition first and then argue my side?
___ make my method of organization clear?
___ link related ideas with parallelism, transitions, and repetition of key words?

Logic: Did I...

___ back up my opinions with facts, statistics, and expert opinions?
___ use specific and correct information?
___ analyze cause and effect correctly?
___ make sense?

Diction: Did I...

___ correctly understand the connotation of the words I selected?
___ use diction appropriate to my audience?

___ use nonbiased language?
___ use idioms and idiomatic phrases correctly?
___ use Standard Written English, not substandard usage?

Grammar: Did I...

___ write complete and correct sentences? Did I check for run-ons and fragments?
___ make sure that all verbs agree with their subjects and pronouns with their antecedents?
___ use the active voice to make my writing more direct and effective?
___ correct misplaced and dangling modifiers?

Style: Did I...

___ begin my essay in a compelling way, such as with an interesting fact or anecdote?
___ use the correct word, not its close cousin?
___ use vivid words, especially verbs?
___ revise and edit to eliminate wordiness?
___ use a variety of sentence structures— including simple, compound, complex, and compound-complex sentences?

Mechanics: Did I...

___ use all end punctuation correctly? Did I avoid overusing exclamation marks?
___ use apostrophes correctly, especially with contractions?
___ spell every word correctly? If I wasn't sure how a word is spelled, did I substitute a correctly spelled synonym?
___ use commas, semi-colons, and colons correctly?
___ capitalize proper nouns?
___ proofread my essay and correct all careless errors?

McGraw-Hill's

Praxis I and II

McGraw-Hill's

Praxis I and II

Third Edition

Laurie Rozakis, Ph.D.

New York   Chicago   San Francisco   Lisbon   London   Madrid
Mexico City   Milan   New Delhi   San Juan   Seoul
Singapore   Sydney   Toronto

2 3 4 5 6 8 9 0   QDB/QDB   1 5 4 3 2

ISBN 978-0-07-171668-0
MHID 0-07-171668-8

McGraw-Hill books are available at special quantity discounts to use as premiums and sales promotions, or for use in corporate training programs. To contact a representative, please e-mail us at bulksales@mcgraw-hill.com.

ETS, PPST, and PRAXIS II are registered trademarks of Educational Testing Service (ETS). THE PRAXIS SERIES and PRAXIS are trademarks of ETS. ETS does not endorse and was not involved in the production of this product.

Product or brand names used in this book may be trade names or trademarks. Where we believe that there may be proprietary claims to such trade names or trademarks, the name has been used with an initial capital or it has been capitalized in the style used by the name claimant. Regardless of the capitalization used, all such names have been used in an editorial manner without any intent to convey endorsement of or any other affiliation with the name claimant. Neither the author nor the publisher intends to express any judgment as to the validity or legal status of any such proprietary claims.

This publication is designed to provide accurate and authoritative information in regard to the subject matter covered. It is sold with the understanding that neither the author nor the publisher is engaged in rendering legal, accounting, or other professional service. If legal advice or other expert assistance is required, the services of a competent professional person should be sought.

—From a Declaration of Principles jointly adopted by a Committee of the American Bar Association and a Committee of Publishers

Cataloging-in-Publication data is on file with the Library of Congress.

Contents

Acknowledgments

Many people helped me work on this monumental project, and I could not have done it without them.

- My thanks to editor Barbara Gilson, who welcomed my idea for this book and helped me develop the first edition. Deep thanks to Charles Wall, who steered the third edition to completion.
- Much thanks to Charles Rozakis (AB Princeton, '03) for his extensive and expertly written math section. Bob Rozakis, my brilliant and patient husband, revised the math for this edition.
- My deep gratitude to my first editor and longtime friend Linda Bernbach for doing her usual spectacular first read.
- The wonderful people at Glyph International, including Somya Rustagi, project manager; and Radhey Balabh in production. Kay Mikel, copyeditor; Christine Anderson, proofreader. You're great!

To all these dedicated professionals: I am indebted to your wisdom, expertise, and devotion.

McGraw-Hill's

Praxis I and II

PART 1

The Basics

CHAPTER 1

The Ten-Step Power Study Plan

Myth: *You can't study for a standardized test.*
Reality: *Oh, yes you can.*

Many people believe that you can't improve your score on a standardized test because these tests are designed to assess the knowledge you have gained during many years of education. It is undeniably true that *cramming* for a Praxis or any other standardized test probably won't have a noticeable effect on your score, but you most certainly can significantly improve your score by *studying*.

The Ten-Step Power Study Plan provides guidelines for what to do in the months leading up to the test and the day of the test. It's the easiest and best way to achieve your highest possible score on the Praxis. Here's how to do it.

STEP 1:   Get Serious about the Test
Do any of these statements describe you?

- "I know I'm an excellent teacher, a real natural at it. After all, my cooperating teacher gave me high marks on all my observations during my student teaching. Why do I have to prove that I can teach through a test?"
- "The test doesn't show that I can teach. It just shows that I can take a test."
- "I was working as an accountant/physicist/translator/bassoonist/circus roustabout for decades before I was laid off. Teaching is my encore career. I know math/science/French/music/physical education inside and out, so why do I have to take the Praxis?"
- "The test scares the beejeezus out of me. I hate tests like I hate snakes, deep water, and three-way mirrors in dressing rooms."

Whether you have too much confidence or too little, you're not going to do well on the Praxis unless you get your head around reality. In this case, reality is simple: You *must* take the Praxis test and earn a good enough score to achieve your goal of becoming a teacher. Life isn't always fair. Shake your fist at the sky and rattle the chains on your cage for about an hour. Then adopt a positive attitude and get to work.

STEP 2: Improve Your Reading Comprehension

"Half of the American people have never read a newspaper. Half have never voted for President. One hopes it is the same half."

—GORE VIDAL, AUTHOR

Since 1982, the number of people who read literary works (novels, short stories, etc.) has fallen in all groups and segments. College-aged people (18–24) have had the sharpest drop in reading, to around 40 percent, compared to the nearly 60 percent who were reading 20 years previously. Young adults (25–34) have not been immune to this decline either, as their rate of reading has dropped more than 15 percent during the same time frame.

According to the National Endowment for the Arts, recreational reading is way down. "We've got a public culture which is almost entirely commercial- and novelty-driven," says NEA chairman Dana Gioia. The following sobering statistics bear out Gioia's claim:

- 27 percent of adults did not read a single book for pleasure in 2007.
- 65 percent of college freshmen in 2005 said they read little or nothing for pleasure.
- 70 percent of Americans haven't visited a bookstore in 5 years.
- Only 32 percent of the U.S. population has ever been in a bookstore.

The easiest and most enjoyable way to pump up your score on the Praxis is to read, read, and read some more. Reading increases your vocabulary, reading speed, and overall comprehension. You can't read just anything, however. What you read matters a lot because all reading is not the same.

To get the maximum effect from your reading, choose novels and nonfiction works of recognized literary value, not trashy bestsellers.

STEP 3: Set Up a Study Center

You need a place devoted to study. It doesn't have to be a suite at the Ritz, but it does have to be a quiet place supplied with all the material you need to study. Here's what you need:

- this book
- scratch paper
- pencils or pens
- a watch
- a good light
- a desk and chair

You can set up your study center at a desk in your bedroom, basement, attic, or spare room. If you don't have the space at home, consider a carrel at the library. Most libraries have spaces set aside for quiet reading; these spaces work very well too.

Avoid studying at the dining room or kitchen table, as you're likely to be disturbed by people walking by. You'll have to remove all your papers and notes every times there's a meal as well. Also, don't study on your bed because it's too comfortable. You're likely to doze off.

STEP 4:   Learn the Praxis Test

Familiarize yourself with the content and format of the Praxis test. Studying this book will help you save time on the day of the test. As you work your way through this book, not only will you review your skills, you will also become thoroughly familiar with the test directions and format. On test day you won't waste valuable time puzzling over the directions and orienting yourself to the test content. You'll be able to sit down and get right to work. Here are two areas to concentrate on to get you started:

- *Understand the scoring:* You are not penalized for guessing on the Praxis. Therefore, eliminate answers you know to be wrong and then guess. Never leave an answer blank.
- *Learn the test directions:* Any time that you can save is that much more time you'll have to answer questions. If you learn the test directions for each section, you will save the time you would otherwise have spent reading the directions during the actual test. This extra time will certainly help you earn a better score and could even make a crucial difference in your score.

STEP 5:   Establish a Test Strategy

Approach the Praxis as you would any other large project: devise a strategy. In this instance, you want to choose a test strategy, and there are three ways to approach the Praxis:

Strategy 1: *Work in Chronological Order*
Work from beginning to end, answering every question in order. Answer every single question, even if you have to guess. This is the most common test strategy. It has several advantages, chief among them that it's easy. Further, this strategy helps you keep your place in the test so you don't mismark any answers. However, you run the risk of spending too much time on a difficult question and not answering some easy ones.

Strategy 2: *Go from Easy to Difficult*
With this technique, you answer the easy questions first, and then go back and work on the harder ones. This approach has many advantages. First, it helps you use your time well by getting the most correct answers down quickly. Also, you build confidence as you write down the correct answers. Further, you may think of clues that help you answer the more difficult questions. You may even find the correct answer to a hard question revealed in another test question. You build momentum, which gets your mind into the test mode. You leave time for the harder questions.

Strategy 3: Go from Difficult to Easy

Here, you answer the difficult questions first, and then go back and answer the rest of the questions. This strategy helps you get the most difficult questions out of the way first, but you run the risk of spending too much time on difficult questions and not having the time to finish the test. Thus, you sacrifice the chance of getting some easy points.

None of these test-taking methods is right or wrong, but for most people strategy 2 works best. If you decide to use this test strategy, answer the easy questions first, and then go back to figure out the more difficult ones.

As you work from the beginning to the end, put a check mark next to any question you skip. Write in pencil so you can erase the check marks. When you get to the end of the test, go back to the beginning of the test and start answering the questions you skipped.

Keep moving so you stay within your time limit. Never let yourself get bogged down on one or two questions, especially if they are not worth many points.

As you work through the sample Praxis exams in this book, try each of the three test strategies. Based on your scores, choose the test approach that works best for you.

Regardless of the strategy you adopt, follow these suggestions to get the highest score:

- *Work carefully:* Imagine that you come to question 3 on the English Language, Literature, and Composition Content Knowledge Praxis test. It's a multiple-choice question with four choices: A, B, C, D. You read the test item and choice A. "Ah ha!" you think. "The correct choice is clearly A." Should you write A on your answer sheet? No!

  Even if you think you have spotted the correct answer immediately, read every answer to make sure that you are correct. You might have misread the question, a common mistake. People tend to see what they expect, not what is really on the page.

- *Don't second-guess yourself:* "The short-answer pattern really matters," some people say. "You can never have two Cs (or As, Bs, etc.) in a row," you may have heard. Not true. The pattern of letters on the answer sheet doesn't matter at all. You may have an ABCD, ABCD pattern, an AABBCCDD pattern, another pattern, or no pattern at all. It never matters.

  If you do see a pattern, don't be fooled into changing your answers. Your grade will be higher if you answer questions based on what you know rather than on the way the answers look on the page. If you start to think that you've chosen the incorrect answer, analyze the question rather than the answer pattern. If you can't think of a good reason to change the answer, leave it alone. Studies show that your first analysis is more often the correct one.

STEP 6:   Set Up a Study Routine

To make the most of your study time, get into a study routine. Try these Five Fast Facts:

1. *We Are Creatures of Habit.* Study at the same time every day in the same place. Sit at your desk in your study center to get into the study habit. Try to study for at least 30 minutes at a time. Any less, and you're not apt to get much done.

2. *Start with the Hardest Information.* Study your most difficult material first, when you are the least tired. You get a lot more done and retain more when you're rested.

3. *Ambience Matters.* If your study center has a radio, television, video game system, stereo, or any other distraction—turn it off. "I study better with some noise in the background," you protest. No, you don't. No one does. Turn off the television, radio, or CD when you study. You will study better without distractions. You'll get a lot more done if you devote yourself to studying for the Praxis in a quiet place. Why waste your time?

4. *Go for the Points.* Concentrate on the areas of the test that carry the most credit. Don't obsess over a section that represents only 10 percent of the overall questions. Instead, give more attention to the types of questions that are more heavily represented.

5. *Take a Break—and Give Yourself a Treat.* As you study, give yourself a break. Stretch every 15 minutes or so. Even if you want to soldier through, resting briefly four times an hour helps recharge your batteries. And since you're working hard to succeed on the Praxis, give yourself a treat. It doesn't have to be a designer watch or vacation in the south of France: breakfast with a buddy or an hour in front of the TV provides a lot of pleasure for a lot less money.

STEP 7:   Make a Study Schedule—and Follow It!

A full-day conference at work. A holiday celebration. A hot date. Help! You're pressed for time. Why not leave all your studying to the last minute and cram it all in? Here's why not— cramming doesn't work. It also tends to make you panic when you realize that there's no way you can learn everything you need for the Praxis in a week. Instead of wasting your time cramming, follow this study schedule to earn your highest score:

Six months before the test:
- Review the entire book to get an overview of the Praxis.
- Determine which test(s) to take, when you have to register, at which location you want to take the test(s), and to which schools or colleges to send your scores.

Five months before the test:
- Concentrate on the first part of the test.
- Complete the quizzes to assess your strengths and weaknesses.
- Target your weakest areas that will get you the most points on the Praxis.

Four months before the test:
- Concentrate on the second part of the test.
- Complete the quizzes to assess your strengths and weaknesses.
- Target your weakest areas that will get you the most points on the Praxis.

Three months before the test:
- Concentrate on the last part of the test.
- Complete the quizzes to assess your strengths and weaknesses.
- Target your weakest areas that will get you the most points on the Praxis.

Two months before the test:
- Take the practice tests under test conditions. Use only the amount of time you would be allocated on the real Praxis.
- Score yourself.
- Use this information to decide which areas to review.

The day before the test:
- Set out everything you need.
- Check the directions to the test site.
- Relax.

The night before the test:
- Lay out your clothing, pens or pencils, watch, lunch, and other test supplies. You don't want to be rushing around in the morning. Choose comfortable clothing. Avoid itchy sweaters or new jeans. Your clothes should be loose enough so you're comfortable.
- Get a good night's sleep. Yes, I know you've heard it before, but it really works. A solid 8 hours of sleep can recharge your batteries and give you the winning edge on any test.

The day of the test:
- Review the Fifty Fast Tips for Test Day.
- Be sure to eat breakfast. (You might want to review the Fifty Fast Tips as you eat!) Make sure it's a nourishing breakfast of cereal, fruit, and toast, or perhaps eggs, French toast, or pancakes. Don't make do with a toaster pastry or a doughnut. Too much caffeine can give you the jitters, so avoid caffeinated colas or too many cups of coffee.
- Leave yourself enough time in the morning. This is not the day to be rushing around.

STEP 8: Deal with Special Needs

The Americans with Disabilities Act (ADA) forbids discrimination on the basis of disability in employment, state and local government, public accommodations, commercial facilities, transportation, and telecommunications. This is the law.

To be protected by the ADA, you must have a disability or have a relationship or association with an individual with a disability. The ADA defines a person with a disability "as a person who has a physical or mental impairment that substantially limits one or more major life activities, a person who has a history or record of such an impairment, or a person who is perceived by others as having such an impairment." The ADA does not specifically name all of the impairments that are covered.

Under the ADA, "privately operated entities offering certain types of courses and examinations must provide specific accommodations with persons classified as have a disability. . . . Courses and examinations related to professional, educational, or trade-related applications, licensing, certifications, or credentialing must be provided in a place and manner accessible to people with disabilities, or alternative accessible arrangements must be offered." ETS cooperates fully with these federal regulations.

As a result, ETS offers a wide variety of accommodations for people who qualify. Accommodations available for the Praxis are listed in the following table.

Praxis Test Accommodations for People with Disabilities

Additional rest breaks	Large print answer sheet	Printed copy of spoken directions
Audio test	Large print test book (16 pt.)	Sign language interpreter for spoken directions only
Braille slate and stylus	Listening section omitted	Test reader
Braille test	Oral interpreter	Writer/recorder of answers
Extended testing time	Perkins Braillers	

In addition, ETS offers Monday testing for military or religious reasons. You can also get extended test time if English is not your main language.

For further information:

Phone	1-609-771-7780
Mail	ETS Disability Services
	PO Box 6054
	Princeton, NJ 08541-6054
Web site	www.ets.org/praxis

If you qualify for test accommodations because you have a special need, it is your responsibility to contact ETS with sufficient time to schedule the accommodation. DO NOT WAIT UNTIL THE TEST DAY TO ARRANGE FOR ACCOMMODATIONS.

Being an international student may present some special needs. ETS makes sure that the Praxis I and II are not biased against international test-takers. The test makers pretest all questions by including them in "experimental" test sections given to both U.S. and international test-takers. If statistics prove that any of the new questions put the internationals at a disadvantage, those items do not appear on the test. Still, international test-takers face certain challenges.

Improve Your English

The biggest and most obvious difficulty for nonnative English speakers and international test-takers is the language barrier. The entire test, including instructions and questions, is in English. Your writing, reading comprehension, and grammar skills are directly tested on Praxis I.

Most experts advise nonnative English speakers to read as much in English as they can in the months leading up to the test. Other activities that might help you are creating and using flash cards with difficult English words on them and practicing your English by communicating with others who speak the language. To improve your understanding of spoken English, you can watch American TV shows (often now available online). Keep a journal and express your thoughts about what you have read and seen in writing. Your goal should be to practice presenting evidence in a cohesive and interesting way to support your arguments in the writing section of the exam. When you read items from American publications, pay particular attention to how the writers gather evidence and present it because there are often subtle cultural differences at play. Remember that the quantitative part of Praxis I and the Praxis II math tests also are in English, so it is a good idea to review math formulas and glossaries in English.

Become Familiar with Standardized Tests

Getting acquainted with standardized tests is another must-do for international test-takers. This type of exam is a part of the average American's educational experience but is not necessarily a cultural norm in other parts of the world. Some people outside the United States may be unfamiliar with multiple-choice questions. These are questions in which you are given several choices and asked to select the correct answer. There are strategies for choosing the best one when you're not sure. For example, you can eliminate answers that you know are incorrect and then choose among the remaining choices. This is called "taking an educated guess," and it can improve your chances of picking the correct answer.

Timing is a very important part of standardized tests. Keeping calm is the first step to overcoming the pressure. Taking practice tests is key to learning how to pace yourself to maximize your performance in a limited time period. Taking practice tests will also help you become familiar with the test format; understanding the instructions for each part of the test in advance can save you time during the exam because you won't have to spend time on the instructions in addition to the other reading you have to do.

STEP 9:   Consider Setting Up a Study Group
Studying with classmates can help you in many ways. For instance, group members can take turns summarizing the material aloud or quizzing one another on important topics. Some group members ask questions to help clarify confusing points while other group members provide the answers. Study groups are a staple of MBA and law school programs, but should you form a study group for the Praxis? Use the following chart to help you decide.

Study on your own if you . . .	Study with others if you . . .
Can't concentrate if others are talking	Absorb material better if you hear people talking about it
Talk to yourself as you study	Find you learn better when you explain information to other people
Don't enjoy working with others	Enjoy working with others and have classmates who are serious about the test and can stay on task
Feel relatively confident of your abilities in all the subject areas tested on the Praxis	Feel weak in certain subject areas (such as mathematics or writing) and have classmates who are strong in those areas
Believe your way of studying is the best way (or even the only way!) to approach the test	Are not strong on organization and may be missing important notes
Can set a schedule and stick with it; get annoyed when people don't follow a set schedule	Have difficulty setting down to work and find your mind wanders when you study alone

STEP 10:   Do Your Best on Test Day

The following strategies can help you ace the Praxis.

1. *Follow the directions.* On the day of the test, pay close attention to all directions. Even though you'll be completely familiar with the test format, the proctor may say something very important, such as outlining safety procedures in the event of a fire drill or an actual fire. As a result, it's important to listen closely.

2. *Jot down notes and key facts.* During the test, write down any important details and facts while they are still fresh in your memory. These notes will very likely help you answer questions later on. In addition, having some notes reduces test anxiety because it reminds you that you have learned a lot. Write your notes on scrap paper, inside the test booklet, or in the test margins.

3. *Be creative, but don't overthink.* Sometimes the answer isn't obvious, so you have to think outside the box by analyzing the question from different angles. You have to use creative thinking skills by inferring, analyzing, and drawing conclusions.

   However, when you think creatively, be sure not to overthink. When you overthink, you analyze your answers so deeply that you create relationships that don't really exist. You might get hopelessly lost too.

   When in doubt, go for the most logical and obvious answer. If that doesn't fit, look more deeply into the question to see if you can find an answer that matches your line of thought.

4. *Pace yourself to avoid making careless errors.* Praxis I is both a sprint and a marathon. You have less than a minute, on average, for each question, so it is essential to develop the ability to work through these questions quickly and efficiently. Speed is not enough; Praxis I requires that you have mental stamina so that you can stay focused throughout the test. The best way to prepare yourself is to take practice tests observing strict time limits. There are practice tests included with this book.

During the test, make sure you are wearing a watch or can see a clock. This will help you keep working at the right pace. You want to work quickly, but not so quickly that you throw away points by working carelessly. It's an awful feeling to lose points on questions that you really can answer. You will get the wrong answer if you:

- Misread a question
- Miscalculate a math problem
- Mark the wrong spot on your answer sheet (e.g., you mean to mark C but mark B instead because you're working too fast)

To prevent these careless errors, try to save a few minutes at the end of the test to check the answer sheet against the choices on the test. Read the answer and the letter to yourself. Say the letter in your head.

When you are working on math problems, check that your answers make sense. Are they logical? For example, if you are figuring a discount, make sure that it's not more than the original price.

5. *Check your work.* When you finish the test, always check your work. Even if you have just a minute or two, use your time to look over your papers. Ask yourself these questions as you check the essay part of the Praxis test:

- Have I included all necessary words? People often omit words when they are in a hurry.
- Have I spelled all the words correctly? Check easy words as well as more difficult ones.
- Is my punctuation correct?
- Have I checked my grammar and usage too?
- Can my writing be read easily?

Ask yourself these questions as you check the multiple-choice part of the Praxis test:

- Have I filled in my responses at the correct places on the answer sheet?
- Because I am not being penalized for guessing, did I fill in each blank?
- Did I erase stray marks that might be misread?

Losing your place on an answer sheet is a major disaster that should never happen. Here's how it happens: You're working from the beginning to the end of the test. You get stuck on a few test items, so you skip them and keep on working. You focus on the next question and forget to skip a space on the answer sheet. As a result, you mark the correct answer—but in the wrong spot.

When you get to the last spot on the answer sheet, you have two spaces left. You suddenly realize that when you skipped questions, you forgot to skip the appropriate spaces on the answer sheet—even though you put check marks next to the questions!

You can avoid this disaster by checking your answer sheet each time you skip a question. Keeping your answer sheet next to the test booklet can help you remember to keep checking.

6. *Be neat.* If your writing is difficult to read, consider printing. Don't use all block capitals, however. Instead, use the accepted mix of uppercase and lowercase letters.

7. *Use all your allotted time.* *Never* turn your test booklet in early and leave. Be sure to use all the time you have been given, every single minute. Check your work over and think about your answers. If you are sure you're completely done, set your test aside and take a brief break. A few minutes later, look back at the test and your answers. Errors often become apparent when you've stepped away from the test. You don't want to be out the door and suddenly realize that you have finished so early because you forgot to complete one part of the test.

8. *Deal with test anxiety.* This is covered in detail in Chapter 3.

SUMMARY: THE TEN-STEP POWER PLAN

Step 1　Get Serious about the Test

Step 2　Improve Your Reading Comprehension

Step 3　Set Up a Study Center

Step 4　Learn the Praxis Test

Step 5　Establish a Test Strategy

Step 6　Set Up a Study Routine

Step 7　Make a Study Schedule—and Follow It!

Step 8　Deal with Special Needs

Step 9　Consider Setting Up a Study Group

Step 10　Do Your Best on Test Day

CHAPTER 2

Overview of the Praxis Tests

Created and administered by Educational Testing Service (ETS), the Praxis tests ("The Praxis Series: Professional Assessment for Beginning Teachers") can help you achieve two goals:

1. *Earn a license to teach.* Many state education agencies use Praxis tests as part of their process of licensing teachers. According to ETS, approximately 80 percent of the states that include tests as part of their licensing process use the Praxis Series for this purpose. Previously, the National Teachers Examination (NTE) was used for this purpose. Praxis has replaced the NTE.
2. *Gain entry to a teacher education program.* Some colleges and universities use select Praxis tests to qualify candidates for entry to teacher education programs.

THE THREE PRAXIS TESTS

There are three different Praxis tests, as follows:

1. Praxis I: Pre-Professional Skills Tests (PPST)
2. Praxis II: Principles of Learning and Teaching (PLT) and Subject Assessments
3. Praxis III: Teacher Performance Assessments

Which tests do you need to take at which times in your teaching career? Always consult with your state education department for specific requirements, as these vary from state to state. The following chart provides basic guidelines:

Praxis Test	When to Take it
Praxis I: Pre-Professional Skills Tests (PPST)	• when you are entering a teaching training program • when you have graduated from college and seek to earn a state teaching license
Praxis II: Principles of Learning and Teaching (PLT) and Subject Assessments	• when you have graduated from college and seek to earn a state teaching license
Praxis III: Teacher Performance Assessments	• when you are a beginning teacher

Each Praxis test is different. Let's look at them all, so you can decide which one or ones you need to take at this point in your career.

Praxis I: Pre-Professional Skills Tests (PPST)

Praxis I is a test of *basic knowledge,* what the test makers have determined is the fundamental information that all teachers should possess. Praxis I has three parts, each of which is called a test:

- Reading
- Writing
- Mathematical skills

Praxis II: Principles of Learning and Teaching (PLT) and Subject Assessments

This test has two parts. "Principles of Learning and Teaching" assesses your knowledge of teaching methodology. The "Subject Assessments" tests what you know about the *specific subjects* you will teaching.

Principles of Learning and Teaching

This is the test you take to get licensed to teach a specific age group. Here are the three age groups for which you can be licensed:

- Grades K–6
- Grades 5–9
- Grades 7–12

Subject Assessments

Praxis II also includes Subject Assessments (content area tests). These cover the different subject areas that a person can teach, such as biology, French, or mathematics. Currently, Praxis II includes more than 100 Subject Assessments. The following list shows some of the content areas tested by Praxis II:

Elementary Subject Assessments
- Curriculum, instruction, and assessment
- Content area exercises
- Content knowledge
- Curriculum, instruction, and assessment (K–5)

Subject Assessments
- Art
- Biology
- English language, literature, and composition
- French
- Mathematics
- Music
- Physical education
- Physics
- Science
- Social studies
- Spanish
- Special education

Thus, you might take Praxis I as an admission requirement for a college of education. After you graduate, you might take the Praxis II Principles of Learning and Teaching for grades 5 to 9 and then the Praxis II in social studies. When you pass all these tests, you would be licensed to teach social studies to students in grades 5 to 9. Later, you might complete a master's degree in special education, take the Praxis II in that subject, and earn that certification as well. Candidates seeking multiple certifications at the same time can take the Multiple Subjects Assessments for Teachers (MSAT).

Currently, Praxis II is offered only in paper-and-pencil format, not in a computer-based format.

Praxis III: Teacher Performance Assessments

This test has three parts:

- Direct classroom assessment; you will be observed teaching
- Interviews
- A portfolio review

Praxis III is *not* covered in this book because you cannot study for it. Rather, it involves direct classroom teaching experience.

To find out which Praxis test(s) to take, click on the State Testing Requirements in the Praxis area of the ETS Web site: www.ets.org/praxis

Check with your college or university and state education department before you sign up for the Praxis to confirm the ETS information. Make sure you are taking the appropriate test at the appropriate time in your career.

SCORING SCALE

Each state sets its own passing scores. As mentioned earlier, always check with your state education department to find out the passing score in your state.

FORMAT OF THE PPST

The PPST is offered in paper-and-pencil format as well as a computer-based format. Both test formats measure the same academic skills.

How does the paper-and-pencil version of the PPST compare to the computerized version? Which one should you take?

On both the paper-and-pencil version and the computer version:

- The items are the same format.
- The same skills are assessed.
- The scoring is the same.
- The questions are linear. (The questions vary in difficulty, but this does not depend on the answers you give.)
- You can mark an answer or skip an answer and return to it later.

On the paper-and-pencil test, you can leave answers blank and return to them later. You can put a question mark next to an item and return to it later. Be sure to erase all stray marks, however. Otherwise, your answers might be marked incorrectly.

Likewise, on the computer-based test, by using a special tool that marks answers, you can leave a question blank and return to it later. In addition, you can mark a question you answered and go back to review or change it. A review screen tells you whether a question has been answered, not yet seen, or is marked for review.

Paper-and-Pencil Format of the PPST

If you have taken the PPST previously, you will notice that the number of items and skills have changed, as ETS has revised the exam. The number of test items and time allocated for the paper-and-pencil version of the PPST is as follows:

Test	Number of Test Items	Time
PPST in Reading	40	60 minutes
PPST in Mathematics (Code 0730)	40	60 minutes
PPST in Writing (Code 0720)	38 multiple-choice items 1 essay	30 minutes 30 minutes (60 minutes total)

Here is the specific breakdown of test items:

PPST in Reading

Specific Content Area	Number of Test Items (May vary slightly from test to test)	Percentage of Test Items (May vary slightly from test to test)
Literal understanding	18	45%
Inferential and critical understanding	22	55%

PPST in Mathematics

Specific Content Area	Number of Test Items (May vary slightly from test to test)	Percentage of Test Items (May vary slightly from test to test)
Operations and numbers	13	32%
Algebra	8	20%
Geometry and measurement	9	22%
Probability, Data Analysis	10	25%

PPST in Writing

Specific Content Area	Number of Test Items (May vary slightly from test to test)	Percentage of Test Items (May vary slightly from test to test)
Grammar and usage	13	17%
Sentence structure	14	18.5%
Mechanics (punctuation, capitalization)	11	14.5%
Diction (word choice)		
Essay	1	50%

Computerized Format of the PPST

The number of test items and time allocated for the computerized version of the PPST is as follows:

Test	Number of Test Items	Time
PPST in Reading (Code 5710)	46	75 minutes
PPST in Mathematics (Code 5730)	46	75 minutes
PPST in Writing (Code 5720)	44 multiple-choice items 1 essay	38 minutes 30 minutes (68 minutes total)

Here is the specific breakdown of test items:

PPST in Reading

Specific Content Area	Number of Test Items (May vary slightly from test to test)	Percentage of Test Items (May vary slightly from test to test)
Literal understanding	21	45%
Inferential and critical understanding	25	55%

PPST in Mathematics

Specific Content Area	Number of Test Items (May vary slightly from test to test)	Percentage of Test Items (May vary slightly from test to test)
Operations and numbers	15	32%
Algebra	9	20%
Geometry and measurement	10	22%
Probability, Data Analysis	12	25%

PPST in Writing

Specific Content Area	Number of Test Items (May vary slightly from test to test)	Percentage of Test Items (May vary slightly from test to test)
Grammar and usage	15	17%
Sentence structure	16	18.5%
Mechanics (punctuation, capitalization)	13	14.5%
Diction (word choice)		
Essay	1	50%

Each part of the computer-based test includes additional time for computer tutorials and the collection of background information from you. You will actually spend about 4 1/2 hours at the testing site.

The Computerized PPST in Reading, Mathematics, and Writing is also offered as a combined test that you can take at a single testing session. The combined test has four separately timed sections: Reading, Mathematics, Multiple-Choice Writing, and Essay Writing. There is an optional 15-minute break between the Mathematics and Writing sections. The ETS score report that you receive will have individual scores for Reading, Mathematics, and Writing.

At this time, Praxis II: Principles of Learning and Teaching (PLT) and the Praxis II Subject Assessments are available only in the paper version.

HOW THE TESTS ARE SCORED

Paper-and-pencil test: You complete the test, the proctor collects it, and it is scored by ETS or an agency that ETS has hired for that purpose. You must wait for the score to be posted online. You must wait even longer to receive your official score by mail. The scoring usually takes several weeks, at a minimum.

Computer-based test: You receive your unofficial score when you complete the test. You still have to wait for the official score to arrive by mail, however.

A great deal of confusion has arisen over the computerized scoring. On both the paper-and-pencil test and the computer-based test, each test item has a different value. For example, item 1 might be worth 2 points, item 2 might be worth 4 points, item 3 might be worth 1.5 points, and so on. The point value varies with each version of the test.

When you take the computer-based version, the test will end when/if you reach the passing score for your state. The number of questions you must answer to pass depends on the point value for each question and the passing rate for your state. For instance, you might be finished when you answer 26 questions correctly, 30 questions correctly, or 42 questions correctly. Or you might have to complete the entire test. You have no way of knowing this because you don't know how much each question is weighted.

On the paper-and-pencil test, however, you have to complete the entire test, even if you have already achieved the passing score. That's because you have no way of knowing if you have passed.

This confusion has led some people to believe that the computer-based version of the PPST is a computer-adaptive test. This means that the questions get easier or more difficult depending on your level of skill. The PPST is not and never has been a computer-adaptive test. ETS has no plans to make it one. The computer-based test and the paper-and-pencil test are the same linear tests. They are simply offered in different formats.

In either type of test, your score is based on the number of questions you answer correctly. There is no penalty for answering a question incorrectly. Thus, it's a good idea to write down an answer for every question. Don't leave any blanks.

Take the paper-and-pencil version if . . .
- You are not comfortable working on computers or with this technology.
- You think it will unnerve you if the test suddenly stops (meaning that you passed).
- You think you will earn a higher score this way.

Take the computer-based version if . . .
- You are comfortable working on computers.
- You want your unofficial score immediately.
- You can't wait for the next paper-and-pencil test date.
- You think you will earn a higher score this way.

HOW OFTEN THE TESTS ARE OFFERED

Paper-and-pencil test: This version is offered five times a year, as of publication date. These dates are in November, January, March, April, and July. You choose the time and place when you register.

Computer-based test: This version is offered much more frequently. You make an appointment through Prometric Testing Centers. To arrange an appointment, call Prometric candidate services at 1-800-853-6773.

TEST COSTS

At this time, the fees for the Praxis tests are as follows.

Praxis I

Computer-based test fees

1 Test	$80
2 Tests	$120
3 Tests	$160
Combined Test	$130

Paper-based test fees

Registration per test date (only on paper-based tests)	$50
PPST Reading	$40
PPST Mathematics	$40
PPST Writing	$40

Important! As far as ETS is concerned, a "year" runs from September to July, *not* from January to January. Thus, if you intend to take the Praxis more than once in a "year," do your best to take the test within ETS's year to avoid paying the $50 registration fee twice.

Praxis II

Subject Assessment tests vary from $65–$115 each. Most are in the $80–$90 range.

In addition, there are all sorts of extra fees. There is a state surcharge fee on paper-based tests in Nevada, for example. In addition, special services are steep: late registration ($45), changes to test date or location ($45), telephone registration ($35), scores by phone ($30 per request), additional score reports ($40 each), score verification ($40 for multiple-choice, $55 for constructed response, $80 for teaching foundations).

Thus, the least expensive way to take the PPST is to register online for the computer-based test. Don't make any changes in your test date or location. This doesn't mean it is the best way for you to take the test—just that it is the most economical way.

FREQUENTLY ASKED QUESTIONS (FAQs)

Q: Which test(s) should I take?

A: The test(s) you take depends entirely on your state and college requirements. ETS has a link to each state's requirements. Check with your college teacher certification office to determine its requirements. Remember: Each state and each college has its own requirements.

Q: How do I register for the test?

A: You can obtain registration forms in several ways.

1. Contact the Educational Testing Service online at its Web site: www.ets.org/praxis (or ⟵ e-mail: praxis@ets.org).

   You cannot register online if . . .

   - You need services for students with disabilities.
   - You are registering the first time for Sunday testing.
   - You are testing in certain countries (including Taiwan, Nigeria, Benin, Togo, Ghana, and Kenya).

2. Write to the Educational Testing Service at this address:

   ETS-The Praxis Series
   P.O. Box 6051
   Princeton, NJ 08541-6051

3. Obtain an application from your college department of education.

   - ETS will reduce fees for students who can demonstrate financial need. Do not send money to ETS.
   - Your university's department of education or financial aid office will have this information.

Q: Where should I take the test?

A: As with all ETS tests, the paper-and-pencil version of the Praxis is administered at colleges, universities, high schools, and civic centers. As mentioned earlier, the computer-based test is given at Prometric Testing Centers as well as at select colleges and universities.

Register for a convenient location close to your home. This will help you reduce test anxiety. If you have to go to an inconvenient site, try to visit it prior to the test to get your bearings. If you don't meet the registration deadline, don't despair. Most test centers accept walk-in test takers if they have space. As mentioned earlier, you'll pay an extra fee for this service, but at least you'll be able to take the test on the day you wish.

Q: What do I have to bring with me on test day?

A: You will need the following items to take the test:

   - If you register by phone or mail, your admission ticket   ⟵

ETS will send this to you. But . . . if you registered for a paper-based Praxis test by mail or phone and didn't receive your admission ticket at least 1 week before the test date, contact ETS to confirm your test appointment.

- If you register online, your e-ticket

ETS has taken a page from the airlines and gone to ticketless travel: candidates who register online will no longer be mailed a printed paper ticket. Instead, if you register online, you must print out an e-ticket from the online registration system.

- A photo ID

The following documents are acceptable:

> Passport
> Driver's license
> State ID
> National identification
> Military identification

- Sharpened number 2 pencils and an eraser
- A calculator, if you are allowed to use one on the test you are taking. Be sure to check this ahead of time, as not all of the Praxis mathematical tests allow you to use a calculator at this time.
- A watch. Do *not* assume that you will be able to use your cell phone as a watch or that the test room will have a clock on the wall. Test takers are not allowed to bring their cell phones into the test rooms because of the possibility of downloading information that can be used to obtain answers. In addition, many test rooms do not have clocks—and if they do, you can't assume that they work!

Q: What types of questions will I have to answer on the PPST?
A: Remember that the PPST is designed to measure basic skills in reading, writing, and mathematics. Expect questions similar to those on the SAT.

Q: What can I expect on the reading part of the PPST?
A: Fortunately, there are no surprises here because this is a standard ETS reading test: a series of reading passages followed by multiple-choice questions with five answer choices each. Reading passages range from just a few sentences to about 500 words each. As you learned earlier in this book, the reading skills tested can be divided as follows:

Finding literal details: about 45%
Making inferences: about 55%

This means that about half the questions require you to go back into the passage to find the answers. The information you need will be directly stated. The other questions will require you to read between the lines to find the answers. You'll combine story clues with what you know to infer the answers. This is explained in detail in Part 3, "PPST: Reading Test."

Q: What can I expect on the mathematics part of the PPST?
A: Again, you'll be dealing with multiple-choice questions with five answer choices. You'll be tested on a wide variety of mathematical concepts.

Naturally, you'll want to allocate your study time accordingly, spending more time not only on your weakest areas but also on the areas that will get the most emphasis on the test.

Q: Can I use a calculator on the mathematics part of the PPST?
A: Alas, no. The calculator has to stay at home.

Q: What can I expect on the writing part of the PPST?
A: Remember that this test has two parts: multiple-choice questions and an essay. (The number of multiple-choice questions is different on the paper-and-pencil and the computerized versions of the test, but the breakdown of the skills is the same.) Each part of the test counts 50 percent of your final score.

The multiple-choice part of the test has usage questions and sentence correction questions. Each type of question has a different format.

Usage questions

These questions have four answer choices consisting of underlined words or groups of words. The fifth choice is always "No error." Here is a sample question:

The <u>top three winners</u> in the <u>state competition</u> <u>goes</u> to the national finals

          A   B   C

<u>to be held</u> this year in San Francisco, California. <u>No error</u>

    D   E

Answer: C. The underlined word in choice C, <u>goes,</u> should be <u>go,</u> since the plural subject <u>winners</u> required the plural verb <u>go</u>.

Sentence correction questions

These questions have some or all of the words underlined. Each sentence is followed by five choices: The first is the same as the underlined part, and the others are revisions. You must decide whether the original or one of the rewrites is best. Here is a sample question:

Dr. Seuss, one of the world's most famous children's book <u>authors, he has written</u> books for adults and advertising copy as well.
(A) authors, he has written
(B) authors, written by him has been
(C) authors him has written
(D) authors written
(E) authors, has written

Answer: E. As written, the sentence is incorrect because there is no reason to include the pronoun <u>he</u>. As you approach these questions, always start by looking for the easiest and least convoluted way of revising the sentence. The easiest way is to delete the pronoun he. The other choices create wordy, awkward, and incorrect sentences. The correct sentence reads: *Dr. Seuss, one of the world's most famous children's book authors, has written books for adults and advertising copy as well.*

The essay part of the test

You will be given a topic (the "writing prompt") to write on. You do not have a choice: there is one prompt and one prompt only. NEVER make up your own writing prompt. If you do, you won't receive any credit on this part of the test. Directly respond to the prompt given to you.

Q: What can I expect if I decide to take the computer-based version of the PPST?
A: As explained earlier, this form of the test is the same as the pencil-and-paper test. It's just transferred to a computer version.

Q: What can I expect on the Praxis II Principles of Learning and Teaching (PLT)?
A: Remember that this test consists of three different tests, depending on the grade level at which you intend to teach:

- Grades K–6
- Grades 5–9
- Grades 7–12

Each test follows the same format: First you will read three descriptions of teaching situations. Then you will answer 7 multiple-choice questions and 2 short-answer questions based on the descriptions. In addition, each test contains 24 multiple-choice items not based on the descriptions. According to ETS, the areas that you will be tested on can be divided as follows:

- Creating an environment for student learning
- Organizing content for student learning
- Teaching for student learning
- Teacher professionalism

The PLT tests take 2 hours each.

Q: What can I expect on the Praxis II Subject Assessments?
A: Remember that there are more than 100 different Subject Assessments. These tests assess how well you know your subject and teaching skills. Chapter 17, "Subject Assessments," reviews many of these areas.

These tests usually take 2 hours.

Q: If I don't know the answer, should I guess?

A: On many of the other ETS tests, such as the SAT, you are penalized for guessing. This is not the case on the Praxis. Only questions answered correctly count toward the reported score. Therefore, it is better to guess than to leave an answer blank.

Q: How do I get my score?

A: Starting in September 2009, your official scores will be available online at the ETS site 45 days after you take the test. You can also call to get your score, but this costs $30 extra. In addition, you can request your score by mail. Further information is available on the ETS Web site.

ETS will send your score to three certification agencies, colleges, or other agencies without charge. You designate these agencies when you register for the test. For more than three reports, you have to pay an extra fee. At this time, the fee is $40 per request.

ADDITIONAL INFORMATION

For additional information about the Praxis tests, you can contact ETS.

E-mail:	praxis@ets.org
Web site:	www.ets.org/praxis
Phone:	United States, U.S. Territories, and Canada 1-800-772-9476
	All other locations 1-609-771-7395
	TTY: 609-771-7714
Mail:	ETS-The Praxis Series, P.O. Box 6051, Princeton, NJ 08541-6051
Fax:	1-609-771-7906; 1-609-530-0581

CHAPTER 3

Deal with Nerves

"The only thing we have to fear is fear itself," said President Franklin Delano Roosevelt. President Roosevelt was right, but try telling that to all the butterflies in your stomach the night before the Praxis.

Start by building your self-confidence. Getting yourself all upset before the test will make you feel more nervous. It can also rob you of the confidence you need to succeed. Remind yourself that you have prepared well so you will do well. A positive attitude yields great results.

LEARN TECHNIQUES FOR HANDLING TEST JITTERS

Fortunately, there are many effective ways to deal with test jitters. Here are some of my most effective techniques.

1. *Downplay the test.* It's natural to feel nervous before a high-pressure situation; in fact, some scientists think we're hardwired to get an adrenaline rush when we're in a tight spot. These scientists theorize that tension under pressure comes from ancient days when we faced bison and other gigantic creatures. The adrenaline gave us the power we needed to run away. Now, however, we can't run away; we have to stay and face the pressure. So how can you deal with this flood of tension? Start by downplaying the test. Instead of referring to the Praxis as "The Worst Day of My Life" (or "Doomsday," "The Kiss of Death," "My Personal Waterloo," etc.), think about the Praxis as one more hurdle to overcome. Be casual when you talk about it, and don't let your classmates, parents, partner, or instructors push your panic button.

2. *Don't dismiss your fears.* In your attempt to downplay the test, don't go to the opposite extreme of saying, "Oh, this old Praxis doesn't mean a thing. I can still become a teacher if I bomb the test." Recognize that the Praxis does matter. Nonetheless, even in the most pressurized test situations, the test will never be the sole measure of your qualifications. And the Praxis certainly has nothing to do with your worth as a human being.

3. *Learn (and use) relaxation techniques.* Use visualization and breathing techniques to overcome your fear of failure. Visualize or imagine yourself doing well, filling in the blanks, or writing the essays with confidence. Imagine receiving a high score on the Praxis. Visualizing success puts you in control.

Breathing techniques can also help, especially during a test. If you feel yourself losing control, take slow, deep breaths to calm yourself. If you have time before the test, try to get in some exercise. It's a great way to reduce tension. Even 10 minutes of jogging can take the edge off.

4. *Be optimistic.* We can't all be little rays of sunshine, especially when faced with a big, important test. Nonetheless, studies clearly show that people who approach tense situations with an upbeat attitude do better than those who trudge in already defeated. Imagine achieving success rather than automatically dooming yourself to failure.

Quick Tip

Right before a big test, stay away from people who bring you down by preying on your stress and anxiety. You don't need them pulling you down with their doom-and-gloom scripts.

OVERCOME PANIC

What if none of my suggestions work for you and panic strikes during the Praxis? Start by recognizing that panic is a natural reaction to a pressure situation. Nonetheless, panic can prevent you from doing your best, so let's reduce or banish it. Here are some techniques that can help you deal with panic:

- *Don't panic if . . .* some questions seem much harder than others. They probably are. That's the way the test was designed. Accept this and do the best you can. Remember that you don't have to answer each question to do well. That's because you're not being marked against yourself; rather, you're being judged against all other test takers. Furthermore, they're feeling the same way you are.
- *Don't panic if . . .* you can't get an answer. Just skip the question and move on. If you have enough time, you can return to the question later. If you run out of time before you can return to it, you were still better off answering more questions than wasting time on a question you didn't know.
- *Don't panic if . . .* you freeze and just can't go on. If this happens, remind yourself that you have studied and so you are well prepared. Remember that every question you have answered is worth points.

Reassure yourself that you're doing just fine. After all, you are. Stop working and close your eyes. Take two or three deep breaths. Breathe in and out to the count of five. Then, go on with the test.

Quick Tip

Take comfort from this: A minor case of nerves can actually help you do well in a test (especially a standardized test) because it keeps you alert and focused on the task at hand.

PART 2

Three Diagnostic Pretests

Before you begin your review for the Praxis tests, you need to assess your knowledge of the skills being tested. These diagnostic pretests have been designed to help you do just that.

To get the most use from these diagnostic tests, take them under Praxis test conditions. Work in a quiet room and time yourself carefully. Then score the test with the answer keys, which follow each test.

CHAPTER 4

Reading Diagnostic Test

ANSWER SHEET

1 Ⓐ Ⓑ Ⓒ Ⓓ Ⓔ   8 Ⓐ Ⓑ Ⓒ Ⓓ Ⓔ   15 Ⓐ Ⓑ Ⓒ Ⓓ Ⓔ
2 Ⓐ Ⓑ Ⓒ Ⓓ Ⓔ   9 Ⓐ Ⓑ Ⓒ Ⓓ Ⓔ   16 Ⓐ Ⓑ Ⓒ Ⓓ Ⓔ
3 Ⓐ Ⓑ Ⓒ Ⓓ Ⓔ   10 Ⓐ Ⓑ Ⓒ Ⓓ Ⓔ   17 Ⓐ Ⓑ Ⓒ Ⓓ Ⓔ
4 Ⓐ Ⓑ Ⓒ Ⓓ Ⓔ   11 Ⓐ Ⓑ Ⓒ Ⓓ Ⓔ   18 Ⓐ Ⓑ Ⓒ Ⓓ Ⓔ
5 Ⓐ Ⓑ Ⓒ Ⓓ Ⓔ   12 Ⓐ Ⓑ Ⓒ Ⓓ Ⓔ   19 Ⓐ Ⓑ Ⓒ Ⓓ Ⓔ
6 Ⓐ Ⓑ Ⓒ Ⓓ Ⓔ   13 Ⓐ Ⓑ Ⓒ Ⓓ Ⓔ   20 Ⓐ Ⓑ Ⓒ Ⓓ Ⓔ
7 Ⓐ Ⓑ Ⓒ Ⓓ Ⓔ   14 Ⓐ Ⓑ Ⓒ Ⓓ Ⓔ   21 Ⓐ Ⓑ Ⓒ Ⓓ Ⓔ

22 Ⓐ Ⓑ Ⓒ Ⓓ Ⓔ   29 Ⓐ Ⓑ Ⓒ Ⓓ Ⓔ   36 Ⓐ Ⓑ Ⓒ Ⓓ Ⓔ
23 Ⓐ Ⓑ Ⓒ Ⓓ Ⓔ   30 Ⓐ Ⓑ Ⓒ Ⓓ Ⓔ   37 Ⓐ Ⓑ Ⓒ Ⓓ Ⓔ
24 Ⓐ Ⓑ Ⓒ Ⓓ Ⓔ   31 Ⓐ Ⓑ Ⓒ Ⓓ Ⓔ   38 Ⓐ Ⓑ Ⓒ Ⓓ Ⓔ
25 Ⓐ Ⓑ Ⓒ Ⓓ Ⓔ   32 Ⓐ Ⓑ Ⓒ Ⓓ Ⓔ   39 Ⓐ Ⓑ Ⓒ Ⓓ Ⓔ
26 Ⓐ Ⓑ Ⓒ Ⓓ Ⓔ   33 Ⓐ Ⓑ Ⓒ Ⓓ Ⓔ   40 Ⓐ Ⓑ Ⓒ Ⓓ Ⓔ
27 Ⓐ Ⓑ Ⓒ Ⓓ Ⓔ   34 Ⓐ Ⓑ Ⓒ Ⓓ Ⓔ
28 Ⓐ Ⓑ Ⓒ Ⓓ Ⓔ   35 Ⓐ Ⓑ Ⓒ Ⓓ Ⓔ

READING DIAGNOSTIC TEST

40 questions, 60 minutes

Directions: Each of the following passages is followed by questions. Answer the questions based on what is directly stated or suggested in each passage. Indicate your answers by filling in the corresponding circle on your answer sheet.

Questions 1–2

In 1997, Vermont state representative Sydney Nixon was seated as an apparent one-vote winner, 570 to 569. Mr. Nixon resigned when the State House determined, after a recount, that he had actually lost to his opponent, Robert Emond, 572 to 571. In 1989, a Lansing, Michigan, school district proposition failed when the final recount produced
(5) a tie vote, 5,147 to 5,147. In the original vote count, votes against the proposition were 10 more than those in favor. The result meant that the school district had to reduce its budget by $2.5 million.

1. Which sentence best summarizes the content of this passage?

(A) It's not as important to vote as you might think.

(B) Even minor elections can have very important outcomes.

(C) As Americans, we are very fortunate to have the right to vote.

(D) The voting process is laborious and time-consuming, but in the end it is worth the time and trouble.

(E) Just one vote can and often does make a difference in the outcome of an election.

2. The numbers "572 to 571" mentioned in the second sentence serve to emphasize

(A) how close the outcome was

(B) how few people exercise their right to vote

(C) the insignificance of this particular election

(D) why we need Internet voting rather than paper ballots

(E) how the voters decided that Nixon was a better candidate than Emond

Questions 3–5

Often teachers despair at the lifelessness of student writing about literature. Students need to be encouraged to find and explore their own topics in relation to literature and to maintain their own voices. Some teachers who have extensively used exploratory/response writing have been frustrated that the liveliness of the student's
(5) own voice can sometimes disappear when he or she moves from the relative privacy and

free form of journal writing into the formal essay. This is something we need to continue to analyze and work on—encouraging students to maintain their personal and unique connection to the material, even as they write for an audience.

3. According to the author, what happens when students shift from personal writing to public expression?

(A) Their voice gets lost.
(B) They become more confident and skilled writers.
(C) Their tone becomes more vivacious.
(D) They are able to create their own, unique topics.
(E) They become less private and more free with their topics.

4. Which of the following best describes the organization of the passage?

(A) The writer uses chronological order.
(B) The writer uses cause and effect.
(C) The writer makes an assertion and backs it up with specific details.
(D) The writer introduces a current debate and then presents both sides.
(E) The writer begins with a summary of the research and then proposes the thesis.

5. The writer of this selection is most likely

(A) a parent
(B) a classroom teacher or educational scholar
(C) a member of the parent-teacher association
(D) a member of the board of education
(E) a student

Questions 6–8

Why is everyone interested in solar energy now? The reason is that the fuels we use are very expensive, and the supply of these fuels is shrinking every day. The cost of home heating oil, for example, has gone up more than 50 percent in the past decade. The figures are not much better for natural gas and electric power. As our oil and
(5) natural gas reserves shrink further, the price can only climb higher.

6. What is causing the price of heating oil to increase?

(A) an interest in solar energy
(B) an increase in the price of electric power
(C) the increased cost of natural gas
(D) decreased supplies
(E) the development of safe and efficient alternative forms of energy

7. Which of the following statements, if true, would weaken the author's arguments?

(A) Fuel prices continue to increase at the same or an even higher rate.
(B) The supply of oil continues to decline.
(C) The supplies of natural gas and electric power do not increase.
(D) An expected oil embargo will further decimate supplies.
(E) Fuel prices decrease as new supplies of fossil fuels are discovered.

8. The main idea of this essay is best stated as

(A) Heating oil and gas are expensive.
(B) Solar energy is collected in special photoelectric cells.
(C) Solar energy is important now because we are running out of fuel, and fuel costs are higher.
(D) Our supply of fossil fuels is shrinking.
(E) Solar energy is only one possible alternative energy source.

Questions 9–10

Men are like plants; the goodness and flavor of the fruit proceeds from the peculiar soil and exposition in which they grow. We are nothing but what we derive from the air we breathe, the climate we inhabit, the government we obey, the system of religion we profess, and the nature of our employment. Here in America, you will find but few (5) crimes; these have acquired as yet no root among us.

9. In the second sentence, the main effect of using parallel phrases that elaborate on one another is to

(A) emphasize the amount of time and effort it takes for a person to mature
(B) make the writing vigorous and logical
(C) establish the author's solemn and scholarly tone
(D) convince people to move to America
(E) temper the author's enthusiasm with unquestionable scientific facts

10. Based on the details, you can conclude that this essay reveals the author's

(A) gratitude that he or she is not an American
(B) belief that Americans are an easily influenced group of people
(C) distrust of foreigners, especially immigrants
(D) mild support for America and Americans
(E) affection for and deep faith in the promise of America and Americans

Question 11

11. Teachers have discovered that one practical way in which students can develop a working knowledge of grammar is to start with writing and move into matters of grammar as such problems arise in students' writing. The time to help students learn grammar is when they need help in revising the structure of their sentences.

According to the preceding statement, the author most likely

(A) believes that grammar is not relevant in today's electronic world
(B) is not a teacher
(C) would argue in favor of a return to traditional grammar instruction
(D) doesn't know much about grammar
(E) seizes "teachable moments" by having students correct grammar errors in context

Question 12

12. *Themes* connote broad-based concepts for examination that stretch across a range of disciplines, and this is a very legitimate focal point for study, but there are other forms. Some people focus literature-based interdisciplinary studies around *issues,* or *problems,* or *topics.* Sometimes beginning with an *author study* can lead into some other arenas.

According to the author, a thematic approach to literature

(A) should not be taken in a restrictive sense
(B) is the only legitimate method of studying classics
(C) is the same as an author study
(D) should not be confused with an interdisciplinary study based on issues, problems, or topics
(E) is the recommended way to teach fiction to young adults

Questions 13–16

Damage to rangeland is only one measure of the destructiveness of current grazing patterns. Forests also suffer from livestock production, as branches are cut for fodder or entire stands are leveled to make way for pastures. The roster of impacts from forest clearing includes the loss of watershed protection, loss of plant and animal species, and
(5) on a larger scale, substantial contributions of the greenhouse gas carbon dioxide to the atmosphere. Latin America has suffered the most dramatic forest loss due to inappropriate livestock production. Since 1970, farmers and ranchers have converted more than 20 million hectares of the region's moist tropical forests to cattle pastures.

13. Damage to rangeland is caused by all of the following except

(A) increasing the greenhouse effect
(B) losing plant and animal species
(C) building too many homes and office buildings on land formerly set aside for pasture
(D) mowing down acres of trees to create new pastures and cutting branches to use as cattle fodder
(E) raising cattle in detrimental ways

14. The author's purpose is most likely to

(A) convince people to leave the big cities and become ranchers
(B) describe a problem that affects third-world nations far more than it affects developed industrial nations
(C) force the government to stop leasing public land to ranchers until the situation with poor grazing practices is resolved
(D) alert people to a serious problem and press for change
(E) show that this problem affects only grazing land in Europe, not the United States

15. The author develops the argument by using

(A) personal experiences
(B) chronological order
(C) causes and effects
(D) comparison and contrast
(E) a series of examples

16. This excerpt would most likely be published

(A) in a college textbook
(B) on a commercial Web site
(C) in a popular magazine
(D) in a trade publication for home builders
(E) in a newspaper article for meatpackers

Question 17

17. The way individuals concentrate on and remember new and difficult information is related to their global versus their analytical cognitive processing styles. Some students learn easily when information is presented step by step in a cumulative, sequential pattern that builds toward conceptual understanding. Others learn easily when they either understand the concept first and then concentrate on the details or are introduced to the information with a humorous story or an anecdote related to their experiences and replete with examples and graphics. Both types of learners reason and learn equally well, but they do so through different strategies.

According to the author,

(A) there is one best way to learn
(B) the way people learn new information is related to their attitude toward school
(C) teaching approaches should be tailored to an individual's learning style
(D) teachers should incorporate more humor into their lectures
(E) the way people learn is a complex and not easily understood topic

Questions 18–21

There is a great deal of confusion over what the 40 different species that belong to the family Delphinidae are called. For example, is a small cetacean a "dolphin" or a "porpoise"? Some people distinguish a dolphin as a cetacean having a snout or beak, while a porpoise usually refers to one with a smoothly rounded forehead. The larger members
(5) of this porpoise and dolphin family are called "whales," but they nonetheless fit the same characteristics as their smaller relatives. The number of different names for these creatures reflects the confusion of long-ago sailors as they tried to classify them. Unfortunately, identifying them in their home in the sea is not easy, for the main differences between members of the species is in their skeletal structure.

18. The 40 different species that belong to the family Delphinidae have been referred to as all of the following designations except

(A) dolphin
(B) porpoise
(C) shrimpers
(D) cetacean
(E) whales

19. What is the main idea of this passage?

(A) People have trouble telling dolphins, porpoises, and whales apart.
(B) People long ago thought that dolphins were fish.
(C) Porpoises have smoothly rounded foreheads.
(D) There are many different varieties of cetaceans.
(E) Whales, which are very large, are not very similar to their smaller cousins, dolphins and porpoises.

20. According to the passage, which of the following is true of dolphins?

(A) They have a smoothly rounded forehead.
(B) They may be any one of 50 different species.
(C) They are sweet and affectionate creatures.
(D) They have a snout or beak.
(E) They can be trained to do tricks and often appear at water parks.

21. According to the passage, whales

(A) are not the same as cetaceans
(B) is the name we give to large porpoises and dolphins
(C) do not bear much similarity to porpoises and dolphins
(D) are not members of the Delphinidae family
(E) are beloved by sailors in the present as well as the past

Questions 22–30

It is for want of self-culture that the superstition of Traveling, whose idols are Italy, England, Egypt, retains its fascination for all educated Americans. They who made England, Italy, or Greece venerable in the imagination, did so by sticking fast where they were, like an axis of the earth. In manly hours we feel that duty is our place. The
(5) soul is no traveler; the wise man stays at home, and when his necessities, his duties, on any occasion call him from his house, or into foreign lands, he is at home still and shall make men sensible by the expression of his countenance that he goes, the missionary of wisdom and virtue, and visits cities and men like a sovereign and not like an interloper or a valet.
(10)   I have no churlish objection to the circumnavigation of the globe for the purposes of art, of study, and benevolence, so that the man is first domesticated, or does not go abroad with the hope of finding somewhat greater than he knows. He who travels to be amused, or to get somewhat which he does not carry, travels away from himself, and grows old even in youth among old things. In Thebes, in Palmyra, his will and mind have
(15) become old and dilapidated as they. He carries ruins to ruins.
   Traveling is a fool's paradise. Our first journeys discover to us the indifference of places. At home, I dream that at Naples, at Rome, I can be intoxicated with beauty and lose my sadness. I pack my trunk, embrace my friends, embark on the sea, and at last wake up in Naples, and there beside me is the same sad self, unrelenting, identical, that
(20) I fled from. I seek the Vatican and the palaces. I affect to be intoxicated with sights and suggestions, but I am not intoxicated. My giant goes with me wherever I go.

22. What purpose does the following sentence serve? "They who made England, Italy, or Greece venerable in the imagination, did so by sticking fast where they were, like an axis of the earth."

(A) It introduces the essential conflict in the essay.
(B) It underscores the immaturity of Europeans when compared to the sophistication of Americans.
(C) It berates people who choose to visit Europe before they tour America.
(D) It unifies the essay's imagery.
(E) It conveys the impression that the world revolves around Europe rather than America.

23. In the end of the first paragraph, the writer compares someone who travels for the wrong reasons to a

   (A)   great ruler
   (B)   weak monarch
   (C)   statue
   (D)   servant
   (E)   brave and masculine traveler

24. The connotation of the word domesticated in the phrase "so that the man is first domesticated" is

   (A)   trained
   (B)   educated and well-informed
   (C)   subdued
   (D)   tame
   (E)   well-mannered

25. The sentence "He carries ruins to ruins" in paragraph 2 refers to

   (A)   stealing valuable artifacts from foreign countries and smuggling them to America
   (B)   elderly people traveling to dangerous old cities
   (C)   traveling too much, which will result in premature aging
   (D)   traveling for the wrong reasons, which will deplete your sense of purpose and intelligence
   (E)   ruining the trip for others by traveling for selfish reasons

26. The writer believes that travel

   (A)   provides a unique educational opportunity for people of all ages, but especially for the mature and seasoned individual
   (B)   is too expensive to be undertaken without great thought
   (C)   can bridge the gap between the "haves" and the "have-nots"
   (D)   enables people to run away from themselves and their inner lives
   (E)   enriches our soul by giving us a wider view of people who are different from us

27. The writer's topics and themes include all of the following except

   (A)   knowledge and wisdom
   (B)   cultural appreciation
   (C)   self-awareness
   (D)   spiritual growth
   (E)   nature and the natural world

28. The writer of this essay would be least likely to

    (A) take a year-long tour of Europe for pleasure and diversion
    (B) stay home during his annual vacation to write and study
    (C) travel to a foreign land to help the victims of a terrible natural tragedy such as an earthquake or flood
    (D) engage in contemplation and introspection
    (E) encourage a young person to study abroad

29. Who or what is the "giant" of the last line?

    (A) people who travel too much
    (B) the self that is unable to find beauty at home and cannot be affected by the simple experiences of daily life
    (C) our conscience
    (D) the guilt we carry as citizens of the richest nation on earth
    (E) depression

30. Which sentence best summarizes the writer's main point?

    (A) There's no substitute for seeing the world.
    (B) Travel is wasted on the young because they are too inexperienced to appreciate the wonders they see.
    (C) No matter where we travel, we can never escape from ourselves.
    (D) Travel is a delightful diversion for people of all ages.
    (E) Only the young should travel; it is too dangerous for the elderly.

Questions 31–32

> Writing presents several problems for English as a Second Language learners (ESL) and Limited English Proficient (LEP) students. Difficulties arise from limited English vocabulary and internalized grammar patterns from the students' first language. Writing-as-a-process strategies are helpful to ESL and LEP students if these strategies
> (5) are comprehensible. Often, students do not understand an assignment because they do not understand many of the words in the writing prompt.

31. According to the author, what problems do English language learners face?

    (A) insufficient vocabulary, primarily
    (B) an inability to learn grammar
    (C) problems understanding writing strategies
    (D) having to be prompted to write
    (E) having insufficient vocabulary and poor command of structure

32. Which statement would the author most likely endorse?

(A) Nonnative English speakers can benefit from structured writing assignments, written in language they can understand.
(B) Everyone should learn a foreign language.
(C) Total immersion is better for ESL students than other forms of English instruction.
(D) Nonnative English speakers should be taught to write English before they are taught to speak it.
(E) Learning to write English is more difficult than learning to speak it.

Questions 33–37

> Eventually the whole business of purveying to the hospitals was, in effect, carried out by Miss Nightingale. She, alone, it seemed, whatever the contingency, knew where to lay her hands on what was wanted; she alone possessed the art of circumventing the pernicious influences of official etiquette. On one occasion 27,000 shirts arrived, sent out at her
> (5) insistence by the Home Government, and were only waiting to be unpacked. But the official "Purveyor" intervened; "I could only unpack them," he said, "with an official order from the Government." Miss Nightingale pleaded in vain; the sick and the wounded lay half-naked, shivering for want of clothing; and three weeks elapsed before the Government released the shipment. A little later, on a similar occasion, Miss
> (10) Nightingale ordered a Government consignment to be forcibly opened, while the "Purveyor" stood by, wringing his hands in departmental agony.

33. The use of the phrase "she alone" gives the reader an idea of Miss Nightingale's

(A) loneliness
(B) conceit
(C) femininity
(D) uniqueness
(E) inefficiency

34. Describing the influence of official etiquette as "pernicious" reveals the author's awareness of the

(A) dangers of red tape
(B) efficiency of command procedure
(C) lack of blood plasma
(D) women's liberation movement
(E) horrors of war

35. The description of the sick and wounded as "half-naked" and "shivering" serves as

(A) a metaphor
(B) weather information
(C) historic documentation
(D) a contrast to bureaucratic lack of concern
(E) irony

36. The Purveyor seems concerned only with

(A) humanity
(B) the ill men
(C) men's needs
(D) departmental procedure
(E) Miss Nightingale's requests

37. The tone of the phrase "departmental agony" is

(A) ironic
(B) despairing
(C) serious
(D) tragic
(E) funny

Question 38

38. Desktop publishing really encourages a sense of ownership and allows children to make a lot of decisions about layout, about what to put into a particular layout, and how to format the final document—so that when it's printed, there's really a great sense of creation. There's a lot of discussion, too, and a lot of cooperative learning—children get excited about what they are doing, and they go over to see what other children are doing. Students can be talking, listening, and working at the same time.

The author would most likely endorse

(A) organizing a multigrade classroom
(B) seating children in rows to discourage too much talking
(C) inviting parents into the classroom on a regular basis
(D) having students write daily
(E) integrating technology into the classroom

Questions 39–40

One of the rarest and most prized animals in the United States is the key deer. This tiny creature was once hunted without mercy. It was not uncommon for a single hunter to kill more than a dozen key deer in one day. Often, hunters set grass fires to drive the creatures out of hiding; other times, they were attacked with harpoons while they were
(5) swimming. In the 1950s, conservationists—led by the Boone and Crockett Club—saved the key deer from extinction. Today, the surviving key deer are protected by the U.S. government in the Key Deer National Wildlife Refuge, created in 1957.

39. Which of the following is implied in the passage?

(A) Species become at risk of dying out when they are hunted too extensively.
(B) The government is still the most effective way to safeguard the environment because it has the resources to establish effective programs.
(C) Endangered species will be saved only if they become a priority.
(D) Government officials and private citizens must work together to help the environment.
(E) The key deer is valuable for its beautiful coat.

40. According to the passage, today the key deer is

(A) protected by the government
(B) still endangered
(C) hunted without mercy
(D) not especially valuable
(E) extinct

STOP. This is the end of the Reading Diagnostic Test.

READING DIAGNOSTIC TEST: ANSWERS

1. E.   The entire passage demonstrates how just one vote can and often does make a difference in the outcome of an election.

2. A.   The numbers "572 to 571" in line 4 serve to emphasize how close the outcome was. Since we don't know how many people live in the town, we cannot conclude that few people exercise their right to vote (choice B). In fact, if the town had only 1,500 eligible voters, this turnout would be quite robust. The number of votes does not indicate that this particular election was significant or insignificant (choice C). The numbers have nothing to do with the issue of Internet voting rather than paper ballots (choice D). Finally, the vote actually shows that the voters decided that Emond was a better candidate than Nixon because Emond won the election, so choice E cannot be valid.

3. A.   The author argues that students lose their voice when they shift from personal writing to public expression. You can find the relevant details in this sentence: "Some teachers who have extensively used exploratory/response writing have been frustrated that the liveliness of the student's own voice can sometimes disappear when he or she moves from the relative privacy and free form of journal writing into the formal essay."

4. C.   The writer makes an assertion and backs it up with specific details. You can find the assertion in the second sentence: "Students need to be encouraged to find and explore their own topics in relation to literature and to maintain their own voices." Among the details that follow is this statement: "Some teachers who have extensively used exploratory/response writing have been frustrated that the liveliness of the student's own voice can sometimes disappear when he or she moves from the relative privacy and free form of journal writing into the formal essay."

5. B.   The scholarly tone and evident knowledge of classroom methodology suggest that the writer is either a classroom teacher or an educational scholar.

6. D.   The cost of heating oil is increasing because "the supply of these fuels is shrinking every day." This detail is directly stated in the passage.

7. E.   The author argues that everyone is interested in solar energy now. However, if fuel prices decrease as new supplies of fossil fuels are discovered, people's interest in alternative forms of energy is likely to decrease.

8. C.   The main idea is directly stated in the first two sentences: "Why is everyone interested in solar energy now? The reason is that the fuels we use are very expensive, and the supply of these fuels is shrinking every day." Eliminate choices A and D because they are details, and thus are too narrow to be the main idea. Eliminate choices B and E because they are not included in the information given in the paragraph.

9. B. The parallel phrases that elaborate on one another make the writing vigorous and logical. Think about famous quotes that use parallelism, such as John F. Kennedy's call in his inaugural address: "Ask not what your country can do for you but what you can do for your country."

10. E. Based on the details about the sweet air and lack of crime, you can conclude that this essay reveals the author's affection for and deep faith in the promise of America and Americans.

11. E. The author most likely seizes "teachable moments" by having students correct grammar errors in context. You can infer this from the statement "The time to help students learn grammar is when they need help in revising the structure of their sentences."

12. A. From the word *broad-based* in the first sentence, you can infer that this approach is not restrictive. This is the opposite of choices B and E, so you can eliminate them. Choices C and D are a misreading of the information in the passage.

13. C. Damage to rangeland is caused by all of the following *except* building too many homes and office buildings on land formerly set aside for pasture. Every other choice can be found in the passage. Choice A is found in the sentence "The roster of impacts from forest clearing includes . . . substantial contributions of the greenhouse gas, carbon dioxide to the atmosphere." Choice B is found in the same sentence: "The roster of impacts from forest clearing includes . . . loss of plant and animal species." Choice D comes from the sentence "Forests also suffer from livestock production, as branches are cut for fodder or entire stands are leveled to make way for pastures." Choice E comes from the sentence ". . . dramatic forest loss due to inappropriate livestock production."

14. D. The author's purpose is most likely to alert people to a serious problem and press for change. Choice C is too specific. The writer does not propose any specific solution. Choices B and E cannot be correct because the writer shows that the problem is worldwide and affects wealthy people as well as disadvantaged ones. There is no support for choice A.

15. E. The author develops the argument through a series of examples. With the exception of the topic sentence, the entire passage is a series of examples.

16. A. The serious, scholarly tone and specific examples suggest that this excerpt would most likely be published in a college textbook. The information about the destruction of grazing land would not be appropriate in a publication for home builders, who would most likely be looking for new land to develop. The same is true for choice E.

17. C. According to the author, teaching approaches should be tailored to an individual's learning style. You can infer this from the last sentence: "Both types of learners reason and learn equally well, but they do so through different strategies." The fact that there are two types of learning styles shows that choice A cannot be correct. Choice B is wrong because the way people learn new information is related to "their global versus their analytical cognitive processing styles," not their attitude toward school, according to this author. Some people do learn better with humor, the author states, but we cannot conclude from this that teachers should incorporate more humor into their lectures (choice D) because not all students respond to humor and not all topics are suited to humor. Last, choice E is incorrect because the author clearly defines different learning styles.

18. C.   The 40 different species that belong to the family Delphinidae have been referred to as all of the following designations *except* shrimpers. Shrimpers catch shrimp; they are not themselves fish.

19. A.   The main idea is that people have trouble telling dolphins, porpoises, and whales apart. This is especially clear in the last sentence: "Unfortunately, identifying them in their home in the sea is not easy, for the main differences between members of the species is in their skeletal structure."

20. D.   The detail that dolphins have a snout or beak can be found in the following sentence: "Some people distinguish a dolphin as a cetacean having a snout or beak." Choices C and E may be true but are not stated in the passage.

21. B.   The answer is directly stated in this sentence: "The larger members of this porpoise and dolphin family are called 'whales'..."

22. E.   The sentence conveys the impression that the world revolves around Europe rather than America. This is conveyed through the phrase "like an axis of the earth." The simile does not introduce the essential conflict in the essay (choice A) because the essay does not have a conflict. The author, Ralph Waldo Emerson, is expressing his opinion on travel and trying to convince us that his point of view is correct or at least deserves serious consideration. Choice B is wrong because neither the simile nor the essay underscores the immaturity of Europeans when compared to the sophistication of Americans. Indeed, the topic of immaturity never comes up. Choice C is wrong because Emerson does not berate people who choose to visit Europe before they tour America; rather, he believes that we should look into our souls for enlightenment rather than seeking diversion through travel. Choice D is wrong because this simile does not serve to unify the essay's imagery.

23. D.   At the end of the first paragraph, the writer compares someone who travels for the wrong reasons to a servant. You can figure this out by knowing that a valet is a servant. The information is found in the following line: "... and visits cities and men like a sovereign and not like an interloper or a valet." Choice A is a result of misreading the preceding line.

24. B.   The connotation of the word *domesticated* in the phrase "so that the man is first domesticated" is "educated and well-informed." This is a difficult question because *domesticated* has several different meanings. Choices A and C are synonyms with the most common meaning but not with the meaning that fits the context. Choice C does not make sense in context. Choice E is wrong because Emerson does not discuss how Americans act when they travel abroad, only that such travel rarely serves its purpose of enlightenment.

25. D.   The phrase "He carries ruins to ruins" in paragraph 2 refers to traveling for the wrong reasons, which will deplete your sense of purpose and intelligence. A close reading of the passage reveals Emerson's belief that someone who "travels to be amused, or to get somewhat which he does not carry, travels away from himself" and will find his soul grows weary through the useless search.

26. D.   The writer believes that travel enables people to run away from themselves and their inner lives. Of course, you only think you are running away. In fact, your problems go with you. You can infer this from the second paragraph as well as from sentences such as this one: "Traveling is a fool's paradise." Choice A is wrong because Emerson believes just the opposite of this statement: travel does *not* provide a unique educational opportunity for people of all ages, but especially not for the mature and seasoned individual. Choice E is again the opposite of Emerson's thesis: Travel does *not* enrich our soul by giving us a wider view of people who differ from us. Emerson never deals with the issue of cost, so choice B cannot be correct. The same is true for choice C.

27. E.   The writer's topics and themes include all of the following *except* nature and the natural world. Emerson treats knowledge and wisdom (choice A) at great length, as shown in this quote: ". . . by the expression of his countenance that he goes, the missionary of wisdom and virtue, and visits cities and men like a sovereign and not like an interloper or a valet." He also discusses cultural appreciation (choice B), revealed in this passage: "I have no churlish objection to the circumnavigation of the globe for the purposes of art, of study, and benevolence. . . ." The entire passage focuses on self-awareness (choice C) and spiritual growth (choice D), as shown in the passages cited earlier in this explanation.

28. A.   The writer of this essay would be *least* likely to take a year-long tour of Europe for pleasure and diversion because that is precisely what he condemns. This is evident in the following passage: "He who travels to be amused, or to get somewhat which he does not carry, travels away from himself, and grows old even in youth among old things." He is in favor of looking inward to find knowledge, so choice B is wrong. He would be in favor of traveling to a foreign land to help the victims of a terrible natural tragedy such as an earthquake or flood, so choice C is wrong. This is shown in the sentence "I have no churlish objection to the circumnavigation of the globe for the purposes of art, of study, and benevolence." The word *contemplation* shows that choice D cannot be correct. The same is true for choice E because of the prepositional phrase "of study."

29. B.   The "giant" of the last line is the self that is unable to find beauty at home and cannot be affected by the simple experiences of daily life. We carry this with us always because it defines who we are. Since Emerson does not travel too much (or at all, if he can avoid it), choice A cannot be correct. Choice C is close, but choice B is more precise. Since he does not discuss the unequal distribution of assets, choice D cannot be correct. Choice E is too big a leap, for we have no proof at all that he is depressed; on the contrary, he seems quite content with his life of study and introspection at home.

30. C.   The theme is best stated by choice C: No matter where we travel, we can never escape from ourselves. You can see this especially in the last two sentences: "I affect to be intoxicated with sights and suggestions, but I am not intoxicated. My giant goes with me wherever I go." Choice A is wrong because it is the opposite of the writer's theme. The same is true of choice D. There is no support for choice B.

31. E.   According to the author, ESL and LEP students have inadequate vocabulary and don't know the structure of their second language. You can find this detail in the following sentence: "Difficulties arise from limited English vocabulary and internalized grammar patterns from the students' first language." Choice A is partially correct. The other choices represent misreading of the passage.

32. A. You can infer that the author believes that nonnative English speakers can benefit from structured writing assignments, written in language they can understand. The textual clue is this: "Writing-as-a-process strategies are helpful to ESL and LEP students if these strategies are comprehensible. Often, students do not understand an assignment because they do not understand many words in the writing prompt." There is insufficient support for the other choices.

33. D. The use of the phrase "she alone" gives the reader an idea of Miss Nightingale's uniqueness. The first sentence reveals that she alone is responsible for the welfare of the sufferers.

34. A. *Pernicious* means "exceedingly harmful." Describing the influence of official etiquette as "pernicious" reveals the author's awareness of the dangers of red tape. The incident concerning the delay in unpacking shirts already in the hospital shows the author's feelings about red tape, the official tendency to make things more difficult than they need be.

35. D. The description of the sick and wounded as "half-naked" and "shivering" contrasts to bureaucratic lack of concern. The author underscores the same point with the example of the shirts being unreleased.

36. D. The Purveyor seems concerned only with departmental procedure. That he could stand by and watch people suffer shows this. The final incident is another example of his disregard for people's suffering.

37. A. The tone is ironic because the Purveyor feels agony not because of any real wartime suffering, but rather because his authority is being usurped.

38. E. You can tell that the author would most likely endorse integrating technology into the classroom from the tone of the opening: "Desktop publishing really encourages a sense of ownership and allows children to make a lot of decisions about layout. . . ." Other details such as "children get excited about what they are doing" add to this first impression.

39. C. The passage implies that endangered species will be saved only if they become a priority. The key deer escaped extinction only when conservationists, led by the Boone and Crockett Club, took measures to protect the animal. Choice A clearly applies to the key deer, but a species can also become endangered when its habitat disappears or when members fall prey to disease. Thus, choice A is too general. Choice B is another gross generalization. Choice D is wrong because either group can accomplish much on its own. Further, we do not know whether the conservationists and Boone and Crockett Club members are government employees or private citizens. Finally, choice E is not supported by evidence in the passage. It may have been hunted for sport or for its meat.

40. A. The answer is directly stated in the last sentence: "Today, the surviving key deer are protected by the U.S. government in the Key Deer National Wildlife Refuge, created in 1957."

Skills Spread

Skill Type	Item Numbers
Literal understanding	3, 6, 12, 13, 15, 17, 18, 19, 20, 21, 23, 24, 25, 26, 27, 29, 35, 40
Inferential and critical understanding	1, 2, 4, 5, 7, 8, 9, 10, 11, 14, 16, 22, 28, 30, 31, 32, 33, 34, 36, 37, 38, 39

CHAPTER 5

Writing Diagnostic Test

ANSWER SHEET

1 Ⓐ Ⓑ Ⓒ Ⓓ Ⓔ
2 Ⓐ Ⓑ Ⓒ Ⓓ Ⓔ
3 Ⓐ Ⓑ Ⓒ Ⓓ Ⓔ
4 Ⓐ Ⓑ Ⓒ Ⓓ Ⓔ
5 Ⓐ Ⓑ Ⓒ Ⓓ Ⓔ
6 Ⓐ Ⓑ Ⓒ Ⓓ Ⓔ
7 Ⓐ Ⓑ Ⓒ Ⓓ Ⓔ

8 Ⓐ Ⓑ Ⓒ Ⓓ Ⓔ
9 Ⓐ Ⓑ Ⓒ Ⓓ Ⓔ
10 Ⓐ Ⓑ Ⓒ Ⓓ Ⓔ
11 Ⓐ Ⓑ Ⓒ Ⓓ Ⓔ
12 Ⓐ Ⓑ Ⓒ Ⓓ Ⓔ
13 Ⓐ Ⓑ Ⓒ Ⓓ Ⓔ
14 Ⓐ Ⓑ Ⓒ Ⓓ Ⓔ

15 Ⓐ Ⓑ Ⓒ Ⓓ Ⓔ
16 Ⓐ Ⓑ Ⓒ Ⓓ Ⓔ
17 Ⓐ Ⓑ Ⓒ Ⓓ Ⓔ
18 Ⓐ Ⓑ Ⓒ Ⓓ Ⓔ
19 Ⓐ Ⓑ Ⓒ Ⓓ Ⓔ
20 Ⓐ Ⓑ Ⓒ Ⓓ Ⓔ
21 Ⓐ Ⓑ Ⓒ Ⓓ Ⓔ

22 Ⓐ Ⓑ Ⓒ Ⓓ Ⓔ
23 Ⓐ Ⓑ Ⓒ Ⓓ Ⓔ
24 Ⓐ Ⓑ Ⓒ Ⓓ Ⓔ
25 Ⓐ Ⓑ Ⓒ Ⓓ Ⓔ
26 Ⓐ Ⓑ Ⓒ Ⓓ Ⓔ
27 Ⓐ Ⓑ Ⓒ Ⓓ Ⓔ
28 Ⓐ Ⓑ Ⓒ Ⓓ Ⓔ

29 Ⓐ Ⓑ Ⓒ Ⓓ Ⓔ
30 Ⓐ Ⓑ Ⓒ Ⓓ Ⓔ
31 Ⓐ Ⓑ Ⓒ Ⓓ Ⓔ
32 Ⓐ Ⓑ Ⓒ Ⓓ Ⓔ
33 Ⓐ Ⓑ Ⓒ Ⓓ Ⓔ
34 Ⓐ Ⓑ Ⓒ Ⓓ Ⓔ
35 Ⓐ Ⓑ Ⓒ Ⓓ Ⓔ

36 Ⓐ Ⓑ Ⓒ Ⓓ Ⓔ
37 Ⓐ Ⓑ Ⓒ Ⓓ Ⓔ
38 Ⓐ Ⓑ Ⓒ Ⓓ Ⓔ

WRITING DIAGNOSTIC TEST

SECTION 1: MULTIPLE-CHOICE QUESTIONS

38 questions, 30 minutes

Directions: The following sentences require you to identify errors in grammar, usage, punctuation, and capitalization. Not every sentence has an error, and no sentence will have more than one error. Every sentence error, if there is one, is underlined and lettered. If the sentence does have an error, select the one underlined part that must be changed to make the sentence correct and blacken the corresponding circle on your answer sheet. If the sentence does not have an error, blacken circle E. Elements of the sentence that are not underlined are not to be changed.

Part A

21 questions, suggested time: 10 minutes

1. <u>Grasshoppers</u> are the <u>most commonly</u> consumed <u>insect, wasps</u> have the highest
    A   B   C

   protein content—<u>81 percent</u>—of all edible insects. <u>No error</u>.
                D   E

2. <u>Her influence</u> over the next <u>forty years</u> was tremendous, <u>as she writes</u> essays,
    A   B   C

   lectured, and espoused the cause of fine <u>children's books</u> all over New York
                                       D

   and New England. <u>No error</u>.
                   E

3. <u>Today's</u> mild weather was <u>more comfortable</u> than yesterday's brisk <u>weather, so</u>
    A   B   C

   the teacher <u>decided to hold</u> class outdoors. <u>No error</u>.
               D   E

4. The <u>dietitian thinks</u> that salmon is the <u>better</u> of all fish because
        A   B

   <u>it is healthful and tasty,</u> as well <u>as being easily</u> available. <u>No error</u>.
       C   D   E

5. The principal <u>knows</u> of no other teacher <u>who</u> is as intelligent as <u>her</u>, and so has
              A   B   C

   recommended <u>her</u> for a raise. <u>No error</u>.
                 D   E

6. Louise and I have <u>decided to take</u> the PPST this <u>Spring</u>, because <u>we have</u>
       A   B   C   D

   studied for weeks. <u>No error</u>.
                    E

7. <u>As he</u> <u>was walking</u> near the boarded-up shopping complex <u>in the center</u> of
   A   B   C

   town, <u>a gold bracelet</u> was found by Herman. <u>No error</u>.
             D   E

8. First <u>it rained</u> a great deal, then <u>it hailed</u> for a few minutes<u>, and</u> <u>finally snow</u>.
        A   B   C   D

   <u>No error</u>.
     E

9. <u>Making startling new discoveries in science during the Renaissance</u>,
                           A

   <u>when people</u> <u>made</u> startling <u>new discoveries</u> in science. <u>No error</u>.
      B   C   D   E

10. <u>Nourishing</u>, low-calorie foods such as fresh fruits<u>, vegetables, lean meats, and</u>
      A   B

   seafood <u>is rarely served</u> in homes <u>where people do not have</u> enough money.
             C   D

   <u>No error</u>.
     E

11. <u>Some people claim</u> <u>this is</u> the decade of fitness<u>; but</u> at least one-third of
             A   B   C

   the American population <u>is classified</u> as obese. <u>No error</u>.
                       D   E

12. <u>During the graduation ceremonies</u>, the superintendent of schools told the story of
               A

   the desks and <u>cites their cleaning</u> <u>as evidence</u> of a new spirit of responsibility
                    B   C

   <u>among students</u>. <u>No error</u>.
        D   E

13. The twins are fond of peanuts and <u>eating ice cream,</u> <u>but their parents</u> are loath
                                                                A   B

to give <u>the children</u> snacks <u>between meals.</u> <u>No error.</u>
                    C   D   E

14. The real estate broker <u>promised to notify</u> my <u>partner and I</u> as soon as the house
                                              A   B

<u>was put up for sale</u> so <u>we could make</u> any necessary repairs to the structure. <u>No error.</u>
              C   D   E

15. Either the witness or the defendant <u>was lying,</u> but <u>the judge was</u> unable to
                                                              A   B

determine <u>which</u> of the two men was <u>committing prejudice.</u> <u>No error.</u>
                        C   D   E

16. <u>A close friend of the family,</u> the patient <u>was referred</u> to a psychologist
              A   B

<u>with several emotional problems</u> to <u>receive counseling.</u> <u>No error.</u>
                          C   D   E

17. The speaker <u>didn't say nothing</u> that the audience had not already <u>heard; as a result,</u>
                              A   B

the <u>audience quickly</u> lost interest in his speech and <u>began to talk</u> among themselves.
                  C   D

<u>No error.</u>
      E

18. <u>The Word workshop trains</u> employees in maximizing skills to <u>improve</u>
                    A   B

<u>employees' productivity, the Internet</u> training teaches employees <u>how to use the Internet</u>
                          C   D

for product searches and e-mail to worldwide subscribers. <u>No error.</u>
                                                                                              E

19. <u>The recipe was complex</u> but is <u>worth</u> it because chicken and biscuits <u>made this way</u>
                    A   B   C

<u>tastes more deliciously.</u> <u>No error.</u>
              D   E

20. The prominent lawyer won more awards than <u>anyone at</u> the ceremony,
A

<u>which surprised her</u> because <u>she had long taken on</u> unpopular cases <u>and defendants</u>.
B   C   D

<u>No error</u>.
    E

21. <u>We moved</u> our sleeping bags closer to the fire, <u>hanged blankets</u> over the windows,
  A   B

<u>made some hot cocoa</u>, and <u>added more logs to the blaze</u>. <u>No error</u>.
     C   D   E

Part B

17 questions, suggested time: 20 minutes

Directions: Choose the best version of the underlined portion of each sentence. Choice A is the same as the underlined portion of the original sentence. If you think that the original sentence is better than any of the suggested revisions, choose A. Otherwise, choose the revision you think is best. Answers and explanations follow the questions.

22. There have been many controversial World Series, but the <u>most unique one</u> was certainly the thrown World Series of 1919.

(A) most unique one
(B) most one-of-a-kind
(C) unique one
(D) uniquest one
(E) one that was the most unique

23. Derek Bickerton, a noted linguist, described some of the best examples of the innate formation of a grammar <u>system he</u> noted that indentured workers on plantations in the South Pacific needed to communicate with each other in order to carry out practical tasks.

(A) system he
(B) system when he
(C) system, he
(D) system yet he
(E) system; he

24. It was not until 1966 that an African-American <u>become the coach</u> of a major United States professional sports team.

    (A) become the coach
    (B) became the coach
    (C) coaching
    (D) were coaching
    (E) becoming the coach

25. According to the new personnel policy instituted this year, <u>it is necessary for all employees to select a health plan.</u>

    (A) it is necessary for all employees to select a health plan
    (B) it is required that all employees to select a health plan
    (C) because it is necessary all employees to select a health plan
    (D) since it is necessary all employees to select a health plan
    (E) all employees must select a health plan

26. Each morning when the guards checked my shoulder bag and clanked shut the iron door behind me, the old convict in me <u>rose up</u> full of hatred and rage for the guards, the walls, the terrible indecency of the place.

    (A) rose up
    (B) rosed up
    (C) rised up
    (D) risen up
    (E) rise up

27. <u>Tornadoes</u> can pick up a house and drop it hundreds of feet away, these are extremely dangerous storms.

    (A) Tornadoes
    (B) When tornadoes
    (C) If tornadoes
    (D) Since tornadoes
    (E) A tornado

28. The candidate went to political rallies, spoke at meetings, and <u>she shook many hands</u>.

    (A) she shook many hands
    (B) was shaking many hands
    (C) had been shaking many hands
    (D) realized the importance of shaking hands
    (E) shook many hands

29. The conference will provide training to ensure that our employees are kept abreast of the latest technology advancements <u>and is able to</u> function in the information age.

    (A) and is able to
    (B) and was able to
    (C) is able to
    (D) and being able to
    (E) and are able to

30. <u>Temp work is done by actors, models, artists, musicians, and writers in their chosen fields when possible,</u> but often find that temp work in other fields can tide them over during lean times.

    (A) Temp work is done by actors, models, artists, musicians, and writers in their chosen fields when possible,
    (B) Actors, models, artists, musicians, and writers do temp work in their chosen fields when possible,
    (C) Actors, models, artists, musicians, and writers work in their chosen fields when possible,
    (D) In their chosen fields when possible, temp work is done by actors, models, artists, musicians, and writers
    (E) When possible, temp work is done by actors, models, artists, musicians, and writers in their chosen fields

31. <u>A turkey instead of an eagle was first wanted by Ben Franklin as our national symbol.</u>

    (A) A turkey instead of an eagle was first wanted by Ben Franklin as our national symbol.
    (B) First, a turkey instead of an eagle was wanted by Ben Franklin as our national symbol.
    (C) As our national symbol, a turkey instead of an eagle was first wanted by Ben Franklin.
    (D) Ben Franklin first wanted a turkey instead of an eagle as our national symbol.
    (E) By Ben Franklin, a turkey instead of an eagle was first wanted as our national symbol.

32. During a thunderstorm, people who are inside should not talk on the telephone, stand near any open windows, or <u>using large appliances.</u>

    (A) using large appliances
    (B) use large appliances
    (C) have been using large appliances
    (D) used large appliances
    (E) were using large appliances

33. Of all the movies ever made, *The Godfather* has been recognized as one of America's <u>greater movies.</u>

    (A) greater movies
    (B) more great movies
    (C) greatest movies
    (D) more greater movies
    (E) most greater movies

34. Most people who drink coffee do not know where it comes <u>from it is</u> actually the fruit of an evergreen tree.

    (A) from it is
    (B) from, it is
    (C) from it is,
    (D) from; it is
    (E) from it; is

35. Samuel Morse patented the telegraph in 1842. On March 3, 1843, <u>Morse was granted $30,000 from congress to build a trial line between Baltimore and Washington</u>.

    (A) Morse was granted $30,000 from congress to build a trial line between Baltimore and Washington.
    (B) Morse was granted $30,000 from congress to build a trial line between baltimore and washington.
    (C) Morse was granted $30,000 from congress to build a Trial Line between baltimore and washington.
    (D) Morse was granted $30,000 from congress to build a Trial Line between Baltimore and Washington.
    (E) Morse was granted $30,000 from Congress to build a trial line between Baltimore and Washington.

36. We must create a classroom environment that <u>support and encourage</u> experimentation and sharing.

    (A) support and encourage
    (B) supports and encourage
    (C) support and encourages
    (D) supports and encourages
    (E) supporting and encouraging

37. We fund programs like that all around the country, and they are <u>enormous successful.</u>

    (A) enormous successful.
    (B) enormously successful.
    (C) enormous successfully.
    (D) enormously successfully.
    (E) very enormous successful.

38. <u>Our students are becoming more familiar with good poetry</u>, we should give them a chance to write their own poetry.

(A) Our students are becoming more familiar with good poetry,

(B) Since our students are becoming more familiar with good poetry,

(C) While our students are becoming more familiar with good poetry

(D) Our students become more familiar with good poetry,

(E) Our students becoming more familiar with good poetry,

STOP. This is the end of Section 1: Multiple-Choice Questions.

SECTION 2: ESSAY

30 minutes

Directions: Write an essay on the following topic. You will not receive any credit for writing on a topic other than the one given here. Plan your essay carefully and be sure to include specific examples and details that illustrate your point. Write your essay on your own sheets of paper. (On the real Praxis PPST test, paper for writing your essay will be provided.)

You will not receive credit if you write on any other topic. For your response to be scored, you must write in English. you cannot write in a foreign language.

Read the opinion stated:

Fast-food franchises should be allowed in schools.

The space below is for your notes.

WRITING DIAGNOSTIC TEST: ANSWERS

SECTION 1: MULTIPLE-CHOICE

Part A

1. C.   This is a run-on sentence, two independent clauses incorrectly joined. The sentence can be corrected by adding a coordinating conjunction as follows: *Grasshoppers are the most commonly consumed insect, but wasps have the highest protein content—81 percent—of all edible insects.*

2. C.   This sentence has an error in verb tense. Every sentence must be consistent in the use of verb tenses. Because the sentence begins in the past tense (was), the sentence must stay in the past tense (wrote). The correct sentence reads: *Her influence over the next 40 years was tremendous, as she wrote essays, lectured, and espoused the cause of fine children's books all over New York and New England.*

3. E.   This sentence is correct as written.

4. B.   Use the superlative degree, *best*, because more than two things are being compared.

5. C.   *She* is the subject of the understood verb *is*. Therefore, the pronoun is in the nominative case. Read the sentence to yourself this way: *The principal knows of no other teacher who is as intelligent as she [is], and so has recommended her for a raise.*

6. C.   Do not capitalize the names of seasons, unless they are used as the first word in a sentence. Choice (A) is correct because it is in the nominative case, since "Louise and I" is the subject of the sentence. They are doing the action.

7. D.   Avoid the passive construction. The sentence should read: *As he was walking near the boarded-up shopping complex in the center of town, Herman found a gold bracelet.*

8. D.   This is an error in parallel structure (having ideas of the same rank in the same grammatical structure). Parallel each clause to *it rained*. Start with the clause it rained. Here is one correct revision: *First it rained a great deal, then it hailed for a few minutes, and finally it snowed heavily.*

9. A.   This is a dangling modifier. Choice (A) is one correct version of the sentence: *The Renaissance was a time of rebirth when people made startling new discoveries in science.*

10. C.   This question tests your understanding of subject-verb agreement. The plural subject *foods* takes a plural verb. Here, use the plural form of the verb "to be," *are: Nourishing, low-calorie foods such as fresh fruits, vegetables, lean meats, and seafood are rarely served in homes where people do not have enough money.* Ignore the intervening prepositional phrase: such as fresh fruits, vegetables, lean meats, and seafood.

11. C.   The error here is in punctuation. A semi-colon functions the same as a coordinating conjunction used to connect two independent clauses, so using a semi-colon and "but" is redundant. Use one or the other.

12. B.   The error occurs in verb tense. Tenses must be consistent and logical throughout a sentence and a passage. Here, the sentence begins in the past tense (*told*) and so must continue in the same tense. The word *cites* switches to the present tense. Choice D is correct as written because we use *among* when referring to groups of three or more and *between* when referring to two people.

13. A.   This is a parallel structure question: The phrase *eating ice cream* does not parallel the phrase *are fond of peanuts*. The correct sentence reads: *The twins are fond of peanuts and ice cream, but their parents are loath to give the children snacks between meals.*

14. B.   This is a question on pronoun case. Pronouns in English have three cases: nominative, objective, and possessive. In this sentence, *me* (together with *my partner*) is the object of the infinitive to *notify*. Therefore, the pronoun must be in the objective case. The correct sentence reads: *The real estate broker promised to notify my partner and me as soon as the house was put up for sale so we could make any necessary repairs to the structure.*

15. D.   This is a question about diction. The correct word is *perjury*, which refers to lying under oath. It is the word required by the sentence.

16. C.   As written, this sentence contains a misplaced modifier, a phrase, clause, or word placed too far from the word or word it modifies (describes.) The misplaced modifier with several emotional problems implies that the psychologist has emotional problems, not the patient. The correct sentence reads: *A close friend of the family, the patient with several emotional problems, was referred to a psychologist to receive counseling.*

17. A.   The error in this sentence is a double negative: *n't in didn't and nothing*. The correct sentence reads: *The speaker didn't say anything that the audience had not already heard; as a result, the audience quickly lost interest in his speech and began to talk among themselves.* Or: *The speaker said nothing that the audience had not already heard; as a result, the audience quickly lost interest in his speech and began to talk among themselves.*

18. C.   This is a comma splice, two independent clauses (complete sentences) run together with only a comma to separate them. Two complete sentences cannot be joined with only a comma; they require a semicolon or a coordinating conjunction (*for, and, nor, but, or, yet, so*). Here is one correct revision: *The Word workshop trains employees in maximizing skills to improve employees' productivity, while the Internet training teaches employees how to use the Internet for product searches and e-mail to worldwide subscribers.*

19. D.   Use an adjective (*delicious*) rather than an adverb (*deliciously*) after a linking verb (*tastes*). The correct sentence reads: *The recipe was complex but is worth it because chicken and biscuits made this way tastes more delicious.*

20. A. The error here is an illogical comparison. Since the thing you are comparing is part of a group, you have to differentiate it from the group first by using the word *other* or *else*. The correct sentence reads: *The prominent lawyer won more awards than anyone else at the ceremony, which surprised her because she had long taken on unpopular cases and defendants.*

21. B. This is an error in diction. "Hanged" is used to refer to people; "hung" is used to refer to things.

Part B

22. C. Since *unique* is already in superlative degree, it cannot be further modified.

23. B. As written, this is a run-on sentence. Choice B corrects the error by creating a subordinate clause with the subordinating conjunction *when*. Choice C is still a run-on. Choice D does not make logical sense because the conjunction *yet* does not fit in this context. Choice E is technically correct because you can use a semi-colon to join two independent clauses. However, the conjunction in choice B is better because it serves to link ideas logically. The correct sentence reads: *Derek Bickerton, a noted linguist, described some of the best examples of the innate formation of a grammar system when he noted that indentured workers on plantations in the South Pacific needed to communicate with each other in order to carry out practical tasks.*

24. B. The past tense *became* is required to show that the action has already taken place. Choices C (*coaching*) and D (*were coaching*) introduce new errors.

25. E. Choice E is the best answer because it eliminates unnecessary words. Choices C and D create sentence fragments. The correct sentence reads: *According to the new personnel policy instituted this year, all employees must select a health plan.*

26. A. This question tests verbs in the past tense, as required by the sentence. *Rose* is the correct past tense of *to rise*. The correct sentence reads: *Each morning when the guards checked my shoulder bag and clanked shut the iron door behind me, the old convict in me rose up full of hatred and rage for the guards, the walls, the terrible indecency of the place.*

27. D. As written, this is not a complete sentence. The first group of words—*Tornadoes can pick up a house and drop it hundreds of feet away*—must be subordinated to the main clause—*these are extremely dangerous storms. Since* is the most logical subordinating conjunction in context. The correct sentence reads: *Since tornadoes can pick up a house and drop it hundreds of feet away, these are extremely dangerous storms.*

28. E. This is a question on parallel structure. The phrase *shook many hands* parallels *went to political rallies* and *spoke at meetings*. The correct sentence reads: *The candidate went to political rallies, spoke at meetings, and shook many hands.*

29. E. The question tests subject-verb agreement. *Employees* is plural, so it requires the plural verb *are*. The correct sentence reads: *The conference will provide training to ensure that our employees are kept abreast of the latest technology advancements and are able to function in the information age.*

30. C. The sentence should be recast in the active voice to be less wordy and more direct. The most correct version is C: *Actors, models, artists, musicians, and writers work in their chosen fields when possible.* Also notice that this version eliminates the redundancy of saying "temp work" twice.

31. D. As written, the sentence is in the passive voice. In this construction, the subject receives the action. In the active voice, the subject performs the action named by the verb. In general, the active voice is preferable to the passive voice because the active voice is less wordy. The sentence should read: *Ben Franklin first wanted a turkey instead of an eagle as our national symbol.*

32. B. As written, the sentence lacks parallel structure. The sentence should read: *During a thunderstorm, people who are inside should not talk on the telephone, stand near any open windows, or use large appliances.* In the revised sentence, *talk on the telephone* and *stand near any open windows* parallel *use large appliances.*

33. C. Use the superlative case (*-est* or *most*) to compare three or more things, as is the case here, since more than three movies are being compared. Never use *-er* and more or *-est* and most together. The correct sentence reads: *Of all the movies ever made, The Godfather has been recognized as one of America's greatest movies.*

34. D. As written, this is a run-on sentence, two independent clauses run together. Just adding a comma (choice B) creates a comma splice. You can correct the error by adding a semi-colon or a coordinating conjunction (*and, for, but, yet, so, nor, or*). Choice D is the only correct version: *Most people who drink coffee do not know where it comes from; it is actually the fruit of an evergreen tree.*

35. E. As written, this sentence has errors in capitalization. "Congress" should be capitalized when it refers to the House of Representatives and the Senate. However, the word is not capitalized when it refers to a generic group or any other meaning it has. Capitalize the names of cities (*Baltimore, Washington*.) There is no reason to capitalize "trial line" because it is not a proper noun.

36. D. This question tests agreement of subject and verb. Use the singular verbs *supports* and *encourages* to agree (or match) the singular subject *classroom environment.*

37. B. Use an adverb (*enormously*) to modify or describe an adjective (*successful*).

38. B. As written, this is a run-on sentence. Correct the error by subordinating the first clause to the sentence by adding the subordinating conjunction "while."

SECTION 2: ESSAY

The following model essay would receive a 6, the highest score, for its specific details, organization, and style (appropriate word choice, sentence structure, and consistent facility in use of language). It is an especially intelligent and insightful response.

Every student has heard of "mystery meat," that puzzling gray staple of school cafeteria lunches. Students fear and shun mystery meat—with good cause—so it usually gets dumped in the trash. Unfortunately, vegetables, fruits, and juices follow suit, as kids crave burgers, fries, and shakes. Since so much food is wasted, why not give kids what they want to eat in the first place?

Soda companies have already insinuated themselves into school cafeterias, successfully marketing sugar-rich carbonated drinks to students. In many schools, students can't buy soda during the school day, but as soon as classes end, students flock to the soda machines like lemmings to the sea. School districts don't complain about this arrangement because part of the profits from soda sales goes to pay for such "extras" as athletic equipment, lighting, scoreboards, and field trips. But even if the district does not need the money generated from soda machines to fund "extras," soda companies and other fast-food franchises should be able to sell their products in schools to fund essential items such as textbooks, field trips, and school repairs. Further, students should have the right to get the foods and carbonated drinks they want, rather than being forced to eat vile "mystery meat."

On the other hand, former U.S. Surgeon General David Satcher claims that some 300,000 children a year die from illnesses related to obesity. To help kids eat healthful food, Satcher has called for the removal of fast food from schools. Of course, fast foods aren't the only cause of obesity, but these foods are one of the main reasons why Americans are the fattest people on earth. We are fast becoming the least healthy people, too, succumbing from diseases linked to being overweight, such as heart disease and diabetes. Schools should be teaching students the advantages of eating fruits, vegetables, and broiled rather than fried meats.

Fast-food franchises should be allowed in schools only if they sell healthful food. Some possibilities include juices (currently sold at nearly all fast-food chains), BK Broilers, and McDonald's salads. A change in menu would help schools raise much-needed funds as well as teach students healthy eating habits.

Skills Spread

Specific Content Area	Item Numbers
Grammar and usage	2, 4, 5, 10, 12, 14, 20, 24, 26, 29, 33, 36, 38
Sentence structure	1, 7, 8, 9, 13, 16, 18, 23, 27, 28, 30, 31, 32, 34
Mechanics (punctuation, capitalization) Diction (word choice)	3, 6, 11, 15, 17, 19, 21, 22, 25, 35, 37
Essay	1

CHAPTER 6

Mathematics Diagnostic Test

ANSWER SHEET

1 Ⓐ Ⓑ Ⓒ Ⓓ Ⓔ	8 Ⓐ Ⓑ Ⓒ Ⓓ Ⓔ	15 Ⓐ Ⓑ Ⓒ Ⓓ Ⓔ
2 Ⓐ Ⓑ Ⓒ Ⓓ Ⓔ	9 Ⓐ Ⓑ Ⓒ Ⓓ Ⓔ	16 Ⓐ Ⓑ Ⓒ Ⓓ Ⓔ
3 Ⓐ Ⓑ Ⓒ Ⓓ Ⓔ	10 Ⓐ Ⓑ Ⓒ Ⓓ Ⓔ	17 Ⓐ Ⓑ Ⓒ Ⓓ Ⓔ
4 Ⓐ Ⓑ Ⓒ Ⓓ Ⓔ	11 Ⓐ Ⓑ Ⓒ Ⓓ Ⓔ	18 Ⓐ Ⓑ Ⓒ Ⓓ Ⓔ
5 Ⓐ Ⓑ Ⓒ Ⓓ Ⓔ	12 Ⓐ Ⓑ Ⓒ Ⓓ Ⓔ	19 Ⓐ Ⓑ Ⓒ Ⓓ Ⓔ
6 Ⓐ Ⓑ Ⓒ Ⓓ Ⓔ	13 Ⓐ Ⓑ Ⓒ Ⓓ Ⓔ	20 Ⓐ Ⓑ Ⓒ Ⓓ Ⓔ
7 Ⓐ Ⓑ Ⓒ Ⓓ Ⓔ	14 Ⓐ Ⓑ Ⓒ Ⓓ Ⓔ	21 Ⓐ Ⓑ Ⓒ Ⓓ Ⓔ
22 Ⓐ Ⓑ Ⓒ Ⓓ Ⓔ	29 Ⓐ Ⓑ Ⓒ Ⓓ Ⓔ	36 Ⓐ Ⓑ Ⓒ Ⓓ Ⓔ
23 Ⓐ Ⓑ Ⓒ Ⓓ Ⓔ	30 Ⓐ Ⓑ Ⓒ Ⓓ Ⓔ	37 Ⓐ Ⓑ Ⓒ Ⓓ Ⓔ
24 Ⓐ Ⓑ Ⓒ Ⓓ Ⓔ	31 Ⓐ Ⓑ Ⓒ Ⓓ Ⓔ	38 Ⓐ Ⓑ Ⓒ Ⓓ Ⓔ
25 Ⓐ Ⓑ Ⓒ Ⓓ Ⓔ	32 Ⓐ Ⓑ Ⓒ Ⓓ Ⓔ	39 Ⓐ Ⓑ Ⓒ Ⓓ Ⓔ
26 Ⓐ Ⓑ Ⓒ Ⓓ Ⓔ	33 Ⓐ Ⓑ Ⓒ Ⓓ Ⓔ	40 Ⓐ Ⓑ Ⓒ Ⓓ Ⓔ
27 Ⓐ Ⓑ Ⓒ Ⓓ Ⓔ	34 Ⓐ Ⓑ Ⓒ Ⓓ Ⓔ	
28 Ⓐ Ⓑ Ⓒ Ⓓ Ⓔ	35 Ⓐ Ⓑ Ⓒ Ⓓ Ⓔ	

MATHEMATICS DIAGNOSTIC TEST

40 questions, 60 minutes

Directions: Select the best answer for each question and mark your choice on the answer sheet.

1. If the probability of picking a brown sock from your drawer is 0.4, and if you randomly pick 15 socks out of the drawer, about how many would be brown?

  (A) 0
  (B) 4
  (C) 5
  (D) 6
  (E) 8

2. Which pairs of decimals and fractions are equivalent?
  I. 0.15, 1/5   II. 0.5, 4/8   III. 0.6, 3/5

  (A) I only
  (B) II only
  (C) I and II
  (D) II and III
  (E) I, II, and III

3. Which of these fractions is not equivalent to the others?

  (A) 2/3
  (B) 5/15
  (C) 4/6
  (D) 8/12
  (E) 18/27

4. Which answer is closest to 0.0003×12.1?

  (A) 36
  (B) 0.36
  (C) 0.036
  (D) 0.0036
  (E) 0.00036

5. Ken, a theatrical director, said that the skills a performer should have are broken down as shown in the following pie chart. If dancing should constitute about 33 percent of a performer's emphasis, about how much should be on singing?

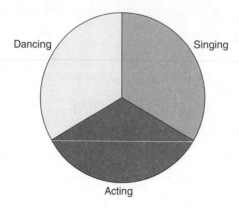

(A) 0 percent
(B) 25 percent
(C) 33 percent
(D) 50 percent
(E) 66 percent

6. If you roll 2 six-sided dice, what is the probability that the combined total shown will be 5?

(A) 1/6
(B) 7/36
(C) 1/12
(D) 1/9
(E) 0

7. Which of these problems have the same numerical answer?
   I. If I need 3 cups of flour to make 1 batch of waffles, how many full batches can I make with 37 cups of flour?
   II. If three people share the $37 cost of a gift evenly, how much does each pay?
   III. If three people divided up 37 pies to take home, how many pies would each person get?

(A) I and II
(B) I and III
(C) II and III
(D) I, II, and III
(E) None of the above

8. On the ruler shown here, the arrow most likely indicates:

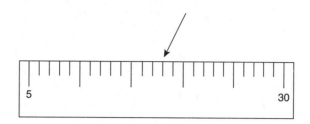

(A) 13
(B) 14
(C) 7 $^3/_5$
(D) 18
(E) 23

9. "Some cubes are red." Which of the following is true according to this statement?

(A) All cubes are red.
(B) All balls are blue.
(C) Some red things are cubes.
(D) No balls are red.
(E) Things that are not red are not cubes.

10. 77,100 is how many times 7.71?

(A) 100
(B) 1,000
(C) 10,000
(D) 100,000
(E) 1,000,000

11. Which answer is closest to 990 × 4,791?

(A) 5,000,000
(B) 9,000,000
(C) 10,000,000
(D) 27,000,000
(E) 45,000,000

12. What are the coordinates of point F?

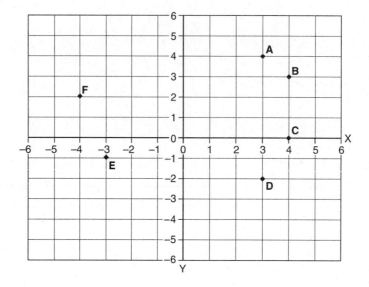

(A) $(2, 4)$

(B) $(4, 2)$

(C) $(2, -4)$

(D) $(-4, 2)$

(E) $(-4, -2)$

13. Which number falls between 3/5 and 7/9?

(A) 75 percent

(B) 0.123

(C) 1/2

(D) 0.9

(E) 36/45

14. What is the mean number of meetings for these 5 days?

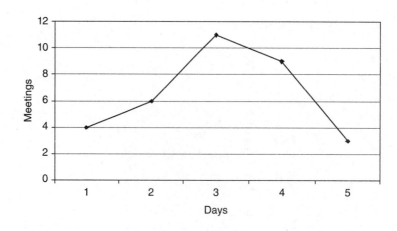

(A) 3
(B) 6.6
(C) 7.5
(D) 8
(E) 11

15. If $x \div 2 = y$, what is $2x$?

(A) y
(B) $y \div 2$
(C) $y \div 4$
(D) $2y$
(E) $4y$

16. Which decimal is greatest?

(A) 0.0034
(B) 0.001567
(C) 0.000998
(D) 0.00457
(E) 0.00001156

17. A teacher has 4 students with red hair, 10 with blond hair, and 10 with dark hair. If she picks one randomly, what is the chance that student will *not* have dark hair?

(A) 10/24
(B) 7/12
(C) 1/6
(D) 5/12
(E) 1/24

18. Three friends go to a restaurant for dinner. When the bill comes, the tax on it is $7.13. If the tax rate is 5 percent, approximately how much should the friends leave as a 15 percent tip?

(A) $7.00
(B) $14.50
(C) $21.00
(D) $25.00
(E) $28.00

19. If there are 12 inches in a foot, and 3 feet in a yard, how do you convert inches to yards?

    (A) Divide by 12, then divide by 3
    (B) Multiply by 12, then multiply by 3
    (C) Divide by 12 and multiply by 3
    (D) Multiply by 12 and divide by 3
    (E) Multiply by 36

20. A map is drawn to the scale 1 inch = 10 miles. If the distance between two points on the map is 7.21 inches, what is the distance in miles?

    (A) 1.39 miles
    (B) 7.21 miles
    (C) 10 miles
    (D) 36.05 miles
    (E) 72.1 miles

21. Which formula describes the relationship between X and Y shown below?

X	Y
2	4
8	7
14	10
20	13
26	16

    (A) $Y = 2X$
    (B) $Y = X + 2$
    (C) $Y = -X - 7$
    (D) $Y = X/2 + 3$
    (E) $Y = X/4 + 3/2$

22. In straight-line distance, it is 5 miles from Chestertown to Centerville, and 12 miles from Centerville to Dover. If the three towns are set up on a map as shown below, what is the approximate straight-line distance between Chestertown and Dover?

    (A) 17 miles
    (B) 14.5 miles
    (C) 13 miles
    (D) 12 miles
    (E) 7 miles

23. How many square feet of carpet would you need to carpet the room pictured below?

(A) 174
(B) 180
(C) 200
(D) 153
(E) 168

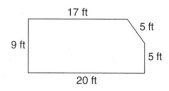

24. Which of the following numbers is a quarter of a million?

(A) 400,000
(B) $1{,}000{,}000 \times 0.25$
(C) $4/1{,}000{,}000$
(D) $1{,}000{,}000/0.25$
(E) $1{,}000{,}000 \times 0.4$

25. The following chart shows the amount of profit a company earns for a given number of employees and customers. If the company earned a profit of 55, how many employees and customers did it have?

		Customers				
		10	**20**	**30**	**40**	**50**
	1	30	32	34	36	38
Employees	**2**	25	60	62	64	66
	3	20	55	90	92	94
	4	15	50	85	120	122
	5	10	45	80	115	150
	6	5	40	75	110	145

(A) 2 employees, 20 customers
(B) 3 employees, 20 customers
(C) 2 employees, 50 customers
(D) 3 employees, 30 customers
(E) 1 employee, 40 customers

26. Five real estate agents received the following commissions. Which commission was the greatest?

(A) 5 percent of $500,000
(B) 4 percent of $600,000
(C) 5 percent of $600,000
(D) 7 percent of $500,000
(E) 6 percent of $500,000

27. If $A = r/4 + 5$, and $r = 8$, then $A =$

    (A) 7
    (B) 3
    (C) 5
    (D) 9
    (E) 17

28. In a deck of 52 cards, 4 of them are kings. What percentage of the cards is kings?

    (A) 4.0 percent
    (B) 7.7 percent
    (C) 13.0 percent
    (D) 13.7 percent
    (E) 52.2 percent

29. Last week, you spent $15 on gasoline. This week, you spent $25. If you know you used the same amount of gasoline both weeks, what is the percent increase in the price of gas?

    (A) 10.0 percent
    (B) 25.0 percent
    (C) 50.0 percent
    (D) 66.7 percent
    (E) 68.3 percent

30. On the dial shown, the arrow most likely indicates:

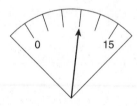

    (A) 3
    (B) 5
    (C) 9
    (D) 10
    (E) 12

31. A wall is 10 feet high and 14 feet long. There is a window set into the wall that is 5 feet high and 3 feet wide. If 1 quart of paint covers 20 square feet, how many quarts of paint are needed to cover this wall?

(A) 7 quarts

(B) 6.25 quarts

(C) 0.75 quarts

(D) 7.75 quarts

(E) 125 quarts

32. Using the ruler shown below, approximately how long is the line?

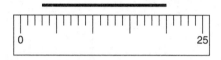

(A) 20

(B) 22

(C) 17

(D) 4

(E) 3 ²/₃

33. Eileen catered a party and made 489 cookies. The party planners were expecting 53 people to come to the party. About how many cookies did Eileen think each person would eat?

(A) 1

(B) 5

(C) 10

(D) 17

(E) 53

34. If 10 fewer people were expected at the party, how many fewer cookies would Eileen have to make?

(A) 30

(B) 63

(C) 75

(D) 100

(E) 127

35. I hate cookies; I prefer that Eileen serve cream puffs instead. If I estimate that each guest will eat 1 cream puff for every 5 cookies they'd otherwise eat, approximately how many cream puffs should Eileen make for 53 guests?

    (A) 100
    (B) 160
    (C) 220
    (D) 190
    (E) 481

36. In a box of 20 cookies, 10 have vanilla cream and 10 have chocolate cream. What percentage has strawberry cream?

    (A) 10 percent
    (B) 50 percent
    (C) 25 percent
    (D) 33.3 percent
    (E) 0 percent

37. If $A = (x/2) - 2$ and $A = 6$, then $x =$

    (A) 12
    (B) 0
    (C) 3
    (D) 18
    (E) 16

38. How many cubic feet of grain can be stored in a cylinder-shaped silo 30 feet in diameter and 30 feet high?

    (A) $27,000\pi$
    (B) $6,750\pi$
    (C) 900π
    (D) $1,125\pi$
    (E) $202,500\pi$

39. If the scale for a dollhouse is 3 inches: 2 feet and a shelf is 6 feet high, how high would you make a dollhouse-scale shelf?

    (A) 1.5 inches
    (B) 2 inches
    (C) 12 inches
    (D) 9 inches
    (E) 3 feet

40. To convert centimeters to meters, you should

(A) divide by 10
(B) multiply by 10
(C) divide by 100
(D) multiply by 100
(E) divide by 1,000

STOP. This is the end of the Mathematics Diagnostic Test.

MATHEMATICS DIAGNOSTIC TEST: ANSWERS

1. D. $0.4 \times 15 = 6$.

2. D. $^1/_6 = 0.16$. Change fractions to decimals by dividing.

3. B. $^5/_{15} = {}^1/_3$.

4. D. Estimate, then multiply and count spaces past the decimal point. $0.0003 \times 12 = 0.0036$.

5. C. The two parts of the pie chart are approximately equal.

6. D. There are four combinations that add up to 5, out of 36 possible combinations.

7. C. This is a remainder interpretation problem. I is 12 batches, II is $12.33, III is $12^1/_3$ pies.

8. D. There are 25 hashes between 5 and 30, so each of the long hashes is 5 units, and each of the small hashes is 1 unit. The arrow is 13 hashes away from 5. $5 + 13 = 18$.

9. C. If some cubes are red, then some cubes are not red, and some red things are cubes. You don't know anything about balls, and you don't know what other shapes might be red or not be red.

10. C. $7.71 \times 10,000 = 77,100$.

11. A. Estimate by rounding to the nearest thousand. $1,000 \times 5,000 = 5,000,000$.

12. D. $(-4,2)$ means 4 left and 2 up.

13. A. The number must fall between 0.6 and 0.78, or between 60 percent and 78 percent.

14. B. $(4 + 6 + 11 + 9 + 3) \div 5 = 6.6$.

15. E. $x = 2y$, so $2x = 4y$.

16. D. Compare the first nonzero place after the decimal point in each number.

17. B. 14 choices out of a possible 24 $(4 + 10 + 10)$. Reduce the fraction to get 7/12.

18. C. Estimate. $7 is about 5 percent of the bill, so 15 percent of the bill would be three times as much.

19. A. 12 inches = 1 foot, 3 feet = 1 yard, so 36 inches = 1 yard. Divide the number of inches by 36 to get the number of yards.

20. E. If 1 inch = 10 miles, 7.21 inches = $7.21 \times 10 = 72.1$ miles.

21. D. Trial and error. Try all of the pairs in each equation and find which one works for all of them.

22. C. The towns are set up in a right triangle, so use the Pythagorean theorem: $5_2 + 12_2 =$ the hypotenuse squared, or 169, and the square root of 169 $=13$.

23. A. This is an area problem. The room is a 20 by 9 rectangle, minus a triangle with legs of 3 (20 – 17) and 4 (9 – 5). $(20 \times 9) - (\frac{1}{2} \times 3 \times 4) = 174$.

24. B. One million times one-quarter (0.25).

25. B. The line for 3 employees and the column for 20 customers meet at 55.

26. D. Multiply (e.g., $0.05 \times \$500,000 = \$25,000$) to find each commission. $35,000 is greatest.

27. A. $8/4 + 5 = 7$.

28. B. As a fraction, 4/52. Convert fractions to decimals by dividing: $4 \div 52 = 0.077.\ 0.077 = 7.7$ percent.

29. D. $25 - 15 = 10, 10 \div 15 = 0.667$.

30. C. There are five hashes between 0 and 15, so each of the hashes is three units. The arrow is about three hashes away from $0.3 \times 3 = 9$.

31. B. There is 140 square feet of wall, minus 15 square feet of window. You need to cover 125 square feet; divide by 20 per quart of paint.

32. C. There are 25 hashes between 0 and 25, so each of the long hashes is 5 units and each of the small hashes is 1 unit. The line begins at 3 and ends at 20. $20 - 3 = 7$.

33. C. Estimate. About 50 people were expected, and there were about 500 cookies, so each person would eat about 10 cookies.

34. D. Estimate. 10 is 1/5 of 50. So you'd need about 1/5 fewer cookies. $500 \times 1/5 = 100$. (If she figured 10 cookies per person, $10 \times 10 = 100$ fewer cookies.)

35. A. $\frac{1}{5}$ the number of cookies: $500 \times \frac{1}{5} = 100$.

36. E. None of them do, so the answer is 0 percent.

37. E. $6 = (x/2) - 2$. Add 2 to both sides to get $8 = x/2$, then cross multiply to get $16 = x$.

38. B. This is a volume problem. $A = \pi r^2 h$. Radius is half of diameter. $15^2 \times 30 \times \pi = 6,750\pi$

39. D. 3 inches = 2 feet. 6 feet = 3×2 feet, so 3×3 inches = 9 inches.

40. C. 1 meter = 100 centimeters.

PART 3

PPST: Reading Test

No matter which Praxis tests you take, pumping up your reading speed and comprehension will help you earn a higher score. Clearly, this is most important on the reading section of the Praxis I Academic Skills Assessment, where reading is directly tested.

CHAPTER 7

Pump Up Your Vocabulary

Increasing your vocabulary is the first step to increasing reading comprehension, so let's start by increasing your word power.

USE CONTEXT CLUES

When you use *context clues,* you interpret a word's specific meaning by examining its relationship to other words in the sentence. To improve your vocabulary, you must understand how a word interacts with other words. Let's look at the four most common types of context clues:

1. Restatement context clues
2. Definitions after colons and transitions
3. Inferential context clues
4. Contrast context clues

Restatement Context Clues

Writers want their words to be understood so their message goes through. As a result, they will often define a difficult word right in the text. Study this example:

> The Army Corps of Engineers distributed 26 million plastic bags throughout the region. Volunteers filled each bag with 35 pounds of sand and then stacked them to create *levees,* makeshift barriers against the floodwaters.

Right after the word *levees,* readers get the definition: "makeshift barriers against the floodwaters."

Definitions After Colons and Transitions

Writers can also provide context clues in the form of definitions after colons and transitions. For example:

The media trumpets our obsession with appearance, claiming that Americans are more fit than ever before. However, just the opposite is true. In fact, at least one-third of the American population is classified as *obese:* being more than 20 percent over a person's ideal body weight.

Directly after the colon, the writer defines *obese:* "being more than 20 percent over a person's ideal body weight."

Inferential Context Clues

Sometimes you will have to *infer* the meaning of a new word by combining what you already know with textual clues to discover the unstated information. As you read the following passage, use context clues to infer what *forerunner* means:

In 1862, in order to support the Civil War effort, Congress enacted the nation's first income tax law. It was a *forerunner* of our modern income tax in that it was based on the principles of graduated, or progressive, taxation and of withholding income at the source.

Here's how to make an inference to define *forerunner:*

Context Clue	+	What I Know	=	Inference
A *forerunner* was the "nation's first income tax law."		*Fore* means "before."		*Forerunner* means "something before or preceding."

Contrast Context Clues

You can also figure out an unknown word when an opposite, or contrast, is presented. When you do this, you're making an inference. For example, you can define *literal* by finding its contrast in the sentence:

It is hard to use *literal* language when talking about nature because people tend to talk about nature using figures of speech.

Literal language must be the opposite of "figures of speech." If you know that figures of speech are words and expressions not meant to be taken at face value, you can infer that *literal* must mean "the strict or exact meaning." Other synonyms would include *verbatim* or *word for word.*

DISTINGUISH BETWEEN MULTIPLE-MEANING WORDS

Building your vocabulary means more than just learning new words. It also means telling the difference between words that you already know. The word *favor,* for example, has many different meanings. Here are six of them: "a kind act," "friendly regard," "being approved," "a gift," "to support," or "to resemble." Here are some additional examples of multiple-meaning words:

Word	Example	Meaning	Example	Meaning
address	home <u>address</u>	residence	graduation <u>address</u>	speech
game	play a <u>game</u>	sport	have a <u>game</u> leg	injured
rash	have a <u>rash</u>	skin problem	<u>rash</u> action	hasty

When you read, you often come across a word that you think you know but that doesn't make sense in the sentence you're reading. That is your clue that the word has more than one meaning. In this case, you must choose the meaning that fits the context.

To do so, follow these three simple steps:

1. Read the sentence and find the word with multiple meanings.
2. Look for context clues that tell you which meaning of the word fits.
3. Substitute a synonym for the word and see if it makes sense. If not, try another meaning for the word. Continue until you find the right meaning.

UNDERSTAND CONNOTATION AND DENOTATION

Every word has a *denotation,* its dictionary meaning. In addition, many words have connotations, or emotional overtones. Two words may have similar denotations but very different connotations. For example, *sobbing* and *blubbering* have the same denotation, "crying." However, *sobbing* suggests pitiful crying, while *blubbering* suggests foolish, overwrought crying. Being able to distinguish connotations is crucial because it helps you understand the writer's point, make inferences, and grasp fine shades of meaning. Remember that about 45 percent of the questions on the reading part of the PPST require you to make inferences. Here are some additional examples of connotation and denotation:

Word Denotation	Positive Connotation	Negative Connotation
confused	puzzled	flustered
without a friend	friendless	reclusive
raw	unrefined	crude
inexperienced	trusting	naive

CHAPTER 8

Be an Active Reader

Reading is an active process that requires you to be engaged with the text. When you're actively involved in reading a passage, you'll boost your comprehension greatly. Active reading involves the following steps:

1. *Previewing the text:* Get an overview of the text by skimming it quickly.
2. *Making predictions:* When you make predictions, you make educated guesses about what's to come in a text. Make, revise, and confirm your predictions to increase your reading comprehension.
3. *Setting a purpose for reading:* Your purpose for reading shapes the way you read. On the Praxis tests, your purpose will be to locate facts, grasp the main ideas, make inferences, draw conclusions, and discover opinions. As a result, you will read more closely than you do when you read for pleasure.
4. *Tapping prior knowledge:* Use what you know to make your reading easier and more productive. Connecting new facts with your prior knowledge helps you remember new information as you read under pressure. This will make it easier for you to answer the questions that follow the passage.
5. *Asking and answering questions:* Ask yourself questions to define unfamiliar words, clarify confusing passages, or locate the main idea. You can also ask yourself questions to isolate the text organization; the author's purpose; or to make, revise, or confirm predictions. Answer the questions based on the information you find by rereading or reading on.

There are a number of excellent ways to get more from your reading. These include *skimming, summarizing,* and *checking comprehension.* With practice, these techniques become second nature. As you increase your reading speed and boost your understanding, your score on the Praxis will improve.

SKIM A TEXT TO GET THE MAIN IDEA

Skimming is a very fast method of reading that lets you glance at a passage to get its main idea or to find a key point. Skimming boosts comprehension because it helps you focus on the important parts of the text. When you go back and read the text in detail, you can zero in on the parts you need.

Follow these steps as you skim a text:

1. Run your eyes across the page. Try to read as fast as you can.
2. Look for the main idea. It will often be in the first and last sentences. Read these parts more slowly.
3. Pause at the end of every paragraph to restate the meaning in your own words.

Quick Tip

Skimming isn't a substitute for a complete reading. Skim *before* you read the text . . . not *instead* of reading it.

SUMMARIZE TO INCREASE COMPREHENSION

To *summarize,* find the most important information and restate it in your own words. Summarize every time you read a passage on the Praxis to help you understand what you read. To be sure you have included all the important details in your summary, check that it answers these questions: *Who? What? When? Where? Why? How?* To summarize a passage:

1. Preview the passage, set predictions, and read the passage.
2. Find the main idea and important details.
3. Explain them in your own words.
4. Skim the passage again to make sure you have included all the important points.

Quick Tip

A summary is shorter than the original passage. You can remember this because both *summary* and *shorter* start with *s.*

CHECK YOUR COMPREHENSION

As you read, check on your understanding. It's especially important to pause and regroup if you get confused. Ask yourself, "What am I having trouble understanding?" Once you know, try some of the following strategies to get back on track:

- Read more slowly.
- Reread any parts that confuse you.
- Use the details in the passage to visualize or imagine the scene you're reading.

- Restate what you have read in your own words.
- Ask yourself, "What is the main idea?" Reread the text for details and clues.

You can also change your reading rate to accommodate the text. Vary your reading rate this way:

Skim the text when . . .

- You need to find a specific fact
- You need only *some* of the information from the text

Read slowly and carefully when . . .

- You're confused about the content or stuck on a specific point
- You've lost the author's main idea
- You want to make sure you understand all of the author's points
- The passage contains a lot of difficult or new words
- The passage contains a lot of new concepts or ideas

PRACTICE MAKES PERFECT

Practice is the best way to boost your critical reading comprehension skills, so read every minute you can. "I don't have the time to read," you say. You may have more time than you think.

Consider the little parcels of time that are otherwise wasted. Read during the time you spend waiting in line at the bus stop, when you are sitting in the dentist's office, or when you are tapping your heels waiting for a late appointment. You can use all of these otherwise lost minutes to read.

To speed the process along, in addition to reading required material such as textbooks, read for pleasure as well. Consider reading best sellers, classic works of fiction and nonfiction, newspapers, and magazines. Reading *anything* is better than not reading at all. Even reading trashy novels will help boost your reading skills.

That said, here are some classic novels and plays, traditional as well as new, that you can use to get started:

The Adventures of Huckleberry Finn	*The Age of Innocence*
All My Sons	*All the Pretty Horses*
Anna Karenina	*Antigone*
As I Lay Dying	*The Awakening*
The Birthday Party	*Beloved*
Billy Budd	*Bless Me, Ultima*
Candide	*Catch-22*
Ceremony	*The Color Purple*
A Clockwork Orange	*Crime and Punishment*
The Crucible	*Cry, the Beloved Country*

Delta Wedding
Dinner at the Homesick
  Restaurant
Dr. Faustus
An Enemy of the People
A Farewell to Arms
The Great Gatsby
Hamlet or *King Lear*
  (or any play by Shakespeare)
The Iceman Cometh
Jane Eyre
The Joy Luck Club
Lord Jim
A Member of the Wedding
Mrs. Dalloway
The Oresteia (or any
  Greek tragedy)
The Piano Lesson
The Portrait of a Lady
Pride and Prejudice
A Raisin in the Sun
The Scarlet Letter
Song of Solomon
The Sound and the Fury
Sula
Things Fall Apart
Waiting for Godot
Wuthering Heights

David Copperfield (or any novel
  by Dickens)
A Doll's House (or any play by Ibsen)
Emma
Equus
The Glass Menagerie
Gulliver's Travels
Heart of Darkness
Invisible Man
Jasmine
Jude the Obscure or *The Mayor of*
  Casterbridge (or any novel by
  Hardy)
A Lesson Before Dying
Moby Dick
Native Son
Our Town
A Portrait of the Artist as a Young Man
Praisesong for the Widow
Pnin
Saint Joan (or any play by Shaw)
The Shipping News
Sons and Lovers
The Stone Angel
Their Eyes Were Watching God
The Turn of the Screw
The Warden
1984

Also consider the following suggestions to help you become a better reader.

- Practice these reading techniques 15 to 20 minutes a day. Follow the schedule and you'll see progress.
- Try reading at the same time every day, in the same place, so you get into a reading routine.
- Keep a "reading diary" by listing all the different things you have read. You'll feel good looking back at all the reading you've done.

CHAPTER 9

The PPST Reading Test

As you learned in Part 1, the reading part of the PPST test consists of a series of reading passages followed by multiple-choice questions with four answer choices each. Some passages are very short, just a few sentences. Other passages run about 100 words each. The longest passages are about 200 words.

The PPST reading test is offered in two versions:

- Paper-and-pencil   60 minutes long with 40 multiple-choice questions
- Computerized   75 minutes long with 46 questions

No matter which version you take, the format and style of the questions will be the same. Thus, you will need the same skills. According to ETS, the reading skills being tested can be divided as follows:

- Finding literal details   About 45%
- Making inferences   About 55%

FIND LITERAL DETAILS

First, let's focus on finding literal details.

How can you recognize details in a passage? Details will fall into these six main categories:

1. Examples   *Examples* illustrate a writer's point. Examples help readers understand a general statement by giving specific information that represents one part of the whole concept.

2. Facts   *Facts* are statements that can be proven. For example, the statement "Samuel Clemens lived from 1835 to 1910" is a fact. It can be verified in reference books such as encyclopedias, and there are no reasonable arguments against it.

3. Statistics   *Statistics* are numbers used to give additional information. Statistics can be presented in different ways, such as charts, graphs, lists, percentages, and decimals.

4. Reasons   *Reasons* are explanations that tell *why* something happened. Reasons may also explain the cause of someone's beliefs or actions.

5. Definitions   *Definitions* are statements that explain what something means.

6. Descriptions   *Descriptions* are words or phrases that tell *how* something looks, smells, tastes, sounds, or feels. Descriptions use sensory words to help readers visualize what they are reading.

The following diagram shows how details back up main ideas:

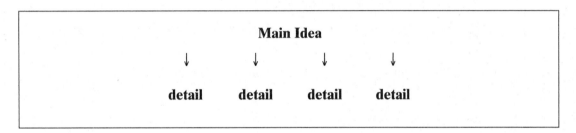

Details support the main idea.

Follow this three-step plan to find the details in a passage.

Step 1. Identify the topic: The *topic* of a paragraph is its subject. It tells what the paragraph is all about, which can be stated in one or two words. Sample topics include *special needs students, school uniforms, state tests, selling fast foods in school cafeterias, medieval painters, supply-side economics, the Supreme Court, sharks, airplane safety.*

Step 2. Identify the main idea: After you find the topic, look for the *main idea.* It may be directly stated, or you may have to infer it from information in the passage. More on this later in this section.

Step 3. Find details that back up the main idea: Look for the details that directly support the main idea. Details will be the small pieces of information that you can use to answer the test questions.

As you read the following passage, isolate the significant details. Then answer the questions.

The federal system of courts in America is like a pyramid, with state courts on the bottom and federal courts in the middle. At the very top of the pyramid is the Supreme Court, the "court of last resort." The nine Supreme Court justices have "original jurisdiction" (the power to try cases that have not been previously tried by a lower court) over very few types of cases. They may try
(5) disputes between two states, for example, or a case involving an ambassador. However, these "original jurisdiction" cases are rare. Instead, most of the Supreme Court's time is spent reviewing decisions that have already been made in lower courts. Each year, the Supreme Court justices receive more than 5,000 petitions to review such decisions. They accept only the most important of these. The Supreme Court considers cases that demand a decision about the
(10) meaning of the Constitution or a specific federal law. The Supreme Court is unique because when the justices reach a decision about a case, their decision is final. The decisions of the Supreme Court result in laws that have an impact on us all.

1. According to the paragraph, how many justices serve on the Supreme Court?

(A) six
(B) nine
(C) 12
(D) 5,000
(E) 10,000

2. Which types of cases do the Supreme Court justices review most often?

(A) disputes between two states that have continuous borders and significant immigration
(B) cases involving ambassadors who have abused the rules of the country they are visiting
(C) cases about national monuments, such as the Lincoln Memorial or Empire State Building
(D) original jurisdiction cases that had ambiguous, contentious, or highly-publicized decisions
(E) decisions that have already been adjudicated in lower courts

3. How many petitions a year are submitted to the Supreme Court?

(A) about nine
(B) at least 200
(C) very few
(D) about 2,500
(E) more than 5,000

4. The Supreme Court's decisions are special because

    (A) they are final and cannot be brought back to court for appeal
    (B) they can be reconsidered at a later date, if new evidence is discovered
    (C) they are not very important to average, everyday people
    (D) they affect only some people in the United States
    (E) they are arcane and difficult for ordinary people to understand

5. The main idea of this passage is

    (A) State courts are the lowest on the pyramid of the federal court system.
    (B) The Supreme Court rarely tries "original jurisdiction" cases.
    (C) The Supreme Court is the "court of last resort."
    (D) The Supreme Court receives many petitions to review cases.
    (E) The Supreme Court's decisions cannot be overturned.

Don't be misled by unnecessary information in the answer choices. Look for the detail you need and disregard information that is wordy or off the topic.

ANSWERS

1. B.   The information is directly stated in this sentence: "The *nine* Supreme Court justices have 'original jurisdiction' . . ."

2. E.   The information is directly stated in this sentence: "Instead, most of the Supreme Court's time is spent *reviewing decisions that have already been made in lower courts.*"

3. E.   The information is directly stated in this sentence: "The Supreme Court justices receive more than *5,000 petitions* to review such decisions."

4. A.   The information is directly stated in this sentence: "The Supreme Court is unique because when the justices *reach a decision about a case, their decision is final.*"

5. C.   The information is directly stated in this sentence: "At the very top of the Supreme Court, the '*court of last resort.*'"

    Try it again with the following passage. As you read, isolate the significant details. Then answer the questions.

By the 1800s, several hundred medicine shows were traveling across America, giving a wide variety of shows. At one end of the scale were simple magic acts; at the other, complicated spectacles. From 1880 to 1910, one of the largest of these shows was "The King of the Road Shows," the Kickapoo Indian Medicine Company. Two experienced entertainers, Charles H. "Texas Charlie"

(5)   Bigelow and John E. "Doc" Healy, had started the company more than two decades before. From their headquarters in New Haven, Connecticut, the partners sent as many as twenty-five shows at a time across America.

Texas Charlie managed the "medicine" end of the production, training the "Doctors" and "Professors" who gave the "Medical Lectures." Doc Healy was in charge

(10)   of hiring the performers—from fiddlers to fire-eaters, including comedians, acrobats, singers, and jugglers. Both Native Americans and Whites were hired. All the Native Americans, including Mohawks, Iroquois, Crees, Sioux, and Blackfeet, were billed as "pure-blooded Kickapoos," a completely fictional tribe.

All the entertainers wore outrageous costumes. The Native Americans were covered in

(15)   feathers, colored beads, and crude weapons. The "Doctors" and "Professors" were equally glittery. Some wore fringed leather coats and silver-capped boots; others, fancy silk shirts, a type of tuxedo jacket called a "frock coat," and high silk hats. One of the most outlandish figures was the glib "Nevada Ned, the King of Gold." Born Ned T. Oliver, this entertainer wore a fancy suit studded with buttons made of gold. On his head he sported a huge

(20)   sombrero dangling 100 gold coins.

During the summer, the Kickapoo shows were presented under enormous tents. When the weather turned chilly, the troupe moved into town halls and opera houses. Most often, the show was free. Occasionally, adults were charged a dime to get in. Where did the profits come from? The sale of "medicine." According to the show's advertisements, these wonder-working Kickapoo

(25)   brews were "compounded according to secret ancient Kickapoo Indian tribal formulas." Among the ingredients were "blood root, feverwort, spirit gum, wild poke berries, slippery elm, white oak bark, dock root, and other natural products." These "medicines" were sold for fifty cents to a dollar a bottle, and were guaranteed to cure all the ills that afflict the human body.

1. According to paragraph 1, the Kickapoo Indian Medicine Show was started by

(A) two men who did not have a lot of experience in the entertainment field
(B) revered senior members of the historic Kickapoo Indian tribe
(C) Charles H. "Texas Charlie" Bigelow, and John E. "Doc" Healy
(D) an organization called The Kings of the Road Shows
(E) traditional Native healers with a large following of true believers

2. According to paragraph 2, the Kickapoo tribe was, in actuality,

(A) a series of highly trained "doctors" and "professors" from all around the country
(B) a group of volunteer fiddlers, fire-eaters, comedians, acrobats, singers, and jugglers
(C) pure-blooded Native Americans who took great pride in their heritage
(D) a completely invented tribe with no basis in historical fact
(E) a group of talented men and women who enjoyed reading fictional literature

3. According to paragraph 3, which performers wore Western clothing such as leather jackets and fancy boots?

(A) the "Doctors" and "Professors"
(B) the Native Americans
(C) "Nevada Ned, the King of Gold"
(D) everyone in the show at one time or another
(E) Ned. T. Oliver, who was the most outrageous of all

4. The main idea of paragraph 3 is

(A) The Native Americans wore the most beautiful costumes of all.
(B) Everyone in the show wore wildly colorful outfits.
(C) One of the most far-out figures was the smooth-talking "Nevada Ned, the King of Gold."
(D) The costumes cost a lot of money and were very difficult to make.
(E) The show would not have been as successful without the costumes.

5. According to paragraph 4, where did the Kickapoo entertainers perform when the weather was warm?

(A) They gave their shows in town halls.
(B) They performed under huge tents.
(C) They acted in opera houses.
(D) They could be found out in the open air, under the stars.
(E) They performed in hospitals, where their medicine was sold.

ANSWERS

1. C. The information is directly stated in this sentence: "Two experienced entertainers, *Charles H. 'Texas Charlie' Bigelow, and John E. 'Doc' Healy, had started the company more than two decades before.*"

2. D. The information is directly stated in this sentence: "All the Native Americans, including Mohawks, Iroquois, Crees, Sioux, and Blackfeet, were billed as *'pure-blooded Kickapoos,' a completely fictional tribe.*"

3. A.   The information is directly stated in this sentence: "The '*Doctors*' and '*Professors*' were equally glittery. Some wore fringed *leather coats and silver-capped boots;* others, fancy silk shirts, a type of tuxedo jacket called a 'frock coat,' and high silk hats."

4. B.   The information is directly stated in this sentence: "All the entertainers wore outrageous costumes." Choice (E) overstates the case and reaches a conclusion not supported by the information in the passage.

5. B.   The information is directly stated in this sentence: "During the summer, the Kickapoo shows were presented under enormous *tents.*"

LOCATE A STATED MAIN IDEA

As you learned in the previous section, sometimes a writer will directly state the main idea. To find the stated main idea in a passage, follow these steps:

1. Find the *topic,* or subject of the passage.
2. Look for a sentence that gives an overview of the topic. It will explain what the entire paragraph is about.
3. Check to see if the sentence tells what the paragraph is about.

Although the stated main idea is often the first sentence, it can be in the middle or end of a paragraph as well. Some examples follow. The main idea is underlined in each one.

Main idea in the *beginning* of a passage:

<u>The Florida landscape boasts a wide variety of plant life—about thirty-five hundred different kinds.</u> Almost half of all the different kinds of trees found in America grow in Florida. Some of Florida's woodlands are filled with majestic coniferous pines. Swamp maples, bald cypresses, bays, and oaks flourish in some of the state's forests. Still other wooded areas are a mix of different types and species of plant life. Dozens of different kinds of subtropical trees can be found in the Florida peninsula and the Keys. The warm climate in these areas nourishes the strangler fig, royal palm, and mangroves, for example.

Main idea in the *middle* of a passage:

Business people are dressed neatly—the women in suits or skirts and blouses and the men in jackets, ties, pressed pants, and stiffly starched shirts. Restaurant servers are polite to tourists and residents alike. Children stand quietly by their parents. <u>Almost all aspects of life on the island are polite and civilized.</u> People hold doors open for one another, wait to get into elevators until everyone has gotten off, and step aside to let those in a rush get by. At noon, the shops close and everyone goes home for a two-hour rest. But if you ask the shopkeepers to stay open a little longer, they will often gladly oblige.

Main idea in the *end* of a passage:

The brown pelican, Florida's most popular bird, can often be seen perched on jetties, bridges, and piers. The state wetlands boast herons, egrets, wood ducks, and roseate spoonbills (often mistaken for flamingos). On the beach you can find sanderlings, plovers, and oystercatchers. The state bird, the mockingbird, likes living in suburban neighborhoods. Offshore, cormorants, black skimmers, and terns look for their dinner. Florida's forests shelter quail, wild turkey, owls, and woodpeckers. <u>In all, more than a hundred native species of birds have been found in Florida.</u>

Find the stated main idea in the following passage.

Tsunamis, or seismic sea-waves, are gravity waves set in motion by underwater disturbances associated with earthquakes. These waves are frequently called "tidal waves" although they have nothing to do with the tides. Tsunamis consist of a decaying train of waves and may be detectable on tide gauges for as long as a week. Near its origin, the first wave of a tsunami may be the largest; at greater distances, the largest is normally between the second and seventh wave.

You can find the stated main idea in the first sentence: <u>Tsunamis, or seismic seawaves, are gravity waves set in motion by underwater disturbances associated with earthquakes.</u>

INFER AN UNSTATED MAIN IDEA

Sometimes writers don't directly state the main idea of a passage. In these cases, you have to make *inferences* to find the main idea. When you *make an inference,* you combine what you already know with spoken or textual clues to discover the unstated information. You may have heard this referred to as "reading between the lines" or "putting two and two together." It's drawing a conclusion from facts and speculation. More than half of the questions on the PPST (55 percent) will require you to make inferences.

To find the unstated main idea in a passage, follow these steps:

1. Find the topic or subject of the passage.
2. Look for details that relate to the topic.
3. Make an inference about the main idea from the details and what you already know about the subject.
4. Consider whether the inference makes sense given the information in the passage and what you already know.
5. Read the answer choices to find the one that matches your inference. If you can't find your inference, repeat this process. Make sure that your inference is logical, given common sense and the content of the passage.

Follow the five steps to infer the unstated main idea in the following passage.

Egypt, a long, narrow, fertile strip of land in northeastern Africa, is the only place in the world where pyramids were built. Back then, all the water for the land and its people came from the mighty Nile River. Natural barriers protected the land from invaders. Around 300 BC, when kings and other high Egyptian officials authorized the building of
(5)   the first pyramids, these natural barriers protected the land from invaders. There were deserts to the east and west that cut off Egypt from the rest of the world. There were dangerous rapids on the Nile to the south. Delta marshes lay to the north. This circle of isolation allowed the Egyptians to work in peace and security. In addition, great supplies of raw materials were needed to build the pyramids. Ancient Egypt had an abundance of
(10) limestone, sandstone, and granite. These rocks were quarried close to the banks of the Nile. But these rocks had to be brought from quarries to the building sites. Egypt's most precious resource—the great Nile River—provided the means for transportation.

1. Find the topic or subject of the passage: *the pyramids of Egypt.*
2. Look for details that relate to the topic.

   - *Natural barriers protected the land from invaders.*
   - *Ancient Egypt had the raw materials: limestone, sandstone, and granite.*
   - *Workers transported the stone on the Nile River.*

3. Make an inference about the main idea from the details: *Ancient Egypt had a unique combination of factors necessary for building the pyramids.*

Now, identify the unstated main idea in the following passage.

Ancient savage tribes played a primitive kind of football. About 2,500 years ago there was a ball-kicking game played by the Athenians, Spartans, and Corinthians, which the Greeks called *Episkuros*. The Romans had a somewhat similar game called *Harpastum*. According to several historical sources, the Romans brought the game with them when
(5)   they invaded the British Isles in the first century AD. The game today known as "football" in the United States can be traced directly back to the English game of rugby, although there have been many changes to the game. Football was played informally on university fields more than a hundred years ago. In 1840, a yearly series of informal "scrimmages" started at Yale University. It took more than twenty-five years, however,
(10) for the game to become part of college life. The first formal intercollegiate football game was held between Princeton and Rutgers teams on November 6, 1869. It was held on Rutgers's home field at New Brunswick, New Jersey, and Rutgers won.

Which of the following BEST states the main idea of this paragraph?

(A) The Romans, Athenians, Spartans, and Corinthians all played a game like football.
(B) Football is a very old game; its history stretches back to ancient days.
(C) American football comes from a British game called "rugby."
(D) Football is a more popular game than baseball, even though baseball is called "America's pastime."
(E) Football is a savage but exciting game, which explains its enduring appeal.

Answer: B. Eliminate choices A and C because they give supporting details, not the main idea. Eliminate choice D because it contains information that is not included in the paragraph. Eliminate choice E because the opinion is not based on information in the passage, even though it may be true.

Practice finding the unstated main idea in the following passage:

What could be easier than grabbing a juicy cheeseburger, a creamy thick shake, and a bag of salty fries from a fast-food drive-in? It's fast and tastes great. These fast foods just seem to hit the spot that lettuce and bean sprouts can't. Unfortunately, in recent years Americans have discovered that many of their favorite fast foods
(5)   are empty calories with no nutrition. Cheeseburgers, shakes, and fries are loaded with salt and fat; fried chicken has more cholesterol than motor oil. But what about people who just can't make it through a week without some fast food? Consider pizza. Although it is usually lumped together with all the other "fast foods"—burgers, fried chicken, hot dogs, and fish sticks—pizza is *not* the same as these foods.
(10)   Pizza contains many of the vitamins and minerals that we need. This is especially true when the pizza is made with fresh ingredients. The crust provides us with carbohydrates, an excellent low-calorie source of energy. The cheese and meat provide our bodies with the building blocks of protein. The tomatoes, herbs, onions, and garlic supply us with vitamins and minerals.

1. What have many Americans learned recently?

(A) Pizza tastes better than other fast foods because it is usually made fresh.
(B) Fast foods have a lot of salt and fat, which is unhealthy for most people.
(C) Pizza costs less than other fast foods, which makes it a great bargain.
(D) Many fast foods taste great, which explain their robust sales worldwide.
(E) Some people are truly addicted to fast foods, which is a dangerous trend.

2. The main idea of this passage is

(A) People should stay away from all junk food if they want to stay well.
(B) Many fast foods are not good for you, but that won't stop people from eating them.
(C) Even though it is a convenience food, pizza is healthier for you than many people think.
(D) Pizza gives us the carbohydrates we need for quick energy, which makes it a useful food.
(E) Pizza truly is the perfect food and it's time that more people realize its benefits.

3. Where would you most likely find this passage?

(A) in a new cookbook aimed at adults
(B) in a travel brochure for Italy
(C) in a scholarly journal for nutritionists
(D) on the inside of a pizza box
(E) in a general-readership magazine

ANSWERS

1. B.   You can infer the answer from this sentence: "Unfortunately, in recent years Americans have discovered that many of their favorite fast foods are empty calories with no nutrition."

2. C.   You can infer the main idea from these two sentences: "Consider pizza" and "Pizza contains many of the vitamins and minerals that we need." The question could also be written this way:

> **2.** Which of the following BEST describes the purpose of this passage?
>
> (A) To inform readers about fast foods
> (B) To persuade readers to avoid all fast foods
> (C) To tell a story about fast food
> (D) To convince readers that pizza has more nutritive value than other fast foods

> If you're having difficulty understanding a question (or a passage, for that matter), restate it in your own words. Often, restating a question will help you understand it more fully.

3. E.   From the general language and common-interest topic, you can infer that this passage would most likely be found in a general-readership magazine. The language is not elevated enough for a scholarly journal, so you can eliminate choice C. Since there's no recipe, it seems unlikely this piece would appear in a cookbook, so you can eliminate choice A. There is no mention of travel or eating pizza abroad, so you can eliminate choice B as well. It seems unlikely that advertisers would pay to write about the advantages of pizza inside the pizza box, since people have already made the purchase. Thus, you can eliminate choice D, too.

CHAPTER 10

Four Steps for Success on the PPST Reading Test

Whether you take the pencil-and-paper version of the test or the computerized version of this Praxis test, the following four-step method will help you do your very best.

1. Skim each passage.
2. Read the questions and answers.
3. Use process of elimination to cross off answers that are obviously wrong. They might represent a misreading of the passage or be illogical, for instance.
4. Read the passage and the remaining choices. Then choose the best answer.

Try this method now with the following passage:

Between Homedale and Lewiston, Idaho, the Snake River writhes its way north, majestically separating the states of Oregon and Idaho. For some distance this river flows through the deepest gorge on the North American continent, Hells Canyon. To the east, the Seven Devils Range in Idaho, volcanic in origin, towers 8,000 feet above
(5)   the river. The western side of the canyon, formed by the flat-topped ridge between the Imnaha and Snake Rivers, rises a stunning 5,500 feet. Jutting out into the canyon are circular rock benches that give a spectacular observation point. From the crest of the ridges, a person can look for miles into Oregon, Washington, Idaho, and Montana, across pretty, grassy plateau country and tumbling masses of mountains. On
(10) a clear day, a person can see into nine national forests. Tourists come from miles around to enjoy the gorgeous view. Higher up, the grass gives way to magnificent clear lakes. Hells Canyon is one of America's most dramatically beautiful places, a 130,000-acre scenic area extending for 22 miles along the Snake River.

1. The deepest gorge in North America is

(A) Seven Devils Range
(B) Snake River
(C) Hells Canyon
(D) Idaho
(E) Lewiston

2. How high is the Seven Devils Range in Idaho?

(A) 5,500 feet
(B) 8,000 feet
(C) 3,500 feet
(D) 2 miles
(E) 130,000 acres

3. The main idea of the passage is BEST stated as

(A) The Snake River flows in a winding path between Idaho and Oregon.
(B) People don't often stop to appreciate America's great natural beauty.
(C) The National Park Service works hard to keep the canyon in good shape.
(D) At one place, the canyon soars high into the air in a breathtaking sight.
(E) Hells Canyon is one of America's great recreation areas.

4. The author would MOST likely agree with which of the following opinions about wildlife conservation?

(A) Natural wonders should be protected so future generations can enjoy them.
(B) Federal parks are overfunded, which is the fault of short-sighted government officials.
(C) Plants and animals can best survive under the careful supervision of the federal government.
(D) We do not need stricter laws to protect our great natural treasures.
(E) Wildlife should be preserved, but we must be fiscally responsible above all else.

5. What would be the BEST title for this passage?

(A) The Snake River
(B) A Sight to Behold
(C) Visit Today!
(D) Hells Canyon
(E) America the Beautiful

ANSWERS

1. **C.** Choice A is wrong because it is a mountain, not a gorge. Choice B is wrong because it is a river, not a canyon. Eliminate choice D because Idaho is a state, not a gorge. Eliminate E because Lewiston is a town, not a gorge.

2. **B.** Only choice B describes Seven Devils Range.

3. **E.** The main idea is directly stated in the last sentence: "Here is one of America's great playgrounds, a 130,000-acre scenic area extending for 22 miles along the Snake River." This is the same as choice B, "Hells Canyon is one of America's great recreation areas." Eliminate choices A and D because they are details not the stated main idea. There is no support for choice C in the passage.

4. **A.** The author's admiring tone in phrases such as "America's most dramatically beautiful places" suggests that he or she would favor conservation. Only choice A has this meaning.

5. **D.** Choice D best summarizes the entire content. Choice A is too narrow; choice B is too vague; choice C is too cheerful in tone. Choice E is too broad to describe the passage clearly.

CHAPTER 11

Practice PPST Reading Exercises

Complete the following sample reading exercises using the techniques you have learned in this chapter. Work in a quiet room, as close to real test conditions as you can get. Circle the letters of your answer choices. Answers and explanations follow the test.

Questions 1–5

> Described as a "swimming and eating machine without peer," the shark has changed little over 60 million years. Sharks are admirable models of efficiency with their boneless skeletons, simple brains, generalized nervous systems, and simple internal structures. Their hydrodynamically designed shapes, razor-sharp replaceable teeth,
> (5) powerful jaws, and voracious appetites make them excellent marauders. Through scavenging and predation, the 250 species of sharks perform a valuable service in maintaining the ecological balance of the oceans. Their well-developed sensory systems enable them to detect extreme dilutions of blood in water, low-frequency sounds of splashing made by a fish in distress, and movements and contrasts in water.

1. Sharks are successful hunters for all of the following reasons *except* for their

(A) hydrodynamically designed shapes
(B) great age
(C) razor-sharp replaceable teeth
(D) powerful jaws
(E) insatiable need to eat

2. Which of the following is an opinion stated by the author?

(A) Sharks have uncomplicated brains and internal organs.
(B) Sharks have razor-sharp replaceable teeth.
(C) There are 250 species of sharks.

(D) Sharks can detect extreme dilutions of blood in water.

(E) Sharks are admirable models of efficiency.

3. Which conclusion can MOST likely be drawn from this paragraph?

(A) The author is very afraid of sharks and with good cause because they are highly dangerous creatures.

(B) People should learn more about sharks because most of us are abysmally ignorant of them.

(C) Sharks have tremendous hunger because there is relatively little food in their natural habitat.

(D) The author admires sharks for many different reasons.

(E) There is no other creature as fascinating as the shark, which is why they are part of popular culture.

4. Which of the following statements represents the main idea of this passage?

(A) A shark's shape is ideally designed for survival in the ocean.

(B) Sharks are very dangerous because they attack humans.

(C) Sharks are expert hunters that help keep the oceans healthy.

(D) Sharks can sense even the smallest amount of blood in the water.

(E) Sharks are a delicious and highly prized food source around the world.

5. What would be the BEST title for this passage?

(A) Sharks: Man's Best Friends

(B) An Evolutionary Success Story

(C) 250 Species of Sharks

(D) Razor-Sharp Teeth

(E) Swim at Your Own Risk

Questions 6–10

Two men were traveling together when a bear suddenly met them on their path. The first traveler climbed up quickly into a tree and concealed himself in the branches. The other, seeing that he must be attacked, fell flat on the ground, and when the bear came up and felt him with his snout and smelled him all over, he held his breath and feigned the appearance of death as much as he (5) could. The bear soon left him, for it is said bears will not touch a dead body. When the bear was quite gone, the other traveler descended from the tree, and jocularly inquired of his friend what it was the bear had whispered in his ear. "He gave me this advice," his companion replied. "Never travel with a friend who deserts you at the approach of danger."

6. What did the second traveler do?

   (A) died of fright when he saw the bear
   (B) smelled the bear all over and then walked away
   (C) fought the bear with all his strength
   (D) climbed a tree and hid in the branches
   (E) lay down, held his breath, and pretended to be dead

7. What pair of adjectives BEST describes the second traveler?

   (A) quick-thinking and brave
   (B) craven and timid
   (C) foolish and overly hasty
   (D) carefree and easygoing
   (E) nasty and selfish

8. Why did the first traveler ask his friend what the bear had said?

   (A) He was sad that he and his friend had come so close to death.
   (B) He was terrified of bears, a fear that he had carried over from childhood.
   (C) He did not take the entire incident and the bear's words seriously.
   (D) He was determined to hunt the bear down so he wanted to know where the bear had gone.
   (E) Curious by nature, he always tended to stick his nose in other people's business.

9. The theme of this fable is BEST stated as

   (A) be very careful of wild creatures
   (B) appearances are deceptive
   (C) never trust your enemy
   (D) one good turn deserves another
   (E) misfortune tests the sincerity of friends

10. This selection is most likely a(n)

   (A) epic
   (B) explanatory essay
   (C) editorial on safety in the woods
   (D) fable
   (E) short story

Questions 11–15

> Dinosaurs roamed the earth for nearly 150 million years; then they suddenly died out. No one knows exactly why. Some observers have suggested that the dinosaurs vanished because of raids by extraterrestrial beings. The dinosaurs could have died because of some mass disease. That seems unlikely, though, because of the way they were dispersed all over the world. Some speculate
>
> (5) that an exploding star bathed the earth in radiation, killing all the dinosaurs. This does not explain why all the other creatures on earth survived. One well-regarded theory concerns food sources. According to these scientists, the dinosaurs ate too many flowering plants and absorbed poisonous chemicals. Since they did not have a well-developed sense of taste, the dinosaurs did not realize that they were eating something that would harm them. These theories remain just
>
> (10) that, however—theories.

11. Based on the information in this passage, which of the following is the MOST plausible cause of the dinosaurs' disappearance?

   (A) They were really creatures from outer space so they returned to their home planet.
   (B) They lived in many different parts of the world so they didn't have the support of one another.
   (C) They ate too much of one type of food that eventually poisoned them.
   (D) They were attacked by larger and fiercer creatures in territorial disputes over food.
   (E) They all suffered from the same disease, which decimated them all at once.

12. All of the following details are part of this passage EXCEPT

   (A) how long dinosaurs inhabited earth
   (B) where on earth the dinosaurs lived
   (C) the fact that the dinosaurs did indeed all die out
   (D) different theories about the dinosaurs' disappearance from earth
   (E) the definitive cause of the dinosaurs' death

13. This passage is MOST likely an excerpt from a

   (A) college science textbook
   (B) middle-school or high-school textbook
   (C) guidebook to a nature part
   (D) commercial Web page
   (E) movie preview

14. Which is the MOST logical conclusion that you can draw from this passage?

(A) The reason for the dinosaurs' disappearance has puzzled many scientists.
(B) The disappearance of the dinosaurs is one of the most important problems facing scientists today and has great impact on other research.
(C) The same exploding star that killed off the dinosaurs also killed off many early cave people.
(D) Most of the theories of the dinosaurs' disappearance are not backed up by sufficient facts to be convincing.
(E) No one will ever know what happened to the dinosaurs, so this puzzle is unsolvable.

15. What is the main idea of this passage?

(A) The dinosaurs will be able to return as soon as we figure out what made them vanish in the first place.
(B) It's a terrible shame and waste to science that dinosaurs became extinct.
(C) Dinosaurs vanished because there were just too many of them in too small a place at the same time.
(D) There are many theories about the dinosaurs' disappearance, but no one theory has been accepted as fact.
(E) Scientists will be able to clone dinosaurs as soon as they extract some DNA from dinosaur bones preserved in amber.

Questions 16–20

> Cleopatra, queen of Egypt, made history when she made a bet that she could eat, at one meal, the value of a million sisterces, many years' wages for the average worker. Everyone thought that her wager was impossible. After all, how could anyone eat so much at a single meal? Cleopatra was able to eat a meal worth so much by putting a million sisterces' worth of pearls into a glass of
> (5) vinegar. Then she set the goblet aside while the dinner was served; the vinegar dissolved the pearls. When it was time for her to fulfill her gamble, she simply drank the dissolved pearls!

16. According to the information in the passage, you can infer that a million sisterces in ancient Egypt was worth

(A) a queen's salary for a year
(B) what an average person would earn in many years
(C) a strand of perfectly matched pearls
(D) a truly excellent meal
(E) about a million dollars today

17. You can infer that Cleopatra

    (A) believed that pearls were going out of fashion soon
    (B) knew that vinegar would not harm pearls
    (C) liked to play practical jokes on people
    (D) was very lucky
    (E) realized that vinegar would dissolve pearls

18. Everyone thought Cleopatra would lose the bet because

    (A) she was the queen of Egypt and she wouldn't cheat her subjects
    (B) she was very slender so she rarely ate much food at a single sitting
    (C) there was so much money involved in the wager
    (D) no one could eat so much at one time
    (E) no one would be foolish enough to make such a bet

19. What conclusions can you draw from this story?

    (A) Cleopatra was a clever woman.
    (B) Cleopatra often made outrageous wagers.
    (C) Vinegar dissolves pearls instantly.
    (D) Vinegar will dissolve all precious gems.
    (E) Vinegar is the all-purpose cleaner.

20. What is the main idea of this story?

    (A) Cleopatra should not gamble, especially with expensive jewelry.
    (B) Vinegar liquefies pearls.
    (C) Cleopatra won the bet.
    (D) Never trust a queen.
    (E) Gamblers need help to overcome their addictions.

ANSWERS

  1. B.   Choices A, C, D, and E all show why sharks are "excellent marauders," or superb hunters. Only detail B has nothing to do with sharks' ability to hunt. Further, it represents a misreading of the passage.

  2. E.   Only choice E is an opinion; all the other choices are facts. Remember: facts can be substantiated by reliable sources such as dictionaries and encyclopedias and/or by direct observation.

3. D. The opening statement—"Described as a 'swimming and eating machine without peer'"— shows the author's admiration for sharks. Details about the sharks' ability to hunt reinforce this conclusion. Eliminate choices A and B because they are generalizations not supported by the information in the paragraph. Choice C is wrong because it is too narrow to apply to the entire paragraph.

4. C. You can infer the main idea that sharks are expert hunters from the detail "excellent marauders." You can infer that they help keep the oceans healthy from the sentence "Through scavenging and predation, the 250 species of sharks perform a valuable service in maintaining the ecological balance of the oceans." Eliminate choices A and D because the statements are too narrow; eliminate choices B and E because the information is not given in the paragraph.

5. B. Sharks are an "evolutionary success story" because they have changed little in 60 million years and are remarkably efficient at what they do. Eliminate choice A because sharks are predators, as stated in the passage. Choices C and D are too specific. Choice E contains information that is not the focus of the passage.

6. E. The word *feigned* means "faked." The traveler pretends to be dead to fool the bear because he believed that bears will not touch dead bodies.

7. A. You can infer that the second traveler is quick thinking and brave because he pretends to be dead to fool the bear. None of the other choices describes his character as shown by his actions.

8. C. *Jocularly* means "in a joking or humorous way." From his humorous tone, you can infer that the traveler was shrugging off the incident. Choices A and B cannot be correct because of the word *jocularly*. There's no support in the passage for choices D and E.

9. E. You can infer this theme from the first traveler's desertion. He had no apparent regard for his friend's safety; rather, he was concerned only for his own skin.

10. D. You can tell this is a fable because it features talking animals, a strong moral, and a simple plot. Choice E is not precise enough because a short story is a general category; a fable is a type of short story so it is a better choice.

11. C. You can find the cause in this sentence: "One well-regarded theory concerns food sources. According to these scientists, the dinosaurs ate too many flowering plants and absorbed poisonous chemicals. Since they did not have a well-developed sense of taste, the dinosaurs did not realize that they were eating something that would harm them." Choice A is a misreading of the passage. The other choices are not logically supported by the information in the paragraph.

12. E. You can infer the answer from the following sentences: "Dinosaurs roamed the earth for nearly 150 million years; then they suddenly died out. No one knows exactly why .... These theories remain just that, however—theories." All the other information is provided in the passage.

13. B. Based on its relatively easy language and level of detail, this passage is probably part of a middle-school or high-school textbook. Thus, you are analyzing the style of the passage to make this inference. You can eliminate choice A because the style and detail are too simplistic. The passage is too long to be part of a movie preview. There is no support in the text for the other choices.

14. A. Only choice A is supported by information in the paragraph. Choices B and C are wrong because they are not supported with information from the passage. Further, you know from prior knowledge that choice C is wrong. Choice D can be eliminated because it is too narrow to apply to the entire paragraph. Be careful of "absolute" words, such as *never, no one, by no means, forever, always,* etc. You cannot conclude that no one will ever know the solution to the dinosaurs' disappearance.

15. D. From the details about the different theories and the final sentence—"The theories remain just that, however—theories"—you can infer that there are many theories about the dinosaurs' disappearance, but no one theory has been accepted as fact. Eliminate choice B because it is too broad to be the main idea; eliminate choice C because it is too narrow to be the main idea. Choices A and E are incorrect because there is no information about them in the passage.

16. B. From the sentence "Cleopatra, queen of Egypt, made history when she made a bet that she could eat, at one meal, the value of a million sisterces," you can find the detail that tells you what a million sisterces is worth. The other choices are a misreading of the information in the passage.

17. E. If Cleopatra didn't know that vinegar would dissolve pearls, she would not have made the bet. She was clearly stacking the deck in her favor.

18. D. The sentence "After all, how could anyone eat so much at a single meal?" gives you the cause. Choices A, C, and E do not make sense; choice B contains information not in the passage.

19. A. Only choice A is supported by information in the paragraph. Choices B and D are wrong because they are not supported with information from the passage. For choice C, just the opposite is true, since Cleopatra had to set the glass aside to give the vinegar time to dissolve the pearls. Choice E may be true, but you cannot infer that from the information given in the passage.

20. B. You can find the unstated main idea by combining the details that Cleopatra proposed the bet and set the cup aside. Choice C is true, but it is too narrow to be the main idea. Choice E has nothing to do with the passage.

PART 4

PPST: Writing Test

The PPST writing test is divided into two sessions. During the first session, you will have to answer 38 multiple-choice items in 30 minutes on the paper-and-pencil version of the test or 44 multiple-choice items in 38 minutes on the computer-based version of the test.

No matter which version of the PPST you take, during the second session, you will have to write an essay. You will have 30 minutes to complete this task.

This part of the PPST assesses your ability to use standard written English and communicate effectively in writing. Let's examine the multiple-choice questions first.

CHAPTER 12

Master the Multiple-Choice Questions

There are two types of multiple-choice questions on the PPST writing test: usage questions and sentence correction questions. The questions test your ability to recognize errors in punctuation, capitalization, grammar, sentence structure, and word choice. There are five answer choices, indicated by the letters A, B, C, D, and E. The topics are as follows:

Grammar

- Identify errors in adjective use.
- Identify errors in adverb use.
- Identify errors in noun use.
- Identify errors in pronoun use.
- Identify errors in verb use.

Sentence structure

- Identify errors in comparison.
- Identify errors in coordination.
- Identify errors in subordination.
- Identify errors in correlation.
- Identify errors in negation.
- Identify errors in parallel structure.

Word choice/idioms, punctuation, and capitalization

- Identify errors in capitalization.
- Identify errors in idioms (phrases peculiar to a group or area).
- Identify errors in punctuation.
- Identify errors in word choice.

Some of the test questions will have errors, while others will not. You will identify correct sentences by choosing E (No error) choice. Happily, you will not be asked to identify the actual grammatical error by name, such as labeling the question "dangling participle" or "faulty pronoun reference."

Spelling is *not* tested on the multiple-choice questions. Everything included on the multiple-choice items will be spelled correctly. Your spelling on the essay *will* count on your grade on that part of the test, however.

ANSWERING USAGE QUESTIONS

Usage questions are sentences with five parts underlined. They look like this:

<u>Fast-food franchises</u> are installing outlets in some <u>high schools</u>_ selling hamburgers_
        A   B   C
chicken, tacos, <u>fries, and sodas.</u> <u>No error.</u>
                    D   E

Remember your only job is to locate the error, not correct it. In general, these questions are focused on specific errors such as capitalization, punctuation, and sentence errors rather than on issues such as ambiguity and wordiness. Those two issues are usually tested in the sentence correction questions, to be discussed later in this chapter.

The answer to the sample question is C, because a comma is needed to set off the first item in a series.

Four-Step Method for Solving Usage Questions

1. Become familiar with the format.

   - A line under a blank space means that you should decide if punctuation is needed there.
   - One small error in an underlined phrase is enough to make the entire phrase incorrect.
   - Every test has some correct sentences. If you think the sentence is correct, don't shy away from marking E (No error).

2. Read the sentence all the way through to get a general sense of its meaning. Read very carefully.

3. Look for an obvious error.

4. If you have to guess, use these methods:

   - First eliminate all choices that are obviously correct.
   - Make the effort to understand *why* you made the choice you did.
   - If you can eliminate even one choice, it is to your advantage to guess. Remember that you are *not* penalized for guessing on the Praxis.

Sample Usage Questions

Try the method now with the following sample usage questions.

1. Bill <u>see</u> the ad in <u>yesterday's newspaper</u> <u>_,_</u> but he now can't seem to find <u>the ad.</u>
        A   B   C   D

   <u>No error.</u>
     E

2. The basement is the <u>larger</u> room in the <u>house, bigger</u> <u>than</u> the eat-in kitchen <u>_and</u> the
                            A   B   C   D

   huge family room. <u>No error.</u>
                      E

3. The mayor, <u>Joe Smith,</u> established a special committee <u>to explore the problems</u> with
                 A   B

   water pressure and <u>appoint</u> three members of the town council <u>to sit on the committee.</u>
                             C   D

   <u>No error.</u>
     E

4. Even the expert <u>couldn't read none</u> of the writing on the faded <u>letters, but</u> the heirs
                                A   B

   <u>were determined</u> to solve the mystery about their <u>grandfather's past.</u> <u>No error.</u>
        C   D   E

5. <u>The lectures</u> and the small discussion groups <u>consist to</u> an hour of instruction twice
        A   B

   a week <u>followed by</u> forty-five <u>minutes of a free</u> exchange of ideas. <u>No error.</u>
             C   D   E

6. <u>Sixty dollars</u> for a pair of jeans <u>are</u> far too much to spend<u>;</u> jeans <u>shouldn't</u> cost more
        A   B   C   D

   than thirty dollars. <u>No error.</u>
                  E

7. <u>Part of our job</u> in multicultural education <u>is to challenge</u> the culture of the school <u>_</u> to
        A   B   C

   <u>create a culture</u> of acceptance and achievement. <u>No error.</u>
        D   E

8. During his lunch hour<u>,</u> Miguel studies for his night classes; <u>later,</u> <u>on the bus,</u> he <u>reviewed</u>
                      A   B   C   D

   his notes and skims the reading assignments. <u>No error.</u>
                                           E

9. <u>Teaching</u> out of state is the <u>most furthest</u> thing from <u>Kristen's</u> mind, since she wants to
    A   B   C   D

stay close to her family and friends. <u>No error.</u>
                                     E

10. <u>According to the latest research,</u> the <u>brain's ability</u> to make connections and absorb
               A   B

knowledge in the first year of life <u>is even greater</u> than <u>previous believed</u>. <u>No error.</u>
                                C   D   E

ANSWERS

1. A. The tense is wrong, since the event occurred in the past. The correct sentence reads: *Bill saw the ad in yesterday's newspaper, but he can't seem to find the page with the ad.*

2. A. Use the superlative form—*largest*—when comparing three or more things.

3. C. The error is in verb tense. The sentence is set in the past ("established") and then switches to the present ("appoint"). The correct form of the verb is *appointed.*

4. A. Don't use double negatives. The sentence should read: *Even the expert couldn't read any . . .*

5. B. The correct idiom is *consist of,* not "consist to."

6. B. This is an error in subject-verb agreement. The singular subject "sixty dollars" requires the singular verb *is,* not the plural verb "are." Don't be confused by the intervening prepositional phrase "for a pair of jeans."

7. E. The sentence is correct as written.

8. D. The error occurs with verb tense. The sentence is set in the present ("studies") and then switches to the past ("reviewed"). The correct form of the verb is *reviews.*

9. B. Never use *-er* or *-est* with *more* or *most.* The sentence should read: *Teaching out of state is the furthest thing . . .*

10. D. Use the adverb *previously* to describe the verb *believed.* The sentence should read: *According to the latest research, the brain's ability to make connections and absorb knowledge in the first year of life is even greater than previously believed.*

ANSWERING SENTENCE CORRECTION QUESTIONS

Sentence correction questions are single sentences with part or all of the sentence underlined. The first answer choice is the same as the underlined part. The other four answer choices present various ways to revise the underlined part. Sentence correction questions look like this:

> In view of the extenuating circumstances and the defendant's youth,
> <u>leniency having been recommended by the judge.</u>
>
>   (A) leniency having been recommended by the judge.
>   (B) leniency was recommended by the judge.
>   (C) the judge recommending leniency.
>   (D) the judge leniency recommended.
>   (E) the judge recommended leniency.

These questions are the opposite of the usage questions: Here, the error is identified for you but you have to correct it. The underlined portion can be one word, a phrase, or even the entire sentence.

The answer to the sample question is E, because the sentence is more direct and clear when written in the active voice.

Four-Step Method for Solving Sentence Correction Questions

1. Read the sentence all the way through to get a general sense of its meaning.
2. Anticipate the answer. Determine how best to revise the sentence.
3. Read the five answer choices. Don't stop reading if you find an answer that seems correct. Always check every one of the choices in context because there may be a choice that corrects the sentence better than the original one you found.
4. If you have to guess, use these methods:

   - Keep it simple. Go for the answer that creates the most direct, least convoluted sentence.
   - Make the effort to understand *why* you made the choice you did.
   - If you can eliminate even one choice, it is to your advantage to guess.

Sample Sentence Correction Questions

Try this method now with the following sample sentence correction questions.

1. The story opens in the Dutch West <u>Indies most of the action</u> takes place on a tiny, isolated *cay* (an island composed mainly of coral and sand) in the Caribbean.

   (A) Indies most of the action
   (B) Indies, most of the action
   (C) Indies, the action mostly
   (D) Indies, when most of the action
   (E) Indies, but most of the action

2. The great explorer's astonishing discovery brought him fame around the world and assured him a lucrative book contract.

(A) explorer's astonishing discovery brought him fame
(B) explorer's astonishing discovery brought them fame
(C) explorer's astonishing discovery brought his company fame
(D) explorer's astonishing discovery brought fame
(E) fame that was brought to the explorer because of his astonishing discovery

3. After the major argument at the wedding, reconciliation was the most furthest thing from their minds.

(A) most furthest thing
(B) furthest thing
(C) more furthest thing
(D) most further thing
(E) further thing

4. The right belongs to every American to vote in elections.

(A) The right belongs to every American to vote in elections.
(B) The right belongs to vote in elections to every American.
(C) To vote in elections to every American the right belongs.
(D) To vote in elections, the right belongs to every American.
(E) The right to vote in elections belongs to every American.

5. Driving through the park at night, the pine trees looked like eerie giants.

(A) Driving through the park at night, the pine trees looked like eerie giants.
(B) Driving through the park at night, the eerie giants looked like pine trees.
(C) Driving through the park at night, we thought the pine trees looked like eerie giants.
(D) The pine trees looked like eerie giants driving through the park at night.
(E) The eerie looked like giants pine trees driving through the park at night.

6. It is still not certain how most animals, particularly birds, find their way on long migrations; however, experiments have shown that many birds use the sun to navigate.

(A) migrations; however, experiments have shown that many birds use the sun to navigate.
(B) migrations however, experiments have shown that many birds use the sun to navigate.
(C) migrations, however, experiments have shown that many birds use the sun to navigate.
(D) migrations; however, experiments are showing that many birds use the sun to navigate.
(E) migrations; however, experiments showing that many birds use the sun to navigate.

7. Each species has adapted itself to a special diet, a varied environment, and <u>predators that are different.</u>

   (A) predators that are different
   (B) predators that act in different ways
   (C) predators that are very dangerous
   (D) different predators
   (E) differently-abled predators

8. In Argentina, <u>you</u> will find many large cattle ranches, beautiful beaches, and a lively nightlife.

   (A) you
   (B) a tourist
   (C) he or she
   (D) they
   (E) them

9. <u>Homesick settlers in Australia got a small shipment of rabbits from England in the mid-19th century triggered one of the world's most devastating ecological disasters.</u>

   (A) Homesick settlers in Australia got a small shipment of rabbits from England in the mid-19th century triggered one of the world's most devastating ecological disasters.
   (B) Homesick settlers in Australia got a small shipment of rabbits from England in the mid-19th century, triggered one of the world's most devastating ecological disasters.
   (C) Homesick settlers in Australia got a small shipment of rabbits from England in the mid-19th century, trigger one of the world's most devastating ecological disasters.
   (D) Got a small shipment of rabbits from England in the mid-19th century, homesick settlers in Australia triggered one of the world's most devastating ecological disasters.
   (E) Homesick settlers in Australia got a small shipment of rabbits from England in the mid-19th century, and triggered one of the world's most devastating ecological disasters.

10. <u>The point of the matter is, permission was not given by Georgia O'Keeffe to display her work at the show that launched her on the road to fame.</u>

   (A) The point of the matter is, permission was not given by Georgia O'Keeffe to display her work at the show that launched her road to fame.
   (B) Georgia O'Keeffe did not give permission to display her work at the show that launched her road to fame.
   (C) Permission was not given by Georgia O'Keeffe to display her work at the show that launched her road to fame.
   (D) Georgia O'Keeffe had not been giving permission by to be displaying her work at the show that launched her road to fame.
   (E) At the show that launched her road to fame, to be displaying her work permission was not given by Georgia O'Keeffe.

ANSWERS

1. **E.** As written, the sentence is a run-on, two incorrectly joined sentences. Merely adding a comma (choice B) creates a comma splice. Choice C rephrases the sentence but does not correct the run-on. Choice D is illogical, because the subordinating conjunction *when* does not make sense in this context. The correct sentence reads: *The story opens in the Dutch West Indies, but most of the action takes place on a tiny, isolated* cay (*an island composed mainly of coral and sand*) *in the Caribbean.*

2. **C.** Do not use a pronoun to refer to a noun's possessive form (the form that shows ownership). In addition, you cannot use a noun's possessive form as the antecedent to a pronoun unless the pronoun is also in the possessive case. Thus, the pronoun *him* cannot be used to refer to the possessive noun *explorer's.* Choice C—"explorer's astonishing discovery brought his company fame"—correctly puts both the noun and the pronoun in the possessive case (*explorer's, his*).

3. **B.** Never add both *-er* and *more* (or *less*) or both *-est* and *most* (or *least*) to a modifier. The corrected sentence should read: *After the major argument at the wedding, reconciliation was the* furthest thing *from their minds.*

4. **E.** This is a misplaced modifier, resulting in a confusing sentence. Moving the modifier (the describing words "to vote in elections") closer to the noun it describes corrects the error.

5. **C.** This is a dangling participle, a phrase that does not describe anything. As a result, the sentence does not make sense. You can usually correct a dangling participle by rewriting the sentence to include the missing modified word, as is the case here. Choices B, D, and E compound the error by creating totally illogical sentences.

6. **A.** This sentence is correct as written.

7. **D.** This is an error in parallel structure. Parallel (or match) the phrase "different predators" to the phrases "a special diet" and "a varied environment."

8. **B.** The pronoun "you" is vague and imprecise. The sentence should read: *In Argentina, a tourist will find.* . . . None of the other choices makes the sentence clear and precise.

9. **E.** As written, this is a run-on. Choice B creates a comma splice because a comma is not a strong enough form of punctuation to join two complete sentences (only a semicolon or a colon can join two independent clauses). Only choice E corrects the error.

10. **B.** As written, this sentence is awkward and wordy. Choice B best streamlines the sentence by removing the wordiness and rewriting the passive construction into the active voice.

CHAPTER 13

Review of English Skills for the PPST

The following is a review of the skills tested on the PPST writing test. Nearly all of these skills will be tested directly on the multiple-choice questions, but *all* of them apply to the essay. Skim this chapter, pausing at the sections that pose the greatest challenge for you.

USE ADJECTIVES AND ADVERBS CORRECTLY

Adjectives and adverbs are called *modifiers* because they modify or change by describing. *Adjectives* are words used to describe a noun or pronoun. By so doing, adjectives give the noun or pronoun a more precise and specific meaning. You can test whether a word is an adjective by seeing if it answers one of these four questions:

What Kind?	*Which One?*	*How Many?*	*How Much?*
red dress	that pencil	an apple	enough money
hot weather	any disk	several guides	more time

Proper adjectives, such as African art, Latin music, Greek architecture, are capitalized. The adjective can come before or after the noun or pronoun it describes. Here are some examples:

Before the noun   The sick   child did not come to school.
                             adjective   noun

After the noun   The child, sick with mumps, did not come to school.
                          noun   adjective

Adverbs are words used to describe a verb, an adjective, or another adverb. By so doing, adverbs give the verb, adjective, or other adverb a more precise and specific meaning. You can test whether a word is an adverb by seeing if it answers one of these four questions:

Where?	*When?*	*In What Manner?*	*To What Extent?*
fell below	left today	danced smoothly	wash completely
went there	quickly left	talked loudly	hardly complained

Adverbs can come before or after the word they describe. Here are some examples:

Before the verb   Do you <u>completely</u> <u>understand</u> the situation?
                              adverb   verb

After the verb   Our neighbors are <u>moving</u> <u>away</u>.
                                        verb   adverb

Many adverbs end in *-ly*. That's because most adverbs are formed by adding *-ly* to an adjective. However, quite a few common adverbs do not end in *-ly*. These include: *almost, always, aside, away, down, ever, everywhere, inside, late, often, overhead, today, then, tomorrow, up, yesterday.* Here are some rules governing the use of adjectives and adverbs.

Use an Adjective After a Linking Verb

A *linking verb* connects a subject with a descriptive word. Here are the most common linking verbs: *be* (*is, am, are, was, were,* etc.), *seem, appear, look, feel, smell, sound, taste, become, grow, remain, stay,* and *turn.*

Example: Chicken cooked this way <u>tastes</u> more *delicious* (not *deliciously*).

Use an Adverb to Describe a Verb, an Adjective, or Another Adverb

Describe a verb   Experiments using dynamite must be done *carefully.*
Describe an adjective   Rick had an *unbelievably large* appetite for pizza.
Describe an adverb   They sang *so sweetly.*

Make Correct Comparisons with Adjectives and Adverbs

- Use the comparative degree (*-er* or *more* form) to compare two things.

   Example: Your test seems <u>longer</u> than mine.
   I don't think it is <u>more difficult</u>, however.

- Use the superlative form (*-est* or *most* form) to compare more than two things.

   Example: This is the <u>longest</u> test I have ever taken.
   It is also the <u>most difficult</u> test I have ever taken.

- Never use *-er* and *more* or *-est* and *most* together.

   Example: No: This is the <u>more longer</u> of the two tests.
   Yes: This is the <u>longer</u> of the two tests.

Adjectives and adverbs have different forms to show degree of comparison: the *positive, comparative,* and *superlative* degrees.

- *Positive degree:* The base form of the adjective or adverb. It does not show comparison.

- *Comparative degree:* The form an adjective or adverb takes to compare *two* things.
- *Superlative degree:* The form an adjective or adverb takes to compare *three* or more things.

	Positive Degree	*Comparative Degree*	*Superlative Degree*
adjective	tall	taller	tallest
	good	better	best
adverb	slowly	more slowly	most slowly
	well	better	best

Use *-er* or *more* (never both!) to form the comparative degree and *-est* or *most* (never both!) to from the superlative degree of most one- and two-syllable adjectives and adverbs. Use *more* or *most* to form the comparative and superlative degrees of all adjectives and adverbs that have three or more syllables. Use *more* and *most* with all adverbs that end in *-ly*. Here are some examples:

Positive Degree	*Comparative Degree*	*Superlative Degree*
high	higher	highest
just	more just	most just
extensive	more extensive	most extensive
prevalent	more prevalent	most prevalent
easily	more easily	most easily
rudely	more rudely	most rudely

Some adjectives and adverbs have irregular comparative and superlative forms, as the following chart shows.

Positive Degree	*Comparative Degree*	*Superlative Degree*
bad	worse	worst
badly	worse	worst
far	farther	farthest
far	further	furthest
good	better	best
ill	worse	worst
late	later	last or latest
little (amount)	less	least
many	more	most
much	more	most
well	better	best

Avoid Misplaced and Dangling Modifiers

Place adjectives and adverbs as close as possible to the noun or pronoun they describe. A *misplaced modifier* is a phrase, clause, or word placed too far from the noun or pronoun it describes. As a result, the sentence fails to convey its exact meaning and can also be unintentionally funny.

Correct a misplaced modifier by placing it as close as possible to the word it describes. Here are two examples:

Misplaced: <u>Coming in for a landing</u>, ground control radioed to the helicopter. (States that ground control is coming in for a landing.)

Corrected: Ground control radioed to the helicopter <u>coming in for a landing.</u>

Misplaced: <u>Smashed beyond repair</u>, Larry saw his tennis racket lying on the court. (States that Larry is smashed.)

Corrected: Larry saw his tennis racket, <u>smashed beyond repair,</u> lying on the court.

A *dangling modifier* is a word or phrase that describes something that has been left out of the sentence. A modifier is said to "dangle" when the word it modifies (describes) is not actually in the sentence.

Correct a dangling modifier by adding a noun or pronoun to which the dangling construction can be attached. Two examples follow:

Dangling: Flying over the countryside, the houses looked like toys. (States that the houses were flying.)

Corrected: As we flew over the countryside, the houses looked like toys. (Added the pronoun *we.*)

Use Vivid and Precise Adjectives and Adverbs in Writing

Colorful and specific modifiers make your writing and speech more specific and descriptive. Study the following example:

A successful actor before he entered politics, Ronald Reagan used his public speaking skills to further his conservative agenda. He lowered taxes, increased defense spending, and reduced social programs, including food stamps and unemployment benefits. Under his economic policy, nicknamed "Reaganomics," the country sank in a recession and the national debt soared. The Iran-Contra scandal, involving illegal weapons sales to Iran and the support of anticommunist "Contra" guerrillas in Nicaragua, failed to tarnish the "Great Communicator's" image.

PRACTICE PPST EXERCISES

Directions: Each of the following sentences has four underlined and lettered portions. Read each sentence and decide whether any of the underlined parts contains an error. If so, write the letter of the portion containing the error in the space provided. If there is no error, write E (No error). No sentence contains more than one error. Answers and explanations follow the questions.

This is the format for Part A, questions 1–21, on the writing part of the PPST.

_____ 1. The messenger spoke to the latest receptionist who delivered the package.
   A   B   C   D
No error.
E

_____ 2. In my opinion, Raul is most intelligent than your student Luisa, but
   A   B
it's plain that they both deserve more recognition than they are
   C   D
receiving. No error.
         E

_____ 3. Driving through the forest late at night, the trees looked more than a
                     A   B   C
little mysterious. No error.
   D   E

_____ 4. A delicious sundae was served to each guest dripping with chocolate
   A   B   C   D
sauce. No error.
      E

_____ 5. This year's principal is more kinder than last year's principal and so is
                            A   B   C
easier to work with on a daily basis. No error.
   D   E

ANSWERS

1. D.   Because of the misplaced modifier, the sentence incorrectly states that the receptionist, not the messenger, delivered the package. The sentence should read: *The messenger who delivered the package spoke to the new receptionist.*

2. B.   Use the comparative form, not the superlative form, to compare two people. The correct word should be *more.*

3. A.   The dangling modifier suggests that the trees were driving through the forest. Here is one way to correct the sentence: *As we were driving through the forest late at night, the trees looked more than a little mysterious.*

4. D.   Because of the misplaced modifier, the sentence incorrectly states that the guests were dripping with chocolate sauce. The sentence should read: *A delicious sundae dripping with chocolate was served to each guest.*

5. A.   Don't use *-er* and *more* or *-est* and *most* together. Here, just use the word *kinder.*

USE NOUNS CORRECTLY

A *noun* is a word that names a person, place, or thing. There are three main types of nouns: *common nouns*, *proper nouns*, and *compound nouns*.

- *Common nouns* name a type of person, place, or thing.
- *Proper nouns* name a specific person, place, or thing. They are always capitalized.
- *Compound nouns* are two or more nouns that work together as one word. A compound noun can be two individual words, words joined by a hyphen, or two words combined.

Common Nouns	*Proper Nouns*	*Compound Nouns*
woman	Eleanor Roosevelt	outside
dog	Rin Tin Tin	out-of-date

Use Possessive Nouns Correctly

In grammar, *possession* shows ownership. Follow these rules to create possessive nouns:

1. With singular nouns, add an apostrophe and an *s.* If the singular noun ends in *-s,* you still add the *'s.* However, when the *'s* makes the word difficult to pronounce, you can add just the apostrophe.

girl	girl's book
student	student's ideas
James	James's eyeglasses or James' eyeglasses

2. With plural nouns ending in *s,* add an apostrophe after the *s.*

girls	girls' books
students	students' ideas

3. With plural nouns not ending in *s,* add an apostrophe and an *s.*

women	women's books
mice	mice's tails

USE PRONOUNS CORRECTLY

Pronouns are words used in place of a noun or another pronoun.

1. *Personal pronouns* refer to a specific person, place, object, or thing. The following chart shows the personal pronouns in the first, second, and third person.

	Singular	*Plural*
First person	I, me, mine, my	we, us, our, ours
Second person	you, your, yours	you, your, yours
Third person	he, him, his she, her, hers, it	they, them, their, theirs, its

2. *Possessive pronouns* show ownership.

   yours   his   hers   its   ours   theirs   whose

3. *Interrogative pronouns* begin a question.

   who   what   which   whom   whose

4. *Indefinite pronouns* refer to people, places, objects, or things without pointing to a specific one. Here are the most common indefinite pronouns:

Singular		*Plural*	*Singular or Plural (depending on context)*
another	anyone	both	all
each	everyone	few	any
much	other	many	more
either	neither	others	most
nobody	nothing	several	none
little	no one	some	
someone	anybody		
anything	one		
somebody	something		
everybody	everything		

Use the Correct Pronoun Case

Case is the form of a noun or pronoun that shows how it is used in a sentence. English has three cases: *nominative, objective,* and *possessive.* The following chart shows the three cases:

Nominative	Objective	Possessive
(pronoun as subject)	(pronoun as object)	(ownership)
I	me	my, mine
you	you	your, yours
he	him	his
she	her	her, hers
it	it	its
we	us	our, ours
they	them	their, theirs
who	whom	whose
whoever	whomever	whoever

- Use the nominative case to show the subject of a verb.

  Example: *We* spoke to the teacher about the test.

- Use the objective case to show the noun or pronoun receives the action.

  Example: The teacher was willing to speak to *us.*

- Use the possessive case to show ownership.

  Example: The book is *mine,* not *yours* or *his.*

Do not confuse possessive pronouns with contractions. Study this chart:

Possessive Pronouns	Contractions
your	you're (you + are)
its	it's (it + is)
their	they're (they + are)
whose	who's (who + is)

PRACTICE PPST EXERCISES

Directions: Choose the best version of the underlined portion of each sentence. Choice A is the same as the underlined portion of the original sentence. If you think that the original sentence is better than any of the suggested revisions, choose A. Otherwise, choose the revision you think is best. Answers and explanations follow the questions.

This is the format for Part B, questions 22–38 on the writing part of the PPST.

1. Have <u>students read the passage from John Steinbecks *Grapes* of *Wrath*.</u>

   (A) students read the passage from John Steinbecks *Grapes'*
   (B) students' read the passage from John Steinbeck's *Grape's*
   (C) student's read the passage from John Steinbeck's *Grapes*
   (D) students read the passage from John Steinbecks' *Grapes*
   (E) students read the passage from John Steinbeck's *Grapes*

2. The teacher gave <u>he</u> a lot of advice for the upcoming test.

   (A) he
   (B) him
   (C) I
   (D) we
   (E) they

3. From <u>who</u> did you buy that book?

   (A) who
   (B) who's
   (C) whom
   (D) whose
   (E) whoever

4. There is no question that <u>your</u> studying hard for the exam.

   (A) your
   (B) your'e
   (C) you
   (D) you're
   (E) you be

5. Technological <u>resources for writing a variety of documents</u> continue to grow rapidly.

   (A) resources for writing a variety of documents
   (B) resources' for writing a variety of documents
   (C) resources for writing a variety of document's
   (D) resources for writing a variety of documents'
   (E) resource's for writing a variety of documents'

ANSWERS

1. **E.** The book *Grapes of Wrath* belongs to John Steinbeck, so the phrase is written as John Steinbeck's *Grapes of Wrath*. Choices B, C, and D are incorrect because we do not use an apostrophe with a noun that ends in *s* unless the noun shows ownership.

2. B. Use the objective case because *teacher* is the subject and *him* is the object. All the other choices are in the nominative case.

3. C. Use the objective case (*whom*) for the object of a preposition (*from*). Choice B is a contraction so it is incorrect in context. Choice D is possessive, incorrect in context, and choice E is in the nominative case.

4. D. Use the contraction you're (*you are*) to make sense in context.

5. A. This sentence is correct as written.

USE VERBS CORRECTLY

Verbs are words that name an action or describe a state of being. There are four basic types of verbs: *action verbs, linking verbs, helping verbs, and verb phrases.*

1. *Action verbs* tell what the subject does.

   Examples: jump kiss laugh

2. *Linking verbs* join the subject and the predicate and name and describe the subject.

   Examples: be feel grow seem smell remain appear sound stay look taste turn become

3. *Helping verbs* are added to another verb to make the meaning clearer.

   Examples: am does had shall has can did may should must could have might will do would

4. *Verb phrases* are made of one main verb and one or more helping verbs.

   Examples: will arrive could be looking

Use the Correct Verb Tense

The *tense* of a verb shows its time. A verb's tense tells when the action took place. For example, a verb's tense tells if the action is finished or is still continuing, whether it began in the past and continues into the present. We form the tenses of English verbs from helping verbs and principal parts, as the following chart shows.

Present	Present Participle	Past	Past Participle
talk	talking	talked	have talked
run	running	ran	have run

Some verbs are *regular.* This means they form the past tense by adding *-d* or *-ed* to the present form. Here are some examples:

Present	Present Participle	Past	Past Participle
play	playing	played	have/had played
reach	reaching	reached	have/had reached

Other verbs are irregular. They form their past tense in many different ways. Pay close attention to irregular verbs because they are easily confused and thus present fertile ground for testing. For example:

Present	Present Participle	Past	Past Participle
be	is	was/were	had/have been
do	doing	did	have/had done
go	going	went	have/had gone
lay	laying	laid	have/had laid
lie	lying	lay	have/had lain
rise	rising	rose	have/had risen
teach	teaching	taught	have/had taught
write	writing	wrote	have/had written

When you *conjugate* a verb, you list the singular and plural forms of the verb in a specific tense, as this chart shows:

Present Tense—Regular Verbs	
I	I
you	you
we walk	we walk
they	they
he, she, it walks	he, she, it walks
Past Tense—Regular Verbs	
I	I
you	you
we walk	we walk*ed*
they	they
he, she, it walks	he, she, it walk*ed*

Use Tenses Consistently

Use tenses logically to show when an action took place. Illogical shifts in tense confuse your readers.

Incorrect: He <u>rushed</u> into the test and <u>slams</u> his books on the floor.
       past tense   present tense

Correct: He <u>rushed</u> into the test and <u>slammed</u> his books on the floor.
       past tense   past tense

Use Can and Could Correctly

Can means <u>am/is/are</u> able. It may be used to show the <u>present tense</u>. Here are two examples:

I can clean the garage this afternoon.
Luc can watch television all afternoon.

Could means "was/were able" when used to show the <u>past tense</u> of *can. Could* also means "might be able, a possibility or wish." Here are two examples:

Last year, Jean could devote more time to community service.
Jean could make the 7:32 train if she hurries.

Can and *could* (along with *might, must, shall, should, will, would*) never change form.

Use Active and Passive Voice Correctly

In the *active voice,* the subject performs the action named by the verb.

Example: Ben Franklin first wanted a turkey instead of an eagle as our national symbol.

In the *passive voice,* the subject receives the action.

Example: A turkey instead of an eagle was first wanted by Benjamin Franklin as our national symbol.

In general, the active voice is preferable to the passive voice because it is more direct and concise.

Make Subjects and Verbs Agree

Agreement means that sentence parts match. Follow these rules to match sentence parts:

1. A singular subject takes a singular verb.

   Example: <u>I</u> *am* staying home to study.

2. A plural subject takes a plural verb.

   Example: <u>Joey and Louis</u> *are* staying home to study.

3. Ignore words or phrases that come between the subject and the verb.

   Example: Too many *onions* in a pot roast often *cause* an upset stomach. The plural subject *onions* requires the plural verb *cause.* Ignore the intervening prepositional phrase "in a pot roast."

4. Subjects that are singular in meaning but plural in form require a singular verb. These subjects include words such as *measles, news, economics,* and *mathematics.*

   Example: The *news* <u>was</u> good.

5. Singular subjects connected by *or, neither . . . nor, and not only . . . but also* require a singular verb.

   Example: Either the witness or the defendant *was* lying.

6. If the subject is made up of two or more nouns or pronouns connected by *or, nor, not only, but also,* the verb agrees with the noun closer to the pronoun.

   Example: Neither the cat nor the <u>dogs</u> *are* house-trained.
   Example: Neither the dogs nor the <u>cat</u> *is* house-trained.

PRACTICE PPST EXERCISES

Directions: Each of the following sentences has four underlined and lettered portions. Read each sentence and decide whether any of the underlined parts contains an error. If so, write the letter of the portion containing the error in the space provided. If there is no error, write E (No error). No sentence contains more than one error. Answers and explanations follow the questions.

1. When <u>my cousin</u> arrived <u>at the bus terminal,</u> the entire family <u>greets</u> him with
          A   B   C

   <u>hugs and kisses.</u> <u>No error.</u>
       D   E

2. All the boys and girls <u>in the fifth grade</u> class <u>does</u> volunteer work <u>in the local</u>
                   A   B   C

   community center on <u>Tuesdays and Thursdays.</u> <u>No error.</u>
                    D   E

3. Around 300 B.C., when the great Egyptian pyramids <u>beginned</u> to be built,
                                        A

   <u>deserts</u> to the <u>east and west</u> cut off Egypt from the rest of the world and
   B   C

   <u>protected the land</u> from invaders. <u>No error.</u>
       D   E

4. Near the top of the closet in the master bedroom are an old electric fan; please
     A   B   C   D

get it for me. No error.
            E

5. Some time near the beginning of the seventh century, so the unproven legend goes,
       A   B

a monk had some dough left over from his baking, which he forms into a looped
                                                               C

twist we know as the "pretzel." No error.
                D   E

ANSWERS

1. C. The sentence begins in the past tense ("arrived") but then illogically switches to the present tense ("greets"). The correct sentence reads: *When my cousin arrived at the bus terminal, the entire family greeted him with hugs and kisses.*

2. B. The plural subject "all the boys and girls" requires the plural verb *do*. Ignore the intervening prepositional phrase "in the fifth grade."

3. A. The correct past tense of "begin" is *began*.

4. C. The singular subject "fan" requires the singular verb *is*.

5. C. The sentence begins in the past tense ("had"), but then illogically switches to the present tense ("forms"). The correct sentence reads: *Some time near the beginning of the seventh century, so the unproven legend goes, a monk had some dough left over from his baking, which he formed into a looped twist . . .*

Write Correct Sentences

To be a sentence, a group of words must . . .

- Have a *subject* (noun or pronoun)
- Have a *predicate* (verb or verb phrase)
- Express a *complete thought*

Recognize Sentence Parts

Every sentence must have two parts: a *subject* and a *predicate*. The subject includes the noun or pronoun that tells what the subject is about. The predicate includes the verb that describes what the subject is doing. Here are some examples of complete sentences:

Sentence Parts	
[You] *(understood subject)*	Leave! *(predicate)*
You *(subject)*	leave! *(predicate)*
You *(subject)*	leave early for the airport to make sure you have enough time to check in. *(predicate)*

- To find the subject, ask yourself, "Which word is the sentence describing?"
- To find an action verb, ask yourself, "What did the subject do?"
- If you can't find an action verb, look for a linking verb. The linking verbs include *to be* (*am, are, was, were, am being,* etc.), *appear, become, feel, grow, look, remain, seem, smell, sound, stay, taste, turn.*

In most sentences, the subject comes *before* the verb. This is not the case with questions. In a question, the subject often comes *after* the verb. Here are some examples:

- *Is the ice cream on the counter?* The subject of the sentence is "ice cream." The verb is "is" (a form of *to be*). The subject comes *after* the verb.
- *Are you staying home tonight?* The subject of the sentence is "you." The verb is "are" (a form of *to be*). The subject comes *after* the verb.

To find the subject in a question, rewrite the question as a statement. The question "Is the ice cream on the counter?" becomes "The ice cream is on the counter." Now the subject, *ice cream,* is in the usual position before the verb.

Identify Sentence Types

There are two types of clauses: *independent* and *dependent.*

- *Independent clauses* are complete sentences because they have a subject and a verb and express a complete thought.
- *Dependent clauses* are not complete sentences because they do not express a complete thought—even though they have a subject and a verb.

Independent and dependent clauses can be used in a number of ways to form the four basic types of sentences: *simple, compound, complex, compound-complex.*

Simple Sentences

A *simple sentence* has one independent clause. That means it has one subject and one verb—although either or both can be compound. In addition, a simple sentence can have adjectives and adverbs. A simple sentence cannot have another independent clause or any subordinate clauses. For example:

- My <u>sister</u>   <u>shops</u>   every day.
  (one subject)   *(one verb)*

- My <u>sister</u> and my <u>mother</u>   <u>buy</u>   many amazing things.
  (compound subject)   *(one verb)*

- My <u>daughter</u>   <u>plays</u> softball and <u>rides</u> her bicycle.
  (one subject)   *(compound verb)*

Compound Sentences

A *compound sentence* consists of two or more independent clauses. The independent clauses can be joined in one of two ways:

- With a coordinating conjunction: *for, and, nor, but, or, yet, so.*
- With a semicolon (;)

As with a simple sentence, a compound sentence cannot have any subordinate clauses. For example:

- Mike grills steak,   and   Nancy sets the table.
  (independent clause)   *(conjunction)*   *(independent clause)*

- Nancy cooks every day   ;   Mike cooks only on weekends.
  (independent clause)   *(semicolon)*   *(independent clause)*

You may also add a conjunctive adverb to this construction, as in this example: Nancy cooks every day; <u>however</u>, Mike cooks only on weekends.

Complex Sentences

A *complex sentence* contains one independent clause and at least one dependent clause. The independent clause is called the *main clause.* These sentences use *subordinating conjunctions* to link ideas. Study these examples:

- When   you take the PPST,   you will have to write an essay.
  (subordinate   (dependent clause)   (independent clause)
  conjunction)

- An essay is included   because   writing is a key skill teachers
                                                                               must possess.

  (independent clause)   *(subordinate)*   *(dependent clause)*
                                      conjunction)

The most common subordinating conjunctions include:

Subordinating Conjunctions					
after	although	as	because	before	even if
even though	if	rather than	since	so	so that
though	unless	until	when	whether	while

Compound-Complex Sentences

A *compound-complex sentence* has at least two independent clauses and at least one dependent clause. The dependent clause can be part of the independent clause. For instance:

- When people want to teach,   they take the PPST   and they study to get the highest possible score.

  (dependent clause)   *(independent clause)*   *(independent clause)*

- Josh got a new car for graduation,   but the transmission broke immediately,   so he took it back to the dealer for repairs.

  (independent clause)   *(independent clause)*   *(dependent clause)*

Identify and Correct Sentence Errors

There are two types of sentence errors: *run-ons* and *fragments*. A *run-on sentence* is two incorrectly joined independent clauses. The sentences can be run together without any punctuation or incorrectly joined with a comma. For example:

- No knowledge ever exists in isolation interest in any field comes from the relationships between ideas.
- The PPST test in writing measures your ability to use grammar and language, it also assesses your ability to communicate effectively in writing.

You can correct a run-on sentence in several different ways, as the following examples show:

Separate the run-on into two sentences with end punctuation such as periods, exclamation marks, and question marks.

- The PPST test in writing measures your ability to use grammar and language. It also assesses your ability to communicate effectively in writing.

Add a coordinating conjunction (*and, nor, but, or, for, yet, so*) to create a compound sentence. Be sure to use a comma before the coordinating conjunction in a compound sentence, unless the two independent clauses are very short.

- The PPST test in writing measures your ability to use grammar and language, and it also assesses your ability to communicate effectively in writing.

Add a subordinating conjunction to create a complex sentence.

- The PPST test in writing measures your ability to use grammar and language, while it also assesses your ability to communicate effectively in writing.

Use a semicolon to create a compound sentence. You may choose to add a conjunctive adverb, such as *however, nevertheless, nonetheless, moreover.*

- The PPST test in writing measures your ability to use grammar and language; it also assesses your ability to communicate effectively in writing.

- The PPST test in writing measures your ability to use grammar and language; in addition, it assesses your ability to communicate effectively in writing.

Rewrite the sentence.

- The PPST test in writing measures your ability to apply grammar, to use language, and to communicate effectively in writing.

Which revision is best? *Choose the way that best suits your purpose, audience, and tone.*

As its name suggests, a *sentence fragment* is a group of words that do not express a complete thought. Most times, a fragment is missing a subject, a verb, or both. Other times, a fragment may have a subject and a verb but still not express a complete thought. Fragments can be phrases as well as clauses.

Fragment missing a subject:

- Unanimously voted today to require the PPST.

Fragment missing a verb:

- The state education department to require the PPST.

Fragment missing a subject and a verb:

- While listening to the radio.

Fragment with a subject and a verb that does not express a complete thought:

- Because it is essential that well-educated people communicate effectively in writing.

You can correct a fragment by adding the missing part to the sentence or by omitting the subordinating conjunction. In some instances, you can also correct a fragment by adding it to another sentence.

Fragment	*Sentence*
Unanimously voted today to require the PPST.	The state education department unanimously voted today to require the PPST.
The state education department to require the PPST.	The state education department voted to require the PPST.
While listening to the radio.	While listening to the radio, Martha practiced the latest dance steps.
Because it is essential that well-educated people communicate effectively in writing.	It is essential that well-educated people communicate effectively in writing.

Eliminate Unnecessary Words

Write simply and directly. Omit unnecessary details or ideas that you have already stated. Use a lot of important detail, but no unnecessary words.

1. Omit unnecessary words.

   Wordy: We watched the big, massive, black cloud rising up from the level prairie and covering over the sun.

   Better: We watched the massive, black cloud rising from the prairie and covering the sun.

2. Rewrite the sentence to eliminate unnecessary words.

   Wordy: Sonnets, which are a beautiful poetic form, have fourteen lines and a set rhythm and rhyme.

   Better: Sonnets are a beautiful poetic form with fourteen lines and a set rhythm and rhyme.

USE PARALLEL STRUCTURE

Parallel structure means putting ideas of the same rank in the same grammatical structure. Words, phrases, and clauses should be parallel. Match each subsequent element to the first part of the sentence.

- Parallel words: A healthful diet contains *fruits, vegetables,* and *protein.*
- Parallel phrases: The state government can afford to *make classes smaller, to repair potholes faster,* and *to pick up trash earlier,* too.

PRACTICE PPST EXERCISES

Directions: Choose the best version of the underlined portion of each sentence. Choice A is the same as the underlined portion of the original sentence. If you think that the original sentence is better than any of the suggested revisions, choose A. Otherwise, choose the revision you think is best. Answers and explanations follow the questions.

1. Scorers will base their judgment of your essay on such factors as clarity, conciseness, and <u>logic they</u> will also check that you have addressed the question directly.

   (A) logic they
   (B) logic, they
   (C) logic. they
   (D) logic, and they
   (E) logic, so they

2. <u>Yew classified</u> as a softwood even though the wood is very strong and durable.

   (A) Yew classified
   (B) Yew, classified
   (C) Yew be classified
   (D) Yew classifying
   (E) Yew is classified

3. <u>When the Minoan civilization of Crete</u> came to a sudden and mysterious end in about 1450 B.C.

   (A) When the Minoan civilization of Crete came
   (B) The Minoan civilization of Crete came
   (C) Since the Minoan civilization of Crete came
   (D) Whether the Minoan civilization of Crete came
   (E) When the Minoan civilization of Crete coming

4. As a student, Harvey was unruly, inattentive, and <u>he had no patience.</u>

   (A) he had no patience
   (B) he lacked patience
   (C) impatient
   (D) didn't have any patience
   (E) he lacked composure

5. At first, Mark Twain was terrified at speaking in <u>public, he</u> did it and was a great success.

    (A) public, he
    (B) public, but he
    (C) public he
    (D) public, so he
    (E) public

ANSWERS

1. D.   Only choice D corrects the run-on. Adding the coordinating conjunction correctly joins the two clauses. Choice E does not make sense.

2. E.   Adding the complete verb corrects the fragment.

3. B.   This is a fragment because the subordinating conjunction *when* creates an incomplete idea. Removing the conjunction corrects the sentence.

4. C.   Use parallel nouns: *unruly, inattentive,* and *impatient.*

5. B.   Correct the run-on by adding the coordinating conjunction *but.* Choice D is a coordinating conjunction, but it does not make sense in context.

USE WORDS CORRECTLY

Here are some words that are often confused and thus used incorrectly.

Word	Definition	Example
accept	take	Accept this gift.
except	leave out	Everyone except him.
affect	influence	This affects your ear.
effect	result	The effect of the law.
already	before	My ride already left.
all ready	prepared	I was not all ready to go.
all together	everyone at once	They finish all together.
altogether	completely	It was altogether wrong.

Word	Definition	Example
altar	table of worship	Put the Bible on the altar.
alter	to change	The tailor alters the suit.
ascent	rising	The rocket's ascent.
assent	agreement	Nod to show assent.
bare	uncovered	The floor was bare.
bear	animal	The bear growled.
	endure	Can you bear the noise?
brake	stop	Use the car's brake.
break	destroy	The dog will break the bowl.
capital	government seat	Visit the capital.
Capitol	where the U.S. legislature meets	Congress meets in the Capitol.
conscience	morally right	Lou won't violate her conscience.
conscious	awake	Jack is conscious during surgery.
desert	leave behind	Don't desert me.
	arid region	Camels travel in the desert.
dessert	sweet	The dessert is gooey.
emigrate	leave a country	They emigrate from Canada.
immigrate	enter a country	They immigrate to America.
lay	put down	*Present:* The dog lies down.
		Past: The dog lay down.
		Future: The dog will lie down.
		Perfect: The dog has lain down.
lie	be flat	*Present:* Lay your book down.
		Past: He laid the book down.
		Future: He will lay the book down.
		Perfect: She has laid the book down.

Word	Definition	Example
lead	writing material	Use a lead pencil.
led	conducted	The usher led us to our seats.
learn	receive facts	We learn math.
teach	give facts	They teach math.
loose	not fastened	The shoelace is loose.
lose	misplace	Don't lose your keys.
passed	moved by, go by	The car passed them.
	complete a class	Rory passed with a B.
	come to an end	The crisis passed.
past	time gone by	They helped in the past.
principal	main	The principal road is Green Street.
	head of a school	The principal gave a speech.
principle	rule	Principles of electronics.
rise	get up	The bread needs an hour to rise.
raise	lift	Raise your arms.
respectfully	with respect	The man bowed respectfully.
respectively	in the stated order	The red, blue, and green ties belong to Mike, Steve, and Lamar, respectively.
stationary	fixed in place	The lion was stationary.
stationery	writing paper	The stationery was cream-colored.
than	comparison	Nick is older than Nora.
then	at that time	Then we will eat.
their	belonging to them	It is their car.
there	place	Put it there.
they're	they are	They're my brothers.
weather	climate	The weather is rainy.
whether	if	Whether or not you attend.

Here is a list of prepositional phrases. *Always* use these prepositional phrases as units; don't substitute other prepositions.

- acquainted with
- addicted to
- agree on (a plan)
- agree to (someone else's idea)
- angry at or about (a thing)
- angry with (a person)
- apply for (a job)
- approve of
- consist of
- contrast with
- convenient for
- deal with
- depend on
- differ from (something)
- differ with (a person)
- displeased with
- fond of
- grateful for (something)
- grateful to (someone)
- identical with
- interested in
- interfere with
- object to
- protect against
- reason with
- responsible for
- shocked at
- similar to
- specialize in
- take advantage of
- worry about

AVOID DOUBLE NEGATIVES

Use only one negative word to express a negative idea. A *double negative* is a statement that contains two negative describing words. Here are some examples.

Double negative: I <u>don't</u> want <u>no</u> more advice.
Correct: I don't want any more advice. *Or,* I don't want more advice.

Here are the most frequently used negative words:

barely	but	hardly	never
n't (the contraction for *not*)	no	no one	none
not	nothing	nowhere	scarcely

USE PUNCTUATION CORRECTLY

Often, as much as the words themselves, punctuation creates meaning. As a result, it's vital to use punctuation correctly.

End Marks

1. *Use a period at the end of a sentence and with abbreviations.* A period is used at the end of a declarative or an imperative sentence. A *declarative sentence* states an idea. An *imperative sentence* is a command. Also, use a period after an initial and most abbreviations. If the abbreviation comes at the end of the sentence, don't add another period.

   - Open your test booklet.
   - Write your notes in the margins.
   - The speaker was Dr. Martin Luther King, Jr.

2. *Use a question mark at the end of a sentence that asks a question.* If the quotation mark is part of dialogue, place it inside the closing quotation marks.

   - What do you want to do today?
   - He said, "What do you want to do today?"

3. *Use an exclamation mark at the end of an* exclamatory sentence, *a sentence that conveys strong emotion.*

   - Don't touch the pie!

Commas

1. *Use a comma to separate the parts of a compound sentence.* The comma goes directly before the coordinating conjunction.

   - The average modern symphony has from 90 to 120 players, but orchestras used to be much smaller.
   - Many people like to play baseball, and even more like to watch it.

2. *Use commas between items in a series.* This rule holds for words, phrases, and clauses. The number of commas you use is always one less than the number of items. For instance, if you have three items, you use two commas.

- We plan to visit Spain, France, and Italy.
- The tourists plan to tour the museums, enjoy the restaurants, and buy many souvenirs.

3. *Use a comma after any introductory word, phrase, or clause.*

   - Yes, we plan to take the Praxis next month.
   - Over the hill, the runners saw a flock of geese rise into the sky.
   - If we study hard, we should earn a good grade.

4. *Use commas to set off nonessential information.*

   - The child was accompanied, of course, by a chaperone.
   - Rick, could you please take out the trash?
   - Charles de Vile Wells, the gambler whose exploits were celebrated in the song "The Man Who Broke the Bank at Monte Carlo," once emptied the Monaco casino's cash reserves six times in three days.

5. *Use a comma after the greeting of an informal letter and the close of any letter.*

   - Dear Lacey,
   - Very truly yours,
   - Sincerely,

6. *Use a comma to set off a direct quotation.*

   - "The test is given in the gym," Stephanie said.
   - Stephanie said, "The test is given in the gym."
   - "The test," Stephanie said, "is being given in the gym."

7. *Use commas with numbers.* Use a comma to separate the parts of an address.

   - Adam lives at 41 Nichol Street, Stony Brook, New York 11743.

Use a comma between the day of the month and the year.

   - August 2, 2004   April 5, 1974

Use commas to separate every three digits.

   - 2,367   291,070   240,681,700

Semicolons

1. *Use a semicolon between independent clauses (complete sentences) when the coordinating conjunction has been left out.*

   - Sailboats have always used the power of the wind; the wind is used as a power source on land as well.

2. *Use a semicolon to join independent clauses when one or both clauses contain conjunctive adverbs or commas.*

- Sailboats have always used the power of the wind; in addition, the wind is used as a power source on land.
- The warmest days of summer, usually from about July 7 to August 15 in temperate latitudes in the Northern Hemisphere, were named the "dog days" by the Romans; the brightest star in the sky at that time was Sirius, the Dog Star, and the Romans associated weather patterns with the stars.

Colons

1. *Use a colon before a list.*

- Debbie had to purchase the following items: pillows, draperies, shades, and carpets.

2. *Use a colon when the second clause explains or defines the first clause.* Capitalize the second clause if it is a complete sentence.

- Pyrite became known as "fool's gold" and was considered worthless, but today it does have a real value: It is used in the large-scale production of sulfuric acid.

3. *Use a colon before a long quotation, a quotation of more than five lines.* Usually, long quotes are indented on either side.

- *A New Look at Children's Literature* (Anderson, 1972) offers the following advice to teachers on selecting books:

No titles should be required. Nor should children be asked to read books for extraliterary, utilitarian reasons—learning moral lessons, improving their personalities, improving reading skills, or preparing for some future job. We reject the notion of some authorities, notably Arbuthnot, that the major purposes of reading literature are to add to a child's life by satisfying his need to know, his need to love and be loved, his need to belong, and his need for change. These are secondary to the major purpose of literature, which is to provide him an artistic or aesthetic experience not found elsewhere in life.

Quotation Marks

1. *Use quotation marks to set off a speaker's exact words.*

- Oscar Wilde said, "Children begin by loving their parents; after a time they judge them; sometimes they forgive them."

2. *Use quotation marks to set off the titles of short works such as poems, essays, songs, short stories, and magazine articles.*

- "The Road Not Taken"
- "America the Beautiful"
- "The Ransom of Red Chief"

Apostrophes

The apostrophe (') is used three ways:

> To show contractions
> To show plural forms
> To show possession (ownership)

1. *Use an apostrophe to show contractions.* A *contraction* is created when two words have been combined by omitting letters from one or both of them.

   - I'm (I am)
   - we're (we are)
   - can't (can not)

2. *Use an apostrophe to show plural forms.* Use an apostrophe and *s* to write the plurals of numbers, symbols, letters, and words used to name themselves.

   - Three 6's and five 9's
   - Two ?'s

3. *Use an apostrophe to show possession.* Add an apostrophe and an *s* to show the possessive case of most singular nouns. If the word ends in *s,* the second *s* can be dropped.

   - Idea of the boy, boy's idea
   - Bone of the dog, dog's bone
   - The car of James, James's car, or James' car

PRACTICE PPST EXERCISES

Directions: Each of the following sentences has four underlined and lettered portions. Read each sentence and decide whether any of the underlined parts contains an error. If so, write the letter of the portion containing the error in the space provided. If there is no error, write E (No error). No sentence contains more than one error. Answers and explanations follow the questions.

1. Millions and millions of chalky <u>skeletons deposited</u> by tiny animals <u>that live in</u>
                                       A   B

   shallow tropical <u>waters, lock</u> together to <u>form coral reefs.</u> <u>No error.</u>
                           C   D   E

2. Fishermen <u>who</u> use lights <u>to attract their catch</u> at night have a flying
               A   B

   <u>counterpart skimmers,</u> ternlike birds <u>that appear to use</u> minute marine
                  C   D

   creatures in the same way. <u>No error.</u>
                                   E

3. We read <u>an interesting short story </u>called <u>The Dead</u> <u>by James Joyce</u> as well as a
        A   B   C

series of poems by other <u>Irish authors</u>. <u>No error</u>.
         D   E

4. Most birds use body heat to incubate their <u>eggs, but</u> the mallee <u>fowl, one</u> of the
               A   B

brush turkey <u>family found in Australia</u> and on many Pacific <u>Islands, keeps</u> its eggs
       C   D

warm by burying them in compost heaps of rotting vegetables. <u>No error</u>.
                       E

5. When <u>my cousin</u> arrived <u>at the bus terminal</u> the entire family <u>greeted</u> him with
    A   B   C

<u>hugs and kisses</u>. <u>No error</u>.
  D   E

ANSWERS

1. **A.** Set off nonessential information with commas. The nonessential information here is the phrase "deposited by tiny animals that live in shallow tropical waters."

2. **C.** Use a colon when the second half of the sentence defines the first.

3. **C.** Set off the titles of short stories in quotation marks.

4. **E.** This sentence is correct as written.

5. **B.** Use a comma to set off an introductory subordinate clause.

CAPITALIZATION

1. *Capitalize the first word in a sentence.* Capitalize the first word of a quotation if the quotation is a complete sentence.

   - The capital of Ethiopia is Addis Ababa.
   - Lena asked, "Are you going to visit Africa?"

2. *Capitalize proper nouns and proper adjectives.* Proper nouns and proper adjectives name a specific person, place, or thing.

   - Richard
   - Niagara Falls
   - Spanish lace

3. *Capitalize a compass point when it identifies a specific area of the country.* Don't capitalize a compass point when it refers to direction.

   - Jake lives in the South.
   - The storm comes from the east.

4. *Capitalize historical events, months, days, holidays.*

   - Revolutionary War
   - June
   - Tuesday
   - Thanksgiving

5. *Capitalize organizations, languages, and religious references.*

   - Lions Club
   - English
   - Heaven

6. *Capitalize special places and items, such as brand names.*

   - Statue of Liberty
   - Nobel Peace Prize
   - Kleenex

7. *Capitalize titles.*

   - Ms. Steinem
   - Rabbi Gold
   - Dr. Smith

8. *Capitalize parts of correspondence.* Capitalize the first word and all nouns in a salutation.

   - Dear Mr. Graves:

9. Capitalize the first word in a complimentary close.

   - Very sincerely yours,

CHAPTER 14

Ace the Essay Question

The essay section tests how well you perform in a pressure situation. Since you clearly won't be able to do any research during this 30-minute test, the topic will require you to tap your own personal experience.

Your score will be based on how well you . . .

- Answer the question
- Organize your ideas
- Develop your ideas with specific examples
- Create unity by linking ideas
- Use language skillfully to communicate your ideas
- Follow the conventions of standard written English

THE BASICS

The PPST writing test is scored *holistically*. This means that readers form an overall impression of your writing ability rather than picking out specific errors and deducting points. The PPST scorers use a 6-point holistic scoring scale. These scales are called *rubrics*. The PPST rubric looks like this:

1	2	3	4	5	6
Lowest score		Middle score		Highest score	

An equivalent in conventional grading would look like this:

F	D	C	B	B+	A
1	2	3	4	5	6
Lowest score		Middle score		Highest score	

Here is what PPST scorers will be looking for as they assess your essay:

Essays that receive a score of 0. The 0 score is reserved for essays that do not answer the topic, no matter how well written the essay may be. Thus, test takers who choose to write about a prompt other than the one they are given will not receive any credit at all.

Essays that receive a score of 1. Papers that receive a score of 1 barely touch on the topic because they lack details and examples. Length is not necessarily the determiner: The papers can be very long and filled with illogical information or very short and equally vague. Often, these essays are not divided into logical paragraphs. Last, the paper will likely earn a score of 1 if it is so badly littered with errors that the writer's point is obscured or completely illegible.

Essays that receive a score of 2. In this case, the writer may try to prove both sides of the topic and, in so doing, prove neither side. In addition, the writer's conclusions may be strange, unrelated, or weird. Further, these essays have serious problems with grammar, usage, punctuation, and capitalization. The papers may be too brief to develop the argument with any detail, or they may be long and meandering. Ideas may not be divided into logical paragraphs.

Essays that receive a score of 3. In these essays, the writer chooses a side and tries to organize the essay, but the structure is flawed and the supporting detail is weak. The writer may ramble and include unnecessary details and information. In addition, the paper shows some serious problems with grammar, usage, and mechanics. These problems get in the way of readers understanding the writer's points.

Essays that receive a score of 4. In these essays, the writer chooses one side of the issue and proves it. The essay contains some valid and specific proof, too, but the writer has not completely considered the issue. As a result, key points may be missing. The style seems plodding and dull, with little variation in sentence structure, word choice, or punctuation. In addition, there are some writing errors that may distract the reader from the argument and the writer's point.

Essays that receive a score of 5. These essays demonstrate solid, logical, and persuasive discussion. Generalizations are supported by specific examples. The essays stay on the thesis, too, and every detail works toward the writer's main idea. The writer includes appropriate word choice and sentence variety. There may be a few writing errors, but these do not distract the reader from the writer's main points. However, these essays lack the originality or insight of the papers that score 6. In addition, the writer does not use words with any evident style or grace, as shown in the papers scoring a 6.

Essays that receive a score of 6. These essays are clearly focused discussions made up of coherent arguments of exceptional clarity. The writers show originality and imagination. These essays leave the reader convinced of the soundness of the discussion, impressed with the quality of the writing style, and stimulated by the writer's intelligence and insight.

PRETEST

Take the following pretest to help you analyze your strengths and weaknesses writing under pressure. It is a sample PPST-style writing prompt. Allow yourself 30 minutes to complete the essay. Try to get as close as possible to actual writing conditions:

- Complete the test in one sitting.
- Work in a quiet room.
- Do not use dictionaries, computerized spell-checkers, or other assistance.

In your essay, take a position on this issue. You can agree with the quote, disagree with it, or qualify it. Be sure to support your opinion with specific facts, details, reasons, and examples. You can begin your essay on the lines below and complete it on additional sheets of paper.

Prompt: **"Standardized testing has harmed rather than improved education."**

_____

_____

_____

_____

_____

_____

_____

_____

_____

_____

_____

_____

_____

_____

_____

_____

_____

_____

_____

_____

_____

_____

_____

HOW TO WRITE A HIGH-SCORING PPST ESSAY

Prompts used for the PPST writing test will:

- Center on a controversial topic
- Require you to take a stand on the issue
- Require you to use facts, details, and examples to support your stand

No matter what topic you are given for the PPST writing test, you will use the same writing and thinking skills. The following suggestions can help you do your very best.

1. *Rephrase the question in your own words.* Before you start writing, be certain that you understand the topic and your task. The easiest way to make sure you understand the question is to rephrase it. Here's a model. Notice how the rephrasing makes the prompt more specific and thus easier to answer successfully.

    Prompt: "Voting should be conducted on the Internet."
    Rephrasing: People should be able to vote in national, state, and local elections on the Internet.

2. *Take a position on the issue.* No matter how well you write, your essay will not get credit if you don't take a position on the issue. If you grasp no other point from this chapter, make it this point: Take a position on the prompt that you are given. Here is an example, using the previous prompt:

    Position: Voting should not be conducted via the Web.

3. *Support your stance on the issue with specific examples.* It's not enough to say that you believe in a certain point. Saying the same thing over and over in different ways won't get you any points, either. Instead of empty air, give specific examples. Let's walk through a model.

    Position: Voting should not be conducted via the Web.
    Reasons:

    - There is too much potential for tampering with votes, especially people casting multiple votes.
    - Not everyone has a computer and knows how to use it, so some people will be disenfranchised.
    - Some people won't be able to figure out how to use the Internet to vote.

4. *Plan your essay.* With only 30 minutes, you don't have time to see where your thoughts will take you. Instead, take a few minutes to write a simple outline. This will help you stay on track. In the following example, each Roman numeral stands for a paragraph.

Outline	*Example*
I. Introduction	Your position on the issue: no to Internet voting
II. First main point	Potential for tampering
III. Second main point	Voters without computers disenfranchised
IV. Third main point	Difficult to use
V. Conclusion	Restating your position and summing up

Outlines are covered in depth later in this chapter.

5. *Consider your audience.* Always remember that you are writing for a very specific set of readers: PPST scorers. Do not write anything that will offend them. Offensive topics include racist, sexist, or bigoted comments. Resist the urge to rant and call names; always keep your tone mature and calm. This is especially important if you feel strongly about the topic. Your essay will be much more effective if you keep a professional tone, and you won't run the risk of alienating your audience.

6. *Use your time well.* Since you have only 30 minutes for your essay, consider spending your time this way:

   2 to 3 minutes planning
   20 minutes writing/revising
   5 to 10 minutes editing/proofreading

7. *Begin writing.* Most people start writing at the beginning with the introduction. What should you do if you can't think of a good topic sentence? Don't waste time staring off into space. Instead, start where you can, with the body paragraphs. The best essay in the world won't score any points if you don't get it down on paper within 30 minutes. If you run out of things to say as you are writing, skip some lines and keep going. If you can't keep writing, take a few deep breaths and gather your wits. Planning carefully can help you stay on track.

8. *Write neatly.* If your writing cannot be read, your papers won't be scored. If your writing is messy or has a lot of crossing out, your scorer might misread a crucial point. If your handwriting is difficult to read, be sure to print neatly and carefully.

9. *Consider your style.* Good writing is concise, vivid, and precise. The key here is *concise.* Effective writers use the simplest and most precise word to express their ideas. In a famous essay entitled "Fenimore Cooper's Literary Offenses," master stylist Mark Twain offered his rules for good writing. Here are the ones relevant to your success on the PPST. They require that the author shall:

   - *Say* what he is proposing to say, not merely come near it.
   - Use the right word, not its second cousin.
   - Eschew surplusage.

- Not omit necessary details.
- Avoid slovenliness of form.
- Use good grammar.
- Employ a simple and straightforward style.

However, it appears that many PPST scores (as with SAT scorers) prefer a wordy style with unnecessarily complex words and overblown diction. Unofficial studies have revealed that test takers who use an inflated style earn a higher score than those who write clean, crisp prose. The choice is yours: write well and gamble that your scorer recognizes good writing, or gamble and throw in some big words to impress the scorer.

10. *Proofread.* No matter how rushed you are for time, always leave a few minutes to proofread your paper. A few minor errors in spelling, grammar, usage, or mechanics are not likely to impact your grade seriously. However, if your paper is riddled with serious errors in sentence construction (fragments and run-ons), logic, and unity, you will lose a significant number of points.

    That is because errors distract your readers and reduce the effectiveness of your arguments. As you proofread your paper, be as careful as you can to read what is there, not what you *think* is there.

11. *Deal with panic and writer's block.* One of the best ways to deal with panic is to be well prepared. Take all the practice tests in this section of the book, writing the essays, and going over them. If you know what to expect and have prepared as well as you can, you will be less likely to lose control during the real Praxis writing test.

    Always remember that scorers reward you for what you do well. They are not looking for perfection. After all, you have only 30 minutes to write your essay. Prepare thoroughly and do the very best you can.

WRITING A PERSUASIVE ESSAY

When you take a stand on an issue and support your position with details and examples, you are writing a persuasive essay. *Persuasive essays* argue a point. You must agree or disagree with the writing prompt and give specific reasons to support your opinion. The PPST writing test requires you to write a persuasive essay.

There are several ways to arrange the information in a persuasive essay. Following are two ways that are especially well suited for the PPST writing test, the *cluster method* and the *point-by-point method.*

The Cluster Method

With this method, you deal with the main points in clusters, as follows:

- All of *their* side (the opposition)
- All of *your* side

Study this outline:

Persuasive Essay Organized by the Cluster Method

   I. Introduction
      A. Topic sentence
      B. Summary of opposition
      C. Summary of your side
      D. Lead-in sentence to the next paragraph

  II. Opposition (one to two points)
      A. Topic sentence
      B. Point 1
      C. Point 2 (if necessary)

 III. Your side of the argument (two to three points)
      A. Topic sentence
      B. Point 1
      C. Point 2
      D. Point 3 (if necessary)

 IV. Conclusion
      A. Topic sentence
      B. Summary of your first main point
      C. Summary of your second main point . . . and so on
      D. Summary of your entire argument

If time permits, you briefly mention the opposition to show the following:

- You understand there are two sides to the issue.
- You are an intelligent thinker.
- The opposing view is not as valid as your opinion.

Although you may bring up the opposition, you do so only to make your point stronger. Your side of the argument is always more fully developed with details and examples than the opposing side. Be sure to save your strongest points for your side to persuade your readers that your point is deserving of more serious consideration.

The following model is a persuasive essay organized according to the cluster method. Follow the sidebars as you read to help you analyze the essay's structure.

***Prompt:* "Students should attend school year-round."**

1   I. A. Topic sentence

2   I. B. Summary of opposition

3   I. C. Summary of your side

4   I. D. Transition to the next paragraph

5   III. A. Topic sentence

6   III. B. Point 1 opposition

7   III. C. Point 2 opposition

8   IV. A. Topic sentence

9   IV. B. Point 1 Your side

10   IV. C. Point 2 Your side

11   IV. B. Point 3 Your side

12   V. A. Topic sentence

13   V. B. Summarize your first main point

14   V. C. Summarize your second main point

15   V. C. Summarize your third main point

16   V. D. Make your point

[1] Recently, there has been a lot of discussion over whether or not students should be required to attend school year round. [2] There's a downside: Forcing high-school students to attend school year round may increase the dropout rate. [3] However, the upside is very compelling: Year-round education helps students learn more and eliminates the need for extended review in autumn. Keeping schools in session in the summer also has significant economic advantages. [4] Let's examine the disadvantages of year-round education first.

[5] There are only a few disadvantages to educating students year round. [6] First, the extra learning from year-round education comes at a very high price: stress. High-school classes such as physics, chemistry, calculus, advanced foreign language, world literature, and economics require enormous concentration. [7] Further, many high-school students take summer jobs to pay for college expenses, cars, and family expenses.

[8] However, the advantages to year-round schooling greatly outweigh the disadvantages. [9] First and most important, students will have more instructional time. Rather than attending 180 days, as is the case now, students will be in classes at least 250 days, resulting in more study time. As a result, elementary-school students will have more time to learn and reinforce basic skills in reading, writing, and 'rithmetic. High-school students will be able to conduct longer chemistry experiments, spend more time in language labs, and drill math problems, for instance. [10] Having year-round school also helps students retain what they learned because they won't forget information over summer vacation. This way, teachers won't have to spend most of September and October reviewing the previous year's work. [11] Last but not least, keeping kids in school year round has significant economic advantages. Parents of young students won't have to spend money for summer camps and other day-care arrangements. This money more than offsets any higher taxes that may occur as a result of increased teachers' salaries and fuel costs. Operating schools full time makes the most use of the physical plant, too, reducing the need for guards during summer, when much vandalism occurs.

[12] In conclusion, there are both advantages and disadvantages to year-round high school, but the advantages of year-round schooling outweigh the disadvantages. [13] First, it seems likely that year-round high school will boost students' knowledge and achievement. Spending more time in class increases learning, allowing greater depth, and breadth of knowledge. [14] Further, eliminating the long summer vacation helps students retain what they learn and eliminates the need for the extensive review that cuts into the autumn. [15] Finally, year-round school makes good economic sense. [16] For these reasons and others, students should attend school all year round.

Practice Test

Now, write an essay on the following prompt. Use the cluster organizational method that you just learned. Begin your essay on the lines below and complete it on additional sheets of paper.

Prompt: **"Parents should be able to use a portion of their tax dollars toward charter schools or private schools for their children."**

_____

_____

_____

_____

_____

_____

_____

_____

_____

_____

_____

_____

_____

_____

_____

_____

_____

_____

_____

_____

_____

_____

The Point-by-Point Method

With this method of organization, you deal with the main points one at a time, as follows:

- First main point

  The opposition
  Your side

- Second main point

  The opposition
  Your side

- Third main point

  The opposition
  Your side

The following outline shows how to organize your essay using the point-by-point method:

Persuasive Essay Organized by the Point-by-Point Method

I. Introduction
    A. Topic sentence
    B. Summary of points to follow
    C. Lead-in sentence to the next paragraph

II. First point
    A. Topic sentence
    B. Opposition
    C. Your side

III. Second point
    A. Topic sentence
    B. Opposition
    C. Your side

IV. Third point (if necessary)
    A. Topic sentence
    B. Opposition
    C. Your side

V. Conclusion
    A. Topic sentence
    B. Summary of your first main point
    C. Summary of your second main point
    D. Summary of your third main point (if necessary)
    E. Making your point

Here is the same essay that you read organized according to the point-by-point method. Follow the sidebars as you read to help you analyze the essay's structure. As you read, decide which method of organization you prefer for this question and why.

1 I. A. Thesis sentence

2 I. B. Summary of points to follow

3 I. D. Transition to the next paragraph

[1] Should high school be in session all year round? [2] Opponents of year-round schooling argue that it has the potential to increase the number of dropouts as well as deny students income from summer jobs. [2] However, year-round education has many compelling advantages. It helps students learn more and eliminates the need for extended review in autumn. It also makes good economic sense. [3] Let's start with the premise that holding high school year round increases learning.

[4] Clearly, the most important issue is the quality of education being offered. [5] Those who oppose year-round education claim that the extra classroom time causes students undue stress, especially in high school, where classes such as physics, chemistry, and calculus are very demanding. They claim this results in a higher dropout rate. [6] However, just the opposite is true. By adding more classroom time—from 180 days to at least 250—students will be better able to learn at their own pace. Demanding high-school classes can be repaced, allowing more time for completing complex labs and reading long novels. In elementary schools, having more class time will help children master important material, especially the "basics" like reading, writing, and 'rithmetic. There will be more time for students to explore interesting topics and perhaps even discover their bliss, too, whether it be painting for an extra few hours, singing more challenging songs, or exploring more complex mathematical problems. Further, year-round high school classes would certainly diminish September and October review sessions.

[7] Next comes the issue of students working while in school. [8] People against year-round high school education also argue that it denies students the opportunity to hold summer jobs. [9] While this is certainly true, students' most important job is learning. A high-school graduate who retires at age 65 faces nearly fifty years of work as an adult! Students should spend their childhood mastering the basics (reading, writing, math, science, history) and exploring other areas of potential interest, such as foreign languages, art, music, and home and career skills. Further, students can still work after school, during some evenings, and on weekends if they so desire.

[10] Last comes the issue of money. [11] Opponents of year-round high school claim that schools cannot be operated more efficiently on a full-year schedule. [12] Keeping a school operating all year makes solid economic sense. It reduces the need for nearly three months of child care, be it summer camp or babysitters. The average summer camp can cost thousands of dollars for the season, which will more than offset any increased costs of teachers' salaries and utilities. Further, keeping the school open year-round will eliminate much (if not all) of the vandalism that occurs when the schools are left unattended during the summer months. This also greatly reduces taxpayers' expenses.

[13] There's no denying that full-year education makes solid sense. [14] Most important, it increases learning, allows students to explore areas of interest, and eliminates the need for tedious and time-wasting autumn review. [15] Further, year-round schooling does not impact students' ability to work, since they still have afternoons, evenings, and weekends free. [16] Further, year-round high school makes good economic sense. [17] For these reasons and others, schools should be in session all year.

Practice Test

Now, write an essay on the following prompt. Use the point-by-point organizational method that you just learned. You can begin your essay below and complete it on additional sheets of paper.

Prompt: "State college tuition should be free for all students who graduate from high school with a B average or above."

_____

_____

_____

_____

_____

_____

_____

_____

_____

_____

_____

_____

_____

_____

_____

_____

_____

_____

_____

Choosing an Organizational Pattern

Both the cluster method and the point-by-point method are equally well suited for the PPST writing test. Now that you have tried both methods for yourself, you have to decide which method to use for the actual test.

Use the cluster organizational pattern when . . .

- You have more points on your side than the opposition
- The opposition is weak
- Your readers don't have a strong position on the topic

Use the point-by-point organizational pattern when . . .

- You have the same number of points on your side and on the opposition's side
- The opposition has many valid points
- Your readers have a strong position on the topic—and it's not your position

Choose an entirely different method when . . .

- It makes logical sense with your topic
- You have been taught an organizational pattern that works for you

Practice Test

A simulated PPST writing test prompt follows. Analyze the question to decide which method of organization you would use.

> *Prompt:* **"All physically able students should be required to take one hour of physical education daily."**

Organizational pattern

_____

Reasons why

_____

_____

_____

Now, write the essay. Start by making a simple outline on the lines below. Then follow the outline as you write, using your own paper for more space.

_____
_____
_____
_____
_____
_____
_____
_____
_____
_____
_____
_____
_____
_____
_____
_____
_____
_____

_____

_____

_____

_____

_____

_____

_____

_____

_____

Supporting Your Main Points

It is vital that you back up your opinions with facts to convince the test scorer that your point of view is valid. When writers are trying to convince you to believe something, they will almost always include a combination of facts and opinions.

- A *fact* is something that can be proven beyond the point of a reasonable argument.
- An *opinion* is a statement that a person thinks is true. It is a personal belief, not something that can be proven. Some people may agree with it, but not everyone.

For example, the statement "The Civil War ended in 1865" is a fact. It can be verified, and no one can argue with it. In contrast, the statement "Studying a foreign language is more important than taking gym class" is an opinion. Some people might argue against this statement, and their opinions could also be valid. You could support either side of the discussion, but you could not prove it conclusively.

Read the following paragraph and then complete the chart that follows. Place an X in the first column if the sentence is a fact and an X in the second column if the sentence is an opinion. Then write your reason.

[1] In 1950, 400 American sportswriters and broadcasters selected Jim Thorpe as the greatest all-around athlete and football player of the first half of the twentieth century. [2] A Sac and Fox Indian, Thorpe was born in Oklahoma in 1888. [3] Although he was a very good high-school athlete, he stunned the entire world with his brilliant performance at the 1912 Olympic Games in Stockholm. [4] There, he won gold medals in both the pentathlon and the decathlon. [5] To date, no other athlete has ever duplicated his amazing achievement. [6] A year later, the International Olympic Committee learned that Thorpe had accepted money in 1911 to play baseball in Rocky Mountain, North Carolina. [7] The International Olympic Committee took away Thorpe's amateur status, stripped him of his gold medals, and erased his achievements from the record books. [8] Many people feel that Thorpe had been treated unfairly. [9] In 1982, the International Olympic Committee agreed to restore Thorpe's amateur status and return his medals. [10] Nearly 30 years after his death, the Olympic records that Thorpe established once again stand in the record books.

Sentence	Fact	Opinion	Reason
[1]			_____
[2]			_____
[3]			_____
[4]			_____
[5]			_____
[6]			_____
[7]			_____
[8]			_____
[9]			_____
[10]			_____

ANSWERS

Sentence	Fact	Opinion	Reason
[1]	X		This statement can be proven.
[2]	X		The statement can be proven.
[3]		X	The statement shows a judgment or belief.
[4]	X		The statement can be proven.
[5]		X	The statement shows a judgment or belief.
[6]	X		The statement can be proven.
[7]	X		The statement can be proven.
[8]		X	The statement shows a judgment or belief.
[9]	X		The statement can be proven.
[10]	X		The statement can be proven.

Connecting Related Ideas

We say that an essay has *unity* and *coherence* when every sentence is on the same idea. To make your essay unified and coherent, follow these guidelines:

- Focus on one topic at a time.
- Link-related ideas with transitions.

Start each paragraph with a topic sentence. Then have every sentence in the paragraph support the topic sentence. Eliminate any word, phrase, or sentence that does not relate to the main idea.

Underline the sentence that does not belong to the following paragraph.

> Studying a foreign language is a waste of time because few college students achieve a useful level of proficiency. Even with four years of concentrated study, most students can do little besides ask for directions, order from a menu, and comment on the weather. My cousin Michelle studies French, but I think Italian is much more useful. Having so little language and thinking that you have achieved mastery is far worse than having no foreign language at all.

Which sentence does not fit?

_____

_____

Why?

_____

_____

The sentence that does not fit is "My cousin Michelle studies French, but I think Italian is much more useful." The sentence is not on the topic of this paragraph as stated in the topic sentence: "Studying a foreign language is a waste of time because few college students achieve a useful level of proficiency."

Transitions are words that connect ideas and show how they are linked. Using transitions helps you create unity and coherence by linking related ideas.

The following chart shows some of these transitions and the relationships they create.

Relationship	*Transition Words*	
Addition	also	and
	besides	too
	in addition to	further
Example	for example	for instance
	thus	namely

Relationship	Transition Words	
Time	next	then
	finally	first
	second	third
	fourth	afterward
	before	during
	soon	later
	meanwhile	subsequently
Contrast	but	nevertheless
	yet	in contrast
	however	still
Comparison	likewise,	in comparison
	similarly	
Result	therefore	consequently
	as a result	thus
	due to this	accordingly
Summary	as a result	in brief
	in conclusion	hence
	in short	finally
Place	in the front	in the back
	here	there
	nearby	

Sample Essays and Scoring Rubrics

Here are some simulated PPST writing prompts, sample essays, the scores they received, and an explanation of the scores. Follow these directions as you complete this part of the chapter. Begin the essay on the lines below. Complete it on your own sheets of paper.

- Write the essay.
- Study these essays, isolating their strengths and weaknesses.
- Read the scores and explanations.
- Evaluate your own essay, based on what you learned.
- Rewrite your essay to prove your point; add details, examples, and facts; achieve unity and coherence; and correct errors.

Prompt: **"Same-sex schools provide a better education than coed schools."**

_____
_____
_____
_____
_____
_____
_____
_____
_____
_____
_____
_____
_____
_____
_____
_____
_____
_____
_____
_____
_____
_____

Sample Essay 1

Most American schools are coed, but some people argue that same-sex schools provide a better education because students can concentrate on their studies rather than getting dates. In your opinion, does a same-sex school provide a better education than a coed school?

Do same-sex schools have an effect on the type of education they are providing? Of course, not. Therefore, I totally disagree with the fact that some people think same-sex schools provide a better education than coed schools.

Now let us begin with education itself. Isn't it something that you learn when you go to school? What has gender got to do with it? No matter what school you go to, either coed or same sex, you get the same type of education.

I understand that most of the time these same-sex school students are said to be the most educated, but guess what. It is the pressure that they put onto them that makes them like that. There are plenty of coed students who are educated as well. I think it is up to you. It does not matter if you go to the same-sex school or not.

Among those schools, mostly private, the students are so frustrated by the supervising. Of course they are going to behave well. When they are all outside the school, they behave and act differently.

Now comes the issue about boys and girls together. I do not think this affects the education at all. Those people who disagree with me might say what about the dating part. But guess what. Now those girls are going to turn out to be weird because there is not going to be boys around. And what are they going to say next?

Like I stated before, it is not about gender. It is about you. If you want to have a good education, you will, but if you don't want, there is nothing they can do about it.

Score: 1
Explanation

- This essay barely touches on the topic because there are no specific details. The first two paragraphs say nothing.
- Further, the writer reached weird conclusions. We can see this in the third paragraph, for instance, where the writer concludes that "No matter what school you go to, either coed or same sex, you get the same type of education." We know that some schools are better than others. In the next-to-last paragraph, the writer attributes serious character flaws to same-sex education when she says: "Now those girls are going to turn out to be weird because there is not going to be boys around." This is an illogical and unsupported conclusion.

Sample Essay 2

Boys and girls are different. The difference is on many levels: physical, emotional, and mental. Boys and girls develop at different rates and at different times. It is these differences that make life interesting and in the long run make us stronger as a species. As a society, we need to acknowledge and affirm these differences to help our children become the best that they can be in their life. One way to help them would be to have same-sex academic classes.

In the past, girls were the discriminated sex in the educational arena. There are centuries of documented accounts on this subject. In the United States, women worked hard in the politics of the country to change the policies that discriminated against gender. The results were: Title IX, and the Gender & Equity Act. Girls have been working hard to achieve their goals and have done a phenomenal job in the last 15 years. Girls now exceed boys in earning degrees in college.

Recent studies are now showing that boys are struggling in school. An alarming number of boys are being diagnosed with attention-deficit hyperactivity disorder and are given medication to compensate. The use of medication to control behavior has increased 500% over the past 10 years, a truly frightening statistic. There are schools where 20% to 25% of the boys are on medication to control behavior. With boys receiving this kind of negative reinforcement about a very natural need, is it any wonder they are having problems. Young men are not interested in going to college because they fail to recognize the value of education.

Educators need to understand and provide an education that acknowledges the different learning abilities of boys and girls. By having same-sex academic classes, the teaching methods can be tailored to each learning style. Such classes will provide an optimal learning environment for students, and teachers will have more creativity in presenting their lessons. Same-sex academic classes allow the teacher to reach students using their strengths, instead of using teaching methods that only reach some students. Keeping schools coed, the students will be able to interact with the opposite sex at lunchtimes, study sessions, and during clubs and activities. This type of school combines the strengths of the same-sex schools and the coed schools. There would be no cost to implement such a system.

Studies are proving that the differences between boys and girls are biological in nature, not environmental. The brain works very differently in boys and girls and they need to learn in different ways. In one area both boys and girls are the same; they need encouragement and approval for who they are and what they achieve. By providing an academic environment that values the differences between boys and girls, society will have citizens that are well adjusted and will become major contributors to a better future for all.

Score: 4

Explanation

- The writer chose one side of the issue and supports it, but the argument is muddy. Stating that boys and girls are different is not the same as proving it. Without this proof, the assertion that boys and girls have different learning styles is not supported.
- There are too many other leaps in logic, too. For example, how is medication for ADHD a form of negative reinforcement? Further, we cannot conclude that "Young men are not interested in going to college because they fail to recognize the value of education" from the information in this passage. Rather, we might conclude that they welcome education but are frustrated by the poor education they are receiving.
- The style is pedestrian and dull, with little variation in sentence structure, word choice, or punctuation.

Sample Essay 3

The purpose of education is not just to provide children with knowledge, but to endow them with useful skills that will allow them to succeed in our society. To do so, the atmosphere in a school should accurately reflect the atmosphere of the society it is preparing children for. Modern America is a nonsegregated society: People of both genders freely intermix, interacting with each other constantly in both professional and social settings. I would argue that the majority of American schools should remain coed, because this atmosphere better prepares students for both the professional and social aspects of the "real world." In addition, I will offer a counterargument to the idea that coed schools are more distracting due to students' romantic inclinations.

School is a child's primary preparation for a future professional role. It is in the classroom that students acquire a work ethic, problem-solving skills, and a propensity for analytical thinking. The classroom is also where students learn teamwork, cooperation, compromise, and similar social skills that are critical to most job functions. However, these skills are only acquired through practice, and thus students must have the opportunity to interact with all manner of people, not just those of the same gender.

The social aspects of modern life are considered by many to be just as rewarding, if not more so, than the professional aspects. The acquisition of friends, the pursuit of romance and marriage, and raising children are highly valued and oft-pursued aspects of our society. Yet all of these things typically hinge upon social interaction with members of the opposite gender. Students must be given the opportunity to acquire confidence, understanding, and level of comfort with the opposite gender in their youth, or they will not be able to use these skills when they're older.

Finally, restricting schools to single-sex will not eliminate the threat of romantic distractions, as after all, homosexual relationships are becoming far more accepted in modern times than ever before. Granted, there will be some reduction in the level of distraction, but the problem will still exist. (Perhaps to the unfair detriment of homosexual students as well, but this is not a discussion on equal treatment.)

School is meant to prepare children for life. For the educational system to have succeeded, they must be fully prepared to deal with the world, not just the half of it with similar chromosomes to theirs.

Score: 6

Explanation

- This essay is clearly focused on the writer's main point as stated in the topic sentence: "The purpose of education is not just to provide a child with knowledge, but to endow them with useful skills that will allow them to succeed in our society."
- The writer brings up the opposition—"the idea that coed schools are more distracting due to students' romantic inclinations"—and shows that it is not as valid as his point.
- The writer provides ample examples to support his point. For instance, note the list of examples in this sentence: "The acquisition of friends, the pursuit of romance and marriage, and raising children are highly valued and oft-pursued aspects of our society. Yet all of these things typically hinge upon social interaction with members of the opposite gender."
- The essay is well organized, moving through the writer's points one by one.
- The language is highly sophisticated, and the writer shows originality and imagination.
- This essay leaves the reader convinced of the soundness of the discussion, impressed with the quality of the writing style, and stimulated by the writer's intelligence and insight.

Practice Writing Prompts

Complete each of the following, writing under test conditions. Be sure to allow yourself no more than 30 minutes for each essay. Pace yourself to make sure you finish the essay in the time required. If you finish with more than a few minutes to spare, you are not spending enough time on details, examples, editing, and proofreading.

1. "Since famous sports figures have a significant influence on adults as well as students, they should act in a socially responsible manner."
2. "All college students should be required to study abroad for a semester."

3. "Handicapped students should be included in regular classes, not segregated into special-education programs."
4. "All students should be required to take a core group of liberal arts classes, at least 36 credits."
5. "The space program is a futile waste of technology, strictly a military byproduct."
6. "Television offers many significant advantages to viewers."
7. "A successful individual is one who has achieved meaningful work and meaningful love."
8. "Doctors, like lawyers, should be expected to provide free professional services at some time in their careers."
9. "Lifetime tenure for teachers should be eliminated."
10. "Students in elementary and high schools should be grouped according to ability."

PART 5

PPST: Mathematics Test

CHAPTER 15

Review of Mathematical Concepts

The PPST Mathematics Test is 60 minutes long and has 40 multiple-choice items. This part of the PPST assesses your ability to use basic mathematical theory, concepts, and formulas. Let's review the basics of mathematics that will help you earn a high score on this test.

REVIEW OF ARITHMETIC

Defining Types of Numbers

Counting numbers: All numbers that don't have decimals or fractions as part of them and are greater than zero, all the way to infinity.

Example: 1, 2, 3, 4 . . .

Whole numbers: All of the counting numbers, including zero.

Example: 0, 1, 2, 3 . . .

Integers: All positive and negative whole numbers.

Example: 1, 18, −3, 0

Real numbers: All positive and negative numbers, including those that have decimal places or fractions.

Example: 3.14, 2¾, −½

Cardinal numbers: Numbers that tell amounts. Any whole number can be a cardinal number.

Example: There are 12 doughnuts in a box, and 3 boxes on the shelf.

Ordinal numbers: Numbers that tell order.

Example: 1st, 2nd, and 3rd person in line to buy doughnuts.

To remember ordinal numbers, try this hint: <u>ord</u>inal numbers tell <u>ord</u>er.

Ordering Numbers

You can compare numbers to one another using symbols. If two numbers are the same, use the *equals* (=) sign.

$5 + 5 = 10$ "Five plus five *equals* ten."

If the numbers are different, use the symbols *less than* (<) or *greater than* (>).

$6 < 12$ "Six is *less than* twelve."
$8 > 2$ "Eight is *greater than* two."
$3 < 5 < 11$ "Three is *less than* five, and five is *less than* eleven."

The arrow points toward the smaller number. Turn a comparison sign into Pac-Man, and remember that he's very hungry, so he wants to eat the biggest number.

$4 < 7$ 4 ⊂ 7

Place Value

Our math system uses *base ten,* which means we write out numbers using a combination of 10 digits: 0, 1, 2, 3, 4, 5, 6, 7, 8, and 9.

When you write a number greater than 9, you move up into the next *place*; 10 means "1 ten and 0 ones," and 27 means "2 tens and 7 ones." The following chart shows the order of the places.

Millions	Hundred thousands	Ten thousands	Thousands	Hundreds	Tens	Ones

Thus, the number 300 is three hundreds; 300,000 is three hundred thousands; 37,501 is 3 ten thousands; 7 thousands, 5 hundreds, and 1 one.

When writing numbers with more than three digits, put a comma (,) in front of every three digits. Example: Write five thousand as 5,000. Write twenty-two million as 22,000,000.

Practice

Identify each item as a counting number, whole number, integer, or real number. Many numbers are more than one of these things, so be sure to say everything that applies.

1. 14
2. −3

3. 0

4. $\frac{1}{2}$

5. 7.33

Put =, <, or > in the space to make the equation true.

6. 6 ____ 9

7. 8 ____ 2

8. 5 ____ 5

9. 15 ____ 13

10. 0 ____ 4

Questions 11 to 15 refer to the number 860231.

11. Where should you put the comma in this number?

12. What number is in the tens place?

13. What number is in the ten-thousands place?

14. What does the 2 in that number stand for?

15. Which place is the 0 in?

ANSWERS

1. Counting, whole, integer, and real

2. Integer and real

3. Whole, integer, and real

4. Real

5. Real

6. <

7. >

8. =

9. >

10. <

11. Between the zero and the two

12. 3

13. 6

14. 200 or two hundreds

15. The thousands place

Arithmetic with Whole Numbers

Addition

First, line up the digits so that similar places are in columns. Then add each column. Remember to carry over ones to the next column.

Example: 459,045 + 34,790

```
 459045
+34790
```

```
  1 1
 459045
+34790
 493835
```

Subtraction

Set this up the same way as addition. Remember that you can "borrow" 10 from the next place.

Example: 508,567 − 14,695

```
 508567
−14695
```

```
 4 74
 508567
−14695
 493872
```

Multiplication

Multiply each place in turn, and remember to bring down a zero with each new line. Then add all of the partial products.

Example: 397 × 27

```
 397
×27
```

First partial product:

```
 264
 397
 ×27
2779
```

Second partial product:

```
  11
 397
 ×27
2779
7940
```

Then add:

```
   111
  2779
 +7940
 10719
```

Division

Set up the problem as illustrated in the example. Divide each part of the number and bring down the remainder.

Example: 542 ÷ 13

```
13)542
```

```
      41  R9
13)542
    52
    22
    13
     9
```

Add:

1. 45	2. 746	3. 892	4. 1438	5. 86
+11	+39	+491	+6720	415
				+133

Subtract:

6. 36	7. 121	8. 713	9. 1456	10. 4070
−24	−98	−496	−837	−2964

Multiply:

11. 12	12. 75	13. 39	14. 274	15. 906
×4	×21	×77	×200	×213

Divide:

16. 4)$\overline{12}$

17. 4)$\overline{344}$

18. 3)$\overline{7251}$

19. 8)$\overline{984}$

20. 11)$\overline{253}$

ANSWERS

1. 56
2. 785
3. 1,383
4. 8,158
5. 634
6. 12
7. 23
8. 217
9. 619
10. 1,106
11. 48
12. 1,575
13. 3,003
14. 54,800
15. 192,978
16. 3
17. 86
18. 2,417
19. 123
20. 23

Remainder Problems

When you divide and are left with a remainder, there are several ways to interpret the remainder. Use common sense when you are left with a remainder for a word problem.

Examples

How many baskets do you need to carry 23 balls, if each basket can carry a maximum of 7 balls?

23 ÷ 7 = 3 R 2

You'll need 4 baskets, because you need a fourth basket to hold the leftover 2 balls.

You need 7 eggs to make a soufflé. You have 23 eggs. How many soufflés can you make?

23 ÷ 7 = 3 R 2

You can make 3 soufflés, as you don't have enough eggs to make a fourth.

You have 23 cookies to split evenly among 7 people. How many cookies does each person get?

23 ÷ 7 = 3 R 2

Each person will get 3⅔ cookies, because you can cut up cookies in order to divide them evenly.

Practice

1. You can fit four milk bottles into a crate. How many crates do you need to hold 34 bottles?
2. There are four workers employed at a factory. The factory operates 34 hours each week, and there must be one worker on duty at all times. If the hours are divided up equally, how long is each worker on duty?
3. In a certain game, each player needs to have four counters. If you have 34 counters, how many people can play?
4. You drink four glasses of water each day. Your watercooler holds a total of 34 glasses of water. How long before you have to refill it?
5. You have 34 horseshoes. A horse needs four shoes to run properly. How many horses can be shod?

ANSWERS

1. 9 crates
2. 8½ hours
3. 8 players
4. 8½ days
5. 8 horses

REVIEW OF EXPONENTS AND SQUARE ROOTS

Exponents are a simple way of showing that you multiply something by itself many times.

Base: The number that is multiplied by itself.
Exponent: The number of times it is multiplied.

Example: $4^3 = 4 \times 4 \times 4 = 64$

This is read as "four to the third power."

Any number raised to the first power equals itself.
$x^1 = x$

Any number raised to the zeroth power (i.e., with zero as an exponent) equals one.
$x^0 = 1$

Arithmetic with Exponents

If exponents have the *same base,* you can multiply them by adding the exponents and divide them by subtracting the exponents.

Examples

$$5^7 \times 5^2 = 5^9$$
$$3^6 \div 3^3 = 3^3$$

You need to perform all operations inside parentheses before exponents. This is discussed later under the head, "Order of Operations."

Practice

1. $7^4 =$
2. $10^5 =$
3. $7^0 =$
4. $14^1 =$
5. $4^5 + 3^2 =$
6. $8^3 - 7^2 =$
7. $5^2 \times 6^3 =$
8. $4^3 \times 4^5 =$
9. $10^2 \div 5^2 =$
10. $8^6 \div 8^4 =$
11. $(7 - 3)^4 =$
12. $(5^2)^2 =$

ANSWERS

1. 2,401
2. 100,000
3. 1
4. 14
5. 1,033
6. 463
7. 5,400
8. $4^8 = 65,536$
9. 4
10. $8^2 = 64$
11. 256
12. 625

Squares and Square Roots

Square of a number: The number raised to the second power. When written out, the exponent is 2.

Square root of a number: Another number that, when raised to the second power, equals the original one.

> *Example:* $4^2 = 16, \sqrt{16} = 4$

The square of 4 is 16. The square root of 16 is 4.

Perfect square: A number whose square root is a whole number.

> *Examples*
> $$\sqrt{1} = 1$$
> $$\sqrt{4} = 2$$
> $$\sqrt{9} = 3$$
> $$\sqrt{16} = 4$$
> $$\sqrt{25} = 5$$

Simplifying Square Roots

The general rule is $\sqrt{(a \times b)} = \sqrt{a} \times \sqrt{b}$.

> *Examples*
> $$\sqrt{45} = \sqrt{(9 \times 5)} = \sqrt{9} \times \sqrt{5} = 3\sqrt{5}$$
> $$\sqrt{147} = \sqrt{(49 \times 3)} = \sqrt{49} \times \sqrt{3} = 7\sqrt{3}$$

Practice

1. $\sqrt{8}$
2. $\sqrt{63}$
3. $\sqrt{150}$
4. $\sqrt{363}$
5. $\sqrt{176}$
6. $\sqrt{832}$
7. $\sqrt{400}$
8. $\sqrt{1,024}$
9. $\sqrt{3,969}$
10. $\sqrt{576}$

ANSWERS

1. $2\sqrt{2}$
2. $3\sqrt{7}$
3. $5\sqrt{6}$
4. $11\sqrt{3}$

5. $4\sqrt{11}$
6. $8\sqrt{13}$
7. 20
8. 32
9. 63
10. 24

ORDER OF OPERATIONS

Order of operations: The order in which you work out the various operations in a problem.

The order is: parentheses, exponents, multiplication, division, addition, and subtraction. First, do everything inside parentheses (starting with the innermost parentheses, if there are several sets). Then solve all of the exponents; then do all of the multiplication and division (from left to right); then do all of the addition and subtraction (from left to right).

A good way to remember the order of operations is the phrase "Please Excuse My Dear Aunt Sally." The first letter of each word stands for the order of operations, like this: **P**lease [**P**arentheses] **E**xcuse [**E**xponents] **M**y [**M**ultiplication] **D**ear [**D**ivision] **A**unt [**A**ddition] **S**ally [**S**ubtraction].

Examples

$$5 + (12 \div 6) = 5 + 2 = 7$$
$$3 \times (4 \times 2 + 4) \div 6^2 = 3 \times (8 + 4) \div 36 = 3 \times 12 \div 36 = 1$$

Practice

1. $1 + 2 \times 3 + 4 - 5 =$
2. $(1 + 2) \times 3 + (4 - 5) =$
3. $3 + 4^2 =$
4. $(3 + 4)^2 =$
5. $4 \times 12 \div 3 + 3 =$
6. $4 \times (12 \div 3 + 3) =$
7. $4 \times 12 \div (3 + 3) =$
8. $7^3 + 3^2 \times 8 =$
9. $(7^3 + 3^2) \times 8 =$
10. $(7 + (8 - 3)^3) \times 2 =$

ANSWERS

1. 6
2. 8
3. 19
4. 49
5. 19
6. 28
7. 8
8. 415
9. 2,816
10. 264

ROUNDING

To round a number to a specific place, look to the place directly to the right of it (i.e., the next lowest place). *If that digit is five or greater, round up; if it's four or less, round down.* When rounding up, add one to the digit in the specified place, and change all the digits to the right of it to zeroes. When rounding down, leave the specified digit as is, and change the lower places to zeroes.

Examples

Round 963,465 to the nearest thousand.

The number 3 is in the thousands place, and 4 is in the place directly to the right of it (the hundreds place). Since 4 is less than 5, we round down. The answer is 963,000.

Round 81.0468 to the nearest hundredth.

4 is in the hundredths place, and 6 is in the place directly to the right of it (the thousandths place). Since 6 is greater than 5, we round up. The answer is 81.05.

Practice

1. Round 9,475 to the nearest ten.
2. Round 48,799 to the nearest thousand.
3. Round 71,146 to the nearest hundred.
4. Round 561,793 to the nearest ten thousand.
5. Round 109,744 to the nearest thousand.
6. Round 67.62 to the nearest one.
7. Round 913.56 to the nearest tenth.
8. Round 67,833.01 to the nearest ten.
9. Round 876.5437 to the nearest thousandth.
10. Round 0.0001 to the nearest hundredth.

ANSWERS

1. 9,480
2. 49,000
3. 71,100
4. 560,000
5. 110,000
6. 68
7. 913.6
8. 67,830
9. 876.544
10. 0

ARITHMETIC WITH INTEGERS

Adding a negative number is the same as subtracting a positive one. When adding integers, remember that if the signs are the same, you're getting farther from zero, and if they're different, you're getting closer.

Here's an easy way to add integers: If the signs are the same, just add the numbers and use the same sign. If the signs are different, subtract the numbers and take the sign of the larger one.

Examples

$$10 + -4 = 6$$
$$4 + -8 = -4$$
$$-7 + -13 = -20$$

When you subtract integers, just change the sign of the number being subtracted by, and then add.

Examples

$$18 - -6 = 18 + 6 = 24$$
$$-10 - 5 = -10 + -5 = -15$$

When multiplying and dividing integers, everything proceeds the same as with whole numbers—until you get to the end. Then, if the two integers you multiplied had the same sign (both positive or both negative), then the answer is positive. If they had different signs (one positive and one negative), then the answer is negative.

Examples

$$-5 \times 3 = -15$$
$$-8 \times -7 = 56$$
$$24 \div -6 = -4$$
$$-18 \div -3 = 6$$

If you have to multiply several integers, try doing them as separate problems.

Example: $-4 \times 6 \times -2$

$$-4 \times 6 = -24, \text{ then } -24 \times -2 = 48$$

You can also count the number of negative signs in a multiplication problem with integers. If it's even, the answer is positive. If it's odd, the answer is negative.

Practice

Add:

1. $15 + -4$
2. $-111 + 37$
3. $-3,578 + -822$
4. $-22 + 984$
5. $-10,000 + 9,999$

Subtract:

6. $50 - -16$
7. $-142 - 121$
8. $-66 - -32$
9. $-75 - -300$
10. $87,645 - -983$

Multiply:

11. 6×-2
12. -1×18
13. -6×-7
14. $-1 \times -7 \times 4$
15. $-5 \times -5 \times -5$

Divide:

16. $-24 \div 4$
17. $-18 \div -6$
18. $27 \div -3$
19. $5 \div -1$
20. $-88 \div -4$

ANSWERS

1. 11
2. −74
3. −4,400
4. 962
5. −1
6. 66
7. −263
8. −34
9. 225
10. 88,628
11. −12
12. −18
13. 42
14. 28
15. −125
16. −6
17. 3
18. −9
19. −5
20. 22

NUMBER THEORY

Factors and Multiples

The *factors* of a number are those numbers that the number can be divided by with no remainder. Every whole number has at least two factors: itself and 1. A number that only has two factors (itself and 1) is called a *prime number*. A number with more than two factors is called a *composite number*.

Examples

The factors of 5 are 1 and 5.
Thus, 5 is a prime number.

The factors of 6 are 1, 2, 3, and 6.
4 and 5 are not factors of 6, because they can't divide into it evenly.
Thus, 6 is a composite number.

The *greatest common factor* (GCF) is the largest factor shared by two numbers. You find the GCF by listing all of the factors of the two numbers and picking the largest ones that match.

Example: Find the GCF of 24 and 28.

>Factors of 24: 1, 2, 3, 4, 6, 8, 12, 24.
>Factors of 28: 1, 2, 4, 7, 14, 28.
>The greatest common factor is 4.

A *multiple* is any number you can find by multiplying something by a whole number. Finding multiples can also be thought of as "counting by" a number.

Examples

>The multiples of 5 are: 5, 10, 15, 20, 25, 30 . . .
>The multiples of 8 are: 8, 16, 24, 32, 40, 48 . . .

The *least common multiple* (LCM) is the smallest multiple shared by two numbers. Like the GCF, you can find the LCM by listing some of the factors of the two numbers and picking the smallest ones that match. Unlike factors, you don't need to list them all. Just list enough until you find a match.

Example: Find the LCM of 8 and 10.

>Multiples of 8: 8, 16, 24, 32, 40, 48 . . .
>Multiples of 10: 10, 20, 30, 40, 50 . . .
>The least common multiple is 40.

Practice

Write the factors of each number:

>1. 12
>2. 5
>3. 36
>4. 256
>5. 210

Find the greatest common factor:

>6. 12, 24
>7. 6, 9
>8. 11, 13
>9. 24, 64
>10. 105, 225

Find the least common multiple:

>11. 3, 5
>12. 2, 8
>13. 6, 15
>14. 12, 16
>15. 28, 35

ANSWERS

1. 1, 2, 3, 4, 6, 12
2. 1, 5
3. 1, 2, 3, 4, 6, 9, 12, 18, 36
4. 1, 2, 4, 8, 16, 32, 64, 128, 256
5. 1, 2, 3, 5, 6, 7, 10, 14, 15, 21, 30, 35, 42, 70, 105, 210
6. 12
7. 3
8. 1
9. 8
10. 15
11. 15
12. 8
13. 30
14. 48
15. 140

Divisibility Rules

If a number is *divisible* by another, that means you can divide it evenly with no remainder—that is, the divisor is one of the factors. Remembering these handy divisibility rules can help you find the factors of large numbers.

- Every even number is divisible by 2.
- Add up the digits: If the sum is divisible by 3, the number is divisible by 3. If the sum is divisible by 9, the number is divisible by 9.
- If a number is divisible by both 2 and 3, then it is also divisible by 6.
- If the last digit is 0 or 5, then the number is divisible by 5. If the last digit is 0, the number is divisible by 10.
- If the last two digits are divisible by 4, the number is divisible by 4. If the last three digits are divisible by 8, then the number is divisible by 8.

Example: What numbers is 7,520,860 divisible by?

The number is even, so it's divisible by 2.

Add up the digits: $7 + 5 + 2 + 0 + 8 + 6 + 0 = 28$.

28 is not divisible by 3 or 9, so the number is not divisible by 3 or 9.

Since the number isn't divisible by 3, it isn't divisible by 6.

The last digit is 0, so the number is divisible by 5 and 10.

The last two digits are 60. 60 is divisible by 4, so the number is divisible by 4.

The last three digits are 860. 860 is not divisible by 8, so the number is not divisible by 8.

7,520,860 is divisible by 2, 4, 5, 10.

Practice

What numbers, for which we have divisibility rules, are these examples divisible by?

1. 43,168
2. 996,633
3. 111,570
4. 3,457,746
5. 938,460

ANSWERS

1. 2, 4, 8
2. 3, 9
3. 2, 3, 5, 6, 10
4. 2, 3, 6, 9
5. 2, 3, 4, 5, 6, 10

REPEATING DECIMALS

Sometimes, you'll encounter a decimal that doesn't end, but instead the decimal portion forms a repeating pattern. This is called a *repeating decimal.*

Example: What is 1 divided by 3? Give a decimal answer.

$$
\begin{array}{r}
0.333 \\
3\overline{)1.000} \\
9 \\
\hline
10 \\
9 \\
\hline
10
\end{array}
$$

You could do the division for the rest of your life and still not reach the end. But the pattern is obvious: Every digit after the decimal point is going to be a three. So this number is expressed as $0.\overline{3}$, which is said as "zero point three repeating." Writing the number this way is called *bar notation.* The bar is placed over whichever numbers repeat.

Examples

$$0.\overline{12} = 0.1212121212\ldots$$
$$0.\overline{456} = 0.456456456456\ldots$$
$$0.12\overline{4} = 0.124444444\ldots$$

Practice

Write these numbers in bar notation:

1. 0.2222222 . . .
2. 1.2424242424 . . .
3. 234.4545454545 . . .
4. 0.1822222222 . . .

Can you write this number in bar notation?

5. 0.5555565587

ANSWERS

1. $0.\overline{2}$
2. $1.\overline{24}$
3. $234.\overline{45}$
4. $0.18\overline{2}$
5. No. It doesn't repeat infinitely.

PERCENTAGES

Percentages are another way of writing numbers smaller than 1. A number followed by the percent sign is actually expressed in hundredths. Changing percentages to and from decimals is easy: To change a decimal into a percentage, move the decimal point two places to the right. To change a percentage into a decimal, move the decimal point two places to the left.

$$0.111 = 11.1\%$$

Examples

$$0.72 = 72\%$$
$$1.344 = 134.4\%$$

$$12\% = 0.12$$
$$93.45\% = 0.9345$$

Practice

Change these decimals into percentages:

1. 0.5   2. 0.14   3. 1.423   4. 0.0034   5. $0.\overline{6}$

Change these percentages into decimals:

6. 17%   7. 42.7%   8. 540%   9. 0.092%   10. 7.$\overline{46}$%

ANSWERS

1. 50%   2. 14%   3. 142.3%   4. 0.34%   5. 66.$\overline{6}$%
6. 0.17   7. 0.427   8. 5.4   9. 0.00092   10. 0.07$\overline{46}$

Remember, when you learn to change decimals into fractions, you'll also know how to change percentages into fractions. Just change the percentages into decimals first!

Finding a Percentage of a Number

If a problem asks you to find the percentage of a number, simply change the percentage into a decimal, and multiply.

Example: What is 17% of 40?

$$0.17 \times 40 = 6.8$$

If the problem asks you to find what percentage one number is of another, divide them to get a decimal, and then change that decimal to a percentage.

Example: 5 is what percentage of 20?

$$5 \div 20 = 0.25 = 25\%$$
5 is 25% of 20.

Practice

1. What is 50% of 20?
2. What is 20% of 75?
3. What is 70% of 49?
4. What is 15% of 50?
5. What is 200% of 6?
6. 4 is what percentage of 20?
7. 7 is what percentage of 40?
8. 3 is what percentage of 18?
9. 22 is what percentage of 11?
10. 2 is what percentage of 44?

ANSWERS

1. 10
2. 15
3. 34.3
4. 7.5
5. 12
6. 20%
7. 17.5%
8. $16.\overline{6}\%$
9. 200%
10. $4.\overline{54}\%$

Percent of Increase and Decrease

If a number increases or decreases by a percentage, first find the percentage of the number, then add or subtract it from the original number.

Examples

150 increased by 50%
50% of 150 = 0.50 × 150 = 75
150 + 75 = 225

40 decreased by 25%
25% of 40 = 0.25 × 40 = 10
40 − 10 = 30

Similarly, if you are asked to find the percentage of increase or decrease, divide that by the original number, then change the resulting decimal into a percentage.

Example: There are 200 people in a crowd. 40 more arrive. What is the percent increase in people?

40 ÷ 200 = 20%

Always read carefully! It's easy to get confused between percent *increase* and percent *of.*

Practice

1. What is 20 increased by 50%?
2. What is 75 increased by 10%?
3. What is 5 increased by 25%?

4. What is 25 decreased by 10%?
5. What is 50 decreased by 15%?
6. I have 30 cookies. I bake 15 more. What is the percent increase in cookies?
7. A child was 40 inches tall. He grows 6 inches. What is the percent increase in height?
8. A couple has 2 children. What is the percent increase in people?
9. There are 8 slices of pie. I eat two of them. What is the percent decrease in pie?
10. I weighed 225 pounds. I lost 35 pounds. What is the percent decrease in weight?

ANSWERS

1. 30
2. 82.5
3. 6.25
4. 22.5
5. 42.5
6. 50%
7. 15%
8. 100%
9. 25%
10. 15.$\bar{5}$%

INTRODUCTION TO FRACTIONS

Fractions, like decimals, are another way of expressing numbers between 0 and 1. A fraction has two parts, the *numerator* and the *denominator*. The numerator is how many pieces you have, and the denominator is how many pieces there are in total.

Example

$^5\!/_8$ numerator/denominator

In this example, there are eight pieces that make up the whole, and you have five of them.

You can remember that *denominator* and *down* start with the same letter to remember that the denominator is the lower part of the fraction.

Improper Fractions and Mixed Numbers

Sometimes, you need to express a number greater than 1 as a fraction. For this, we use *improper fractions* and *mixed numbers*. In an improper fraction, the numerator is greater than the denominator. In a mixed number, you write both a whole number part and a fraction part.

Examples

½ is an improper fraction. 3 is greater than 2, so the entire expression is greater than 1. This is said as, "three halves" or "three over two."

1½ is a mixed number. It is said as "one and one-half."

Equivalent Fractions

Fractions that are equal are said to be *equivalent*. You can change any fraction into an equivalent one by multiplying (or dividing) the numerator and denominator by the same number.

Any fraction that has the same numerator and denominator is equal to 1. As you remember from arithmetic, any number multiplied by 1 equals itself. This is one way to remember how to create equivalent fractions.

Comparing Fractions

You can find out if two fractions are equivalent by *cross multiplying*. Multiply the numerator of each fraction by the denominator of the other fraction, and compare those two numbers.

Example: Compare $\frac{5}{10}, \frac{2}{4}$

$$2 \times 10 = 20, 5 \times 4 = 20$$

$$20 = 20, \text{ so } \frac{5}{10} = \frac{2}{4}$$

You can also tell which fraction is greater by this method. Compare the two products, and use the same symbol for the fractions.

Example: Compare $\frac{5}{10}, \frac{4}{7}$

$$7 \times 5 = 35, 10 \times 4 = 40$$

$$35 < 40, \text{ so } \frac{5}{10} < \frac{4}{7}$$

Always remember to cross multiply upward. That puts the numbers on the proper sides for comparison.

35   40

Practice

Compare these fractions by cross multiplying.

1. $\frac{1}{2}, \frac{3}{4}$ 2. $\frac{3}{9}, \frac{2}{7}$ 3. $\frac{28}{35}, \frac{4}{5}$ 4. $\frac{7}{4}, \frac{5}{3}$ 5. $\frac{17}{20}, \frac{13}{17}$

ANSWERS

1. $\frac{1}{2} < \frac{3}{4}$ 2. $\frac{3}{9} > \frac{2}{7}$ 3. $\frac{28}{35} = \frac{4}{5}$ 4. $\frac{7}{4} > \frac{5}{3}$ 5. $\frac{17}{20} > \frac{13}{17}$

Sometimes you'll get a fraction for an answer, but it won't match any of the choices. Check to see if one of the choices is equivalent to your answer—if it is, that's the one you should pick.

Fractions in Simplest Terms

Simplest terms refers to a special kind of equivalent fraction. In order to put a fraction into simplest terms, find the greatest common factor of the numerator and denominator, and divide both by it. If the GCF is 1, then the fraction is already in lowest terms.

Example: Put $\frac{12}{16}$ into simplest terms.

Factors of 12 are $1, 2, 3, 4, 6, 12$
Factors of 16 are $1, 2, 4, 16$
The greatest common factor is 4, so $\frac{(12 \div 4)}{(16 \div 4)} = \frac{3}{4}$

Put these fractions into simplest terms:

1. $\frac{5}{10}$ 2. $\frac{3}{9}$ 3. $\frac{12}{18}$ 4. $\frac{9}{24}$ 5. $\frac{16}{60}$

ANSWERS

1. $\frac{1}{2}$ 2. $\frac{1}{3}$ 3. $\frac{2}{3}$ 4. $\frac{3}{8}$ 5. $\frac{4}{15}$

Changing Fractions to Mixed Numbers

To change an improper fraction into a mixed number, divide the numerator by the denominator. The answer becomes the whole-number part, and the remainder is left as a fraction.

Example: Change $\frac{22}{5}$ into a mixed number.

$$22 \div 5 = 4, \text{remainder } 2 = 4\frac{2}{5}$$

To change a mixed number into an improper fraction, multiply the denominator by the whole number, and add that to the numerator.

Example

$$3\frac{3}{4} = \frac{(3 \times 4) + 3}{4} = \frac{15}{4}$$

Practice

Change these mixed numbers into improper fractions:

1. $3\frac{1}{10}$ 2. $2\frac{3}{8}$ 3. $4\frac{4}{5}$ 4. $1\frac{7}{24}$ 5. $5\frac{11}{13}$

Change these fractions into mixed numbers in simplest terms:

6. $\frac{5}{2}$ 7. $\frac{22}{7}$ 8. $\frac{24}{18}$ 9. $\frac{54}{9}$ 10. $\frac{241}{26}$

ANSWERS

1. $\frac{31}{10}$ 2. $\frac{19}{8}$ 3. $\frac{24}{5}$ 4. $\frac{31}{24}$ 5. $\frac{76}{13}$ 6. $2\frac{1}{2}$ 7. $3\frac{1}{7}$ 8. $1\frac{1}{3}$ 9. 6   10. $9\frac{7}{26}$

Arithmetic with Fractions

To do arithmetic with fractions, first change all the mixed numbers into improper fractions.

To add and subtract fractions, you must have a *common denominator;* that is, the denominators of the two fractions must be the same. You can find a common denominator by changing the fractions you have into equivalent fractions. A good common denominator is the *least common multiple* of the two denominators. Then just multiply the top and bottom of each fraction by the same number to get equivalent fractions with that denominator.

Example

$$\frac{1}{3} + \frac{3}{4}$$

Multiples of 3: 3, 6, 9, 12, 15, 18
Multiples of 4: 4, 8, 12, 16, 20
The LCM is 12.

$$\frac{(1 \times 4)}{(3 \times 4)} + \frac{(3 \times 3)}{(4 \times 3)} = \frac{4}{12} + \frac{9}{12} = \frac{13}{12} = 1\frac{1}{12}$$

When you practice, put your answers in lowest terms, as answers on the test typically will be.

To multiply fractions, multiply numerator times numerator and denominator times denominator. To divide, take the *reciprocal* of the fraction you're dividing by, and then multiply.

To take the reciprocal of a fraction, just flip it over. When you take the reciprocal of a whole number x, it becomes $1/x$. Any number times its reciprocal equals 1.

Examples

$$\frac{4}{5} \times \frac{2}{3} = \frac{(4 \times 2)}{(5 \times 3)} = \frac{8}{15}$$

$$\frac{3}{8} \div \frac{3}{4} = \frac{3}{8} \times \frac{4}{3} = \frac{(3 \times 4)}{(8 \times 3)} = \frac{12}{24} = \frac{1}{2}$$

Cross canceling: If the same number appears in both the numerator and denominator when you're multiplying fractions, you can cancel them out—remember, any number over itself equals 1.

Practice

Add:

1. $\frac{1}{6} + \frac{4}{6}$ 2. $\frac{4}{9} + \frac{1}{3}$ 3. $\frac{2}{3} + \frac{1}{5}$ 4. $\frac{5}{24} + \frac{6}{9}$ 5. $1\frac{1}{14} + 3\frac{4}{7}$

Subtract:

6. $\frac{5}{9} - \frac{1}{3}$ 7. $\frac{5}{6} - \frac{1}{4}$ 8. $\frac{17}{8} - \frac{4}{5}$ 9. $3\frac{1}{4} - \frac{2}{3}$ 10. $2\frac{7}{10} - 1\frac{2}{9}$

Multiply:

11. $\frac{1}{3} \times \frac{1}{2}$ 12. $\frac{3}{7} \times \frac{7}{3}$ 13. $\frac{7}{5} \times \frac{2}{5}$ 14. $1\frac{3}{4} \times \frac{3}{10}$ 15. $4\frac{1}{5} \times 2\frac{2}{3}$

Divide:

16. $\frac{5}{9} \div \frac{1}{9}$ 17. $\frac{5}{6} \div \frac{1}{2}$ 18. $\frac{7}{8} \div \frac{5}{4}$ 19. $2\frac{1}{5} \div \frac{1}{3}$ 20. $4\frac{2}{4} \div 3\frac{3}{5}$

ANSWERS

1. $\frac{5}{6}$ 2. $\frac{7}{9}$ 3. $\frac{13}{15}$ 4. $\frac{7}{8}$ 5. $4\frac{9}{14}$ 6. $\frac{2}{9}$ 7. $\frac{7}{12}$ 8. $1\frac{13}{40}$ 9. $2\frac{7}{12}$ 10. $1\frac{43}{90}$

11. $\frac{1}{6}$ 12. 1   13. $\frac{14}{25}$ 14. $\frac{21}{40}$ 15. $11\frac{1}{5}$ 16. 5   17. $\frac{5}{3}$ 18. $\frac{7}{10}$ 19. $6\frac{3}{5}$ 20. $1\frac{1}{4}$

Changing Fractions to Decimals

To change a fraction into a decimal, divide the numerator by the denominator. Put in a decimal point, and divide the same way you would a decimal. This will give you a decimal answer. If the decimal repeats, you have to divide only until you see the pattern, as in the example.

To change a fraction into a percentage, change it into a decimal first, and then move the decimal point two places to the right.

Example: Change $\frac{1}{3}$ into a decimal.

$$
\begin{array}{r}
0.333 \\
3\overline{)1.000} \\
\underline{9} \\
10 \\
\underline{9} \\
10 \\
\underline{9} \\
10
\end{array}
$$

If you have to change it into a percentage, $\frac{1}{3} = 0.333 = 33.3\%$

Practice

Change these fractions into decimals:

1. $\frac{5}{10}$ 2. $\frac{1}{4}$ 3. $\frac{15}{6}$ 4. $\frac{9}{24}$ 5. $\frac{2}{3}$ 6. $\frac{19}{18}$ 7. $\frac{30}{36}$ 8. $\frac{6}{40}$ 9. $\frac{11}{121}$ 10. $\frac{22}{7}$

ANSWERS

1. 0.5	2. 0.25	3. 2.5	4. 0.375	5. 0.6
6. 1.05	7. 0.83	8. 0.15	9. 0.09	10. 3.142857

To change a decimal into a fraction, remember the places discussed in earlier sections; 0.3 is "three-tenths," so you can write it as ³⁄₁₀. Change the decimal into an appropriate fraction using this method, and then reduce it to lowest terms.

Example

$$0.25 = \frac{25}{100} = \frac{1}{4}$$

Practice

Change these decimals into fractions in lowest terms:

1. 0.5   2. 0.2   3. 0.375   4. 0.15   5. 0.64

ANSWERS

1. $\dfrac{1}{2}$ 2. $\dfrac{1}{5}$ 3. $\dfrac{3}{8}$ 4. $\dfrac{3}{20}$ 5. $\dfrac{16}{25}$

PROBABILITY

We use fractions to show probability of events—how likely they are to happen. In general, the denominator is how many possibilities there are, and the numerator is how many of them you're looking for. If something will never occur, the probability is 0. If it will always occur, the probability is 1.

> *Example:* A fair coin is flipped. What is the probability of it coming up heads?
>
> There are two possibilities: heads and tails. You're looking for one of them. The probability of heads is ½.

For this test, all coins, dice, and so on, will be referred to as *fair*. This means that there is an equal probability of coming up with each particular answer. An *unfair* coin might be weighted so that heads comes up more often, for example.

If you're looking for the probability of two things, watch carefully for the word *or* or *and*. If you see *or*, you'll usually have to add the two probabilities. If you see *and*, you'll usually have to multiply them.

Example
What is the probability of the coin coming up heads <u>and</u> then heads again?

$$\frac{1}{2} \times \frac{1}{2} = \frac{1}{4}$$

What is the probability of the coin coming up heads <u>or</u> tails?

$$\frac{1}{2} + \frac{1}{2} = 1$$

Sometimes, a problem will use a deck of cards (or something else you pick, such as socks from a drawer). If it says *with* replacement, remember that you'll have the same number of cards for the later draws (the denominator will remain 52). If it says, *without* replacement, then you'll need to decrease the number of cards after each draw (the second draw would have a denominator of 51, the third 50, and so on). Always pay attention to whether there is replacement, because it affects the probabilities and is an easy way to slip up on a problem. Also note that dice, coins, and other things that are not "taken out" are always considered *with* replacement.

Practice

A drawer contains three brown socks, four blue socks, and three black socks. If you reach in and grab a sock at random, what is the probability of picking:

1. A black sock?
2. A blue or brown sock?
3. A red sock?

If you pick out two socks *with* replacement, what is the probability of picking:

4. Two blue socks?
5. One blue sock, and then one black sock?
6. One blue or one black sock?

If you pick out two socks *without* replacement, what is the probability of picking:

7. Two blue socks?
8. One blue sock, and then one black sock?
9. Two blue socks or two black socks?
10. A matched pair?

ANSWERS

1. $\frac{3}{10}$ 2. $\frac{7}{10}$ 3. 0   4. $\frac{4}{25}$ 5. $\frac{6}{50}$ 6. $\frac{49}{100}$ 7. $\frac{2}{15}$ 8. $\frac{2}{15}$ 9. $\frac{1}{5}$ 10. $\frac{4}{15}$

Mean, Median, Mode

The *mean* is what most people call the *average*. Add up all the numbers and then divide by count of numbers.

The *median* is the middle number, when all of the numbers are put into numerical order. If there are two middle numbers, take the mean of those two.

The *mode* is the number that appears most often. Note that some sets of numbers don't have a mode, and some have several.

Examples

2, 4, 5, 5, 7, 7, 7, 9, 12, 12
$2 + 4 + 5 + 5 + 7 + 7 + 7 + 9 + 12 + 12 = 70, 70 \div 10 = 7$
The *mean* is 7.

There are 10 numbers, so the fifth and sixth are both in the middle. $7 + 7 = 14$, $14 \div 2 = 7$
The *median* is 7.

The number 2 appears once, 4 once, 5 twice, 7 three times, 9 once, and 12 twice. The *mode* is 7.

Sometimes you'll be given numbers in order; sometimes you won't. Always put them in order, as that makes finding the median and mode much easier.

Practice

Find the mean, median, and mode of each set:

1. 1, 2, 3, 3, 6
2. 4, 4, 4, 4, 14
3. 1, 5, 5, 9, 10, 12
4. 3, 15, 12, 3, 9, 15, 6, 15
5. 7, 2, 14, 2, 21, 50, 9

ANSWERS

1. Mean: 3; median: 3; mode: 3
2. Mean: 6; median: 4; mode: 4
3. Mean: 7; median: 7; mode: 5
4. Mean: 9.75; median: 10.5; mode: 15
5. Mean: 15; median: 9; mode: 2

Permutations and Combinations

A *permutation* is a way a set of things can be arranged in order. Permutations are written as $n!$, where n is any number. It's pronounced "n factorial." It means the number n, multiplied by all of the numbers smaller than it.

Example: If you have the letters A, B, and C, you can arrange them:

ABC ACB BAC BCA CBA CAB

You have a set of three things, then the possible permutations are 3!, or $3 \times 2 \times 1 = 6$ possible permutations.

A *combination* is a way of choosing a set of things, but the order doesn't matter.

Example: There are three ways of choosing two letters from A, B, and C, but only one way of choosing three letters.

Two letters: AB, AC, BC
Three letters: ABC

You can find the total number of possible combinations from different categories using the *fundamental counting principle*. Just multiply the number of possible choices in each category.

Example: If you have four pairs of pants, eight shirts, and three pairs of shoes, how many outfits can you make?

4 pants × 8 shirts × 3 shoes = 96 outfits

Practice

There are four colored blocks: red, green, blue, and yellow.

1. How many combinations of three are there?
2. How many combinations of two are there?
3. How many permutations of all four are there?

You have a poker hand of seven cards.

4. How many different six-card selections can you put down?
5. How many different ways can you arrange those six cards on the table?

I have four markers, seven stickers, and six colors of posterboard.

6. How many different posters with one color of writing and one sticker on them can I make?
7. How many ways can I arrange the seven stickers in a row on a poster?
8. How many combinations of two marker colors are there?
9. How many different combinations of two stickers are there?
10. How many posters can I make with two of the marker colors, two of the stickers, and one piece of posterboard? (Hint: Think about the last two answers.)

ANSWERS

1. 4
2. 6
3. 4! = 24
4. 7
5. 6! = 720
6. 168
7. 7! = 5,040
8. 6
9. 21
10. 756

SCIENTIFIC NOTATION

Scientific notation is an easy way of writing very large or very small numbers. It expresses numbers in powers of 10, which tell you how far to move the decimal point. If the exponent is positive, move the decimal point that many places to the right. This expresses a very large number. If the exponent is negative, move the decimal point that many places to the left. This expresses a very small number.

Examples

$$1.2 \times 10^4 = 12,000$$
$$3.79 \times 10^{-7} = 0.000000379$$

The proper format for scientific notation is always a decimal number between 1 and 10. There should only be one digit to the left of the decimal point.

Practice

Write these numbers in standard notation:

1. 1.34×10^3
2. 4.09×10^9
3. 2.55×10^{-3}
4. 6.71×10^{-5}
5. 8.909×10^{-6}

Write these numbers in scientific notation:

6. 2,000,000
7. 340,000
8. 0.042
9. 0.0000153
10. 0.0065001

ANSWERS

1. 1,340
2. 4,090,000,000
3. 0.00255
4. 0.0000671
5. 0.000008909

6. 2.0×10^6

7. 3.4×10^5

8. 4.2×10^{-2}

9. 1.53×10^{-5}

10. 6.5001×10^{-3}

ALGEBRA: SOLVING EQUATIONS

Algebra is math using *variables*, which are letters that stand in for a number you don't know. The letter x is a commonly used variable. When you solve an *algebraic equation* (i.e., an equation that has a variable in it), you're trying to find out what the variable is equal to.

You can solve many simple algebraic equations with a three-step process:

1. Combine like terms.
2. Add or subtract both sides.
3. Multiply or divide both sides.

Examples

$6x - 5x = 16$

Combine $6x$ and $5x$ by subtracting the numerical part.

$6x - 5x = 1x$

$1x = 16$

$x + 5 = 11$

Solve by subtracting 5 from both sides.

$x + 5 - 5 = 11 - 5$

$x = 6$

$3x = 15$

Solve by dividing both sides by 3.

$$\frac{3x}{3} = \frac{15}{3}$$

$\frac{3}{3} = 1$, so $1x = 5$

$4x - 15 = 3 + 2$

Combine like terms: $4x - 15 = 5$

Add to both sides: $4x = 20$

Divide both sides: $x = 5$

Common mistakes with problems like these are not operating on both sides of the equation, or doing the steps out of order. Always add or subtract to both sides before you multiply or divide them.

Practice

Find x.

1. $14 - 8 = x$
2. $3x - 2x = 8$
3. $x + 3 = 17$
4. $6 + x = 2$
5. $x - 15 = 2$
6. $4x = 20$
7. $-7x = 21$
8. $\frac{x}{3} = 6$
9. $15 - x = 8$
10. $2x + 4 = 26$
11. $3x + 7 = 43$
12. $18 - 2x = 12$
13. $\frac{x}{2} - 4 = 7$
14. $13 - \frac{x}{5} = 4$
15. $5x - 2x - 20 = 4 + 3$

ANSWERS

1. $x = 6$
2. $x = 8$
3. $x = 14$
4. $x = -4$
5. $x = 17$
6. $x = 5$
7. $x = -3$
8. $x = 18$
9. $x = 7$
10. $x = 11$
11. $x = 12$
12. $x = 3$
13. $x = 22$
14. $x = 45$
15. $x = 9$

Ratio and Proportion

A *ratio* is a way of comparing two numbers. It means the same thing as a fraction, and is also the same as writing a division problem. The fraction ½ is a ratio. It can also be written as 1:2 or "1 to 2." It means "1 divided by 2."

A *proportion* shows two ratios that have the same value—in other words, it shows equivalent fractions. As explained in the section about comparing fractions, you can tell if two fractions form a proportion by cross multiplying: If the cross products are equal, the fractions form a proportion. Most proportion problems involve writing a proportion to solve a problem.

> *Example:* If it takes 3 hours to do four homework problems, how many hours does it take to do 12 problems?
>
> We'll use the variable x to represent the number of hours we're looking for.
>
> $\frac{3}{4} = \frac{x}{12}$
>
> $3 \times 12 = 4x$
>
> $36 = 4x$
>
> $9 = x$
>
> It takes 9 hours to do 12 problems.

Make sure the two numerators are in the same units—that is, they are both in hours, pounds, bars, or the like. If they're not the same units, you may be setting up the proportion wrong, or you may need to convert to similar units.

Practice

1. A baker can make 4 doughnuts in 2 minutes. How many doughnuts can he make in half an hour?
2. A factory needs 4 bars of steel to make 7 pots. How many bars would it take to make 28 pots?
3. Three hungry college students can eat 8 slices of pizza. How many slices of pizza would you need to feed 18 students?
4. A CD has 15 songs on it. If I have a collection of 105 songs, how many CDs must I have?
5. A recipe for 12 muffins calls for 0.25 cup of sugar. How many cups of sugar would you need to bake 18 muffins?

ANSWERS

1. 60
2. 16

3. 48
4. 7
5. 0.375

GEOMETRY

Lines and Angles

Here are several useful terms you should know:

Parallel lines never touch, even if extended forever in both directions.

Perpendicular lines meet and form a 90° angle.

An *acute* angle is less than 90°.

A *right* angle is exactly 90°.

An *obtuse* angle is more than 90°.

When one line *bisects,* or cuts, another, opposing angles are equal, and adjacent angles add up to 180°. In the diagram, $a = d, b = c, a + b = 180°, c + d = 180°$.

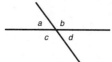

Area, Perimeter, Surface Area, and Volume

In a two-dimensional shape, the *perimeter* is the distance around the shape (going along the edges), and the *area* is the space contained inside it. In a three-dimensional shape, the *surface area* is the space covered by the edges, and the *volume* is the area inside.

Triangle: Any shape with three sides and three angles. Right triangles, which contain a 90° angle, have special rules discussed later.

Area = $\frac{1}{2}$(base × height)

Perimeter = $side_1 + side_2 + side_3$

Square: A four-sided figure with four right angles and sides of equal length.
Area = side^2
Perimeter = side $\times$ 4

Rectangle: A four-sided figure with four right angles. All squares are also
rectangles.
Area = length $\times$ width
Perimeter = $2l + 2w$

Parallelogram: A four-sided figure with two pairs of sides that are the same
length. All rectangles are also parallelograms.
Area = base $\times$ height
Perimeter = $2b + 2h$

Trapezoid: A four-sided figure with two sides that are parallel to each other. All
parallelograms are also trapezoids.
Area = $\frac{1}{2}$(base$_1$ + base$_2$)
Perimeter = base$_1$ + base$_2$ + side$_1$ + side$_2$

Circle: The radius of a circle (*r*) is the distance from the center to any edge. The
diameter (*d*) is the distance from one edge to another, passing through the
center. $d = 2r$.
Area = πr^2
Perimeter = $2\pi r$

Cube: A six-sided figure with sides that are all the same length and all angles
are right angles.
Volume = s^3
Surface area = $6s^2$

Rectangular prism: A six-sided figure where all angles are right angles. All
cubes are also rectangular prisms.
Volume = length $\times$ width $\times$ height
Surface area = $2lw + 2lh + 2wh$

Sphere: Volume = $\frac{4}{3}\pi r^3$

Cone: Volume = $\frac{1}{3}\pi r^2 h$

Cylinder: Volume = $\pi r^2 h$
   Surface area = $2\pi r(h + r)$

If you forget the formulas or see a figure you don't recognize, remember that for most figures, you can find the perimeter simply by adding up the lengths of each side. You can find the area by dividing up a larger shape into smaller, recognizable ones.

Pi (written as π) is a universal constant used to find the area of a circle. It is a nonrepeating decimal that goes on infinitely, but it is often approximated as 3.14.

Example: The radius of a cone is 3 and the height is 4. What is the volume?

$$\text{Volume} = \tfrac{1}{3}\pi r^2 h = \tfrac{1}{3}\pi(3)^2(4) = \tfrac{1}{3} \times \pi \times 9 \times 4 = 12\pi \approx 37.68$$

Practice

1. What is the area of a square whose sides each measure 4 inches?
2. What is the area of a parallelogram with a base that measures 5 inches and a height of 3 inches?
3. What is the surface area of a cube that is 4 inches per side?
4. What is the volume of a rectangular prism that is 3 inches long by 7 inches wide by 4 inches high?
5. What is the volume of a cylinder with radius 5 inches and height 12 inches?

ANSWERS

1. 16 square inches
2. 15 square inches
3. 96 square inches
4. 84 cubic inches
5. $300\pi \approx 942$ cubic inches

Pythagorean Theorem

The *Pythagorean theorem* is a special rule for right triangles, which contain a 90° angle. It states that the sum of the squares of the two legs equals the square of the hypotenuse. The *hypotenuse* is the side opposite the right angle, and it is always the longest side.

$$a^2 + b^2 = c^2$$

Example: If the legs of a right triangle are 4 inches and 3 inches, what is the length of the hypotenuse?

$$4^2 + 3^2 = c^2 = 16 + 9 = c^2 = 25 = c^2 = 5 = c$$

The hypotenuse is 5 inches long.

If you see a right triangle, the Pythagorean theorem should always jump into your head. However, problems you may need it for may try to trick you by hiding the right triangles. Remember that if you split a rectangle diagonally, it forms two right triangles. Also be careful about other kinds of triangles—if there's no right angle, you can't use the Pythagorean theorem.

Practice

1. The legs of a right triangle are 12 inches and 5 inches long. What is the length of the hypotenuse?
2. The length of the hypotenuse of a right triangle is 5 inches and one of the legs is 3 inches long. How long is the other leg?
3. The length of the hypotenuse of a right triangle is 10 inches and one of the legs is 8 inches long. How long is the other leg?
4. The legs of a right triangle are 2 inches and 7 inches long. What is the length of the hypotenuse?
5. A square is 4 inches to a side. How long is the diagonal distance between two opposing corners? (Hint: That distance splits the square into two triangles. Draw a picture.)

ANSWERS

1. 13 inches
2. 4 inches
3. 6 inches
4. $\sqrt{53} \approx 7.28$ inches
5. $\sqrt{32} \approx 5.66$ inches

MEASURING SYSTEMS

There are two commonly used measuring systems: the *metric system* and the *U.S. customary system*. While most of the world uses the metric system at this point, Americans still use the U.S. customary system.

The metric system is based on multiples of 10 and has a common system of prefixes for the three units, which are meters for length, grams for weight, and liters for volume. You multiply by the number listed to get how many base units are in one of the prefix units. Or just count the number of places between the two on this chart, and move the decimal point in the number that many places.

milli	centi	deci	(no prefix)	deca	hecto	kilo
0.001	0.01	0.1	1	10	100	1,000

Examples

There are 1,000 meters in 1 kilometer.
There are 10 meters in a decameter.
There are 10 millimeters in a centimeter and 100 centimeters in a meter.

Practice

1. How many meters are in 1 hectometer?
2. How many centimeters are in 1 decimeter?
3. 18 meters is how many decameters?
4. 44 meters is how many centimeters?
5. 800 millimeters is how many decameters?

ANSWERS

1. 100
2. 10
3. 1.8
4. 4,400
5. 0.08

The U.S. units are not as regular and generally have to be memorized:

Units of Length

12 inches = 1 foot
3 feet = 1 yard
5,280 feet = 1,760 yards = 1 mile

Units of Weight

16 ounces = 1 pound (lb)
2,000 pounds = 1 ton

Units of Volume (for Liquids)

8 fluid ounces = 1 cup

2 cups = 1 pint

2 pints = 1 quart

4 quarts = 1 gallon

You can change between units by multiplying ratios (i.e., by multiplying fractions).

Examples

How many cups are in 1 gallon?

$$\frac{1 \text{ gallon}}{4 \text{ quarts}} \times \frac{1 \text{ quart}}{2 \text{ pints}} \times \frac{1 \text{ pint}}{2 \text{ cups}} = \frac{1 \text{ gallon}}{16 \text{ cups}}$$

On a map or a scale model, you will sometimes be told "an inch is equal to 10 feet" or something similar. Don't get confused into thinking you need to know the units in this section. Set up the problem as equivalent fractions and solve from there.

Practice

1. How many inches are in a yard?
2. How many fluid ounces are in a pint?
3. 7 quarts is how many cups?
4. 2.5 miles is how many feet?
5. 32,000 ounces is how many tons?

ANSWERS

1. 36 inches
2. 16 fluid ounces
3. 28 cups
4. 13,200 feet
5. 1 ton

Time and Temperature

The standard system of measuring time, like U.S. customary measurements, basically requires memorizing.

60 seconds = 1 minute

60 minutes = 1 hour

24 hours = 1 day

7 days = 1 week

365 days = 52 weeks = 1 year

As with measurements of length or weight, you can change between measurements of time by multiplying ratios.

If you are asked to do problems involving a clock, remember that just like any circle, it measures 360° around. There are 12 numbers on any clock and 60 minutes in an hour. By setting up equivalent fractions, you can solve any problem of this type.

Example: A clock is showing 4:15. How many degrees will the minute hand move by 4:35?

There are 60 minutes in an hour, and 360° around the clock.

$\frac{60}{360} = \frac{20}{x}$, $60x = 7{,}200$, $x = 120$

The minute hand will move 120°.

There are two commonly used measurements of temperature: *Celsius* and *Fahrenheit.* Here are some notable temperatures on each scale:

Degrees Celsius	*Degrees Fahrenheit*	
0	32	Freezing point of water
20	68	Room temperature
37	98.6	Human body temperature
100	212	Boiling point of water

The formula for converting between the two is $F = \frac{9}{5}C + 32$. This formula works like any of the others you've seen, such as the formulas for area and perimeter. Fill in the numbers you have, and solve from there.

Example: 54°F is what temperature Celsius?

$54 = \frac{9}{5}C + 32 \Rightarrow 22 = \frac{9}{5}C \Rightarrow 12.22 = C$

COORDINATE GEOMETRY

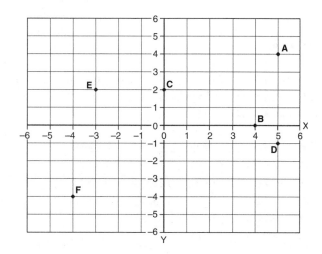

The figure shown here is called a *coordinate plane.* The horizontal line is the *x* axis; the vertical line is the *y* axis. The point where they meet is called the *origin.*

Each point on the graph is represented by a set of *coordinates,* written in the form (x, y). The first number tells how far to the right on the *x* axis the point is; the second number tells how far up on the *y* axis the point is. In both cases, you start counting from the origin, which has the coordinates (0,0). If the coordinates are negative, you count to the left or down, instead.

Example: The point labeled A on the graph has the coordinates (5,4). It is five spaces to the right of the origin and four spaces up.

A common mistake is to mix up the two coordinates. Remember that you write the *x* coordinate first, then the *y* coordinate—it's in alphabetical order.

Practice

Give the coordinates of these five points:

1. B
2. C
3. D
4. E
5. F

ANSWERS

1. $(4, 0)$
2. $(0, 2)$
3. $(5, -1)$
4. $(-3, 2)$
5. $(-4, -4)$

CHARTS AND GRAPHS

Charts and graphs represent visual ways of presenting information. This simple chart shows several stock tickers on the left and various dates on the top. The numbers in the chart are the stock prices on each given date.

	1-Jan	1-Feb	1-Mar	1-Apr	1-May
EBAY	64.61	66.93	69.23	72.25	81.64
MSFT	27.37	27.65	26.70	25.08	27.54
F	16.00	14.54	13.99	13.42	15.59
X	35.02	34.05	39.16	37.03	34.89
IBM	92.68	99.23	97.04	92.37	90.62

Example: The price of EBAY on March 1 was $69.23, which is the number in the EBAY row and the March 1 column.

Practice

1. What was the price of Ford (F) on January 1?
2. What was the price of IBM on April 1?
3. In which month was the price of U.S. Steel (X) highest?
4. Which stock had the highest price in March?
5. The lowest price on the chart is 13.42. Which stock had it, and during which month?

ANSWERS

1. 16
2. 92.37
3. March
4. IBM
5. Ford (F) in April

Here, the same information is presented in two ways: as a *line graph* and as a *bar graph*.

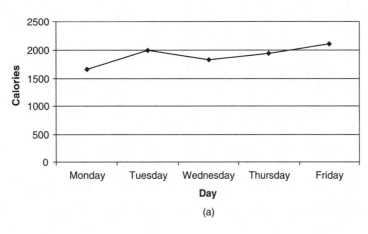

(a)

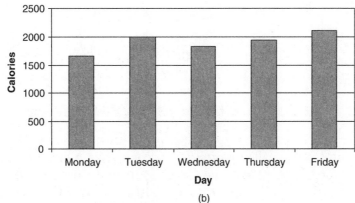

(b)

Both of these graphs show how many calories Gloria ate over a five-day period. In the line graph, each day is represented by a point, and the points are connected by a line to make them easy to compare. In the bar graph, each day is represented by a bar—the higher the bar, the more calories Gloria ate that day.

Example: How many calories did Gloria eat on Tuesday?

On the line graph, the Tuesday point is on the 2,000 line, so she ate 2,000 calories that day.

On the bar graph, the top of the Tuesday bar matches the 2000 line, so the answer is the same.

Practice

1. Did Gloria eat more or fewer calories on Tuesday than Wednesday?
2. On which day did Gloria eat the greatest number of calories?
3. On which days did she eat fewer than 2,000 calories?
4. On which day did Gloria eat 1,625 calories?
5. Based on the line graph, do you think Gloria will eat more or fewer calories on Saturday than Friday?

ANSWERS

1. She ate more on Tuesday than Wednesday.
2. Friday.
3. Monday, Wednesday, and Thursday.
4. Monday.
5. More. The line is going upward.

You may need to match a bar or line graph to the chart that matches it. Here is the actual data chart for the two graphs.

Monday	1650
Tuesday	2000
Wednesday	1825
Thursday	1950
Friday	2100

The following chart is called a *pie chart* because, like a pie, it is divided into slices. This chart shows the percentage of the total Chuck, Burt, and Alice receive. Reading a pie chart is very straightforward; just remember that percentages always add up to 100 percent.

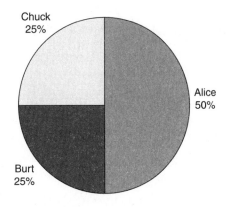

Practice

1. If the pie represents a total of 40, what is Chuck's share?
2. If Burt received 5, what is the total?
3. If Burt received 8, what is Alice's share?
4. If Alice's share was increased to 60%, how much would be taken away from Burt and Chuck?
5. If the total changed from 50 to 80, but everyone's share stayed the same, would the chart change?

ANSWERS

1. 10
2. 20
3. 16
4. 10%
5. No.

Another common form of visual data is a *pictograph.* Pictures are used to represent one or more objects.

Number of Comic Books Owned

Jimmy	☺☺☺☺
Billy	☺☺
Steve	☺☺☺☺☺

Each ☺ represents 4 comic books.

Example

How many comics does Jimmy own?

There are four symbols next to Jimmy's name, and each represents four comics, so he owns 16 comics.

Practice

1. How many comics does Billy own?
2. How many comics does Steve own?
3. If there were a half ☺ in the chart, what would it represent?
4. Chuck owns 12 comic books. How many ☺s would that be on the chart?
5. If each ☺ represented 6 comics, how many would Billy own?

ANSWERS

1. 8
2. 24
3. 2 comics
4. 3
5. 12

Determining Relationships from Charts

x	y
2	9
6	25
13	53
17	69
22	89

This chart shows a relationship between x and y. The test may ask you to find that relationship. In this case, it will be best to work backward from the answers. You will see that in each case, $y = 4x + 1$.

Reading Statistics from Charts

Occasionally you will see a chart that gives statistical data, and you will be asked to find the mean, median, and mode or to work out probabilities. You already know how to do that from the statistics section; you just have to be careful reading the chart.

Example

Score	Students
1	3
2	10
3	23
4	9
5	5

The left column gives a score on the AP math exam, and the right column is the number of students who received that score. Three students received a score of 1; 11 students received a score of 2; and so on. There were 50 students, total.

Practice

1. How many students scored a 3 or higher?
2. What is the mean score?
3. What is the median score?
4. What is the mode score?
5. If you pick a random student, what is the probability they scored a 4?

ANSWERS

1. 37
2. 3.06
3. 3
4. 3
5. $\frac{9}{50}$

LOGIC

You may need to use simple deductive reasoning to solve some problems. Pay careful attention to certain key words: *all, some,* and *none.* When determining whether a statement is true or false, one those three words is usually the key to the answer.

The other important rule to remember is the *law of contrapositives:* Written in logical language, if $a \rightarrow b$ is true, then $\sim b \rightarrow \sim a$ is true. Watch out for the key word *some*—if you see it, it usually means you can't use this rule.

Examples

If all squares are rectangles (true), then a shape that is not a rectangle is also not a square (also true).

If I go out, I always dance (true); I did not dance, therefore I didn't go out (also true).

All gleebs are shnorks, and some shnorks are oglops. Are all gleebs oglops?

False, because while *all* gleeks are shnorks, only *some* (not all) shnorks are oglops, so not *all* gleebs are oglops.

Practice

Write whether the statement is true or false.

1. All triangles have three sides.
2. Some triangles have three equal sides.
3. All triangles contain a right angle.
4. Some prime numbers are divisible by two.
5. All balls are round; therefore all round things are balls.

ANSWERS

1. True
2. True
3. False
4. False
5. False

TEST-TAKING TIPS FOR THE PPST MATHEMATICS

Circle key words: When doing word problems, look for key words that will indicate what you're supposed to do. Also, if you can find information that you don't need, cross it out.

Addition: *sum, more than, and, increased*

Subtraction: *minus, difference, less than, except, decreased*

Multiplication: *of, times, product*

Division: *per, quotient, shared*

Negative number: *opposite, away*

Equals: *is, equals, equivalent*

Draw a picture: Especially for problems involving geometry, it's often helpful to examine the problem visually. Feel free to draw a sketch in the test book or on scrap paper—it doesn't have to be great art, or even to scale, as long as it helps you visualize the problem.

Estimate: Estimating is a good way to make sure your answer is reasonable. Round the numbers to the highest (or lowest, if you're working with small decimals) place and do the easier calculations with those numbers. If your final answer comes out close to your estimated answer, it's likely to be correct.

Work backward: The questions on the test are multiple choice, so when in doubt, start with the possible answers and work backward through the problem. This technique is especially useful for algebra-based questions, where you're trying to find a variable. Use each possible answer in place of the variable and see which one works.

Make an educated guess: If it comes down to guessing, try to eliminate some choices first. If you can knock out a few of the possible answers as wrong, the chances of guessing the correct one are better. (If you can get an answer, especially by working backward, don't guess!)

Mathematics Practice Test

On the following pages you will find a full-length PPST Mathematics practice test. Take this test for additional practice and to help you review what you learned in this chapter. Mark your answers by circling the letter of your choice.

MATHEMATICS PRACTICE TEST

40 questions, 60 minutes

Directions: Select the best choice for each item. Circle the letter of your choice.

1. What are the coordinates of point D?

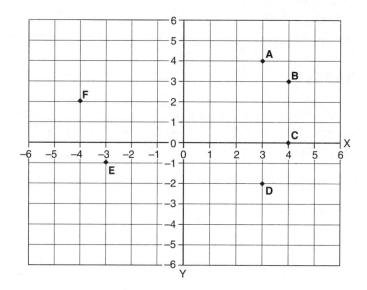

(A) $(2, 3)$
(B) $(3, 2)$
(C) $(3, -2)$
(D) $(-3, 2)$
(E) $(-3, -2)$

2. If $x \div 5 = y$, what is $2x$?

(A) y (B) $y \div 5$ (C) $y \div 10$
(D) $5y$ (E) $10y$

3. Elmont is 12 miles due west of Farmingdale. The beach is 5 miles due south of Elmont. What is the approximate straight-line distance from Farmingdale to the beach?

(A) 7 miles
(B) 14.5 miles
(C) 13 miles
(D) 12 miles
(E) 17 miles

4. In a deck of 52 cards, there are four equal suits: clubs, heart, spades, and diamonds. What percentage of the cards is made up of hearts and diamonds?

(A) 4.0%   (B) 50.0%   (C) 25.0%

(D) 13.0%   (E) 52.0%

5. On the gas gauge shown, the arrow indicates that the tank is:

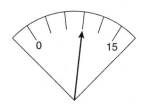

(A) full
(B) $^3/_4$ full
(C) $^1/_4$ full
(D) more than $^1/_2$ full
(E) less than half full

6. In a box of 20 cookies, 8 have vanilla cream and 12 have chocolate cream. What percentage have strawberry cream?

(A) 10%   (B) 50%   (C) 25%

(D) 33.3%   (E) 0%

7. If A = $x/2 - 2$, and A = 6, then $x =$

(A) 12   (B) 0   (C) 3

(D) 18   (E) 16

8. If the scale for a dollhouse is 3 inches: 2 feet and a shelf is 6 feet high, how high would you make a dollhouse-scale shelf?

(A) 1.5 inches
(B) 2 inches
(C) 12 inches
(D) 9 inches
(E) 3 feet

9. The number of sandwiches sold in the deli each weekday is represented by the chart below. What is the approximate mean number of sandwiches for the week?

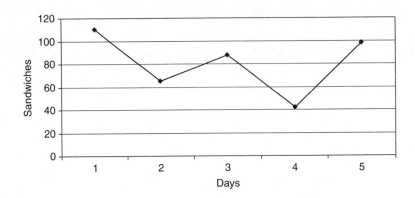

(A) 40 (B) 80 (C) 60

(D) 100 (E) 65

10. Which of these problems have the same numerical answer?

   I. If you need 4 eggs to make a soufflé, and you have 18 eggs, how many soufflés can you make?

   II. If you need 4 sandwiches to feed everyone at a picnic, how many picnics could you go on if you have 18 sandwiches?

   III. If you can fit 4 glasses in a box, how many boxes do you need to hold 18 glasses?

   (A) I and II

   (B) I and III

   (C) II and III

   (D) I, II, and III

   (E) None of the above

11. If there are 8 forks, 8 spoons, and 6 knives in a drawer, and you pick one at random, what is the probability of picking a spoon?

   (A) 1/3 (B) 4/11 (C) 6/22

   (D) 8/24 (E) 1/8

12. 3,640,000 is how many times 3.64?

   (A) 1,000

   (B) 10,000

   (C) 100,000

   (D) 1,000,000

   (E) 10,000,000

13. Which of the following numbers is a third of a million?

(A) 300,000
(B) 1,000,000 × 0.3
(C) 3/1,000,000
(D) 1,000,000/3
(E) 1,000,000/3.3

14. Which decimal is least?

(A) 0.0034   (B) 0.0956   (C) 0.000998
(D) 0.00475   (E) 0.0001156

15. The following chart shows the amount of profit a company earns for a given number of employees and customers. If the company has 30 customers, how many employees should it hire in order to have the greatest profit?

	Customers				
	10	**20**	**30**	**40**	**50**
1	30	32	34	36	38
2	25	60	62	64	66
3	20	55	90	92	94
4	15	50	85	120	122
5	10	45	80	115	150
6	5	40	75	110	145

(Employees listed along the left side 1–6)

(A) 1   (B) 2   (C) 3
(D) 4   (E) 5

16. The gauge on the oil tank looks like this. Approximately how full is the tank?

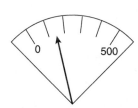

(A) 75%   (B) 50%   (C) 90%
(D) 15%   (E) 30%

17. If $A = 5x + 5$, and $A = 35$, then $x =$

(A) 6   (B) 5   (C) 35
(D) 10   (E) 200

18. A large group of your friends takes you out to a restaurant for a birthday dinner. When the bill comes, the tax on it is $24.96. If you know the tax rate is 8.75 percent, approximately how much should they leave as an 18 percent tip?

   (A) $25.00   (B) $40.00   (C) $45.00
   (D) $50.00   (E) $87.50

19. If the scale on a dollhouse is 1 inch to 2.5 feet and a coat rack is 5.5 feet high, how high would you make a dollhouse-scale coat rack?

   (A) 0.45 inch
   (B) 2.2 inches
   (C) 13.75 inches
   (D) 1.15 feet
   (E) 2.2 feet

20. Which pairs of decimals and fractions are equivalent?
   I. 0.125 and 1/7   II. 0.25 and 2/8   III. 0.60 and 12/18   IV. 1.25 and 5/4

   (A) I and III
   (B) II only
   (C) II and III
   (D) I, II, and IV
   (E) II and IV

21. Which of the following is true?

   (A) 9/7 < 1.1
   (B) 5/4 = 1.25
   (C) 7/14 = 7.14
   (D) 5/6 > 78%
   (E) 1/10 > 0.1

22. Three groups of voters are represented by the chart below. If a majority is required for a motion to pass or be defeated, which of the following is not true?

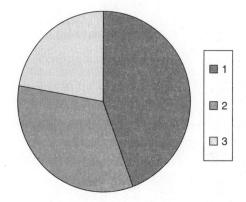

(A) Groups 1 and 3 together could pass a motion.

(B) Groups 2 and 3 together could defeat a motion.

(C) Group 3 cannot defeat a motion.

(D) Group 2 can pass a motion.

(E) Group 1 has the most members.

23. If $2x + 4 = 9x - 10$, then $x =$

(A) 2   (B) 6   (C) 10

(D) 12   (E) 18

24. The chart below represents five baseball games between the Yankees and the Angels. How many runs did the Angels score in all?

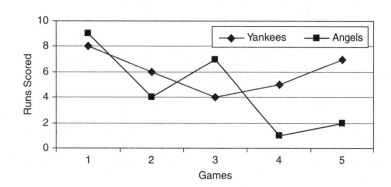

(A) 30   (B) 23   (C) 15

(D) 9   (E) 27

25. If the team that scored more runs won the game, how many games did the Yankees win?

(A) 1   (B) 2   (C) 3

(D) 4   (E) 5

26. What is the average number of runs the Yankees scored per game?

(A) 4   (B) 5   (C) 6

(D) 7   (E) 8

27. There is a fruit bowl in the cafeteria. Based on the chart below, how many peaches and pears are in the bowl?

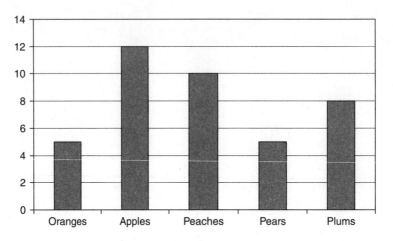

(A) 13 (B) 12 (C) 15
(D) 17 (E) 10

28. The students eating lunch take 3 oranges, 10 apples, 2 peaches, 3 pears, and 1 plum. How many pieces of fruit are left in the bowl?

(A) 11 (B) 22 (C) 24
(D) 21 (E) 35

29. The bowl is refilled with 3 of each type of fruit added to those that remained. Of which type of fruit will there be the most in the bowl?

(A) Oranges
(B) Apples
(C) Peaches
(D) Pears
(E) Plums

30. Coach Torres is storing the practice footballs on a shelf in the locker room. He can fit 6 footballs on a 4-foot-long shelf. If he has 21 footballs, how much shelving does he need to store them all?

(A) 14 feet
(B) 12 feet
(C) 16 feet
(D) 24 feet
(E) 21 feet

31. Four friends order a pizza and have it cut into 12 equal slices. Based on the chart below, who has eaten the most slices?

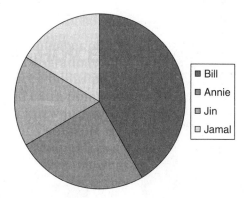

(A) Bill   (B) Annie   (C) Jin

(D) Jamal   (E) They all ate the same number.

32. Based on the chart in the previous question, who ate 3 pieces of the pizza?

(A) Bill   (B) Annie   (C) Jin

(D) Jamal   (E) Jin and Jamal

33. If $x = 3y$, $x + 7 = z$ and $y = 11$, what is the value of z?

(A) 10   (B) 21   (C) 26

(D) 40   (E) It cannot be determined

34. What is the value of 1/10th of 1 percent of 5,000,000?

(A) 50   (B) 500   (C) 5,000

(D) 50,000   (E) 500,000

35. The area of a room is 120 square feet. Which of the following rugs would cover 60 percent of the floor?

(A) $6' \times 10'$ rug

(B) $10' \times 12'$ rug

(C) $5' \times 11'$ rug

(D) $8' \times 9'$ rug

(E) $7' \times 11'$ rug

36. A cube measures 27 cubic inches. Two of its faces are painted red. How many square inches are painted red?

(A) $13\frac{1}{2}$ (B) 9   (C) 27

(D) 12   (E) 18

37. Four to the fourth power plus 3 to the third power is equal to . . .

(A) 17   (B) 283   (C) 145
(D) 256   (E) 77

38. One hundred students were asked to choose their favorite sports and were told they could pick one or two sports. Based on the chart below, how many students named two sports?

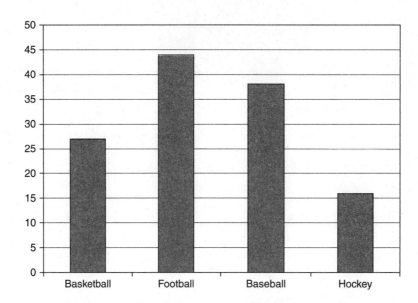

(A) 50   (B) 10   (C) 100
(D) 25   (E) 0

39. If the previous chart represents an accurate sampling of the 2,000 students at the university, how many university students are hockey fans?

(A) 320   (B) 640   (C) 160
(D) 64   (E) 500

40. If all the students in the class wearing red shirts are brown-haired and most brown-haired students wear glasses, which of the following is true?

(A) No blond-haired students wear glasses.
(B) Some students are wearing red shirts and glasses.
(C) All students with glasses have red shirts.
(D) Some brown-haired students have green shirts.
(E) There is not enough information to make a determination.

ANSWERS

1. C. Three to the right, then 2 down.

2. E. $x = 5y$, so $2x = 10y$

3. C. The trip is a right triangle, so use the Pythagorean equation. $12^2 = 144$. $5^2 = 25$. $144 + 25 = 169$. The square root of 169 is 13.

4. B. There are 13 cards in each suit, so two suits is 26 cards. 26 is 50% of 52.

5. D. Each line on the gauge represents 3, so the arrow is at 9 gallons. This is more than half, but less than $^3/_4$, so there is only one correct answer.

6. E. None of the cookies has strawberry cream, which equals 0%.

7. E. $16/2 = 8$, $8 - 2 = 6$

8. D. 2 feet = 3 inches, so 6 feet = 9 inches.

9. B. $110 + 65 + 90 + 40 + 100 = 405$. $405/5 = 81$

10. A. This is a remainder interpretation problem. I is 4 soufflés; II is 4 picnics; III is 5 boxes.

11. B. Eight chances out of a possible 22 $(8 + 8 + 6)$, reduced to lowest terms.

12. D. $1{,}000{,}000 \times 3.64$

13. D. One-third of a million is 1,000,000 divided by 3.

14. E. Find the number with the most leading zeroes, then compare the first nonzero place if two are tied.

15. C. Three employees give a profit of 90, which is higher than any of the other possibilities.

16. E. Each line on the gauge represents 100, so the tank contains about 150 gallons of oil. $150/500 = 30\%$.

17. A. $35 = 5x + 5$, so subtract from both sides to get $30 = 5x$, then divide both sides to get $6 = x$.

18. D. Estimate. $25 is about 9 percent of the bill, so 18 percent of the bill would be twice as much.

19. B. Use equivalent fractions: $1/2.5 = x/5.5$, so $2.5x = 5.5$, and $x = 2.2$.

20. E. $1/7 = 0.143$, $12/18 = 0.667$

21. B.   Convert fractions to decimals by dividing.

22. D.   None of the groups has a majority.

23. A. $2x + 4 = 9x - 10$, subtract $2x$ from both sides so $4 = 7x - 10$, add 10 to both sides so $14 = 7x$, then divide both sides by 7, $x = 2$.

24. B.   They scored 23 runs in all.

25. C.   The Yankees won 3 games.

26. C.   The Yankees scored 30 runs in all, an average of 6 per game.

27. C.   There are 10 peaches and 5 pears.

28. D.   There were 40 pieces of fruit in total and 19 were taken.

29. C.   There will be 11 peaches, 10 plums, and 5 each of apples, oranges, and pears.

30. A. $6/4 = 21/x$. Solve for x. $x = 14$.

31. A.   Bill ate the largest number of pieces.

32. B.   Annie ate $^1/_4$ of the pie. One quarter of 12 pieces is 3.

33. D.   40. $x = 3(11) = 33$. $33 + 7 = 40$.

34. C.   5,000,000 divided by 1000

35. D.   60% of 120 square feet is 72 square feet. An $8' \times 9'$ rug would be 72 square feet.

36. E.   A cube of 27 cubic inches would have 3-inch sides. Each face would measure $3 \times 3 = 9$ square inches. Two faces would equal 18 square inches.

37. B.   Four to the fourth power = 256, 3 to the third = 27. $256 + 27 = 283$.

38. D.   There are 125 responses shown. Therefore, 25 of the students named a second sport.

39. A.   16 of the sampled students are hockey fans. The total student body is $20 \times$ the number of responses or 320.

40. E.   None of the statements made can be proven.

PART 6

Praxis II Content Tests

As you learned in Chapter 2, the Praxis II tests are subject assessments. These tests include Principles of Learning and Teaching tests and content tests. Let's discuss the Principles of Learning and Teaching tests first.

Principles of Learning and Teaching

Principles of Learning and Teaching includes four separate tests:

- Early Childhood (30521)
- Grades K–6 (30522)
- Grades 5–9 (30523)
- Grades 7–12 (30524)

You take the test or tests that apply to the areas in which you wish to be certified. Each test follows the same format:

Test	Time	Number of Questions	Question Format
Principles of Learning and Teaching	*2 hours each*	*12 short-answer* *24 multiple-choice*	*4 case histories, followed by 3 short-answer questions; 24 multiple-choice in 2 sections of 12 questions each*

According to ETS, the skills you'll be tested on are divided as follows:

Type of Question	Percentage of Test
Students as learners (multiple-choice)	11%
Instruction and assessment (multiple-choice)	11%
Teacher professionalism (multiple-choice)	11%
Students as learners (short-answer)	22%
Instruction and assessment (short-answer)	22%
Communication techniques (short-answer)	11%
Teacher professionalism (short-answer)	11%

The following topics are covered on these tests:

1. *Student Development and the Learning Process*

   - How students construct knowledge, acquire skills, and develop habits of mind
   - The writings of important scholars in the field and their theories
   - How students grow and mature and the effect of their development on their learning
   - How development in one area (such as physical growth) may affect development in another area (such as social interactions)
   - Differences in the ways that students learn, such as the theory of multiple intelligences (interpersonal, intrapersonal, kinesthetic, linguistic, musical, etc.), gender factors, and cultural expectations
   - How student learning is affected by problems in speech, vision, hearing, attention-deficit/hyperactivity, developmental delays, mental retardation, and so on
   - The laws regarding students with disabilities, including the Americans with Disabilities Act (ADA) and the Individuals with Disabilities Education Act (IDEA)
   - Ways to accommodate various learning styles, including the requirements for testing modification
   - English as a second language acquisition
   - How to help students become self-motivated
   - The principles of effective classroom management, including ways to establish daily routines, classroom rules, resolving conflicts effectively, keeping accurate records, communicating with students' families and guardians, arranging the classroom to maximize learning, and structuring and pacing lessons

2. *Instruction and Assessment*

   - Student learning processes, including literal, analytical, and critical thinking skills
   - Instructional strategies, including cooperative learning, direct instruction, dividing the class into groups, learning centers, and so on
   - Using a variety of resources and materials, including computers, audiovisual materials, local experts, primary documents, field trips, and libraries
   - State and local standards for instruction and behavioral objectives
   - Methods of teaching, including tapping prior knowledge, predicting, connecting, and analyzing
   - Assessment methods, including scoring techniques

3. *Communication Techniques*

   - Basic verbal and nonverbal ways to communicate with students, including ways to help students express their ideas in a constructive manner

4. *The Teaching Profession and the Community*

   - Materials available for professional development, including professional literature, colleagues, and professional associations

- The role of the school in the community, especially teachers as a resource
- Factors in the students' environment that influence their learning, including family circumstances, health, and economic conditions
- The major laws that relate to teachers' responsibilities and students' rights, including privacy and confidentiality and reporting possible child abuse

Model Test Questions

Case History: 7–12

Directions: The case history is followed by two short-answer questions. Write your response on the blank lines provided on the answer sheet.

Mr. Taylor worked as a reporter for a major city newspaper for 25 years. An Ivy League graduate with a master's degree in journalism and several minor awards to his credit, he left journalism to begin a second career as a senior high school English teacher. He is teaching in a very upscale community where more than 90 percent of the students are expected to go on to college.

Mr. Taylor prepares for class very carefully and grades all writing assignments thoroughly and promptly. He returns the assignments the next day and conferences with his students. Available for extra help before and after school, Mr. Taylor has never been absent or late. His classes are lively, engaging, and filled with solid learning.

He grades his students on a strict bell curve. He also deducts points when students are absent from class because of family vacations and extracurricular activities such as band trips and science fairs. He does not allow makeup assignments or extra-credit work.

Mrs. Sanderson has repeatedly called the principal to complain about her daughter's low grades. "Last year in Honors English, Jill earned straight As," Mrs. Sanderson says. "She is working twice as hard this year and only earning low Bs. How is she going to get into a good school with English grades like that? She got a 650 on her English PSAT, so it's clear that she's an outstanding English student."

Dr. Singh called to complain that his son should be able to miss a day or two of class to attend a family reunion. "Why can't Sanjay make up the work?" he asked. "My family reunion comes only once a year and my son must be with us. Mr. Taylor is being rigid and unreasonable," he concludes.

Other parents are upset that Mr. Taylor requires his students to complete a 20-page research paper and write at least three papers a week. Dr. Washington is furious that her son had to take a test when he returned to class after being absent for a week. Further, many of Mr. Taylor's colleagues bitterly resent his hard work, which they feel makes them look lazy in comparison.

Question 1

- Identify two ways that Mr. Taylor could reduce the amount of criticism he is getting from parents.
- Explain how each action will benefit his students. Cite specific principles of teaching and learning and the role of the school in the community.

Question 2

- What actions could Mr. Taylor reasonably take to improve his relationship with his colleagues?
- You may wish to discuss communication methods.

CHAPTER 17

Content Tests

Praxis II also includes content (subject area) assessments. These tests assess your knowledge of the different subject areas that a person can teach, such as biology, French, and mathematics. You take the content test or tests that apply to the areas in which you wish to be certified.

> *Always check with your state education department to determine which test or tests to take.*

The tests are between 1 hour and 2 hours long and follow different formats. Some tests are multiple choice, others are short answers, and still others are essay tests. The multiple-choice tests may have any number of test items, such as 60, 80, 120, 140, 148, 150, or 157 questions. Some content tests require calculators; others contain listening or speaking sections.

Currently, Praxis II includes the following tests (this list is subject to change at any time):

Subject Assessments
- Art Education
- Athletic Trainer
- Audiology
- Biology and General Science
- Biology: Content Essays
- Biology: Content Knowledge
- Business Education
- Chemistry: Content Essays
- Chemistry: Content Knowledge
- Chemistry, Physics, and General Science
- Citizenship Education: Content Knowledge
- Communication
- Cooperative Education
- Driver Education
- Early Childhood Education

- Earth Science: Content Knowledge
- Economics
- Education in the Elementary School
- Education of Deaf and Hard of Hearing Students
- Education of Exceptional Students: Core Content Knowledge
- Education of Exceptional Students: Learning Disabilities
- Education of Exceptional Students: Mild to Moderate Disabilities
- Education of Exceptional Students: Severe to Profound Disabilities
- Education of Students with Mental Retardation
- Education of Young Children
- Educational Leadership: Administration and Supervision
- Elementary Education: Content Area Exercises
- Elementary Education: Curriculum, Instruction, and Assessment
- English Language, Literature, and Composition: Content Knowledge
- English Language, Literature, and Composition: Essays
- English Language, Literature, and Composition: Pedagogy
- English to Speakers of Other Languages
- Environmental Education
- Family and Consumer Sciences
- Foreign Language Pedagogy
- French (contains listening section)
- French: Content Knowledge
- French: Linguistic, Literary, and Cultural Analysis
- French: Productive Language Skills (contains speaking section)
- General Mathematics
- General Science
- General Science: Content Essays
- General Science: Content Knowledge
- Geography
- German (contains listening section)
- German: Content Knowledge (contains listening section)
- German: Productive Language Skills (contains speaking section)
- Gifted Education
- Government/Political Science
- Health and Physical Education: Content Knowledge
- Health Education
- Introduction to the Teaching of Reading
- Latin
- Library Media Specialist
- Life Science: Pedagogy
- Marketing Education
- Mathematics (calculator allowed)

- Mathematics: Content Knowledge (graphing calculator required)
- Mathematics: Pedagogy
- Mathematics: Proofs, Models, and Problems, Part 1 (graphing calculator required)
- Mathematics: Proofs, Models, and Problems, Part 2 (graphing calculator required)
- Middle School: Content Knowledge (calculator allowed)
- Middle School English Language Arts
- Middle School Mathematics (calculator allowed)
- Middle School Science
- Middle School Social Studies
- Music: Analysis (contains listening section)
- Music: Concepts and Processes
- Music: Content Knowledge (contains listening section)
- Music Education (contains listening section)
- Physical Education: Content Knowledge
- Physical Education: Movement Forms—Analysis and Design
- Physical Education: Movement Forms—Video Evaluation (contains video section)
- Physical Science: Content Knowledge
- Physical Science: Pedagogy
- Physics
- Physics: Content Essays
- Physics: Content Knowledge
- Pre-Kindergarten Education
- Psychology
- Reading across the Curriculum: Elementary
- Reading across the Curriculum: Secondary
- Reading Specialist
- Safety/Driver Education
- School Guidance and Counseling (contains listening section)
- School Psychologist
- School Social Worker: Content Knowledge
- Social Sciences: Content Knowledge
- Social Studies: Analytical Essays
- Social Studies: Content Knowledge
- Social Studies: Interpretation and Analysis
- Social Studies: Interpretation of Materials
- Social Studies: Pedagogy
- Sociology
- Spanish: Content Knowledge (contains listening section)
- Spanish: Linguistic, Literary, and Cultural Analysis
- Spanish: Pedagogy
- Spanish: Productive Language Skills (contains speaking section)
- Special Education

- Special Education: Application of Core Principles across Categories of Disability
- Special Education: Knowledge-Based Core Principles
- Special Education: Preschool/Early Childhood
- Special Education: Teaching Students with Behavioral Disorders/Emotional Disturbances
- Special Education: Teaching Students with Learning Disabilities
- Special Education: Teaching Students with Mental Retardation
- Speech Communication
- Speech-Language Pathology
- Teaching Foundations: History–Social Science
- Teaching Foundations: Mathematics
- Teaching Foundations: Multiple Subjects
- Teaching Foundations: Reading/Language Arts
- Teaching Foundations: Science
- Teaching Speech to Students with Language Impairments
- Teaching Students with Emotional Disturbance
- Teaching Students with Learning Disabilities
- Teaching Students with Orthopedic Impairments
- Teaching Students with Visual Impairments
- Technology Education
- Theater
- Vocational General Knowledge
- World and U.S. History
- World and U.S. History: Content Knowledge

Following is additional information about some of the content tests taken most often and sample questions.

ENGLISH

Currently, the Praxis offers four English tests:
- English Language, Literature, and Composition: Content Knowledge (10041)
- English Language, Literature, and Composition: Essays (20042)
- English Language, Literature, and Composition: Pedagogy (30043)
- English to Speakers of Other Languages (20360)

English Language, Literature, and Composition: Content Knowledge (10041)

This test is designed for people who want to teach English in a secondary school. The 2-hour test has 120 multiple-choice questions that test literature, reading, the English language, composition, and rhetoric (the use of language). Approximately 66 questions test reading and understanding text, approximately 18 questions test language and linguistics, and approximately 36 questions test composition and rhetoric.

Practice Test Questions

Directions: Choose the correct answer to each question.

1. All of the following were American writers from 1607 to 1750 except

    (A) Anne Bradstreet
    (B) Edward Taylor
    (C) Cotton Mather
    (D) Emily Dickinson
    (E) Michael Wigglesworth

2. Which of the following best describes the significant common features of *The Jungle* by Upton Sinclair and *Mrs. Warren's Profession* by George Bernard Shaw?

    (A) Both are three-act stage plays performed often by amateur as well as professional theater groups.
    (B) Both were written to bring about social reform for serious social and political issues.
    (C) Both resulted in significant legislation to protect health and safety of the public.
    (D) Both are light and humorous, featuring amusing slapstick, farce, and clever wordplay.
    (E) Both were derided in their day for their amateur style but now recognized as classic literature.

3. "George Orwell" is the pen name of the author of which novel?

    (A) *Alice's Adventures in Wonderland*
    (B) *Great Expectations*
    (C) *1984*
    (D) *A Connecticut Yankee in King Arthur's Court*
    (E) *Heart of Darkness*

4. Charles Dickens is most famous for

    (A) hilarious, insightful sketches of clerical life among landed gentry in the Victorian era
    (B) showing the effects of genetics and environment on common people set adrift in a cold, uncaring world
    (C) being a strong supporter of British imperialism and the greatest short story writer that England has ever produced
    (D) peeling back the thin veneer of man's social persona as well as exposing the evils of 19th century imperialism
    (E) depicting the working class of British society in the Victorian era while showing the dark side of the Industrial Revolution

5. Theodore Dreiser, Frank Norris, and Jack London are classified as

   (A) naturalists
   (B) romantic writers
   (C) Gothic horror writers
   (D) local colorists
   (E) transcendentalists

6. William Shakespeare's play *Romeo and Juliet* is classified as a

   (A) comedy
   (B) tragedy
   (C) romance
   (D) problem play
   (E) history

7. "Call me Ishmael" is the first line of

   (A) Mark Twain's novel *The Adventures of Huckleberry Finn*
   (B) Philip Roth's novel *Portnoy's Complaint*
   (C) Edgar Allan Poe's short story "The Tell-Tale Heart"
   (D) Jane Austen's novel *Pride and Prejudice*
   (E) Herman Melville's novel *Moby Dick*

8. What literary technique is used in the following lines?
   All things within this fading world hath end,
   Adversity doth still our joys attend

   (A) rhyme
   (B) allegory
   (C) mixed metaphor
   (D) personification
   (E) anaphora

9. Walt Whitman and Emily Dickinson are most famous for their mastery of

   (A) the novel
   (B) the short story
   (C) free verse
   (D) sonnets
   (E) personal essays

10. Ballads are characterized by

   (A) their form (14 lines), metrics (iambic pentameter), and fixed rhyme scheme
   (B) a fictional speaker caught at a critical moment in his or her life

(C) praise of a person or thing

(D) rhythmic stories told in song-like form

(E) praise that glorifies a person, place, or thing

ANSWERS

1. **D**

2. **B**

3. **C**

4. **E**

5. **A**

6. **B**

7. **E**

8. **A**

9. **C**

10. **D**

English Language, Literature, and Composition: Essays (20042)

This test is designed for people who want to teach English in a secondary school. The test is 2 hours long and assesses your ability to analyze and evaluate literature. The test consists of four different types of essays, and each essay counts as 25 percent of your total score. It is assumed that you will spend 30 minutes on each essay.

Essay 1	Analyze a poem.
Essay 2	Analyze a prose work (not poetry).
Essay 3	Evaluate the rhetoric of a passage that addresses an issue in the study of English.
Essay 4	Take and defend a position on an issue in the study of English. Here, you must refer to other works of literature.

The passages can be taken from British, American, or World Literature and may be entire works or excerpts from longer works. The essays are graded holistically, based on their overall quality rather than on individual merits. The score ranges from 6 (highest) to 0 (lowest).

Practice Test Question on Analyzing a Poem

Directions: Read the following poem carefully. Then, in a well-organized essay, discuss how the speaker uses tone and form to convey meaning in the poem. Be sure to use at least three specific examples from the poem to support your points.

Sonnet 130

My mistress' eyes are nothing like the sun;
Coral is far more red than her lips' red;
If snow be white, why then her breasts are dun;
If hairs be wires, black wires grow on her head.
I have seen roses damask'd, red and white,
But no such roses see I in her cheeks;
And in some perfumes is there more delight
Than in the breath that from my mistress reeks.
I love to hear her speak, yet well I know
That music hath a far more pleasing sound;
I grant I never saw a goddess go;
My mistress, when she walks, treads on the ground.
And yet, by heaven, I think my love as rare
As any she belied with false compare.
                                        —William Shakespeare

Sample Response

The tone of the first 12 lines of Shakespeare's "Sonnet 130" contrasts sharply to the tone of the final two, and this difference establishes the theme of the entire work. In presenting his theme this way, Shakespeare is working within the convention of the English sonnet, in which the "turn," or point, is presented in the final couplet.

The first 12 lines of the poem parody the form and content of the typical love sonnet, as the woman fails to measure up to any of the traditional emblems of love and devotion. Thus, her eyes, the time-honored windows of the soul, lack the clear radiance of the sun, and her lips, the deep, rosy tint of coral. "My mistress' eyes are nothing like the sun," the poet playfully notes in line 1, and we learn in line 2 that "Coral is far more red than her lips' red." Her skin is mottled and dark; her hair, coarse wires. If that's not bad enough, she has bad breath ("And in some perfumes is there more delight/Than in the breath that from my mistress reeks") and has a voice that is far from melodious ("I love to hear her speak, yet well I know/That music hath a far more pleasing sound.") Lines 11 to 12 reveal that his beloved "treads on the ground" rather than floating ethereally above it as a goddess should.

The tone is playful and mocking, as Shakespeare inverts all the accepted tools of the love sonneteers trade to construct a series of false analogies. The tone of the final two lines, however, differs sharply. As mentioned earlier, the final couplet of an English sonnet frequently serves to sum up the meaning of the preceding 12 lines and establish the author's theme. Such is the case here, for the couplet's tone and meaning differ markedly from the rest of the sonnet. These two lines are serious, not light and playful, as the author declares his love for the lady he has just pilloried at the stake of false comparison. He wrote this poem, he says in the couplet, to parody her tendency to compare their love to objects and in so doing, establish false analogies. Their love is a rare and serious thing, he states, not to be diminished through "false compare."

The sonnet form is well suited to this difference in tone, as the couplet in the end gives Shakespeare the opportunity to sum up the first 12 lines and establish the theme. Here, he abjures the parody of the first 12 lines to declare his love firmly and seriously. In so doing, he both mocks and embraces the poetic conventions of his day.

Evaluation

This response would receive a 6 on the grading scale because it directly answers the question, shows an impressive knowledge of literature, and is unified, coherent, and complete.

The introduction addresses both parts of the question—tone and form, to convey the theme—and demonstrates a sophisticated use of language. In paragraphs 2 and 3, the writer uses specific examples to describe the theme and its relationship to the poem's form. Note especially how smoothly the writer weaves in specific quotes from the sonnet to prove the thesis. The writer clearly demonstrates familiarity with the conventions of the English (also called "Elizabethan" or "Shakespearean") sonnet. The conclusion to the third paragraph is clear, succinct, and effective. The overall conclusion is brief but adds a graceful and intelligent note, pulling together all aspects of the question. This well-written essay fully answers the question by using specific examples, vivid word choice, and sophisticated syntax.

Practice Test Question on Analyzing a Prose Passage

This prose analysis question is very similar to the poetry question, in that you will

1. Be asked to analyze literary techniques
2. Have the literary passage in front of you to use as reference
3. Be expected to make references to the text as you write

Directions: Carefully read the following passage from a novel by Rebecca Harding Davis. Then write a well-organized essay in which you show some of the ways the author recreates the experience of life in the iron mills. You might wish to consider such literary techniques as imagery, figures of speech, and diction, for example.

A cloudy day: do you know what that is in a town of iron-works? The sky sank down before dawn, muddy, flat, immovable. The air is thick, clammy with the breath of crowded human beings. It stifles me. I open the window, and, looking out, can scarcely see through the rain the grocer's shop opposite.

The idiosyncrasy of this town is smoke. It rolls suddenly in slow folds from the great chimneys of the iron-foundries, and settles down in black, slimy pools on the muddy streets. Smoke on the wharves, smoke on the dingy boats, on the yellow river, —clinging in a coating of greasy soot to the house-front, the two faded poplars, the faces of the passers-by. The long train of mules, dragging masses of pig-iron through the narrow street, have a foul vapor hanging to their reeking sides. Here, inside, is a little broken figure of an angel pointing upward from the mantel-shelf; but even its wings are covered with smoke, clotted and black. Smoke everywhere! A dirty canary chirps desolately in a cage beside me. Its dream of green fields and sunshine is a very old dream, —almost worn out, I think.

From the back-window I can see a narrow brickyard sloping down to the riverside, strewed with rain-butts and rubs. The river, dull and tawny-colored, drags itself sluggishly along, tired of the heavy weight of boats and coal-barges. What wonder? Masses of men, with dull, besotted faces bent to the ground, sharpened here and there by pain or cunning: skin and muscle and flesh begrimed with smoke and ashes; stooping all night over boiling caldrons of metal, laired by day in dens of drunkenness and infamy; breathing from infancy to death an air saturated with fog and grease and soot, vileness for soul and body. What do you make of a case like that, amateur psychologist? You call it an altogether serious thing to be alive: to these men it is a drunken jest, a joke, —horrible to angels perhaps, to them commonplace enough. My fancy about the river was an idle one: it is no type of such a life. What if it be stagnant and slimy here? It knows beyond there waits for it odorous sunlight, —quaint old gardens, dusky with soft, green foliage of apple-trees, and flushing crimson with roses, —air, and fields, and mountains. The future of the Welsh puddler [one who refines metal] passing just now is not so pleasant. To be stowed away, after his grimy work is done, in a hole in the muddy graveyard, and after that, —*not* air, nor green fields, nor curious roses.

Sample Response

From the first image of a "muddy, flat, immovable" sky to the last image of being buried in "a hole in the muddy graveyard," Rebecca Harding Davis paints a grim picture of life for workers in the iron mills. Through images, figures of speech, and syntax, the author describes a brutally hard life in a filthy, polluted town. Her language is so vivid that readers feel themselves a part of this tragically dead-end life.

The "thick, clammy" air, stale with "the breath of crowded human beings," plunges readers into a stifling world marked by lost hopes and lives. The air is so polluted that the narrator cannot even see the grocery shop across the street. The images of the thick black smoke that fills the town appeal to different senses. We see it roll "suddenly in slow folds" and settle "down in black, slimy pools on the muddy streets." We feel it "clinging in a coating of greasy soot to the house-front" and smell its "foul vapor" hanging to the reeking sides of a long train of mules. Symbolically, the smoke covers even the "little broken figure of an angel," extinguishing all hope of beauty or salvation.

In the next paragraph, the author personifies the river as a living thing, dragging itself "sluggishly along, tired of the heavy weight of boats and coal-barges." This figure of speech drags down the reader, too, with the weariness of endless toil and filth. Describing the men as "bent to the ground" makes them seem like animals, an image that is reinforced by the vision of them "laired by day in dens of drunkenness and infamy." By using the noun "lair" as a verb, the author suggests the men are mere brutes, animals living in dens. The people are as "stagnant and slimy" as the river, going nowhere, covered by layers and layers of muck and filth.

The images in the ending are especially grim, as the Welsh mill worker is denied salvation even in death. Instead of passing on to a glorious heaven of "odorous sunlight, —quaint old gardens, dusky with soft, green foliage of apple-trees, and flushing crimson with roses," he will be "stowed away" in a hole in the ground. No air, green fields, or flowers for him. Rebecca Harding Davis recreates the experience of life in the iron mills through many literary techniques, including imagery, figures of speech, and diction. She succeeds in plunging readers into a suffocating world of toil, filth, and hopelessness.

Evaluation

This response would receive a 6 on the grading scale. The writer opens with specific images from the selection to prove the thesis: "Rebecca Harding Davis paints a grim picture of life for workers in the iron mills." This is right on target with the task, to "show some of the ways the author recreates the experience of life in the iron mills." The writer uses all three literary elements listed in the prompt (imagery, figures of speech, and diction), although the words "You might wish to consider such literary techniques as . . ." and "for example" give you leeway to select other literary techniques. This writer decides to play it safe, a very smart thing to do on a Praxis content test (or any standardized test).

The following paragraphs are filled with specific details that directly support the thesis. Isolating details that target each individual sense (sight, touch, and smell) shows a close, thoughtful analysis. The passage on symbolism is also quite perceptive. Notice how the writer weaves in personification, a figure of speech. This directly addresses "figures of speech" mentioned in the directions. The writer's discussion of the word "laired" is astute and again shows a close reading of the passage and a deep understanding of the author's style and purpose.

Practice Test Question on Literary Issues

> The writer's main function is to teach readers crucial life lessons, such as the importance of living up to one's responsibilities.

Directions: Choose *one* work of literature and write a well-organized essay in which you support the preceding statement. Be sure that your references include specific details.

Sample Response

When a person avoids the normal responsibilities of his or her position in life, human relationships will likely collapse. This is true of Macbeth in William Shakespeare's play *Macbeth.* In the beginning of the play, Macbeth is a loyal warrior to his king, Duncan, but as the play progresses he shuns his responsibilities and thus fails in human relationships.

As King Duncan's kinsman, Macbeth is one of the most trusted generals. His reputation was burnished by his many loyal and brave acts during battle. When Macbeth upholds his reputation by fighting bravely for the king against the traitorous Thane of Cawdor's armies, Duncan rewards him with the title of the defeated Thane of Cawdor. This shows how Duncan is a fair and decent king, rewarding his men justly and generously for their bravery. It also shows how Macbeth fights with distinction in the beginning of the play, fulfilling the expected responsibilities as a loyal thane. But all this changes right after the battle, when Macbeth encounters three witches.

As they journey home from battle, Macbeth and his friend Banquo come upon three weird sisters. The witches tell Macbeth that he shall have a glorious future as Thane of Cawdor (he does not yet know he is to receive the title) and eventually king. Intrigued, Macbeth continues on his journey home to learn that he has indeed been given the title of the disloyal thane. This sparks his ambition and he first begins thinking about killing the king to hasten any chance he may have to become king himself. He tells his wife, Lady Macbeth, what has happened and she fans his ambition, plotting how to kill Duncan. They accomplish the heinous deed that night, stabbing the good and generous king and planting the daggers on his guards. Macbeth has clearly deviated from his normal responsibilities as a loyal servant to his king, for killing one's king is treacherous indeed. From this point on, the play describes the destruction of all of Macbeth's relationships.

All suspected enemies are killed to help Macbeth maintain his shaky power base. Macbeth even has his close friend Banquo murdered, for the witches had prophesied that Banquo's heirs would become king. He had intended to kill both Banquo and his son, Fleance, but Fleance escaped the murderers during the fray. He also murders Macduff's family in Act IV, Scene 2, for the loyal Macduff, another of Duncan's original soldiers, organized the rebellion against the now power-crazed Macbeth. The scene where Macbeth's soldiers murder Macduff's family—all the little "chickens"—shows us again how far Macbeth has moved away from his responsibility, how fully he has failed in human relationships.

Macbeth's denial of his normal responsibilities as a loyal soldier to the good King Duncan result in the destruction of all human relationships. By the end of the play he has become a murderous tyrant, devoid of all humanness. Fortunately, few people cause as much devastation as Macbeth did when he shattered individual families and left Scotland in ruins. However, irresponsible people can still cause havoc and sorrow when they avoid their expected responsibilities. The tragedy of Macbeth's life and the havoc he caused illustrate the writer's main function: to teach readers crucial life lessons, such as the importance of living up to one's responsibilities.

Evaluation

This response would receive a six on the grading scale. The introduction divides the answer into two parts: Macbeth's loyalty to the good King Duncan in the beginning of the play, and his later denial of his proper role as kinsman and thane. This structure is maintained throughout the essay, as paragraph 2 discusses the first point and paragraph 3 the second point. The student explains Macbeth's behavior during battle and describes how the good king rewards him. This is crucial, for it must be shown that Macbeth is slaying a good king and thus committing a heinous deed. The setting aside of normal responsibilities would make no sense if Macbeth were killing an evil person—witness Macduff's actions in the end of the play. The final part of this paragraph is especially good, as the writer specifically says, "This shows how . . .".

Try to include phrases such as "This proves . . .", "This illustrates . . .", "This is an example of . . ." to keep yourself on topic.

In paragraph 3, the writer does a very good job of showing that in killing the king, Macbeth has violated the duties of any subject, much less a sworn supporter. The sentence "Macbeth has clearly deviated from his normal responsibilities as a loyal servant to his king . . ." is especially good, for it ties together the rest of the paragraph and makes the point. The final sentence explains that the rest of the essay will show how all of Macbeth's relationships are destroyed.

The writer proves the rest of the thesis by showing how Macbeth's relationships with Banquo, Fleance, and Macduff were destroyed when Macbeth set aside his normal and expected human responsibilities. The reference to "chickens"—recalling Macduff's impassioned speech upon hearing of the murder of his family—is an effective specific detail. The final sentence restates the topic and makes the point clear.

English Language, Literature, and Composition: Pedagogy (30043)

This test is 1 hour long and contains two essay questions. You are given 40 minutes to answer one question and 20 minutes to answer the other question. The first question concerns the teaching of literature; the second, a response to student writing.

Practice Test Question on Teaching Literature

Assume that you are teaching literature to seventh graders. Your task is to convey a love of literature while teaching literary elements, such as plot, theme, setting, and characterization. You can choose from the following literary works:

- *The Phantom Tollbooth* by Norton Juster
- *Tuck Everlasting* by Natalie Babbitt
- *Hatchet* by Gary Paulsen
- *Roll of Thunder, Hear My Cry* by Mildred D. Taylor
- *Catherine, Called Birdy* by Karen Cushman
- *Of Mice and Men* by John Steinbeck
- *The Outsiders* by S. E. Hinton

Choose one work from this list and describe two literary features that you would teach from the novel. Explain how you would teach these elements and what barriers might stand in the way of students' comprehension. Describe two activities you would include as part of your lesson, such as projects, speeches, or writing assignments.

English to Speakers of Other Languages (20360)

This 2-hour test, which contains a 30-minute listening section, has 120 multiple-choice questions, of which 20 are based on the listening section. You can expect the questions to be allocated as follows: analysis of student language production (~30 questions), theory of linguistics (~28 questions), teaching English to nonnative speakers (~36 questions), testing (~18 questions), and issues about teaching (~8 questions).

For the format of the questions, refer to the English Language, Literature, and Composition: Content Knowledge sample test questions.

HISTORY, SOCIAL STUDIES, GEOGRAPHY

Currently, the Praxis offers 10 tests in these related subject areas:

- Geography (30920)
- Government/Political Science (10930)
- Social Studies: Analytical Essays (20082)
- Social Studies: Content Knowledge (10951)
- Social Studies: Interpretation and Analysis (20085)
- Social Studies: Interpretation of Materials (20083)
- Social Studies: Pedagogy (30084)
- World and U.S. History (10940)
- World and U.S. History: Content Knowledge (10941)

All the tests in these related subject areas are designed to assess whether you are ready to teach secondary school history, social studies, government, and/or geography. The differences among the tests concern the format and content.

- *Format:* Some tests are all multiple choice, while others contain short-answer questions and/or essay questions. Some tests are solely essays.
- *Content:* Some tests are based on specific topics (American history, world history, government, etc.), while others contain many different related topics as well as visuals such as maps, charts, and photographs. Some of the tests in this subject area are based heavily on recall, while others involve more higher-order critical thinking, such as analysis, synthesis, and hypothesis. The Social Studies: Pedagogy test, for instance, requires you to choose topics in American or world history and plan units and lessons for high school students.

Let's look at individual tests in this subject area.

Geography (30920)

This 2-hour test contains 120 multiple-choice questions. At this time, only 100 of the 120 questions will be scored. ETS is pretesting the other 20 questions, so they are not scored. You can expect the questions to be allocated as follows: reading a map (24 questions), physical geography (25 questions), human geography (35 questions), and regional geography (36 questions).

For the format of the questions, refer to the Social Studies: Content Knowledge sample test questions.

Government/Political Science (10930)

This 2-hour test contains 120 multiple-choice questions. At this time, only 100 of the 120 questions will be scored. ETS is pretesting the other 20 questions, so they are not scored. You can expect the questions to be allocated as follows: U.S. constitutional theory (15 questions), U.S. government (62 questions), U.S. politics (23 questions), and comparative politics (20 questions).

For the format of the questions, refer to the Social Studies: Content Knowledge sample test questions.

Social Studies: Analytical Essays (20082)

This 1-hour test consists of solely of essays, as the title indicates. There are two essays, and they count 50 percent each. You can expect one essay on U.S. history or contemporary issues and one essay on world history or contemporary issues.

Since you will have 1 hour in which to write the essays, figure on spending 30 minutes per essay.

As with the other tests in this subject area, the Social Studies: Analytical Essays test is designed to evaluate the competency of a novice social studies teacher in a secondary school. Questions may also include topics in sociology, anthropology, and psychology. One of the essay prompts is based on a map, chart, graph, table, cartoon, diagram, quotation, or a passage from a document.

Practice Test Question

"I don't care what the papers write about me—my constituents can't read, but, damn it, they can see pictures!"

—WILLIAM "BOSS" TWEED

Cartoon by Thomas Nast for Harper's Weekly
(New York; 1876).

Using what you know about Boss Tweed and Tammany Hall, write an essay in which you explain the cartoonist's position regarding the New York political climate in the late nineteenth century. Then argue whether or not political cartoonists such as Thomas Nast wield significant political power.

Social Studies: Content Knowledge (10951)

This 2-hour test contains 130 multiple-choice questions. About 60 percent are recall questions and 40 percent involve critical thinking. The test includes visuals such as charts, maps, and photographs. You can expect the questions to be allocated as follows: U.S. history (29 questions), world history (29 questions), government/political science (21 questions), geography (19 questions), economics (19 questions), and behavioral sciences (13 questions).

Practice Test Questions

Directions: Choose the correct answer to each question.

1. The Babylonian king Hammurabi, who lived circa 1800 B.C., is best known for

    (A) developing a code of law
    (B) waging war with the Hyksos
    (C) expanding trade to other parts of North America
    (D) developing the Torah
    (E) building the pyramids and the Sphinx

2. Why is it significant that Napoleon crowned himself emperor of the first French Empire in 1804?

    (A) As the first of his line, he was demonstrating that a new monarchy was being established.
    (B) Since the Senate had named him "Emperor of the French," he was acknowledging the legitimacy of the new Senate.
    (C) He was making a symbolic gesture to show his independence.
    (D) Because of the Concordat of 1801, the clergy refused to participate in the ceremony.
    (E) His action reestablished the hereditary Bourbon line of French tradition.

3. The revolution in psychology at the end of the nineteenth century was spearheaded by

    (A) Karl Marx and Friedrich Engels
    (B) Martin Heidegger
    (C) Carl Jung
    (D) Henri Bergson
    (E) Sigmund Freud

4. At the end of Charlemagne's reign, in the early 800s, mainland Europe came under attack by

    (A) French insurgents
    (B) Crusaders
    (C) the Spanish Armada
    (D) Vikings, people from Scandinavia
    (E) Hannibal

5. Which war resulted in the greatest number of American casualties?

    (A) World War I
    (B) the American Civil War
    (C) the Vietnam War
    (D) World War II
    (E) the Korean War

6. According to the Declaration of Independence, Americans have a right to change or abolish a government if that government

    (A) is a limited monarchy
    (B) favors one part of the country over another
    (C) violates natural law
    (D) makes alliances with other countries
    (E) violates the system of checks and balances

7. The United States followed a policy of unrestricted immigration for Europeans during most of the nineteenth century to

    (A) bring in unskilled workers
    (B) attract capital and investment from overseas
    (C) create a more multicultural society
    (D) relieve the strain of overpopulation in Europe and Asia
    (E) save subjugated people from further oppression

8. Who posted the Ninety-Five Theses on the church door in Germany in 1517?

    (A) Martin Luther
    (B) Queen Elizabeth
    (C) King James
    (D) William Shakespeare
    (E) Thomas Wolsey

9. Harry Truman justified using atomic bombs on Japan in 1945 on the grounds that

    (A) it was necessary to test the bombs
    (B) the Axis deserved total annihilation
    (C) Americans demanded the bombs to be used
    (D) the act would end World War II early and thus save many lives
    (E) such action would serve as the most effective deterrent to all further wars

10. The Ottoman victory at Constantinople in 1453

   (A) began the Reformation, which brought reform to the Church in Rome
   (B) ushered a great wave of oppression across Europe, especially of women
   (C) created a republic in which citizens elected leaders to run the government
   (D) made Rome the leading power in the Mediterranean region
   (E) ended the Byzantine Empire and began a new era of Muslim rule in certain parts of Europe

ANSWERS

   1. **A**

   2. **C**

   3. **E**

   4. **D**

   5. **B**

   6. **C**

   7. **A**

   8. **A**

   9. **D**

   10. **E**

Social Studies: Interpretation and Analysis (20085)

This 2-hour test contains five short-answer questions and two essays. The short-answer questions are based on visuals (maps, charts, and excerpts). The essay questions concern recall and analysis of history, government, geography, and related issues. Unlike many of the other Praxis studies tests, this test relies very heavily on analysis, synthesis, and critical thinking. To earn a high score on this test, you will have to make connections among ideas in varying related disciplines, such as historical artifacts, economic trends, and culture.

You can expect the questions to be allocated as follows: U.S. and world history (two short-answer questions, counting as 20 percent of your score); social science, government, economics, and geography (three short-answer questions, counting as 30 percent of your score); analysis of U.S. social studies (one essay question, counting as 25 percent of your score); and analysis of world social studies (one essay, counting as 25 percent of your score).

Practice Test Questions

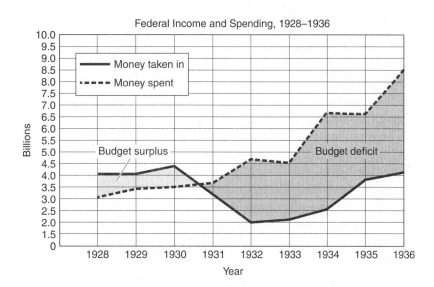

This chart shows federal income and spending from 1928 to 1936. Using the chart and what you know about the political and economic situation in the United States during this time period, answer the following questions.

1. Explain what accounts for the difference between federal income and spending as shown on this chart.
2. Analyze the implications of this trend on the economy of the era as well as the repercussions in our own day.

Social Studies: Interpretation of Materials (20083)

This 1-hour test has 5 two-part essay questions. Each question is counted equally, as one-fifth of the total. The topics covered include U.S. history, world history, government, geography, and economics. Notice that this test is concerned solely with American history and social studies.

Usually, the test contains one question on each of the five areas. The essays are based on documents such as graphs, charts, cartoons, and maps. As with the other tests in this series, it is designed for beginning teachers.

Practice Test Questions

U.S. Foreign Aid, 1946–1954
(Billions of Dollars)

NONMILITARY	YEAR	MILITARY
$ 4.0	1946	$ 0.7
$ 5.8	1947	
$ 5.0	1948	$ 0.1
$ 5.7	1949	$ 0.4
$ 4.3	1950	$ 0.2
$ 3.3	1951	$ 1.1
$ 2.8	1952	$ 1.8
$ 2.0	1953	$ 4.4
$ 1.7	1954	$ 3.5

1. Describe what the graph indicates about nonmilitary foreign aid given from 1947 to 1950.

2. Based on what you know about American history, identify and describe a few of the major factors that affected U.S. military and nonmilitary aid from 1946 to 1954.

Social Studies: Pedagogy (30084)

The test is 1 hour long and contains 2 five-part case studies. Not surprisingly for a test on pedagogy, this assessment focuses on teaching methods. Each case study counts as half of the total score. One question concerns a sample history unit that you might teach in a high school, while the second question describes a single history lesson.

This test is as straightforward as it seems. For example, the first case study offers you the choice of teaching a unit on American history or a unit on world history. Once you make this choice, you will be asked to plan a 2-week unit. Your planning will require five separate steps, such as deciding on a focus for the unit, choosing the overriding theme, and justifying your choices. In addition, you will have to write questions on the lesson and complete other tasks as well. The actual test asks you to answer these questions, as in "Identify a key social studies concept that you wish to teach your students."

World and U.S. History (10940)

This 2-hour Praxis test is designed for prospective teachers of world and U.S. history in schools in the state of Tennessee. The test has 130 multiple-choice questions, which cover historical facts and movements in ancient and non-Western civilizations, Western civilization, U.S. history to 1828, U.S. history from 1828 to 1914, and U.S. history from 1914 to the present. Questions assess your knowledge of facts, movements, trends, the general social/cultural setting, and individuals of historical significance.

Topics include:

- Ancient civilizations before A.D. 500
- Non-Western civilizations from A.D. 500 to the present (China, Japan, India, the Middle East, Southeast Asia, Africa, and Latin America)
- Western civilization (medieval, Renaissance and Reformation, the early modern period, the French Revolution, nationalism, industrialism, reform, Marxism, imperialism, World War I to 1939, World War II to the present, the Holocaust, and the cold war)

- U.S. history to 1828 (Native American life, the colonial and revolutionary period, slavery, the Revolutionary War, the early national period, the Constitution, and the War of 1812)
- U.S. history 1828–1914 (Sectionalism, slavery and abolition, the Civil War and Reconstruction, Jacksonian democracy, the Monroe Doctrine, Manifest Destiny, industrialism, and immigration)
- U.S. history 1914–present (World War I, the Harlem Renaissance, the Depression, the New Deal, Fundamentalism, World War II, the cold war, the Korean War, McCarthyism, civil rights, Vietnam, Watergate, and feminism)

You can expect the questions to be allocated as follows: ancient civilizations (17 questions), Western civilization (35 questions), U.S. history to 1828 (26 questions), U.S. history 1828–1914 (19 questions), and U.S. history 1914–present (33 questions).

World and U.S. History: Content Knowledge (10941)

This 2-hour test is designed for prospective teachers of world and U.S. history in secondary schools. The test has 120 multiple-choice questions (10 fewer questions than the other version of the test). About half the questions deal with world history and half with U.S. history. This test also assesses critical thinking, asking you to determine the causes and effects of specific events, look at events from different points of view, and analyze the results of specific historical events. This test includes visuals such as maps, charts, cartoons, graphs, and photographs.

You can expect the questions to be allocated as follows: prehistory to 1400 C.E. world history (24 questions), world history 1400–1914 (22 questions), world history 1914–present (14 questions), U.S. history to 1791 (18 questions), U.S. history 1791–1877 (18 questions), and U.S. history 1877–present (24 questions).

Practice Test Questions

Directions: Choose the correct answer to each item.

1. The Aztec civilization began its decline

(A) directly after the American Revolution concluded
(B) before the establishment of the ancient Greek civilization
(C) around 3100 B.C., with the reign of King Menes
(D) at approximately the same time as the fall of the Holy Roman Empire
(E) in 1519 when Spanish explorer Hernán Cortés arrived in Mexico

2. When the French people created their *cahiers* (list of grievances) in 1789 for the Estates General to accept, which of the following would not have been MOST unlikely?

(A) The peasants wanted a reduction in feudal dues.
(B) The nobles wanted more power.
(C) The clergy wanted monastic lands protected.
(D) The bourgeoisie wanted access to high public office.
(E) The intelligentsia wanted Cardinal Richelieu to establish the Académie française.

3. What can you infer about William Penn's plans for the city of Philadelphia from his original plans as shown in this map?

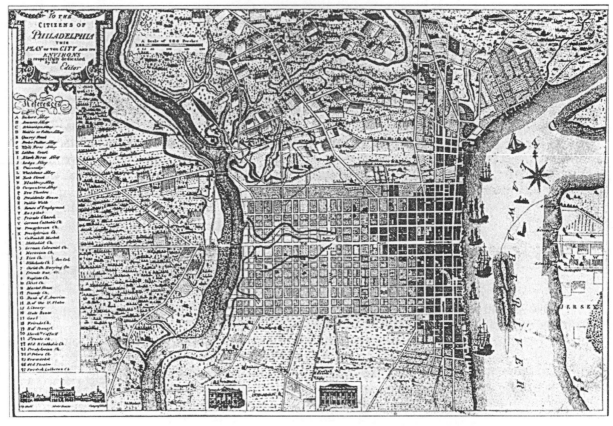

Map division, New York Public Library

(A) He wanted to keep invaders out so he included many walls and other fortifications.
(B) He did not have time to plan the city very carefully, so he copied other colonial villages.
(C) He modeled the city on the villages in England, with winding lanes and narrow alleys.
(D) He planned the city carefully to make it easy to navigate.
(E) He strongly believed that the most important aspect of the new city was its park-like atmosphere.

4. Hieroglyphics, ancient Egyptian picture writing, was finally deciphered after the discovery of

(A) long-lost Macchu Picchu
(B) papyrus
(C) the Ark of the Covenant
(D) King Tut's tomb
(E) the Rosetta stone

5. Which was NOT a provision of the Treaty of Versailles?

(A) Germany accepted total responsibility for starting World War I.
(B) Germany was disarmed.

(C) The Rhineland was demilitarized.

(D) Germany acquired Alsace-Lorraine from France.

(E) The League of Nations was established.

6. What is the best estimate of the number of Jews and non-Jews systematically murdered by the Nazis by gassing, shooting, and starvation?

(A) 10,000

(B) 100,000

(C) 2 million

(D) 6 million

(E) 60 million

7. What is the social importance of women working in factories during World War II?

(A) Women were found to be better at close detail work than men.

(B) The contributions of women during the war helped liberate them from their traditional roles as wives and homemakers.

(C) Only women would accept such arduous and tedious work.

(D) Women were finally granted the right to vote.

(E) Women henceforth refused to return to their traditional roles as homemakers.

8. The ancient African kingdom of Ghana is known for its achievement in what area?

(A) the first written language on the African continent

(B) architecture, notably huge, cone-shaped buildings

(C) the arts, especially sculpture cast in brass through the lost-wax method

(D) the oral tradition of storytelling through griots

(E) the acquisition of great wealth, mainly gold, through trading

9. A common purpose of the Truman Doctrine, the Marshall Plan, and the Eisenhower Doctrine was to

(A) provide medical aid to Latin American countries

(B) limit the proliferation of nuclear weapons

(C) carry out the U. S. policy of preventing the spread of communism

(D) ensure the survival of the newly independent nations in Africa and Asia

(E) reduce air, water, and soil pollution around the world

10. Which of the following was the major result of the Indo-European migration of the Vedic Aryans into India around 1500 B.C.?

(A) the establishment of the salt route across the Sahara Desert into the Middle East

(B) the creation of the Indian social system and Hinduism

(C) the building of the pyramids at Gaza and Abu Simbel

(D) the Mayan culture and society

(E) the development of a rich musical tradition

ANSWERS

1. **E**

2. **B**

3. **D**

4. **E**

5. **D**

6. **D**

7. **B**

8. **E**

9. **C**

10. **B**

Social Sciences: Content Knowledge (10951)

This 2-hour test contains 120 multiple-choice questions. You can expect the questions to be allocated as follows: sociology (48 questions), psychology (48 questions), and anthropology (24 questions). For the format of the questions, refer to the Social Studies: Content Knowledge sample test questions.

MATHEMATICS

Currently, the Praxis offers five tests in these related subject areas:

- Mathematics (calculator allowed) (10060)
- Mathematics: Content Knowledge (graphing calculator required) (10061)
- Mathematics: Pedagogy (30065)
- Mathematics: Proofs, Models, and Problems, Part 1 (graphing calculator required) (20063)
- Mathematics: Proofs, Models, and Problems, Part 2 (graphing calculator required) (30064)

Mathematics (Calculator Allowed) (10060)

This 2-hour test contains 110 multiple-choice questions. You can expect the questions to be allocated as follows: basic (precollege) mathematics (~42 questions), precalculus (~30 questions), advanced college mathematics (~27 questions), and teaching mathematics (~11 questions).

Mathematics: Content Knowledge (Graphing Calculator Required) (10061)

This 2-hour test contains 50 multiple-choice questions. You can expect the questions to be allocated as follows: basic mathematics (~17 questions); functions and calculus (~12 questions); and probability, linear algebra, discrete mathematics, computer science, and mathematical reasoning (~21 questions).

Practice Test Questions

Directions: Choose the correct answer to each item.

1. Which of the following is satisfied by integers under multiplication?
  I.   Closure
  II. Associativity
  III. Commutativity

  (A) I only
  (B) II only
  (C) II and III
  (D) I, II, and III
  (E) I and II

2. Which of the following is equal to i^{47}?

  (A) 1
  (B) -1
  (C) i
  (D) 1.1
  (E) $-i$

3. What is the exact angle between the hour and minute hands of a clock showing the time as 3:15?

  (A) 0°
  (B) 45°
  (C) 7.5°
  (D) 30°
  (E) 60°

4. If you flip a fair coin 20 times, what is the probability that it will come up heads every time?

  (A) 1/2
  (B) 1/20
  (C) $\left(\dfrac{1}{2}\right)^{20}$
  (D) $20^{1/2}$
  (E) 20%

5. $\lim\limits_{x\to\infty} \dfrac{x^7}{x^8 - 500}$ is ...

(A) ∞

(B) $-\infty$

(C) 0

(D) $-\dfrac{1}{500}$

(E) 1

6. A student at Princeton decided to estimate the population of squirrels on the campus. He captured and tagged 75 squirrels, which were then released. The following week, the student caught another 75 squirrels, and discovered that 15 of them were tagged. Assuming a random sample and that no squirrels died during that week, what is a good estimate of the squirrel population?

(A) 125

(B) 810

(C) 890

(D) 1,000

(E) 375

7. In which of the following intervals is the function $f(x) = \cos(x + \pi)$ strictly increasing?

(A) $\left(-\dfrac{\pi}{2}, \dfrac{\pi}{2}\right)$

(B) $(0, \pi)$

(C) $(0, 2\pi)$

(D) $(-\pi, \pi)$

(E) $(\pi, 0)$

8. At how many points on the xy plane do the graphs of $y = 0.25x^3 - x^2 + 4x$ and $y = 3x^2 - 5$ intersect?

(A) None

(B) One

(C) Two

(D) Three

(E) Four

9. Find the area of the region between the curve $y = 3x^2 - 2x^3$ and the x axis.

(A) 0.72

(B) 1.03

(C) 1.00

(D) 1.14

(E) 0.84

10. How many points with integral coordinates lie inside or on the boundary of the region bounded by $y = 0, x = 0$ and $y = -2x + 12$?

(A) 36
(B) 42
(C) 49
(D) 65
(E) 123

ANSWERS

1. D

2. E

3. C

4. C

5. C

6. E

7. B

8. D

9. E

10. C

Mathematics: Pedagogy (30065)

This 1-hour test consists of three essay questions, each weighted equally (one-third of the final score). The questions cover planning a lesson, teaching a lesson, and assessing a lesson.

Mathematics: Proofs, Models, and Problems, Part 1 (Graphing Calculator Required) (20063)

This 1-hour test has four parts: one proof (one-third of the final score), one model (one-third of the final score), and two problems (one-third of the final score).

Mathematics: Proofs, Models, and Problems, Part 2 (Graphing Calculator Required) (30064)

This 1-hour test has three parts: one advanced proof or model (one-third of the final score), one basic problem (one-third of the final score), and one advanced problem (one-third of the final score). Areas covered include arithmetic, basic algebra, geometry, functions, probability, discrete mathematics, functions, graphs, calculus, abstract algebra, and linear algebra.

SCIENCE

Currently, the Praxis offers 21 tests in these related subject areas:

- Biology and General Science (20030)
- Biology: Content Essays (30233)
- Biology: Content Knowledge, Part 1 (20231)
- Biology: Content Knowledge, Part 2 (20232)
- Biology: Content Knowledge (20235)
- Chemistry: Content Essays (30242)
- Chemistry: Content Knowledge (20241)
- Chemistry: Content Knowledge (20245)
- Chemistry, Physics, and General Science (10070)
- Earth Science: Content Knowledge (20571)
- General Science (10430)
- General Science: Content Essays (30433)
- General Science: Content Knowledge, Part 1 (10431)
- General Science: Content Knowledge, Part 2 (10432)
- General Science: Content Knowledge (10435)
- Physical Science: Content Knowledge (20481)
- Physical Science: Pedagogy (20483)
- Physics (30260)
- Physics: Content Essays (30262)
- Physics: Content Knowledge (10261)
- Physics: Content Knowledge (10265)

Biology and General Science (20030)

This 2-hour test contains 160 multiple-choice questions. You can expect the questions to be allocated as follows: history of science and technology (16 questions); molecular and cellular biology of prokaryotes and eukaryotes (24 questions); biology of plants, animals, fungi, and protists (32 questions); evolution (19 questions); ecology (21 questions); chemistry (16 questions); physics (16 questions); and earth and space science (16 questions). As you can tell from this list, a little more than half of the questions focus on biology.

Practice Test Questions

Directions: Choose the correct answer to each item.

1. Bacteria are classified as prokaryotes because they

   (A) have membrane-bound organelles
   (B) may be variously unicellular or multicellular
   (C) form colonies of cells incapable of free living
   (D) are human pancreatic cells
   (E) do not have a nucleus

2. All fungi are heterotrophs because they

   (A) provide nutrition for other organisms
   (B) obtain their nutrition from other organisms
   (C) engage in photosynthesis
   (D) do not have the ability to produce enzymes in their hyphae
   (E) are sophisticated multicelled organisms

3. You want to demonstrate Darwin's theory of natural selection to a class. Which of the following is the best visual to display to the class?

   (A) a photo of a flock of ostriches, with one ostrich clearly in the lead
   (B) a painting of gorillas
   (C) a photo of an iguana with its tail cut off
   (D) a slide showing varied kinds of fossils
   (E) a PowerPoint demonstration of Galapagos turtles

4. Who hypothesized that "simple" organisms emerge spontaneously and evolve to greater "complexity"?

   (A) Jean-Baptiste Lamarck
   (B) Charles Darwin
   (C) Charles Bonnet
   (D) Thomas Malthus
   (E) Stephen Jay Gould

5. A metal conductor is used in an electrical circuit. The electrical resistance provided by the conductor could be increased by

   (A) increasing the size of the circuit by 10 percent
   (B) decreasing the applied voltage on the circuit
   (C) decreasing the mass of the conductor
   (D) increasing the temperature of the conductor
   (E) increasing the amount of current flowing

6. Which of the following statements is true?

   (A) Fungi are grouped into one of six divisions, based primarily on their method of digesting nutrients.
   (B) Fungi differ from plants in several distinct ways; for instance, the cell walls of plants are composed of cellulose, whereas the cell walls of almost all fungi contain chitin.
   (C) Fungi reproduce sexually, through budding, regeneration, and spore production.
   (D) Common molds are not structurally unique because their hyphae lack septa, like most plants.
   (E) Molds are classified in a specific taxonomic and phylogenetic grouping.

7. Orthographic lifting occurs when

   (A) heat energy is transferred by movements of liquids and gases
   (B) cool air acts as a barrier over which lighter, warmer air rises
   (C) the percentage of soluble salt changes when passing through membranes
   (D) water changes directly into a solid such as ice
   (E) mountains act as barriers to the flow of air, forcing it to rise to get to the other side

8. A 4.0-kilogram box and a 1.0-kilogram crate fall from a height of 100 meters. After they fall for 2.0 seconds, the ratio of the box's speed to the crate's speed is

   (A) 1:1
   (B) 2:1
   (C) 1:2
   (D) 4:1
   (E) 1:4

9. What quantity of heat must be added to 15 grams of liquid water to raise its temperature by 20°C?

   (A) 30 calories
   (B) 100 calories
   (C) 300 calories
   (D) 900 calories
   (E) 1,200 calories

10. If it is 12:00 noon where you live and the chronometer reads 5:00 P.M. Greenwich time, you are 5 hours away from Greenwich. What is your longitude?

   (A) 5°W
   (B) 7°W
   (C) 175°W
   (D) 57°W
   (E) 75°W

ANSWERS

1. E

2. B

3. A

4. A

5. D

6. B

7. E

8. A

9. C

10. E

Biology: Content Essays (30233)

This 1-hour test contains three questions. The first question assesses your knowledge of molecular and cellular biology, the second question covers genetics and evolution, and the third question concerns biology and ecology. Each question counts as one-third of your total score. The essays are scored holistically on the 0–6 scale, with 0 being the lowest score.

Practice Test Question

Gregor Mendel used garden plants to study how traits were passed from one generation to another. He hypothesized that each trait is controlled by a distinct "factor" that manifests itself in one of at least two ways. How do we account for genes that do not have purely dominant and recessive alleles? What factors influence the way a gene is expressed?

Biology: Content Knowledge, Part 1 (20231)

This 1-hour test contains 75 multiple-choice questions. You can expect the questions to be allocated as follows: basic principles of science (13 questions); molecular and cellular biology (12 questions); genetics and evolution (11 questions); diversity of life, plants, and animals (19 questions); ecology (10 questions); and science, technology, and society (10 questions). The questions are written on the level that you can expect in an introductory college-level biology class.

For the format of the questions, refer to the Biology and General Science sample test questions.

Biology: Content Knowledge, Part 2 (20232)

Like the previous test, this 1-hour test contains 75 multiple-choice questions. You can expect the questions to be allocated as follows: molecular and cellular biology (16 questions); genetics and evolution (18 questions); diversity of life, plants, and animals (28 questions); and ecology (13 questions). The questions are written on the level that you can expect in an introductory college-level biology class.

For the format of the questions, refer to the Biology and General Science sample test questions.

Biology: Content Knowledge (20235)

This 2-hour test contains 150 multiple-choice questions. You can expect the questions to be allocated as follows: basic principles of science (12 questions); molecular and cellular biology (38 questions); genetics and evolution (23 questions); diversity of life, plants, and animals (45 questions); ecology (22 questions); and science, technology, and society (10 questions). While these questions are again written on the level that you can expect in an introductory college-level biology class, here they reflect the National Science Education Standards.

For the format of the questions, refer to the Biology and General Science sample test questions.

Chemistry: Content Essays (30242)

This 1-hour test contains three questions. The first question assesses your knowledge of structure or property correlations, the second question covers chemical reactions, and the third question concerns the impact of chemistry on society and technology. Each question counts as one-third of your total score.

Practice Test Question

Based on the half-cells $Cu°/Cu^{2+}$ (1.0 M) and $Zn°/Zn^{2+}$ (1.0 M) and the following diagram, provide the information asked for.

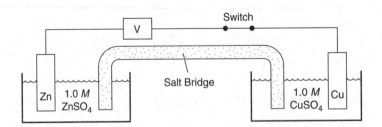

1. Oxidation half-reaction _____.
   Reduction half-reaction _____.
2. Label the anode and cathode.
3. Show the direction of the electron flow.
4. Show the direction of the ion flow.
5. Calculate E° for the cell.

ANSWERS

1. Oxidation: $Zn° \rightarrow Zn^{2+} + 2e^-$ $E° = +0.76$
   Reduction: $Cu^{2+} + 2e^- \rightarrow Cu°$ $E° = +0.34$
2. The diagram shows the copper ion is more easily reduced. Thus, the copper is the cathode and the zinc is the anode.
3. Electrons will flow from the anode (Zn) through the wire to the cathode (Cu).
4. In the salt bridge, positive ions flow toward the cathode and negative ions flow toward the anode.
5. E° for the cell   +0.52
   $\underline{+0.76}$
   1.28V

Chemistry: Content Knowledge (20241)

This 1-hour test contains 50 multiple-choice questions. You can expect the questions to be allocated as follows: atomic structure, chemicals, and chemical reactions (~12 questions); the mole, bonding, and geometry (~11 questions); solutions (~13 questions); and biochemistry and chemical reactions (~14 questions).

Practice Test Questions

Directions: Choose the correct answer to each item.

1. A pure sample of $KClO_3$ contains 71 grams of chlorine atoms. What is the mass of the sample?

   (A) 391 grams
   (B) 180 grams
   (C) 120 grams
   (D) 245 grams
   (E) 300 grams

2. Which of the following substances has the strongest intermolecular forces?

   (A) H_2
   (B) N_3
   (C) NH_3
   (D) CH_4
   (E) NA

3. Why would a chemist use a boiling water bath over a flame?

   (A) It is the traditional way to conduct experiments.
   (B) The water heats up more quickly, transferring the heat to the object in the water.
   (C) The volume of the boiling water does not change.
   (D) It is safer than any other method of heating water to 100°F.
   (E) The water's temperature remains constant.

4. How many calories are absorbed by 30.0 grams of water when the water temperature is raised from 20°C to 40°C?

   (A) 600 calories
   (B) 60 calories
   (C) 6 calories
   (D) 800 calories
   (E) 80 calories

5. Find the mass of 1 mole of glucose, $C_6H_{12}O_6$.

   (A) 18 grams
   (B) 180 grams
   (C) 280 grams
   (D) 800 grams
   (E) 80 grams

6. Calculate how many grams of magnesium are needed to produce 120 grams of magnesium oxide in the reaction $2Mg(s) + O_2(g) \rightarrow 2MgO(s)$.

   (A) 720 grams
   (B) 75 grams
   (C) 120 grams
   (D) 750 grams
   (E) 72 grams

7. The volume of a gas is 342 milliliters at 25.0°C and 730 torr. What is the volume of the gas at 146 torr, with the temperature unchanged?

   (A) 7,300 milliliters
   (B) 171 milliliters
   (C) 1,710 milliliters
   (D) 1,500 milliliters
   (E) 3,700 milliliters

8. Which of the following compounds is ionic?

   (A) $CaCl_2$
   (B) HCl
   (C) SO_2
   (D) N_2O
   (E) H_2O

9. A reaction chamber inside a calorimeter contains 150 grams of water at 19°C. After a reaction takes place in the chamber, the temperature of the water is 29°C. How many calories were released by the reaction?

   (A) 150 calories
   (B) 1,500 calories
   (C) 15 calories
   (D) 3,000 calories
   (E) 300 calories

10. What is the pH of a solution of 0.001 M hydrochloric acid?

   (A) 2.0
   (B) 1.0
   (C) 5.0
   (D) 4.0
   (E) 3.0

ANSWERS

1. D

2. C

3. E

4. A

5. B

6. E

7. C

8. A

9. B

10. E

Chemistry: Content Knowledge (20245)

This 2-hour test contains 100 multiple-choice questions. You can expect the questions to be allocated as follows: matter and energy (~16 questions); atomic energy (~10 questions); the mole, chemical bonding, and solutions (~14 questions); organic chemistry, the periodic table, biochemistry, and chemical reactions (~23 questions); solutions and stability (~12 questions); history of science (~11 questions); and lab procedures and mathematics (~14 questions).

For the format of the questions, refer to the Chemistry: Content Knowledge sample test questions.

Chemistry, Physics, and General Science (10070)

This 2-hour test contains 140 multiple-choice questions. You can expect the questions to be allocated as follows: key concepts in chemistry, physics, energy, and matter (~28 questions); chemistry, the mole, solutions, and safety (~42 questions); heat, electricity, and nuclear physics (~42 questions); earth and space science (~14 questions); and life science (~14 questions).

For the format of the questions, refer to the Chemistry: Content Knowledge sample test questions.

Earth Science: Content Knowledge (20571)

This 2-hour test contains 100 multiple-choice questions. You can expect the questions to be allocated as follows: basic principles of earth and space science (~10 questions), tectonics (~20 questions), earth materials and surface processes (~25 questions), history of the earth and life forms (~15 questions), the atmosphere (~20 questions), and astronomy (~10 questions). All questions are written on the level that you can expect in an introductory college-level earth science class.

Practice Test Questions

Directions: Choose the correct answer to each item.

1. Which of the following is evidence of the earth's shape?

   (A) People weigh less at the poles than at the equator.
   (B) People weigh the same at the equator and at the poles.
   (C) The latitude is the same at the equator and at the poles.
   (D) People weigh the same amount no matter where they stand.
   (E) People weigh more at the poles than at the equator.

2. Which is the softest mineral on the Mohs scale of hardness?

   (A) calcite
   (B) talc

(C) feldspar

(D) topaz

(E) apatite

3. If you wanted to construct a mountain the size of Mt. Everest (8.8 kilometers) to scale on a relief globe, how high would you draw that mountain? Assume the average diameter of the earth is 12,735 kilometers and the relief globe, 20 centimeters. Express your answer in centimeters.

(A) 0.014 centimeters

(B) 0.14 centimeters

(C) 1.4 centimeters

(D) 15 centimeters

(E) 30 centimeters

4. The following graph shows P- and S-wave travel times during an earthquake. Which of the following statements about this graph is true?

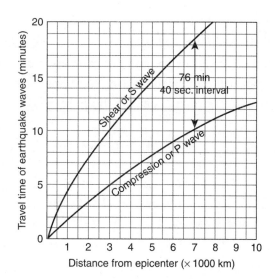

(A) The graph shows that different types of seismic waves travel at the same speeds.

(B) The graph shows that different types of seismic waves arrive at a seismograph station in a definite order: first the S waves and then the P waves.

(C) The graph shows a difference of 7 minutes, 40 seconds, which gives a distance of 40 kilometers from the epicenter.

(D) The graph shows that the sum of the travel times of the P waves and S waves can be used to determine the distance from a seismograph station to the epicenter of an earthquake.

(E) The graph shows that all earthquakes can be predicted and tracked to a remarkable degree of accuracy.

5. What does the information on this diagram indicate?

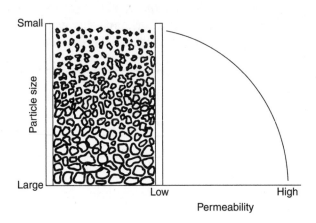

(A) Larger particles will be crushed by the weight of the smaller ones on top.

(B) An aquifer is a natural pipeline through which water can move freely.

(C) The level of the water cycle varies as the zone of saturation changes.

(D) The permeability of a material is directly related to the particle size.

(E) Larger particles have greater porosity because the pore spaces are larger.

6. Which of the following provides evidence of the effect of wind on currents?

(A) Warm currents begin at the South Pole and flow north.

(B) In low latitudes, surface water moves eastward with the trade winds. In higher latitudes, it moves westward with the westerlies.

(C) In high latitudes, surface water moves westward with the trade winds. In lower latitudes, it moves eastward with the westerlies.

(D) In low latitudes, surface water moves westward with the trade winds. In higher latitudes, it moves eastward with the westerlies.

(E) Equal heating of the atmosphere on land and the oceans creates winds and circulation.

7. What happens when liquid is heated at the bottom of a beaker?

(A) The warm liquid rises and the cooler, denser liquid sinks, setting off conduction.

(B) The warm liquid rises and the cooler, denser liquid sinks, setting a convection cell in motion.

(C) The cool liquid rises and the warmer, denser liquid sinks, creating radiation.

(D) The liquid evaporates quickly, leaving a salty residue behind.

(E) The warm liquid rises and the cooler, denser liquid sinks, creating isotherms.

8. What is the relationship between air temperature and atmospheric pressure?

(A) equal
(B) inverse
(C) falling
(D) rising
(E) unrelated

9. The abundance of lakes, valleys, mountains, and fertile soil in North America is evidence of which of the following?

(A) the glaciers that covered parts of the continent during the Pleistocene epoch
(B) natural selection and survival of the fittest
(C) continental drift
(D) contact metamorphism
(E) the inheritance of acquired characteristics

10. The early Greeks felt that the earth was at rest at the center of the universe, a theory called

(A) retrograde
(B) heliocentric
(C) geocentric
(D) orbital
(E) cosmology

ANSWERS

1. E

2. B

3. A

4. C

5. E

6. D

7. E

8. B

9. A

10. C

General Science (10430)

This 2-hour test contains 120 multiple-choice questions. You can expect the questions to be allocated equally, as follows: biology (30 questions), chemistry (30 questions), physics (30 questions), and earth/space science (30 questions).

For the format of the questions, refer to the Biology and General Science sample test questions.

General Science: Content Essays (30433)

This 1-hour test contains three essay questions, one each in physical science, life science, and earth/space science. Each question counts as one-third of your total score.

For the format of the essay questions, refer to the Biology: Content Essay sample test questions.

General Science: Content Knowledge, Part 1 (10431)

This 1-hour test contains 60 multiple-choice questions. You can expect the questions to be allocated equally, as follows: math measurement/data and lab safety (~14 questions), basic principles of science (~14 questions), life sciences (~13 questions), and earth/space science/technology (~19 questions).

For the format of the questions, refer to the Biology and General Science sample test questions.

General Science: Content Knowledge, Part 2 (10432)

This 1-hour test contains 60 multiple-choice questions. You can expect the questions to be allocated equally, as follows: physics (~16 questions), chemistry (~16 questions), life sciences (~11 questions), and earth/space science/technology (~17 questions).

For the format of the questions, refer to the Biology and General Science sample test questions.

General Science: Content Knowledge (10435)

This 2-hour test contains 120 multiple-choice questions. You can expect the questions to be allocated equally, as follows: scientific technology, techniques, and history (~12 questions); physical sciences (~48 questions); life sciences (~24 questions); earth sciences (~24 questions); and science, technology, and society (~12 questions).

For the format of the questions, refer to the Biology and General Science sample test questions.

Physical Science: Content Knowledge (20481)

This 1-hour test contains 60 multiple-choice questions. You can expect the questions to be allocated as follows: methodology—math, measurement; data—science, technology, society (~20 questions); matter and energy, laboratory procedures (~22 questions); and heat/thermodynamics and atomic energy (~18 questions).

For the format of the questions, refer to the Biology and General Science sample test questions.

Physical Science: Pedagogy (20483)

This 1-hour test contains one essay involving instructional strategies and activities, assessment, and follow-up. The essay has several parts.

For the format of the essay, refer to the Biology: Content Essay sample test.

Physics (30260)

This 2-hour test contains 100 multiple-choice questions. You can expect the questions to be allocated as follows: heat/thermodynamics and environmental issues (~28 questions); mechanics (~25 questions); electricity and magnetism (~20 questions); and wave motion and atomic and nuclear physics (~27 questions).

Physics: Content Essays (30262)

This 1-hour test contains three essay questions, each counting as one-third of your grade. One question covers matter and energy, the second question covers fields and waves, and the third question covers science, technology, and society.

Physics: Content Knowledge (10261)

This 1-hour test contains 50 multiple-choice questions. You can expect the questions to be allocated as follows: mechanics (~20 questions), electricity and magnetism (~17 questions), optics and waves and special topics (~13 questions).

Physics: Content Knowledge (10265)

This 2-hour test contains 100 multiple-choice questions. You can expect the questions to be allocated as follows: mechanics (~32 questions), electricity and magnetism (~23 questions), optics and waves (~17 questions), heat and thermodynamics (~8 questions), atomic physics (~8 questions), and history of science (~12 questions).

THEATER

This 2-hour test contains 100 multiple-choice questions. You can expect the questions to be allocated as follows: history of theater and theater literature (19 questions), performance (21 questions), technical concerns (19 questions), production issues (15 questions), teaching theater (10 questions), and creative drama (16 questions).

You are expected to know the important plays throughout history, from the ancient Greek and Roman plays to those of the present. The test also covers children's theater, puppetry, mime, masks, clowning, and rhythm. In addition, the test assesses your knowledge of lighting, costumes, makeup, props, scenery, sound, directing, and producing.

Practice Test Questions

Directions: Choose the correct answer to each item.

1. All of the following refer to parts of a stage *except*

   (A) lobby
   (B) apron
   (C) fly space
   (D) back wall
   (E) the wings

2. *Hubris* is BEST defined as

   (A) a type of crude melodramatic comedy
   (B) perfect indifference to everything
   (C) a sophisticated variation on tragedy
   (D) a hidden trapdoor in the front part of the stage
   (E) excessive pride, often resulting in fatal retribution

3. *Improvisation* is an acting technique that emphasizes

   (A) building a scene carefully, step by step
   (B) giving lines in such a way that another actor can make a point or get a laugh
   (C) the art of acting without using words
   (D) the portrayal of a character or a scene without rehearsal
   (E) drawing from deep reservoirs of emotion and personal experience

4. In the Western world, medieval drama included all of the following types of plays *except*

   (A) miracle plays
   (B) mystery plays
   (C) liturgical dramas
   (D) passion plays
   (E) closet dramas

5. To show surprise, an actor should

   (A) squint the eyes, lower the brows, and close the mouth tightly
   (B) widen the eyes, lift the brows, and open the mouth to an "O" shape

(C) narrow the eyes and drop the lids, sag the facial muscles, drop the jaw and set it firmly

(D) furrow the brow, twist the mouth, and curl the lips outward

(E) close the eyes, pucker the lips, and jut the chin forward

6. The definition of tragedy and the tragic hero originated with

(A) Aristotle
(B) Euripides
(C) William Shakespeare
(D) Sophocles
(E) Aeschylus

7. Who is considered the father of modern drama and the father of realism?

(A) Henrik Ibsen of Norway
(B) Johann Wolfgang von Goethe of Germany
(C) Alexandre Dumas of France
(D) Anton Chekhov of Russia
(E) Eugene O'Neill of America

8. Which of the following playwrights is recognized as a modern master of tragedy?

(A) Edward Albee
(B) Wendy Wasserstein
(C) August Wilson
(D) Athol Fugard
(E) Arthur Miller

9. In general, costumes for musical plays should be

(A) coordinated with a single color scheme, usually red or blue
(B) simple, never elaborate, to allow for quick changes
(C) created in muted colors to prevent distraction
(D) bolder and more exaggerated than those used for straight plays
(E) created with classic lines and colors so they can be reused

10. Which of the following plays is an example of an allegory?

(A) *Romeo and Juliet*
(B) *Cyrano de Bergerac*
(C) *Everyman*
(D) *Man of La Mancha*
(E) *A Doll's House*

ANSWERS

1. A

2. E

3. D

4. E

5. B

6. A

7. A

8. E

9. D

10. C

PART 7

Nine Practice PPST Exams and Answer Keys

READING PRACTICE TEST 1

Answer sheet

1 Ⓐ Ⓑ Ⓒ Ⓓ Ⓔ
2 Ⓐ Ⓑ Ⓒ Ⓓ Ⓔ
3 Ⓐ Ⓑ Ⓒ Ⓓ Ⓔ
4 Ⓐ Ⓑ Ⓒ Ⓓ Ⓔ
5 Ⓐ Ⓑ Ⓒ Ⓓ Ⓔ
6 Ⓐ Ⓑ Ⓒ Ⓓ Ⓔ
7 Ⓐ Ⓑ Ⓒ Ⓓ Ⓔ

8 Ⓐ Ⓑ Ⓒ Ⓓ Ⓔ
9 Ⓐ Ⓑ Ⓒ Ⓓ Ⓔ
10 Ⓐ Ⓑ Ⓒ Ⓓ Ⓔ
11 Ⓐ Ⓑ Ⓒ Ⓓ Ⓔ
12 Ⓐ Ⓑ Ⓒ Ⓓ Ⓔ
13 Ⓐ Ⓑ Ⓒ Ⓓ Ⓔ
14 Ⓐ Ⓑ Ⓒ Ⓓ Ⓔ

15 Ⓐ Ⓑ Ⓒ Ⓓ Ⓔ
16 Ⓐ Ⓑ Ⓒ Ⓓ Ⓔ
17 Ⓐ Ⓑ Ⓒ Ⓓ Ⓔ
18 Ⓐ Ⓑ Ⓒ Ⓓ Ⓔ
19 Ⓐ Ⓑ Ⓒ Ⓓ Ⓔ
20 Ⓐ Ⓑ Ⓒ Ⓓ Ⓔ
21 Ⓐ Ⓑ Ⓒ Ⓓ Ⓔ

22 Ⓐ Ⓑ Ⓒ Ⓓ Ⓔ
23 Ⓐ Ⓑ Ⓒ Ⓓ Ⓔ
24 Ⓐ Ⓑ Ⓒ Ⓓ Ⓔ
25 Ⓐ Ⓑ Ⓒ Ⓓ Ⓔ
26 Ⓐ Ⓑ Ⓒ Ⓓ Ⓔ
27 Ⓐ Ⓑ Ⓒ Ⓓ Ⓔ
28 Ⓐ Ⓑ Ⓒ Ⓓ Ⓔ

29 Ⓐ Ⓑ Ⓒ Ⓓ Ⓔ
30 Ⓐ Ⓑ Ⓒ Ⓓ Ⓔ
31 Ⓐ Ⓑ Ⓒ Ⓓ Ⓔ
32 Ⓐ Ⓑ Ⓒ Ⓓ Ⓔ
33 Ⓐ Ⓑ Ⓒ Ⓓ Ⓔ
34 Ⓐ Ⓑ Ⓒ Ⓓ Ⓔ
35 Ⓐ Ⓑ Ⓒ Ⓓ Ⓔ

36 Ⓐ Ⓑ Ⓒ Ⓓ Ⓔ
37 Ⓐ Ⓑ Ⓒ Ⓓ Ⓔ
38 Ⓐ Ⓑ Ⓒ Ⓓ Ⓔ
39 Ⓐ Ⓑ Ⓒ Ⓓ Ⓔ
40 Ⓐ Ⓑ Ⓒ Ⓓ Ⓔ

READING PRACTICE TEST 1

40 questions, 60 minutes

Directions: Each of the following passages is followed by questions. Answer the questions based on what is directly stated or suggested in each passage. Indicate your answers by filling in the corresponding circle on your answer sheet.

Questions 1–4

The size of the bottlenose dolphin varies considerably from place to place. The largest on record are a 12.7-foot male from the Netherlands and a 10.6-foot female from the Bay of Biscay. The heaviest dolphin on record weighed in at 1,430 pounds. A newborn calf, in contrast, is 38.5 to 49.6 inches long and weighs between 20 to 25 pounds.

(5)   Dolphins are fish eaters. In the wild, the bottlenose feed on squid, shrimp, and a wide variety of fishes. In some waters, the bottlenose have gotten in the habit of following shrimp boats, eating what the shrimpers miss or throw away. They often hunt as a team, herding small fish ahead of them and picking off the ones that don't stay with the rest of the group. A U.N. report claims that a group of dolphins off the California coast

(10) eats 300,000 tons of anchovies each year, whereas commercial fishermen take only 110,000 tons.

1. According to the author, the largest dolphin ever measured was

   (A) a newborn calf
   (B) female
   (C) remarkably similar to smaller whales
   (D) from the Bay of Biscay
   (E) from the Netherlands

2. Which of the following conclusions can you draw from this passage?

   (A) The size to which dolphins grow depends on their location.
   (B) Dolphins are fierce predators, as dangerous as sharks.
   (C) Dolphins are social creatures.
   (D) Dolphins live only in the wild.
   (E) Dolphins can be trained to do tricks and communicate in basic ways with humans.

3. Some dolphins follow shrimp boats because

   (A) dolphins like to eat anchovies
   (B) this is a hunting technique they use
   (C) shrimpers make the dolphins into pets
   (D) dolphins eat a lot
   (E) they pick up the shrimp that the shrimp boats leave behind

4. You can infer from the information in this passage that

(A) dolphins consume a great deal of food
(B) fishermen do not like dolphins
(C) the amount that dolphins eat depends on the season
(D) dolphins eat relatively little, especially when their size is factored in
(E) dolphins are very picky eaters

Questions 5–6

According to the National Academy of Sciences, earth's surface temperature has risen by about 1°F in the past century, with accelerated warming during the past two decades. There is new and stronger evidence that most of the warming over the last 50 years is attributable to human activities. Human activities have altered the chemi-
(5) cal composition of the atmosphere through the buildup of greenhouse gases— primarily carbon dioxide, methane, and nitrous oxide. The heat-trapping property of these gases is undisputed although uncertainties exist about exactly how earth's climate responds to them.

5. The writer repeats the phrase "human activities" for all of the following reasons *except* to

(A) ensure clarity
(B) create emphasis
(C) provide specific details and description
(D) help readers follow the flow of ideas
(E) lead from one idea to the next

6. The next paragraph of this essay will most likely

(A) explain what people can do to stop global warming
(B) trace how the National Academy of Sciences began and elucidate its role today
(C) list other greenhouse gases
(D) suggest ways that the world's meteorological conditions respond to greenhouse gases
(E) illustrate the heat-trapping properties of greenhouse gases

7. Knowing the classics can help us understand the formal rules by which literature is "played." So much of the literature of any generation is a response to earlier models, and knowing these models helps. At the same time, reading the classics and recent literature together can make us aware of how the past differs from our own time. Certain pairings of works have become standard: You read one as a revision of the other or as a way of seeing the same world through entirely different eyes.

Which of the following statements would the author most likely endorse?

(A) Students should learn the classics before they study any modern works.
(B) Students do not understand the value of the classics, to their detriment.
(C) Classics reveal that the past is not as different from the present as we suppose.
(D) Among the most useful books are contemporary novels that rewrite the classics in language and style that students can understand.
(E) The classics and contemporary literature can go hand in hand in a classroom.

Questions 8–10

> To raise meat output, livestock producers in the United States have adopted new, intensive rearing techniques relying on grains and legumes to feed their animals. For example, farmers have moved nearly all of the pigs and poultry in industrial countries into giant indoor feeding facilities. There, they eat carefully measured rations of
> (5) energy-rich grain and protein-rich soybean meal. Cattle everywhere still spend most of their time dining outdoors, although beef producers—particularly in the United States, but also in Russia, South Africa, and Japan—supplement that roughage with grain in the months before slaughter. By contrast, Australian and South American cattle graze their entire lives, and European beef comes mostly from dairy herds, which eat less grain than
> (10) American beef herds.

8. The primary purpose of this passage is to

(A) evaluate the efforts of American livestock farmers to increase cattle production
(B) explain the new methods that livestock farmers use to increase yields
(C) outline the reasons why fresh livestock methods are superior to traditional ones
(D) argue that all livestock should be fed grains rather than recycled meat products
(E) compare and contrast domestic and foreign methods of rearing livestock

9. Which of the following statements best summarizes this passage?

(A) American livestock farmers have raised livestock yield through new techniques, including raising animals indoors on enriched food, while farmers in other countries continue to use older methods.
(B) Australian and South American cattle graze their entire lives, unlike American cattle.
(C) European beef comes mostly from dairy herds, which eat less grain than American beef herds.
(D) Increasingly, livestock are fed precise measures of enriched grain and protein-rich soybean meal.
(E) American beef is far superior to foreign beef—both in yield and in taste—because of our new methods of raising animals.

10. This passage is developed primarily through

(A) time order
(B) comparison and contrast
(C) most to least important details
(D) least to most important details
(E) advantages and disadvantages

11. Technical communication is the process of gathering information from experts and presenting it to an audience in a clear, logical, and easily understandable form. Technical communicators gather knowledge from experts by conducting interviews and reading previously published material. The technical communicator then studies the audience and determines the best way to present the information. Should it be via a Web site? A book? A brochure? An illustration? A chart? The technical communicator reshapes the information so that the audience can easily understand and act upon it.

According to the information in this passage, you can infer that a technical communicator strives to

(A) present the same information in a wide variety of forms
(B) "spin" the information to make the message more acceptable to a wide audience
(C) conduct extensive original research
(D) sell a product or a service to a client
(E) make the writing clear and easy to understand

Questions 12–16

Tell General Howard I know his heart. What he told me before, I have in my heart. I am tired of fighting. Our chiefs are killed. Looking Glass is dead. Toohoolhoolzote is dead. The old men are all dead. It is the young men who say yes and no. He who led on the young men is dead. It is cold and we have no blankets. The little children are freezing to
(5) death. My people, some of them, have run away to the hills and have no blankets, no food: no one where they are—perhaps freezing to death. I want to have time to look for my children and see how many I can find. Maybe I shall find them among the dead. Hear me, my chiefs. I am tired; my heart is sick and sad. From where the sun now stands, I will fight no more forever.

12. Chief Joseph's reasons for deciding to "fight no more forever" include all of the following *except*

(A) the chiefs have been killed
(B) he is dying
(C) it is cold and his people have no shelter
(D) his people are starving
(E) the leader of the young warriors has died

13. Rather than fighting, Chief Joseph wants time to

(A) negotiate honorable surrender terms with the federal government
(B) escape to Canada from the tribe's home in Oregon
(C) fight one last battle and then never fight again
(D) meet with General Howard, with whom he has an understanding
(E) look for his scattered children

14. Who are Looking Glass and Toohoolhoolzote?

(A) young men in the tribe
(B) other Native Americans who are helping the tribe negotiate with the federal government
(C) Chief Joseph's favorite children
(D) great chiefs of his tribe
(E) historical leaders, long dead before the time of this speech

15. The phrase "It is the young men who say yes and no" is best understood to mean

(A) even the young men cannot save them now
(B) Chief Joseph laments the necessity of having the tribe led by inexperienced men
(C) young men are better leaders than older men
(D) Chief Joseph has been forced from power by the young men
(E) young men cannot be trusted as older men can

16. The *tone* of this speech is best described as

(A) ironic
(B) somber and despairing
(C) resigned and thoughtful
(D) hopeful
(E) combative

17. The literature log or response journal is a basic tool for informal, exploratory writing about literature. Here the student uses writing in a spirit of discovery in order to think about the reading. The thinking-on-paper technique can take a wide variety of forms and serve a number of specific purposes, all of which engage the reader personally and meaningfully with the literature being studied and the ideas it suggests. Some useful approaches include noticing, connecting, wondering, and speculating.

It can be inferred from the paragraph that literature logs can be used for all of the following purposes *except*

(A) to write formal research essays
(B) to investigate ideas about a reading
(C) to reflect on a reading
(D) to link ideas in the reading to the reader's own ideas
(E) to theorize about a work of literature

Questions 18–20

Distance learning has come a very long way in just a few short years. When it began, distance learning consisted of simple white papers you could download and tests you could e-mail to a school. Now, distance learning includes interactive instruction in a virtual classroom. Today you can speak to your classmates and instructors, post work, hold
(5) live discussions about the work, and complete group projects online. One online campus, the Virtual University, is even built in three dimensions using the new virtual technology. The university looks like a real campus with buildings, green space, meeting places, and a whole range of services. In the university, people (represented as digital avatars) move around campus and interact with one another.

18. According to this passage, today *distance learning* is best defined as

(A) simple e-mail tests
(B) basic evaluative forms downloaded from the Internet
(C) a traditional three-dimensional classroom with real people
(D) a clever board game
(E) an online meeting place enriched with various collaborative projects

19. Which statement would the author most likely agree with?

(A) Traditional classrooms are far superior to online instruction.
(B) Contemporary online instruction can offer an education comparable to traditional classroom instruction.
(C) The Virtual University is like a video game.
(D) Distance learning has not changed much in the past decade.
(E) Distance learning is much better than traditional classroom instruction.

20. The author of this selection is most likely a

(A) classroom teacher
(B) dissatisfied online student
(C) potential online student
(D) satisfied online instructor
(E) newspaper reporter

21. Recent studies have shown that biological changes that take place in puberty help prevent teenagers from being able to fall asleep as easily as they did when they were younger. On average, teenagers don't feel sleepy until 11:00 P.M. or even midnight. It has to do with circadian rhythms that govern every cell in the body.

The author of this passage will most likely

(A) describe how adults are equally sleep-deprived
(B) argue that sleep is essential to effective functioning

(C) explain ways that teenagers can get the sleep they need

(D) complain how lack of sleep makes adolescents unusually difficult to reason with

(E) argue that adolescents shouldn't be held accountable for their behavior because they are sleep-deprived

> Once I heard a fourth-grade teacher telling the parents of her class students: "In the spring we'll start a bonus program. The children will receive points for each book they read and extra points for classics." This veteran teacher, with 28 years of experience, clearly knew just what she meant by "classics." Moreover, she consid-
> (5) ered them sufficiently valuable reading to offer extra points to those nine-year-olds who read them. But what makes a classic a classic? In order to determine that, it seems necessary to determine what children's literature is supposed to be. By what standards do we judge it? Or is there something else at work? Is it the teachers, or the publishers, or the librarians?

22. Based on this introduction, you can infer that the essay that follows will

(A) castigate teachers for their poor choices of classroom literature

(B) describe some of the author's favorite childhood classics

(C) look at the various ways a classic earns that title

(D) explain the advantages of extra-credit reading projects in the primary grades

(E) compare and contrast contemporary classics and classics of the past

Questions 23–25

> Soon after the world's first oceanarium, Marineland, opened in Saint Augustine, Florida, its manager began to wonder whether a dolphin could be taught tricks to entertain visitors. So in 1949 he hired Adolph Frohn, who trained wild animals for a circus, to educate Flippy, a 200-pound male bottlenose. Within several weeks, Flippy was showing pleasure at being
> (5) educated by leaping into Adolph's arms!

23. Who trained the dolphin?

(A) Adolph Frohn

(B) a 200-pound male bottlenose

(C) the manager of Marineland

(D) Flippy

(E) he trained himself

24. Which statement is a fact?

(A) Marineland is the world's best oceanarium.

(B) Few people train wild animals as well as Adolph Frohn.

(C) Saint Augustine is a good place to vacation because of its many tourist attractions.

(D) Flippy is a very talented dolphin.

(E) Marineland is the world's first oceanarium.

25. What conclusion can be drawn from this passage?

(A) Dolphins' "voices" or "songs" are beautiful.
(B) Some dolphins can be trained in captivity.
(C) Dolphins are intelligent because they have huge brains.
(D) Fish know when dolphins are approaching by their vibrations.
(E) The relationship between brain size and intelligence is not known at this time.

Questions 26–31

... On the 18th of April at 11 at night, about 800 grenadiers and light infantry were ferried across the Bay to Cambridge, from whence they marched to Concord, about 20 miles. The Congress had been lately assembled at that place, and it was imagined that the General had intelligence of a magazine being formed there and that they were going to destroy it.

(5)   The people in the country (who are all furnished with arms and have what they call Minute Companies in every town ready to march on any alarm) had a signal, it is supposed, by a light from one of the steeples in town. Upon the troops' embarking, the alarm spread through the country, so that before daybreak the people in general were in arms and on their march to Concord.

(10)   About daybreak a number of people appeared before the troops near Lexington Common. When they [the American colonists] were told to disperse, they fired on the troops and ran off, upon which the Light Infantry pursued them and brought down about 15 of them. The troops went on to Concord and executed the business they were sent on, and on their return found two or three of their people lying in the agonies of death,

(15) scalped, with their noses and ears cut off and eyes bored out—which exasperated the soldiers exceedingly. A prodigious number of people now occupied the hills, woods, and stone walls along the road. The Light Troops drove some parties from the hills, but all the road being enclosed with store walls served as a cover to the rebels, from whence they fired on the troops. ... In this manner were the troops harassed in their return for 7 or 8 miles.

26. What story does the writer tell of the confrontation on Lexington Common?

(A) When the British told the colonists to disperse, the British fired first and the colonists pursued them. The Native Americans joined the battle on the American side.
(B) The British attacked the colonists, who fought back with great bravery and zeal.
(C) When the British told the colonists to disperse, the colonists fired first but the British pursued them.
(D) An unknown person fired, then a British soldier fired on an unarmed American. Finally, all the British soldiers started firing.
(E) The Americans gathered to fight off the invading British, who greatly outnumbered the rebels.

27. The writer's tone in the second paragraph is best described as

(A) carefully impartial
(B) horrified and dismayed

(C) astonished and amazed

(D) disdainful and condescending

(E) admiring and worshipful

28. The writer refers to the American colonists as *rebels* to

(A) show her sympathy for the British

(B) reveal her secret support for the colonists

(C) further the cause of American independence

(D) address her audience with respect

(E) indicate that the colonists were justified in their actions in this instance

29. The writer is most likely

(A) a British soldier

(B) an American colonist loyal to England

(C) an American rebel

(D) a visitor to America from Europe

(E) someone considering moving to America to join the colonists

30. The author includes the description "lying in the agonies of death, scalped, with their noses and ears cut off and eyes bored out" (lines 14–15) to

(A) convince readers that the difficulties between the British and Americans must be settled as soon as possible, and without any further violence

(B) make her narrative more compelling reading

(C) elicit pity for the rebel soldiers, oppressed by the British

(D) evoke sympathy for the British troops

(E) portray the Native Americans as brutal savages and justify their mass relocation and slaughter

31. This document is most likely a(n)

(A) letter to the editor of a Massachusetts newspaper

(B) plea for peace and moderation

(C) editorial for a colonial newspaper

(D) diary entry

(E) letter to a friend

Questions 32–35
The Donkey and His Purchaser

Aman wished to purchase a donkey, and agreed with its owner that he should try out the animal before he bought him. He took the donkey home and put him in the straw-yard with his other animals, upon which the new animal left all the others and at once joined the one that was most idle and the greatest eater of them all. Seeing this, the man put a halter on him and

(5) led him back to his owner. On being asked how, in so short a time, he could have made a trial

of him, he answered, "I do not need a trial; I know that he will be just the same as the one he chose for his companion."

32. This story is best described as

(A) nonfiction
(B) a legend
(C) a biography
(D) a fable
(E) humorous

33. Why did the man put the donkey with the other animals?

(A) to see how he behaved
(B) to cheat the seller
(C) to determine if the donkey was strong
(D) to see how well he got along with the other animals
(E) to assess his health

34. You can infer that the man is

(A) greedy and sly
(B) wise and careful
(C) nasty and potentially litigious
(D) foolish
(E) not fond of donkeys in general

35. The moral of this story is best expressed as:

(A) Appearances are deceptive.
(B) One good turn deserves another.
(C) It is best to prepare for days of necessity.
(D) Never trust your enemy.
(E) People are known by the company they keep.

Questions 36–40

Those who live near the sea feed more on fish than on flesh and often encounter that boisterous element. This renders them more bold and enterprising; this leads them to neglect the confined occupations of the land. They see and converse with a variety of people; their intercourse with mankind becomes extensive. The sea inspires them with a
(5) love of traffic, a desire of transporting produce from one place to another, and leads them to a variety of resources which supply the place of labor. Those who inhabit the middle settlement, by far the most numerous, must be very different; the simple cultivation of the earth purifies them, but the indulgences of the government, the soft remonstrances of religion, the rank of independent freeholders, must necessarily inspire them
(10) with sentiments, very little known in Europe among people of the same class.

36. In the context of the passage, the phrase "love of traffic" (line 5) most nearly means

(A) a desire to move goods from place to place
(B) an urge to drive
(C) an impulsive nature
(D) a passion for cars
(E) a craving for new sensations

37. According to the author, our character is shaped by all of the following forces *except*

(A) our environment
(B) our government
(C) our career
(D) our genetic background
(E) our religious beliefs

38. The author describes people who live near the sea as

(A) deeply religious
(B) indifferent to their neighbors and other people around them
(C) courageous and adventurous
(D) pure and simple
(E) independent but not physically strong

39. The author would be most likely to describe America as a

(A) "melting pot"
(B) "glorious mosaic"
(C) "crazy quilt"
(D) "salad bowl"
(E) "patchwork of people"

40. You can infer that the writer believes

(A) people in different parts of America will become *less* similar as time passes
(B) people in different parts of America will become *more* similar as time passes
(C) Americans will never get along with one another because they are too individual
(D) people from all over the world will come to America
(E) Americans will deplete their rich natural resources through overfarming, overfishing, and mining

STOP. This is the end of the Reading Practice Test 1.

READING PRACTICE TEST 1: ANSWERS

1. E. The detail is directly stated in this sentence: *The largest on record are a 12.7 foot male from the Netherlands . . .*

2. C. You can conclude that dolphins are social creatures because they work as a team to herd small fish ahead of them.

3. E. Some dolphins follow shrimp boats because they pick up the shrimp that the shrimp boats leave behind. This is directly stated here: *In some waters, the bottlenose have gotten in the habit of following shrimp boats, eating what the shrimpers miss or throw away.* Do not confuse this with choice B—*this is a hunting technique they use.* Eating leftover shrimp is not a hunting technique; rather, it's scavenging.

4. A. You can infer from the information in this passage that dolphins consume a great deal of food. The information comes from the following sentence: *A U.N. report claims that a group of dolphins off the California coast eat 300,000 tons of anchovies each year, whereas commercial fishermen take only 110,00 tons.* The contrast between the two amounts shows that dolphins are voracious eaters.

5. C. The repetition cannot provide specific examples, since only the same phrase is repeated.

6. D. The last sentence—*The heat-trapping property of these gases is undisputed although uncertainties exist about exactly how earth's climate responds to them*—provides a clear transition into ways the world's climate will respond to greenhouse gases. Thus, the second paragraph is most likely to suggest ways the world's meteorological conditions respond to greenhouse gases, as stated in choice D.

7. E. You can infer that the author believes the classics and contemporary literature can go hand in hand in a classroom from this statement: *At the same time, reading the classics and recent literature together can make us aware of how the past differs from our own time.*

8. B. The primary purpose of this passage is to explain the new methods that livestock farmers use to increase yields. The author states this in the first sentence: *To raise meat output, livestock producers in the United States have adopted new, intensive rearing techniques. . . .* The author is explaining these techniques, not judging their effectiveness, so choices A, C, and D are incorrect. The author does compare and contrast domestic and foreign methods of rearing livestock (choice E), but only to explain these methods more fully.

9. A. Choices B, C, and D are details, not the main idea. Choice E misrepresents the passage. While American beef may taste better, this passage does not say so—nor can this information be inferred from the details.

10. B. The author compares and contrasts American and foreign methods of raising livestock to explain how America's techniques are different.

11. E.   According to the information in this passage, you can infer that a technical communicator strives to make the writing clear and easy to understand from the following statements: *The technical communicator then studies the audience and determines the best way to present the information* and *The technical communicator reshapes the information so that the audience can easily understand and act upon it.* Choice A is incorrect because the technical writer is trying to find the best way to present the information. The technical writer doesn't distort the facts, so choice B is wrong. Much of the research is not original because it comes from secondary sources, so choice C is incorrect. Choice D is wrong because there's no mention of selling a product.

12. B.   Chief Joseph's reasons for deciding to "fight no more forever" include all of the following *except* that he is dying. Chief Joseph says: "I am tired; my heart is sick and sad." You cannot infer from this that he is dying, however. All the other choices are directly stated in the speech.

13. E.   Rather than fighting, Chief Joseph wants time to look for his scattered children. This is directly stated in the line: *I want to have time to look for my children and see how many I can find.* Choice B is partly correct—his Nez Perce tribe did try to escape to Canada from their home in Oregon—but this cannot be inferred from Chief Joseph's words. Choice A is again historically correct, since the tribe had negotiated honorable surrender terms with the federal government, but these terms were ignored. This question illustrates the importance of reading a text closely and not bringing in outside information, which may be factually or historically correct, but neither correct nor relevant in context.

14. D.   Looking Glass and Toohoolhoolzote are great chiefs of his tribe. This comes from the line: *Our chiefs are killed. Looking Glass is dead. Toohoolhoolzote is dead.*

15. B.   As used in context, the phrase "It is the young men who say yes and no" is best understood to mean that Chief Joseph laments the necessity of having the tribe led by inexperienced men. You cannot assume that he does not trust these leaders (choice E) or that Chief Joseph has been forced from power by the young men (choice D). In fact, just the opposite must be true if he has been charged with surrendering to the federal government. Since you can infer from the passage that older leaders are more valued than younger ones, choice A—*even the young men cannot save them now*—is not valid.

16. B.   The tone of this speech is best described as *somber and despairing.* The next closest choice—*resigned and thoughtful* (choice C)—is not quite as accurate a description. The other choices are far off the mark.

17. A.   Since the writer clearly explains that a literature log or response journal is a place for *informal, exploratory writing,* choice A—*to write formal research essays*—cannot be correct.

18. E.   According to this passage, today *distance learning* is best defined as an online meeting place enriched with various collaborative projects. You can infer this from the following detail: *Today you can speak to your classmates and instructors, post work, hold live discussions about the work, and complete group projects online.* "The Virtual University" is just that—existing solely online—so choice C (*a traditional three-dimensional classroom with real people*) is false.

19. B. The author would most likely agree that contemporary online instruction can offer an education comparable to traditional classroom instruction. Choice A is incorrect because the author describes the new elements of online instruction in a positive way, while choice E overstates the case. Choice D is contradicted in the first sentence; choice C denigrates online instruction, which is not the author's purpose.

20. D. Because of the positive tone, the most logical answer is *satisfied online instructor*. Since a newspaper reporter should have an unbiased tone, you can eliminate choice E.

21. C. Based on the factual tone, the author of this passage will most likely explain ways that teenagers can get the sleep they need. There is no support in the topic sentence for choice A, since the entire passage concerns teenagers, not adults. Since everyone knows that sleep is essential to effective functioning, choice B is illogical. Choices D and E are not in keeping with the neutral, dispassionate tone.

22. C. Based on this introduction, you can infer that the essay that follows will look at the various ways a classic earns that title. You can draw this conclusion from these questions: *But what makes a classic a classic? By what standards do we judge it? Or is there something else at work? Is it the teachers, or the publishers, or the librarians?*

23. A. The detail is directly stated in the following sentence: "*. . . he hired Adolph Frohn, who trained wild animals for a circus, to educate Flippy.*"

24. E. The only statement that can be verified in a valid reference source is contained in choice E: *Marineland is the world's first oceanarium.* Every other statement is an opinion, open to interpretation.

25. B. The only logical conclusion from the information here is that some dolphins can be trained in captivity. There isn't enough detail to support the other conclusions, even though some of them (such as choice E) are likely valid.

26. C. The writer says, "When they [the American colonists] were told to disperse, they fired on the troops and ran off, upon which the Light Infantry pursued them." There are no Native Americans in the account at all, so choice A cannot possibly be correct.

27. D. The writer's tone in the second paragraph is best described as *disdainful and condescending*. This is shown especially in the phrases *and have what they call Minute Companies* and *it is supposed*. This directly contradicts choice A, as the author is clearly biased toward the British. The writer is not *horrified and dismayed* or *astonished and amazed* until the brutality in paragraph 3, eliminating choices B and C. Overall the writer admires the British (choice E), but the tone of this passage is not worshipful toward them.

28. A. The writer clearly sets forth the events on that fateful day to convince readers that the colonial rebels are barbarians and the British soldiers were justified in their actions. This shows her sympathy for the British.

29. B. The writer's sympathetic account of the problems the British soldiers faced at the hands of American rebels and her familiarity with the situation suggests that she is a colonist loyal to the British. This directly contradicts choice C, *an American rebel.* A British soldier would most likely use the first-person point of view, so choice A cannot be correct. Choice D, *a visitor to America from Europe,* would not be as familiar with the situation. The same is true of choice E, *someone considering moving to America to join the colonists.*

30. D. Since the American rebels attacked the British and left them *lying in the agonies of death, scalped, with their noses and ears cut off and eyes bored out,* this description serves to evoke sympathy for the British troops, choice D. This is the direct opposite of choice C, *elicit pity for the rebel soldiers oppressed by the British.* Therefore, choice C cannot be correct. The description does make her narrative more compelling reading, choice B, but it is more than mere gratuitous violence. There are no Native Americans mentioned in the article, so choice E—*portray the Native Americans as brutal savages and justify their mass relocation and slaughter*—cannot be correct. Finally, while the writer may indeed want the difficulties between the British and Americans settled as soon as possible, there is no indication that she wishes to convince her readers of this, nor that she believes that further violence must be avoided. Therefore, choice A cannot be correct.

31. E. The informal tone suggests the document is a letter to a friend, choice E. The next best choice is D, *a diary entry,* but the tone suggests the document was intended for a specific audience. The writer would not be foolish enough to publish these sentiments in an *editorial for a colonial newspaper* (choice C) or *a letter to the editor of a Massachusetts newspaper* (choice A), with emotions running so high and such bloodshed going on. Since the document has such a marked bias toward the British, it cannot be *a plea for peace and moderation,* choice B.

32. D. Fables are short, easy-to-read, straightforward stories that teach a lesson, usually stated as a moral. Fables often feature animals that talk and act like people, although that is not the case here.

33. A. The man put the donkey with the other animals to see how he behaved before he finalized the sale. He discovered that the donkey was greedy and lazy. Choice D—*to see how well he got along with the other animals*—is close, but choice A is more precise.

34. B. That he would test the donkey's behavior before he finalized the sale shows that the man is wise and careful. Thus, choice D cannot be correct. He is not trying to cheat the seller in any way, just protect himself, so you can eliminate choices A and C. His feelings about all donkeys are not revealed—just his realization that this particular donkey is no good, so choice E is wrong.

35. E. By the donkey's behavior, you can infer that the moral of this story is best expressed as *People are known by the company they keep.*

36. A. In the context of the passage, the phrase *love of traffic* most nearly means a desire to move goods from place to place, which the author defines in context.

37. D. According to the author, our character is shaped by everything except our genetic background. All the other elements are explicitly mentioned in the passage.

38. C. The author describes people who live near the sea as courageous and adventurous. You can infer this from the following sentence: *Those who live near the sea feed more on fish than on flesh and often encounter that boisterous element. This renders them more bold and enterprising.*

39. A. The author would be most likely to describe America as a "melting pot" as Americans blend together to form a new nation.

40. D. From his admiring tone, you can infer that the writer believes people from all over the world will come to America.

Skills Spread

Skill Type	Item Numbers
Literal understanding	1, 3, 5, 6, 8, 10, 12, 13, 14, 17, 23, 24, 26, 28, 33, 34, 37
Inferential and critical understanding	2, 4, 7, 9, 11, 15, 16, 18, 19, 20, 21, 22, 25, 27, 29, 30, 31, 32, 35, 36, 38, 39, 40

WRITING PRACTICE TEST 1

Answer sheet

1 Ⓐ Ⓑ Ⓒ Ⓓ Ⓔ
2 Ⓐ Ⓑ Ⓒ Ⓓ Ⓔ
3 Ⓐ Ⓑ Ⓒ Ⓓ Ⓔ
4 Ⓐ Ⓑ Ⓒ Ⓓ Ⓔ
5 Ⓐ Ⓑ Ⓒ Ⓓ Ⓔ
6 Ⓐ Ⓑ Ⓒ Ⓓ Ⓔ
7 Ⓐ Ⓑ Ⓒ Ⓓ Ⓔ

8 Ⓐ Ⓑ Ⓒ Ⓓ Ⓔ
9 Ⓐ Ⓑ Ⓒ Ⓓ Ⓔ
10 Ⓐ Ⓑ Ⓒ Ⓓ Ⓔ
11 Ⓐ Ⓑ Ⓒ Ⓓ Ⓔ
12 Ⓐ Ⓑ Ⓒ Ⓓ Ⓔ
13 Ⓐ Ⓑ Ⓒ Ⓓ Ⓔ
14 Ⓐ Ⓑ Ⓒ Ⓓ Ⓔ

15 Ⓐ Ⓑ Ⓒ Ⓓ Ⓔ
16 Ⓐ Ⓑ Ⓒ Ⓓ Ⓔ
17 Ⓐ Ⓑ Ⓒ Ⓓ Ⓔ
18 Ⓐ Ⓑ Ⓒ Ⓓ Ⓔ
19 Ⓐ Ⓑ Ⓒ Ⓓ Ⓔ
20 Ⓐ Ⓑ Ⓒ Ⓓ Ⓔ
21 Ⓐ Ⓑ Ⓒ Ⓓ Ⓔ

22 Ⓐ Ⓑ Ⓒ Ⓓ Ⓔ
23 Ⓐ Ⓑ Ⓒ Ⓓ Ⓔ
24 Ⓐ Ⓑ Ⓒ Ⓓ Ⓔ
25 Ⓐ Ⓑ Ⓒ Ⓓ Ⓔ
26 Ⓐ Ⓑ Ⓒ Ⓓ Ⓔ
27 Ⓐ Ⓑ Ⓒ Ⓓ Ⓔ
28 Ⓐ Ⓑ Ⓒ Ⓓ Ⓔ

29 Ⓐ Ⓑ Ⓒ Ⓓ Ⓔ
30 Ⓐ Ⓑ Ⓒ Ⓓ Ⓔ
31 Ⓐ Ⓑ Ⓒ Ⓓ Ⓔ
32 Ⓐ Ⓑ Ⓒ Ⓓ Ⓔ
33 Ⓐ Ⓑ Ⓒ Ⓓ Ⓔ
34 Ⓐ Ⓑ Ⓒ Ⓓ Ⓔ
35 Ⓐ Ⓑ Ⓒ Ⓓ Ⓔ

36 Ⓐ Ⓑ Ⓒ Ⓓ Ⓔ
37 Ⓐ Ⓑ Ⓒ Ⓓ Ⓔ
38 Ⓐ Ⓑ Ⓒ Ⓓ Ⓔ

WRITING PRACTICE TEST 1

SECTION 1: MULTIPLE-CHOICE QUESTIONS

38 questions, 30 minutes

Directions: The following sentences require you to identify errors in grammar, usage, punctuation, and capitalization. Not every sentence has an error, and no sentence will have more than one error. Every sentence error, if there is one, is underlined and lettered. If the sentence does have an error, select the one underlined part that must be changed to make the sentence correct and blacken the corresponding circle on your answer sheet. If the sentence does not have an error, blacken circle E. Elements of the sentence that are not underlined are not to be changed.

Part A
21 questions

suggested time: 10 minutes

1. Yesterday afternoon, the writer read from his new book wearing glasses.
   .......A...............B...........C...................................D
   No error.
   ..E

2. Although some may disagree, it's true that the charms of conversation are
   ....A...................B
   more overpowering than beautifulness. No error.
   .........C.........................D...............E

3. Facing down hostility and prejudice with unshakable dignity and
   ....A.............................B
   playing that was superb, Robinson was named Rookie of the Year. No error.
   .........C.........................D.............................E

4. The small items sold well, but Strauss found himself stuck with the rolls of
   ....A...............................B
   canvass it was not heavy enough to be used for tents. No error.
   .....C.......................D.............................E

5. The glittering necklaces of Lisa Chin has earned high praise not only from the
   .........A...........................B.........................C
   critics but also from jewelry collectors the world over. No error.
   ....D...E

6. <u>Although</u> you use a computer spreadsheet <u>to keep track</u> of your
      A   B

    <u>investments, debts, and budget,</u> <u>one</u> must not overspend and rely on credit
                C   D

    to make up the shortfall. <u>No error.</u>
                       E

7. <u>The vacationers saw</u> the Ruyterkade schooner market in <u>Curaçao; in addition,</u>
          A   B

    they danced at <u>the carnival</u> in Charlotte Amalie, Saint Thomas, and <u>nearly spoke</u> to two
                  C   D

    dozen real West Indian sailors. <u>No error.</u>
                              E

8. At your <u>earliest</u> convenience, please take the time <u>to look over</u>
             A   B   C

    <u>the pamphlet that is enclosed with your family.</u> <u>No error.</u>
                    D   E

9. Just before midnight on <u>April 14, 1912,</u> one of the <u>more dramatic</u> and famous
                              A   B

    of all maritime disasters <u>occurred, the</u> sinking of <u>the</u> *Titanic*. <u>No error.</u>
                          C   D   E

10. After Louis <u>fractured</u> his leg in <u>a skiing accident,</u> he <u>is absent</u> from school
                  A   B   C

    <u>for a full</u> semester. <u>No error.</u>
      D   E

11. If <u>you</u> are upset over an <u>insult or affront</u>—even if it <u>occurred intentionally</u>
      A   B   C

    and maliciously—<u>one</u> should try not to hold grudges. <u>No error.</u>
                  D   E

12. Masses of white clouds <u>hanging</u> low above the <u>flat marshy plain</u> and
                          A   B

    <u>seemed to be</u> tangled in the tops of <u>distant palm</u> and cypress trees. <u>No error.</u>
      C   D   E

13. <u>During a fierce rainstorm,</u> <u>lightning</u> turns nitrogen in the atmosphere into an
            A   B

    <u>oxide the</u> nitrogen then falls with the rain and <u>fertilizes the soil.</u> <u>No error.</u>
      C   D   E

14. Hector has <u>scarcely no</u> money because he <u>is saving</u> all his <u>spare cash</u> to buy a
                    A   B   C
car; in addition, he <u>is contributing</u> to the family budget. <u>No error.</u>
                              D   E

15. One reason <u>for the abundance</u> of fresh produce in our <u>grocery stores</u> <u>is</u>
                          A   B   C
speeding trucks that carry food <u>great distances.</u> <u>No error.</u>
                                            D   E

16. Two bond traders, <u>Alice and her,</u> <u>were given</u> very large bonuses because
                              A   B
<u>their accounts</u> had performed <u>unusually well.</u> <u>No error.</u>
        C   D   E

17. You are <u>welcome to visit</u> the cemetery where <u>famous French composers,</u> artists,
                      A   B
and writers <u>lie buried</u> <u>daily except Sunday.</u> <u>No error.</u>
                    C   D   E

18. The resolution that <u>has just been</u> <u>agreed with</u> by the school board members will
                                  A   B
<u>result in</u> a 5 percent tax increase <u>in the upcoming</u> year. <u>No error.</u>
      C   D   E

19. Computerized grammar checkers <u>are software programs</u> that flag errors or
                                            A
doubtful usage <u>in a passage</u> so that <u>you can correct</u> these <u>writing problems.</u>
                        B   C   D
<u>No error.</u>
    E

20. <u>During the graduation ceremonies</u> the superintendent of schools told the story of
                          A
the desks and <u>cited their cleaning</u> <u>as evidence of</u> a new spirit of responsibility
                          B   C
<u>among students.</u> <u>No error.</u>
          D   E

21. The twins are fond of peanuts and <u>eating ice cream,</u> <u>but their parents</u> are loath
                                                  A   B
to give <u>the children</u> snacks <u>between meals.</u> <u>No error.</u>
              C   D   E

Part B
17 questions

suggested time: 20 minutes

Directions: Choose the best version of the underlined portion of each sentence. Choice A is the same as the underlined portion of the original sentence. If you think that the original sentence is better than any of the suggested revisions, choose A. Otherwise, choose the revision you think is best. Answers and explanations follow the questions.

22. Not only did people starve during the Irish potato famine in 1845 <u>but</u> they had no seed potatoes to use to grow the next year's crop, no food to fatten the pig or cow, and no money for the rent.

    (A) but   (B) but also   (C) so
    (D) also   (E) and

23. <u>A difficult time is had by many young people today</u> finding careers that are both pleasurable and profitable.

    (A) A difficult time is had by many young people today
    (B) Today, a difficult time is had by many young people
    (C) A difficult time is being had by many young people today
    (D) By many young people today, a difficult time is being had
    (E) Many young people today are having a difficult time

24. <u>The point that I am trying to make is that the</u> lists of the highlights in each genre of twentieth-century children's literature in the textbook *Discovering Children's Literature* echo the Bechtel and Egoff and Newbery selections almost title for title.

    (A) The point that I am trying to make is that
    (B) The
    (C) In a very real sense
    (D) That is to say
    (E) As a matter of fact

25. *Distance learning*, the business of helping people learn using online tools and delivery systems, <u>have grown</u> tremendously in recent years.

    (A) have grown   (B) has grown   (C) has grow
    (D) has growed   (E) have grow

26. Technical communicators can have a variety of job titles, such as writer, editor, illustrator, or Web designer <u>they work</u> in different media as the situation dictates.

    (A) designer they
    (B) designer, they
    (C) designer: They
    (D) designer; but they
    (E) designer; since they

27. Orphaned at age fourteen, Jackson became a war hero when he defeated <u>the British during the War of 1812.</u>

    (A) British during the War of 1812.
    (B) British during the war of 1812.
    (C) British during the War Of 1812.
    (D) British during the war Of 1812.
    (E) british during the War of 1812.

28. The 1961 Bay of Pigs invasion of Cuba, a revolt against Castro led by Cuban exiles, was a complete disaster, a serious blow to Kennedy at the beginning of <u>his'</u> administration.

    (A) his'   (B) his's   (C) he's   (D) his   (E) he

29. The book describes how parades help Americans <u>observe holidays celebrate their culture honor national and local heroes and mark historical events such as presidential inaugurations.</u>

    (A) observe holidays celebrate their culture honor national and local heroes and mark historical events such as presidential inaugurations.
    (B) observe, holidays celebrate, their culture honor, national and local, heroes and mark historical events such as presidential inaugurations.
    (C) observe holidays, celebrate their culture, honor national and local heroes, and mark historical events such as presidential inaugurations.
    (D) observe holidays, celebrate their culture, honor national, and local heroes, and mark historical events such as presidential inaugurations.
    (E) observe, holidays, celebrate their culture, honor national, and local heroes, and mark historical events, such as presidential inaugurations.

30. Once I heard a fourth-grade teacher tell the parents of her class: <u>In the spring we'll start a bonus program. The children will receive points for each book they read and extra points for classics.</u>

    (A) In the spring we'll start a bonus program. The children will receive points for each book they read and extra points for classics.
    (B) In the spring "We'll start a bonus program." The children will receive points for each book they read and extra points for classics.
    (C) "In the spring we'll start a bonus program." "The children will receive points for each book they read and extra points for classics."
    (D) "In the spring we'll start a bonus program. The children will receive points for each book they read and extra points for classics".
    (E) "In the spring we'll start a bonus program. The children will receive points for each book they read and extra points for classics."

31. The judges of the writing contest had eliminated all but three of the original candidates, and now their only problem was choosing the winner <u>from among</u> the remaining entrants.

    (A) from among   (B) from within   (C) from between
    (D) from inside   (E) to among

32. <u>You should learn how the sun can provide heat for buildings. There are</u> a few facts about your home's heating system that you should know.

    (A) You should learn how the sun can provide heat for buildings. There are

    (B) Before you learn how the sun can provide heat for buildings, there are

    (C) You should learn how the sun can provide heat for buildings there are

    (D) Learning by you should occur concerning how the sun can provide heat for buildings because there are

    (E) You should learn how the sun can be providing heat for buildings, so there are

33. It was so cold that the <u>mens'</u> noses, cheeks, and toes could turn black with frostbite in seconds.

    (A) mens'   (B) mens   (C) men's   (D) man's   (E) man

34. Consequently, they change careers after a <u>few years they may return to school for retraining or learn</u> new skills on their own.

    (A) a few years they may return to school for retraining or learn

    (B) a few years, they may return to school for retraining or to learn

    (C) a few years, for they may return to school for retraining or learn

    (D) a few years, may return to school for retraining or to learn

    (E) a few years, returning to school for retraining or learning

35. <u>Although it</u> has been estimated that many people are deprived of much-needed medical care in this country, especially follow-up visits and preventative medication.

    (A) Although it   (B) Since it   (C) In spite of the fact that it

    (D) It   (E) If it

36. According to some <u>sources nearly</u> one-third of all American children go to bed hungry each night, despite social welfare programs designed to combat hunger.

    (A) sources nearly

    (B) sources: nearly

    (C) sources, nearly

    (D) sources—nearly

    (E) sources; nearly

37. College financial aid officers claim the money would all be used if applicants looked <u>more thorough</u> for funds.

    (A) more thorough

    (B) thorough

    (C) more, thorough

    (D) more thorougher

    (E) more thoroughly

38. Have you ever heard the famous old <u>saying, "Lightning never strikes twice in the same place"</u>?

   (A) saying, "Lightning never strikes twice in the same place"?
   (B) saying, Lightning never strikes twice in the same place?
   (C) saying, "Lightning never strikes twice in the same place?"?
   (D) saying, "Lightning never strikes twice in the same place?"
   (E) saying "Lightning never strikes twice in the same place?"

STOP. This is the end of Section 1: Multiple-Choice Questions.

SECTION 2: ESSAY

30 minutes

Directions: Write an essay on the following topic. You will not receive any credit for writing on a topic other than the one given here. Plan your essay carefully and be sure to include specific examples and details that illustrate your point. Write your essay on your own sheets of paper. (On the real Praxis PPST test, paper for writing your essay will be provided.)

> You will not receive credit if you write on any other topic. For your response to be scored, you must write in English. You cannot write in a foreign language.

Read the opinion stated below:

> "Whenever you are asked if you can do a job, tell 'em, 'Certainly I can!' Then get busy and find out how to do it."
>
> —THEODORE ROOSEVELT

In an essay, agree or disagree with this statement. But be sure to support your opinion with specific examples from reading, your experiences, your observations, or the media.

The space below is for your notes.

WRITING PRACTICE TEST 1: ANSWERS

SECTION 1: MULTIPLE CHOICE

Part A

1. D.   This is a misplaced modifier: The modifier (describing words) is in the wrong place. The correct sentence should read: *Yesterday afternoon, the writer wearing glasses read from his new book.*

2. D.   This is a lack of parallel structure. The correct sentence reads: *Although some may disagree, it's true that the charms of conversation are more overpowering than the charms of beauty.*

3. C.   Remember that all elements in a sentence have to be in the same grammatical form. This is called parallel structure. *Superb playing*—not *playing that was superb*—parallels *unshakable dignity*, since both phrases comprise a noun modified by an adjective. The correct sentence reads: *Facing down hostility and prejudice with unshakable dignity and superb playing, Robinson was named Rookie of the Year.*

4. C.   This is a run-on sentence, the error occurring between the two independent clauses. Correct the sentence as follows: *The small items sold well but Strauss found himself stuck with the rolls of canvass because it was not heavy enough to be used for tents.*

5. B.   This question tests your knowledge of subject-verb agreement. The subject—*necklaces*—is plural. Thus, it requires a plural verb—*have earned*. All the other choices are incorrect. The correct sentence reads: *The glittering necklaces of Lisa Chin have earned high praise not only from the critics but also from jewelry collectors the world over.*

6. D.   This question tests consistency of pronoun use: Don't switch point of view in the middle of a sentence or passage. Since the sentence begins with the word *you*, the writer cannot switch to one in the middle of the sentence. The correct sentence reads: *Although you use a computer spreadsheet to keep track of your investments, debts, and budget, you must not overspend and rely on credit to make up the shortfall.*

7. D.   This is a misplaced modifier. The phrase *nearly spoke* means that the tourists <u>almost</u> spoke to the sailors. Since this sentence refers to the events the vacationers did indeed complete, the phrase should read *spoke to nearly*. The correct sentence should read: *The vacationers saw the Ruyterkade schooner market in Curaçao; in addition, they danced at the carnival in Charlotte Amalie, Saint Thomas, and spoke to nearly two dozen real West Indian sailors.*

8. D.   As written, the sentence states that the pamphlet is enclosed with the family. The writer means to say that the person should look over the pamphlet with their family. Here is a correct revision: *At your earliest convenience, please take the time to look over the enclosed pamphlet with your family.*

9. B.   Use the superlative degree (*most*) to show the comparison is among three or more objects or instances, which is the case here.

10. C. Use consistent tenses in a sentence. The past tense *fractured* requires the past tense *was* rather than the present tense *is*.

11. D. Use a consistent pronoun person. Since the sentence starts with the pronoun *you,* do not switch to the pronoun one. Rather, stay with the pronoun *you.*

12. A. This is a fragment because it is missing a complete verb. The sentence should read *were hanging* or *hung.*

13. C. This is a run-on sentence, two sentences incorrectly joined. Here are two correct versions of this sentence: *During a fierce rainstorm, lightning turns nitrogen in the atmosphere into an oxide; the nitrogen then falls with the rain and fertilizes the soil. During a fierce rainstorm, lightning turns nitrogen in the atmosphere into an oxide, and the nitrogen then falls with the rain and fertilizes the soil.*

14. A. The error is a double negative. Use *scarcely* (with *any*) or *no,* but not both together in the same sentence.

15. C. The plural subject *trucks* agrees with the plural verb *are,* not the singular verb *is.* Do not be misled by the singular predicate nominative *reason.* (A predicate nominative is a noun or a pronoun used after some form of *to be.*)

16. A. A pronoun used in apposition to a noun is in the same case as the noun. An appositive is a noun or pronoun placed after another noun or pronoun to identify or explain it. Here, the pronoun *she* must be in the nominative case because it is in apposition with the noun *bond traders,* which is also in the nominative case.

17. D. This sentence has a misplaced modifier, a phrase, clause, or word placed too far from the noun or pronoun it describes. As a result, the sentence fails to convey its intended meaning. As written, this sentence implies that the famous French composers, artists, and writers come back to life on Sundays! The sentence should read: *Daily, except Sunday, you are welcome to visit the cemetery where famous French composers, artists, and writers lie buried.*

18. B. The correct idiom is *agreed to,* not *agreed with.* The correct sentence reads: *The resolution that has just been agreed to by the school board members will result in a 5 percent tax increase in the upcoming year.*

19. E. The sentence is correct as written.

20. A. Place a comma after an introductory prepositional phrase (the preposition is *during*).

21. A. To correct the error in parallel structure, the sentence should read: *The twins are fond of peanuts and ice cream.*

Part B

22. B. Correlative conjunctions are used in pairs. The correlative conjunction is *not only . . . but also.*

23. E. Only choice E recasts the sentence in the active voice. Remember that the active voice is more concise and vigorous than the passive voice.

24. B.   Every one of the phrases listed is wordy. The sentence is best stated without any of the redundant openings.

25. B.   Use the singular verb *has* to agree with the singular subject *distance learning*.

26. C.   As written, the sentence is a run-on, two sentences run together without the correct punctuation. Since the second independent clause defines the first one, use a colon. If the second independent clause is a complete sentence, it is capitalized.

27. A.   The sentence is correct as written: Capitalize the names of nationalities and the primary words in the title of a battle.

28. D.   Since the administration belongs to Kennedy, a possessive pronoun is needed. This eliminates choice E. Possessive pronouns do not take an apostrophe, eliminating choices A and B. Choice C is wrong because it is a contraction for "he is."

29. C.   Separate items in a series with commas. Here, the items are clauses consisting of a verb, a noun, and (in some instances) some modifiers. Be sure to set off the complete clause. You can test the logic of your sentence by reading it aloud.

30. E.   Enclose all of the speaker's exact words with quotation marks. Thus, the sentences are incorrect as written. Also, choice B is wrong because it is not everything the speaker said. Choice C is incorrect because there is no reason to break this quotation into two parts. Periods are placed inside the quotation marks, so choice D is incorrect.

31. A.   This is a usage question. The sentence is correct as written because among is used to show a relationship among three or more people or things.

32. B.   Choice B correctly subordinates the first independent clause by using the subordinating conjunction *before*.

33. C.   To show possession in the plural noun *men*, add an apostrophe and an *s*.

34. E.   As written, the sentence is a run-on, that is, two sentences run together. Choice B does not correct the error because a comma is used within a sentence, not to join two sentences. The coordinating conjunction *for* is illogical, so you can eliminate choice C. Choice D does not make sense. Only choice E is correct and logical.

35. D.   As written, the sentence is a fragment, created by the subordinating conjunction *although*. Choices B, C, and E are all subordinating conjunctions, so they do not correct the error. By eliminating the subordinating conjunction—choice D—the sentence is correct.

36. C.   Use a comma after an introductory subordinate clause.

37. E.   Use an adverb (*thoroughly*) to modify or describe a verb (*looked*).

38. A.   The sentence is correct as written. Set off a direct quotation with a comma and quotation marks. The question mark goes outside the closing quotation marks because the entire expression is a question, not just the part in quotes.

Skills Spread

Specific Content Area	Item Numbers
Grammar and usage 13	1, 5, 6, 9, 10, 11, 15, 16, 25, 28, 31, 33, 37
Sentence structure 14	2, 3, 4, 7, 8 , 12, 13, 17, 21, 23, 26, 32, 34, 35,
Mechanics (punctuation, capitalization)	14, 18, 19, 20, 22, 24, 27, 29. 30, 36, 38
Diction (word choice) 11	
Essay	1

SECTION 2: ESSAY

The following model essay would receive a 6, the highest score, for its specific details, organization, and style (appropriate word choice, sentence structure, and consistent facility in use of language). It is an especially intelligent and insightful response.

Theodore Roosevelt said: "Whenever you are asked if you can do a job, tell 'em, 'Certainly I can!' Then get busy and find out how to do it." I fully agree with Roosevelt's statement; in fact, I have found it to be a credo for being successful in life.

My junior year in college, I started looking for a job to earn some extra money. I looked around at the various jobs available, but since I had never held a job before, I didn't have any useful skills. Eventually, I applied for a job in a supermarket as a cashier, where the manager asked me, "Can you work a cash register?" I responded truthfully, "I've never done it before, but I bet I could learn." For any business, hiring someone who needs training is always a risky venture. It costs the business money to train the new employee, and the employee could quit the next day or simply prove to be unwilling or unable to complete the tasks required by the job. I was able to complete the training quickly and was a very productive employee. I think the supermarket likely took the chance on me because I was eager and willing to learn new skills.

This past summer, I worked in an office, inputting data, making copies, sending faxes, and generally doing odd tasks that saved time for others. One day, my boss approached me with the address of a Web site and said, "There's a bunch of data on this site that I need sorted out and put into pie charts. Do you know how to do that?" I replied, "No, but I'm sure I can figure it out." She gave me a smile and as she walked off, said, "That's what makes you such a great employee—you're such a 'can-do' guy."

After two calls to tech support and one to the site administrator, I was able to retrieve the data from the site and make it into exactly the charts my boss needed.

My own experience shows that with determination, courage, and some hard work, you can get ahead on the job. Embracing challenges is the crucial factor in this equation, because it shows you have that "can-do" attitude. Theodore Roosevelt's bravery got him up San Juan Hill during the Spanish-American War. That same determination can help you climb every mountain, too!

MATHEMATICS PRACTICE TEST 1

Answer sheet

1 (A) (B) (C) (D) (E)
2 (A) (B) (C) (D) (E)
3 (A) (B) (C) (D) (E)
4 (A) (B) (C) (D) (E)
5 (A) (B) (C) (D) (E)
6 (A) (B) (C) (D) (E)
7 (A) (B) (C) (D) (E)

8 (A) (B) (C) (D) (E)
9 (A) (B) (C) (D) (E)
10 (A) (B) (C) (D) (E)
11 (A) (B) (C) (D) (E)
12 (A) (B) (C) (D) (E)
13 (A) (B) (C) (D) (E)
14 (A) (B) (C) (D) (E)

15 (A) (B) (C) (D) (E)
16 (A) (B) (C) (D) (E)
17 (A) (B) (C) (D) (E)
18 (A) (B) (C) (D) (E)
19 (A) (B) (C) (D) (E)
20 (A) (B) (C) (D) (E)
21 (A) (B) (C) (D) (E)

22 (A) (B) (C) (D) (E)
23 (A) (B) (C) (D) (E)
24 (A) (B) (C) (D) (E)
25 (A) (B) (C) (D) (E)
26 (A) (B) (C) (D) (E)
27 (A) (B) (C) (D) (E)
28 (A) (B) (C) (D) (E)

29 (A) (B) (C) (D) (E)
30 (A) (B) (C) (D) (E)
31 (A) (B) (C) (D) (E)
32 (A) (B) (C) (D) (E)
33 (A) (B) (C) (D) (E)
34 (A) (B) (C) (D) (E)
35 (A) (B) (C) (D) (E)

36 (A) (B) (C) (D) (E)
37 (A) (B) (C) (D) (E)
38 (A) (B) (C) (D) (E)
39 (A) (B) (C) (D) (E)
40 (A) (B) (C) (D) (E)

MATHEMATICS PRACTICE TEST 1

40 question, 60 minutes

Directions: Select the best choice for each item and mark the answer on your answer sheet.

1. In a deck of 52 cards, 13 of them are spades. What percentage of the cards are spades?

(A) 4 percent
(B) 13 percent
(C) 25 percent
(D) 40 percent
(E) 52 percent

2. On the ruler shown, the arrow most likely indicates:

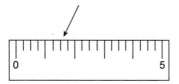

(A) $1^1/_2$
(B) $1^5/_8$
(C) $6^1/_2$
(D) $6^5/_8$
(E) $7^1/_2$

3. Which number falls between $^1/_4$ and $^4/_7$?

(A) 75%
(B) 0.1116
(C) 0.444
(D) $^{10}/_{14}$
(E) $^2/_3$

4. How many cubic feet of air are in a spherical balloon with a diameter of 6 feet?

(A) 9π
(B) 27π
(C) 36π
(D) 216π
(E) 288π

5. Five waitresses received the following tips. Whose was the least?

  (A) 15 percent of $100
  (B) 15 percent of $200
  (C) 10 percent of $200
  (D) 20 percent of $150
  (E) 15 percent of $150

6. Which point on the graph is located at (4,3)?

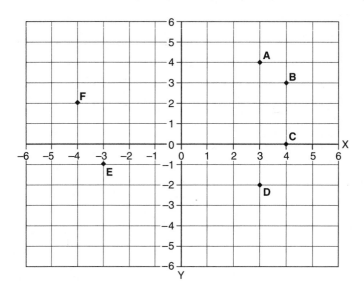

  (A) A   (B) B   (C) C
  (D) D   (E) F

7. If *y* is greater than *x*, and *x* is less than *z*, which of the following statements is true?

  (A) Quantity *z* is less than *y*.
  (B) Quantity *y* is equal to *z*.
  (C) Quantity *x* is the least of the three numbers.
  (D) Quantity *y* is the greatest of the three numbers.
  (E) None of these statements can be proven true.

8. If the hour hand of a clock is at exactly a 90° angle with 12, what time must it be?

  (A) 3:00   (B) 3:15   (C) 6:00
  (D) 12:15   (E) 9:45

9. If $x \div 3 = y$, what is $x \div 6$?

  (A) *y*   (B) $y \div 2$ (C) $y \div 3$
  (D) 2*y*   (E) 6*y*

10. In a fish tank, 4 fish are black, 3 are brown, and 5 are orange. What percentage are black?

(A) 4 percent
(B) 12 percent
(C) 25 percent
(D) 33.3 percent
(E) 40 percent

11. If the scale on a dollhouse is 1 inch = 1 yard, and a doorframe is 2.2 yards high, how high would you make a dollhouse-scale doorframe?

(A) 0.45 inches
(B) 1 inch
(C) 2.2 inches
(D) 4.4 inches
(E) 2.2 feet

12. How many square feet of carpet would you need to carpet the room pictured here?

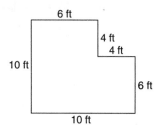

(A) 100   (B) 36   (C) 136
(D) 84   (E) 116

13. Which formula describes the relationship between X and Y?

X	Y
2	2
6	14
13	35
17	47
22	62

(A) $Y = X$
(B) $Y = 2X - 2$
(C) $Y = 3X - 4$
(D) $Y = \dfrac{X}{2} + 1$
(E) $Y = 2X + 2$

14. If $A = \frac{1}{8}r + 7$, and $r = 16$, then $A =$

(A) 2   (B) 9   (C) $2\frac{7}{8}$
(D) 3   (E) $\frac{7}{8}$

15. The floor of a room is 13 feet by 15 feet. Part of the floor is covered by a rug that measures 5 feet by 8 feet. If 1 quart of lacquer covers 10 square feet, how many quarts of lacquer are needed to lacquer the uncovered part of the floor?

(A) 4   (B) 6.25   (C) 15.5
(D) 19.5   (E) 23.5

16. Which pairs of decimals and fractions are equivalent?
I. $0.4, \frac{1}{4}$ II. $0.45, \frac{9}{20}$ III. $0.55, \frac{2}{5}$

(A) I only
(B) II only
(C) I and III
(D) I and II
(E) I, II, and III

17. Three friends go to a restaurant for dinner. When the bill comes, the tax on it is $4.47. If you know the tax rate is 8.75 percent, approximately how much should you leave as a 15 percent tip?

(A) $6.50   (B) $7.00   (C) $7.50
(D) $8.00   (E) $8.50

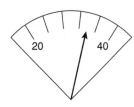

18. On the dial shown, the arrow most likely indicates:

(A) 23.5   (B) 24   (C) 34
(D) 36   (E) 38

19. Which of these fractions is the greatest?

(A) $\frac{3}{7}$ (B) $\frac{8}{5}$ (C) $\frac{13}{20}$
(D) $\frac{14}{5}$ (E) $\frac{11}{6}$

20. If $A = 6x - 2$, and $A = 22$, then $x =$

(A) 6   (B) 2   (C) 2.75
(D) 4   (E) 130

21. This graph represents 1 week of a store's performance. Using this graph, which statement can you determine is true?

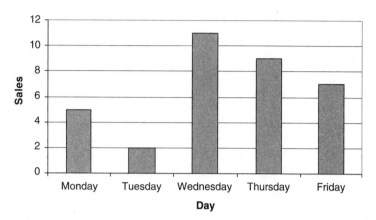

(A) Days with low sales always come before days with high sales.
(B) Wednesdays are always the best.
(C) Sales always decrease near the end of the week.
(D) The store will have very few sales on the following Monday.
(E) There were 34 total sales for this week.

22. A map is drawn to a scale of 1 inch = 4 miles. If the distance between two points on the map is 2.75 inches, what is the actual distance?

(A) 0.69 mile
(B) 1.45 miles
(C) 2.75 miles
(D) 4 miles
(E) 11 miles

23. If the probability of picking a blue sock from your drawer is 0.1, and you randomly pick 20 socks out of the drawer, about how many would be blue?

(A) 0   (B) 1   (C) 2
(D) 10   (E) 20

24. Which of these problems have the same numerical answer?
I. If you need 4 eggs to make a soufflé, and you have 18 eggs, how many soufflés can you make?
II. If you need 4 sandwiches to feed everyone at a picnic, how many picnics could you go on if you have 18 sandwiches?
III. If you can fit 4 glasses in a box, how many boxes do you need to hold 18 glasses?

(A) I and II
(B) I and III
(C) II and III
(D) I, II, and III
(E) None of the above

25. To convert meters to centimeters, you should:

    (A) Divide by 10
    (B) Multiply by 10
    (C) Divide by 100
    (D) Multiply by 100
    (E) Divide by 1,000

26. Which answer is closest to 0.0023×0.4?

    (A) 0.08
    (B) 0.008
    (C) 0.0008
    (D) 0.00008
    (E) 0.000008

27. Last week, you spent \$26 on gasoline. This week, you spent \$30. If you know you used the same amount of gasoline both weeks, what is the percent increase in the price of gas?

    (A) 13.3 percent
    (B) 15.4 percent
    (C) 26.0 percent
    (D) 86.7 percent
    (E) 115.4 percent

28. Using the ruler shown, approximately how long is the line?

    (A) $3^{1}/_{2}$ (B) $4^{1}/_{4}$ (C) $^{3}/_{4}$
    (D) 17   (E) 14

29. Which answer is closest to $2{,}991 \times 14{,}874$?

    (A) 4,500,000
    (B) 4,700,000
    (C) 43,000,000
    (D) 45,000,000
    (E) 470,000,000

30. If you roll 2 six-sided dice, what is the probability that the combined total shown will be less than 5?

    (A) $^{1}/_{6}$ (B) $^{7}/_{36}$ (C) $^{1}/_{12}$
    (D) $^{3}/_{36}$ (E) 0

31. Jennifer catered a party and made 300 cream puffs. The party planners were expecting 147 people to come to the party. About how many cream puffs did Jennifer estimate each person would eat?

(A) 1   (C) 2   (E) 3
(B) 1.5   (D) 2.5

32. If 52 more people were expected at the party, how many more cream puffs would Jennifer have to make?

(A) 25   (C) 75   (E) 150
(B) 50   (D) 100

33. I know that the partygoers are all on a diet and don't want two cream puffs each. I think they'll eat only $^3/_4$ of a cream puff each. How many should Jennifer make for my 300 guests?

(A) 100   (C) 225   (E) 600
(B) 147   (D) 300

34. The following pie chart refers to donations to a children's charity. If there were 400 donations in total, how many were books?

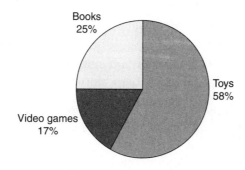

(A) 25   (C) 225   (E) 400
(B) 100   (D) 325

35. If there are 12 inches in a foot, and 3 feet in a yard, how do you convert yards to inches?

(A) Divide by 3, then by 12.
(B) Multiply by 3, then by 12.
(C) Divide by 3 and multiply by 12.
(D) Multiply by 3 and divide by 12.
(E) Divide by 36.

36. If there are 8 forks, 8 spoons, and 6 knives in a drawer, and you pick one at random, what is the probability of picking a spoon?

(A) $^1/_3$ (C) $^6/_{22}$ (E) $^1/_8$
(B) $^4/_{11}$ (D) $^8/_{24}$

37. 3,640,000 is how many times 3.64?

(A) 1,000
(B) 10,000
(C) 100,000
(D) 1,000,000
(E) 10,000,000

38. Which of the following numbers is a third of a million?

(A) 300,000
(B) $1,000,000 \times 0.3$

(C) $\dfrac{3}{1,000,000}$

(D) $\dfrac{1,000,000}{3}$

(E) $1,000,000 \div 0.3$

39. Which decimal is least?

(A) 0.0034
(B) 0.0956
(C) 0.000998
(D) 0.00475
(E) 0.0001156

40. The following chart shows the amount of profit a company earns for a given number of employees and customers. If the company has 30 customers, how many employees should it hire in order to have the greatest profit?

	Customers				
	10	**20**	**30**	**40**	**50**
1	30	32	34	36	38
2	25	60	62	64	66
3	20	55	90	92	94
4	15	50	85	120	122
5	10	45	80	115	150
6	5	40	75	110	145

(A) 1
(B) 2
(C) 3
(D) 4
(E) 5

STOP. This is the end of Mathematics Practice Test 1.

MATHEMATICS PRACTICE TEST 1: ANSWERS

1. **C.** As a fraction, $^{13}/_{52}$. Convert fractions to decimals by dividing: $^{13}/_{52} = 0.25$. $0.25 = 25$ percent.

2. **B.** There are 20 hashes between 0 and 5, so each of the long hashes is 1 unit, each of the small hashes is $^1/_4$ unit. The arrow is $6^1/_2$ hashes away from 0, which is halfway between the $1^1/_2$ and $1^3/_4$ mark.

3. **C.** The number must fall between 0.25 and 0.57, or 25 percent and 57 percent.

4. **C.** This is a volume problem. $V = ^4/_3\pi r^3$. Radius is half of diameter. $^4/_3\pi(3)^3 = 36\pi$.

5. **A.** Multiply to find each tip. $15 is the least.

6. **B.** (4,3) means 4 over and 3 up.

7. **C.** Quantities y and z are both greater than x, but we don't know anything about their relationship to each other. Either one could be greater.

8. **A.** If the hand is at a 90° angle, it is exactly on the 3, which means it must be 3:00.

9. **B.** $x = 3y$, so $x \div 6 = y \div 2$.

10. **D.** As a fraction, $^4/_{12}$. Convert fractions to decimals by dividing: $^4/_{12} = 0.333$. $0.333 = 33.3$ percent.

11. **C.** Use equivalent fractions. $\dfrac{1}{1} = \dfrac{x}{2.2}$, $x = 2.2$.

12. **D.** This is an area problem. The room is a 10×10 square minus a 4×4 square $(10 \times 10) - (4 \times 4) = 84$.

13. **C.** Trial and error. Try all of the pairs in each equation and find which one works for all of them.

14. **B.** $(^1/_8 \times 16) + 7 = 9$.

15. **C.** The floor area is 195 square feet, minus 40 square feet of rug. You need to cover 155 square feet, divide by 10 per quart of lacquer.

16. **B.** $0.4 = ^2/_5$ and $0.55 = ^{11}/_{20}$. Change fractions to decimals by dividing.

17. **C.** Estimate: 4.50 is 9 percent of the bill, so the bill is about $50, and 15 percent of $50 is $7.50.

18. **C.** There are 5 hashes between 20 and 40, so each of the hashes is 4 units. The arrow is about $4^1/_2$ hashes away from 20. $20 + (4.5 \times 4) = 34$.

19. **D.** Choices A and C are less than 1. $^{14}/_5 > ^8/_5$. Cross multiply to show $^{14}/_5 > ^{11}/_6$.

20. **D.** Since $22 = 6x - 2$, add to both sides to get $24 = 6x$, then divide both sides to get $4 = x$.

21. E. You cannot find an overall trend or make predictions from 1 week. Add up the sales for each day to find the total for that week.

22. E. Use equivalent fractions. $\frac{1}{4} = \frac{2.75}{x}$, $x = 11$.

23. C. 0.1×20.

24. A. This is a remainder interpretation problem. I is 4 soufflés; II is 4 picnics; III is 5 boxes.

25. D. 1 meter = 100 centimeters.

26. C. Estimate by rounding to the nearest thousandth, then count spaces past the decimal point. $0.002 \times 0.4 = 0.0008$.

27. B. $30 - 26 = 4$, $4 \div 26 = 0.154$, or 15.4%.

28. A. There are 20 hashes between 0 and 5, so each of the long hashes is 1 unit and each of the small hashes is $\frac{1}{4}$ unit. The line begins at the $\frac{3}{4}$ hash and ends at $4\frac{1}{4}$, and $4\frac{1}{4} - \frac{3}{4} = 3\frac{1}{2}$.

29. D. Estimate by rounding to the nearest thousand: $3,000 \times 15,000 = 45,000,000$.

30. A. There is one combination that adds up to 2 (1, 1), two for 3 (1, 2 and 2, 1), and three for 4 (1, 3, 3, 1, and 2, 2), out of 36 possible combinations.

31. C. Estimate. About 150 people were expected, so each person would eat 2 cream puffs.

32. D. Estimate: 52 is about $\frac{1}{3}$ of about 150. So you'd need about $\frac{1}{3}$ more cream puffs, and $300 \times \frac{1}{3} = 100$. (Alternatively, 52 is about 50. If each person eats 2 cream puffs, she would need 50×2, or 100 more cream puffs.)

33. C. $300 \times \frac{3}{4} = 225$.

34. B. $400 \times 0.25 = 100$.

35. B. 12 inches = 1 foot, 3 feet = 1 yard. You can also multiply by 36.

36. B. Eight choices out of a possible 22 (8 + 8 + 6), reduced to lowest terms.

37. D. $3.64 \times 1,000,000 = 3,640,000$.

38. D. One million divided by three.

39. E. Find the number with the most leading zeroes, then compare the first nonzero place if two are tied.

40. C. Three employees give a profit of 90, which is higher than any of the other possibilities.

READING PRACTICE TEST 2

Answer sheet

1 (A) (B) (C) (D) (E)
2 (A) (B) (C) (D) (E)
3 (A) (B) (C) (D) (E)
4 (A) (B) (C) (D) (E)
5 (A) (B) (C) (D) (E)
6 (A) (B) (C) (D) (E)
7 (A) (B) (C) (D) (E)

8 (A) (B) (C) (D) (E)
9 (A) (B) (C) (D) (E)
10 (A) (B) (C) (D) (E)
11 (A) (B) (C) (D) (E)
12 (A) (B) (C) (D) (E)
13 (A) (B) (C) (D) (E)
14 (A) (B) (C) (D) (E)

15 (A) (B) (C) (D) (E)
16 (A) (B) (C) (D) (E)
17 (A) (B) (C) (D) (E)
18 (A) (B) (C) (D) (E)
19 (A) (B) (C) (D) (E)
20 (A) (B) (C) (D) (E)
21 (A) (B) (C) (D) (E)

22 (A) (B) (C) (D) (E)
23 (A) (B) (C) (D) (E)
24 (A) (B) (C) (D) (E)
25 (A) (B) (C) (D) (E)
26 (A) (B) (C) (D) (E)
27 (A) (B) (C) (D) (E)
28 (A) (B) (C) (D) (E)

29 (A) (B) (C) (D) (E)
30 (A) (B) (C) (D) (E)
31 (A) (B) (C) (D) (E)
32 (A) (B) (C) (D) (E)
33 (A) (B) (C) (D) (E)
34 (A) (B) (C) (D) (E)
35 (A) (B) (C) (D) (E)

36 (A) (B) (C) (D) (E)
37 (A) (B) (C) (D) (E)
38 (A) (B) (C) (D) (E)
39 (A) (B) (C) (D) (E)
40 (A) (B) (C) (D) (E)

READING PRACTICE TEST 2

40 questions, 60 minutes

Directions: Each of the following passages is followed by questions. Answer the questions based on what is directly stated or suggested in each passage. Indicate your answers by filling in the corresponding circle on your answer sheet.

Questions 1–4

In a field one summer's day a grasshopper was hopping about, chirping and singing to its heart's content. An ant passed by, bearing along with great toil an ear of corn he was taking to the nest.

"Why not come and chat with me," said the grasshopper, "instead of toiling in that
(5) way?"

"I am helping to lay up food for the winter," said the ant, "and recommend you to do the same."

"Why bother about winter?" said the grasshopper, "we have got plenty of food at present." But the ant went on its way and continued its toil. When the winter came the
(10) grasshopper had no food and found itself dying of hunger, while it saw the ants distributing every day corn and grain from the stores they had collected in the summer.

1. This story is best described as

(A) a fairy tale
(B) a myth
(C) a biography
(D) a fable
(E) light and amusing

2. The story's style and content show that it would likely appeal to

(A) literary critics
(B) science fiction fans
(C) children
(D) animals
(E) spendthrifts

3. The ant is best described as

(A) farseeing
(B) a victim of peer pressure
(C) worried
(D) dying of hunger
(E) a close friend of the grasshopper

4. The moral of this story is best expressed as

(A) Appearances are deceptive.
(B) It is best to prepare for the days of necessity.
(C) Don't worry, be happy.
(D) Never trust your enemy.
(E) People are known by the company they keep.

5. When I use the word *didactic,* I mean it in a general sense. Many of you have thought I meant "moral instruction"—the teaching of social or spiritual values. I mean *didactic* in the sense of teaching *anything*—be it values, a sense of what the world is like, introduction to ideas that the reader was unfamiliar with before reading this particular book . . . in the case of children's literature, authors are aware that they are writing to an audience that is in the process of getting to know the world.

The writer uses the term *didactic* to mean all of the following *except*

(A) pedagogy in general
(B) instructing students about social and religious values
(C) educating about the world
(D) preteaching the content of a specific book
(E) explaining how to write and publish children's literature

Questions 6–7

> Solar energy is heat and light that comes from the sun. Thousands of years ago, some people used this energy to heat their homes. Today, solar energy is again helping to heat buildings. Solar energy can also be used to heat water and cook food. As our supply of precious gas and oil gets smaller, we will find new uses for energy from the sun.

6. According to the passage, which of following information is *not* true?

(A) The sun creates solar energy.
(B) Ancient people heated their homes with solar energy.
(C) Water can be heated and food can be cooked with solar energy.
(D) Solar energy is the best energy source to use.
(E) Solar energy is a promising new fuel source.

7. What conclusion can be drawn from this paragraph?

(A) Solar energy is more expensive than fossil fuels.
(B) Solar energy is likely to be a valuable energy source in the future.
(C) Solar energy is still a theory, not a reality.
(D) One way to boil water is through solar energy.
(E) Solar energy, like other energy sources, has its drawbacks as well as its strengths.

8. Currently, tuition, room, board, and expenses at an elite Ivy League university run about $38,000 per year. The average private university charges around $22,000 per year; state universities, around $10,500. Because the cost of goods and services continues to rise, college costs are projected to rise about 3 to 4 percent per year. Many students who count on getting financial aid often receive far less than they projected.

Based on the information, you can conclude that

(A) A college education is not worth the investment.
(B) A disproportionate number of college students go to Ivy League schools.
(C) The majority of college students take out loans to pay the cost of their education.
(D) A state college education is the same as a private college education.
(E) College should be free for all students.

Questions 9–14

It stretches, snaps, and shatters when hit with a heavy object. If you press a blob of it against a comic book or newspaper, it picks up the image. It can be used to build strength in a person's hands and remove lint from clothing. Astronauts use it to hold tools to space capsule surfaces during the weightlessness of space travel. What is it?

(5)   That's the question James Wright asked himself in the early 1940s when he created the odd stuff. As an engineer for General Electric, Wright had been trying to develop a rubber substitute to do his part to help the Allies during World War II. Instead of rubber, he created a blob of sticky stuff that bounced when he dropped it. It had no use, but everyone liked to play with it.

(10)   A few years later, Peter Hodgson decided to try to market this odd clay. He called it "Silly Putty" and featured it in a 1949 toy store catalog. Silly Putty was an instant hit, but Hodgson had bigger ideas. He borrowed some money, packed Silly Putty into egg cartons, and drove from city to city showing off his Silly Putty. The product has since become a classic children's toy.

9. According to paragraph 1, the mysterious substance can do everything *except*

(A) break when hit with a hammer
(B) anchor objects to a wall
(C) remove lint from clothing
(D) help build up a person's hands
(E) seal small leaks in hoses

10. What is the main idea of paragraph 1?

(A) This unnamed substance has many unusual properties.
(B) This strange substance is very important to the space race.
(C) You can shatter this substance with a sharp object.
(D) The substance must be very expensive to produce.
(E) It is an excellent substitute for rubber.

11. What is the result of dropping Silly Putty?

(A) It gets sticky.
(B) It becomes useful for the war effort.
(C) It turns into a blob.
(D) It bounces.
(E) It transforms into rubber.

12. What conclusion can you draw from the information in paragraph 2?

(A) Silly Putty can be used in place of rubber.
(B) James Wright was disappointed with his creation.
(C) Silly Putty is useful rather than fun.
(D) James Wright was an engineer during World War II.
(E) James Wright went on to invent a successful rubber substitute.

13. Why did Peter Hodgson decide to sell Silly Putty on the road?

(A) He liked to play with the gooey stuff himself.
(B) It was in a toy store catalog.
(C) He borrowed some money to use for this purpose.
(D) He knew that Silly Putty could be an even bigger success.
(E) He was a traveling salesman and enjoyed being with people.

14. The main idea in paragraph 3 is:

(A) Peter Hodgson sold Silly Putty by driving around the country.
(B) You can sell just about everything with enough time and effort.
(C) Silly Putty was first advertised in 1949.
(D) Silly Putty costs very little to produce.
(E) Silly Putty will continue to be a hit with buyers.

15. Research shows that kids who play sports or who are physically active are more likely to practice healthful behaviors. However, only about 38 percent of all teenagers get enough exercise, which means that the other 62 percent are setting themselves up for a sedentary life and all the problems that come with it.

The author's attitude toward exercise is likely

(A) negative
(B) neutral
(C) highly positive
(D) mildly positive
(E) hostile

Questions 16–18

The concept of gastric surgery to control obesity grew out of results of operations for cancer or severe ulcers that removed large portions of the stomach or small intestine. Because patients undergoing these procedures tended to lose weight after surgery, some doctors began to use such operations to treat morbid obesity. A type of intestinal

(5) bypass, first used 40 years ago, caused weight loss through malabsorption, a decreased ability to absorb nutrients from food because the intestines were removed or bypassed. Because this surgery caused a loss of essential nutrients and its side effects were unpredictable—and sometimes fatal—the procedure is no longer used.

The two types of surgical procedures now used to promote weight loss are:

- *Restrictive surgery:* A section of the stomach is removed or closed, which limits the amount of food it can hold. This causes the patient to feel full although he or she eats very little.
- *Gastric bypass:* The small intestine is shortened and/or changed where it connects to the stomach. This limits the amount of food that is completely digested or absorbed, causing malabsorption.

16. According to the passage, restrictive surgery

(A) is no longer used
(B) involves shortening the small intestines
(C) results in food not being absorbed by the body
(D) should not be used if the patient has cancer or severe ulcers
(E) results in the patient having a feeling of satiety even though he or she has not eaten much

17. According to the information in this passage, you can infer that the author

(A) highly endorses gastric bypass surgery in selected cases
(B) does not wish to take a stand on the different surgeries and their outcomes
(C) feels that restrictive surgery is better than gastric bypass surgery
(D) believes that gastric bypass surgery is better than restrictive surgery
(E) understands that none of these surgeries is safe

18. Which is the best summary of this passage?

(A) Gastric surgery began about 40 years ago as a result of operations done on cancer patients. Intestinal bypass, first used back then, caused weight loss through malabsorption, but this process has been proven unsafe so it is no longer used.

(B) Gastric surgery is a highly effective way to control obesity; indeed, it is the only method that results in significant weight loss. Both restrictive surgery and gastric bypass surgery have equally successful outcomes.

(C) Even though gastric bypass surgery and restrictive surgery are widely used, neither can be considered safe, as shown by the long-term results of the first procedures done 40 years ago on cancer and ulcer patients.

(D) Using gastric surgery to control obesity started about 40 years ago. Today, there are two main types: *restrictive surgery* (the size of the stomach is reduced) and *gastric bypass* (the small intestine is shortened, causing malabsorption).

(E) If you are contemplating surgery to control obesity, you're in luck: Both restrictive surgery and gastric bypass surgery are widely used today to control this medical condition. Gastric surgery began about 40 years ago as a result of operations done on cancer patients. Do not get the older method of surgery because it is not as effective as the newer methods.

Questions 19–24

> We know that the White man does not understand our ways. One portion of land is the same to him as the next, for he is a stranger who comes in the night and takes from the land whatever he needs. The earth is not his brother but his enemy, and when he has conquered it, he moves on. He leaves his fathers' graves, and his children's birthright is
> (5) forgotten. He treats his mother, the earth, and brothers, the sky, as things to be bought, plundered, sold like sheep or bright beads. His appetite will devour the earth and leave behind only a desert.
> There is no quiet place in the White man's cities. No place to hear the unfurling of leaves in spring, or the rustle of an insect's wings. The clatter only seems to insult the
> (10) ears. And what is there to life if a man cannot hear the lonely cry of the whippoorwill or the arguments of the frogs around a pond at night? I prefer the soft sound of the wind darting over the face of a pond, and the smell of the wind itself, cleansed by rain or scented with the pine cone.

19. The statement "The earth is not his brother but his enemy, and when he has conquered it, he moves on" adds to the development of the passage by

(A) contrasting the White and Native American view of the land
(B) showing that the Native Americans will not be conquered by the Whites
(C) aggressively insulting the White man
(D) portraying the Whites as barbarians
(E) focusing on a specific statement rather than vague generalities

20. The speaker is most likely a

(A) poet
(B) naturalist
(C) Native American
(D) White man
(E) contemporary social commentator

21. This passage is primarily developed by

(A) an extended metaphor
(B) comparison
(C) deductive reasoning
(D) inductive reasoning
(E) contrast

22. You can infer that the speaker

(A) prefers the city to the country
(B) prefers the country to the city
(C) lives in the country but wishes to live in the city
(D) used to live in the city but moved to the country
(E) has traveled widely across America

23. The images in the last paragraph combine to create an impression of

(A) the joys of the wilderness
(B) conflict and misunderstanding
(C) fear and hostility
(D) arrogant superiority
(E) life and death

24. What is the author's purpose?

(A) to warn the White man against encroaching on Native American land
(B) to plead for the White man's understanding
(C) to inform the Whites that the land is sacred to persuade them to keep it holy
(D) to persuade the Whites to change their way of looking at nature before it is too late
(E) to tell a story about the glory of nature

25. A good total fitness activity program contains three types of exercises: strength exercises, flexibility exercises, and heart exercises. The following are just a few of the simple and effective exercises that you can do. For best results, you want to do this program two to four times per week, at a level of intensity that you are comfortable with. If you are feeling any significant pain, stop immediately and consult with your doctor before resuming this program.

According to this statement, you should exercise

(A) every day
(B) several times a week
(C) after you have seen your doctor
(D) as hard as you can
(E) as often as you can

Questions 26–28

Twins have fascinated people for centuries. Legend has it that the twin founders of Rome, Romulus and Remus, were nursed by a she-wolf—after surviving an attempt to drown them! Twins are born about 1 out of 90 births in America. They are more rare among the Chinese, whose rate is about 1 out of 300. However, twins are surprisingly
(5) common among the Yoruba of Nigeria, who have a set of twins for every 22 births. The different rates are accounted for by an inherited tendency to release more than one egg a month, resulting in nonidentical siblings being born at the rate of about 4 out of 1,000 births regardless of ethnic background or family history, for the tendency of a single egg to separate into two is not inherited. Triplets, quadruplets, and sextuplets may be fraternal or
(10) identical, and sometimes a combination of both.

26. In which culture are twins most common?

(A) the Yoruba of Nigeria
(B) the Chinese
(C) Americans
(D) Romans
(E) Chinese-Americans

27. What explains the varying rates for twin births?

(A) your birthplace
(B) your genetic makeup
(C) ethnic background
(D) family history
(E) both ethnic background and family history

28. How many different types of multiple births are there?

(A) one
(B) two
(C) three
(D) four
(E) five

Questions 29–30

In 1862, in order to support the Civil War effort, Congress enacted the nation's first income tax law. During the Civil War, a person earning from $600 to $10,000 per year paid tax at the rate of 3 percent. Those with incomes of more than $10,000 paid taxes at a higher rate. Additional sales and excise taxes were added, and an "inheritance" tax also made its debut.
(5) In 1866, internal revenue collections reached their highest point in the nation's 90-year history—more than $310 million, an amount not reached again until 1911.

29. You can infer that the first income tax was

(A) difficult to collect
(B) hotly contested
(C) a flat tax
(D) grossly unfair
(E) similar to our current system, a graduated scale

30. Which of the following statements best describes the organization of the passage?

(A) causes and effects
(B) advantages and disadvantages
(C) least to most important details
(D) chronological order
(E) compare and contrast

Questions 31–33

An old man on the point of death summoned his sons around him to give them some parting advice. He ordered his servants to bring in a bundle of sticks, and said to his eldest son: "Break it." The son strained and strained, but with all his efforts was unable to break the bundle. The other sons also tried, but none of them was successful. "Untie
(5) the bundle," said the father, "and each of you take a stick." When they had done so, he called out to them: "Now, break," and each stick was easily broken. "You see my meaning," said their father.

31. The primary purpose of the passage is to

(A) teach a lesson
(B) entertain readers
(C) persuade people to treat the aged with respect
(D) explain how people lived in the past
(E) describe a real-life incident

32. The father is concerned that his sons

    (A) preserve his estate
    (B) continue to cut wood for a living
    (C) treat the servants well
    (D) build their physical strength
    (E) stay united as a family

33. What is the moral of this story?

    (A) Nature exceeds nurture.
    (B) Little friends may prove great friends.
    (C) Union gives strength.
    (D) You can't please everyone.
    (E) Misery loves company.

Questions 34–35

Described as a "swimming and eating machine without peer," the shark is considered an evolutionary success story, having changed little over 60 million years. Sharks are models of efficiency with their boneless skeletons, simple brains, generalized nervous systems, and simple internal structures. Their hydrodynamically designed shapes, razor-sharp replaceable
(5) teeth, powerful jaws, and voracious appetites make them excellent marauders. Through scavenging and predation, the 250 species of sharks perform a valuable service in maintaining the ecological balance of the oceans. Their well-developed sensory systems enable them to detect extreme dilutions of blood in water, low-frequency sounds of splashing made by a fish in distress, and movements and contrasts in water.

34. All of the following contribute to the shark's success as a hunter *except*

    (A) hydrodynamically designed shape
    (B) great age
    (C) powerful jaws
    (D) voracious appetite
    (E) razor-sharp replaceable teeth

35. Which conclusion is best supported by this passage?

    (A) The author is very afraid of sharks.
    (B) The author admires sharks.
    (C) People should learn more about sharks.
    (D) Sharks are not very intelligent.
    (E) Sharks are very dangerous because they attack humans.

Questions 36–37

The Congressional Medal of Honor is awarded for actions that are above and beyond the call of duty in combat against an armed enemy. The medal was first awarded by the Army on March 25, 1863, and then by the Navy on April 3, 1863. In April 1991, President Bush awarded posthumously the Medal of Honor to World War I veteran Army Cpl. Freddie
(5) Stowers. He was the first African-American soldier to receive the nation's highest honor for valor in either world war. Recipients of the medal receive $400 per month for life, a right to burial in Arlington National Cemetery, admission for them or their children to a service academy if they qualify and if quotas permit, and free travel on government aircraft to almost anywhere in the world, on a space-available basis.

36. This essay is constructed primarily according to

(A) time order
(B) least to most important details
(C) cause and effect
(D) comparison and contrast
(E) spatial order

37. What can be inferred about the Congressional Medal of Honor from this passage?

(A) It is a relatively minor award.
(B) Many soldiers have received this award.
(C) Someone must nominate a recipient.
(D) All recipients of the award have died in battle.
(E) It is a very prestigious award.

Questions 38–40

Physician assistants (PAs) provide health care services under the supervision of physicians. PAs are formally trained to provide diagnostic, therapeutic, and preventive health care services, as assigned by a physician. Working as members of the health care team, PAs take medical histories, examine and treat patients, order and interpret laboratory tests and
(5) x-rays, and make diagnoses. They also treat minor injuries by suturing wounds, splinting breaks, and casting limbs. PAs record progress notes, instruct and counsel patients, and order or carry out therapy. In 47 states and the District of Columbia, PAs may also prescribe medications. PAs may be the primary health care providers in rural or inner-city clinics, where a physician is present for a day or two a week. PAs also may make house calls
(10) or go to hospitals and nursing homes to check on patients and report back to the physician.

38. According to the passage, PAs can do all of the following *except*

(A) check a patient for a sore throat or ear infection
(B) talk with the patient about his or her past illnesses and current complaints
(C) treat major illnesses and wounds
(D) diagnose a patient's illness
(E) set a broken shoulder

39. This passage is developed through

    (A) advantages and disadvantages
    (B) summary
    (C) cause and effect
    (D) examples
    (E) comparison and contrast

40. You can infer that the duties of PAs

    (A) are determined by the supervising physician and by state law
    (B) are the same in all states
    (C) vary with the age and experience of the PA
    (D) include serving as a primary care physician or a specialist
    (E) leave them unsupervised a great deal of the time

STOP. This is the end of Reading Practice Test 2.

READING PRACTICE TEST 2: ANSWERS

1. D.   Fables are short, easy-to-read, and straightforward stories that teach a lesson, usually stated as a moral.

2. C.   The simple language, everyday diction, and straightforward plotline suggest that this story would likely appeal to children. There's not enough "deep meaning" for literary critics, so you can eliminate choice A. Choices B and D are illogical, and *spendthrifts* (choice E) would likely be offended by their portrayal in this fable.

3. A.   Since the ant plans for the future, we can describe her as *farseeing*. While all the other ants act the same way, there's no evidence in the story of peer pressure (choice B) or fear (choice C). Rather, the ant seems confident that she will have enough for the future.

4. B.   The moral of this story is best expressed as "It is best to prepare for the days of necessity." The contrast between the fates of the ant and the grasshopper show this.

5. E.   Each example except the last can be found in the passage.

6. D.   The author does not argue that solar energy is the best energy source to use, the author simply means that it is a promising energy source to explore further.

7. B.   You can infer from the last sentence that solar energy is likely to be a valuable energy source in the future.

8. C.   Based on the last line, you can conclude that the majority of college students take out loans to finance their education. Since state tuition is reasonable, choice A cannot be correct; there is no proof for choices C and D. Choice E is a nice idea, but the writer does not address this issue at all.

9. E.   Every detail except E—*seal small leaks in hoses*—is directly mentioned in the paragraph.

10. A.   Infer the main idea by adding all the details together. Eliminate choice E because it relates to the second paragraph.

11. D.   The detail is directly stated: *Instead of rubber, he created a blob of sticky stuff that bounced when he dropped it.*

12. B.   You can conclude that James Wright was disappointed with his creation because during World War II, a rubber substitute could have greatly helped the Allies. Choices A and C are directly contradicted by the information in the passage. Choice D is a fact in the passage, not a conclusion. There is no support for choice E.

13. D.   Peter Hodgson decided to sell Silly Putty on the road because he suspected that Silly Putty could be an even bigger success. Choices A, B, and C do not make logical sense in a cause-and-effect relationship; there is no support for choice E.

14. A. Peter Hodgson sold Silly Putty by driving around the country. Choice B is too big a stretch, given the facts in the passage; choices C and D are details, not main ideas. Choice E seems a likely prediction, but it is not the main idea of the passage.

15. C. Since the author argues that—*However, only about 38 percent of all teenagers get enough exercise, which means that the other 62 percent are setting themselves up for a sedentary life and all the problems that come with it*—he or she would likely be very enthusiastic about exercise and endorse it for sedentary (but otherwise healthy) adolescents.

16. E. According to the passage, restrictive surgery results in the patient's having a feeling of satiety even though he or she has not eaten much. The detail is directly stated: *Restrictive surgery: A section of the stomach is removed or closed, which limits the amount of food it can hold. This causes the patient to feel full although he or she eats very little.*

17. B. From the factual, neutral tone, you can infer that the author does not wish to take a stand on the different surgeries and their outcomes.

18. D. This summary includes all the important information in a nonbiased manner. Choice A is incomplete. Choices B, C, and E are biased and do not accurately reflect the contents of the passage.

19. A. The statement—*The earth is not his brother but his enemy, and when he has conquered it, he moves on*—develops the passage by contrasting the White and Native American views of the land. This contrast sets the stage for the writer's main idea: the different ways the White man and Native American regard the land.

20. C. You can infer that the speaker is most likely a Native American from lines such as this one: *We know that the White man does not understand our ways.*

21. E. The writer contrasts the Native American and White view of the land, showing how they are different.

22. B. You can infer that the speaker prefers the country to the city from the last line: *I prefer the soft sound of the wind darting over the face of a pond, and the smell of the wind itself, cleansed by rain or scented with the pine cone.* You can eliminate choices A and C because they are the opposite. There is no proof for choice D; he might have visited the city but not lived there, for instance. There is not enough support for choice E.

23. A. The images in the last paragraph convey the joys of the wilderness, especially *the unfurling of leaves in spring, rustle of an insect's wings, lonely cry of the whippoorwill, arguments of the frogs around a pond at night, soft sound of the wind darting over the face of a pond, the smell of the wind itself, cleansed by rain or scented with the pine cone.* There are no images of conflict and misunderstanding (B) or fear and hostility (C). The speaker is not arrogant, so choice D is wrong; there are images of life but not death, so choice E is wrong.

24. D. From the images in the last paragraph, you can infer that the author is trying to persuade the Whites to change their way of looking at nature before it is too late. There's no warning, so choice A is incorrect. The tone is not pleading, so choice B is wrong. The writer does not go into the holiness of the land, so choice C is incorrect. Last, the writer is not telling a story about the glory of nature, choice E. Rather, he is using a description of the glories of nature to make his point.

25. B. You can find the answer in this sentence: *For best results, you want to do this program two to four times per week, at a level of intensity that you are comfortable with.*

26. A. Twins are most common among the Yoruba, as the following sentence shows: *However, twins are surprisingly common among the Yoruba of Nigeria, who have a set of twins for every 22 births.*

27. B. The answer is in the following sentence: *The different rates are accounted for by an inherited tendency to release more than one egg a month.*

28. C. There are three different types of multiple births: fraternal, identical, and sometimes a combination of both.

29. E. From the following two sentences, you can infer that the first income tax was similar to our current system, a graduated scale: *During the Civil War, a person earning from $600 to $10,000 per year paid tax at the rate of 3 percent. Those with incomes of more than $10,000 paid taxes at a higher rate.* This directly contradicts choice C. Choice A is wrong because so much money was collected. There is no support for choice B. Choice D is incorrect because the tax seems fair.

30. D. The passage is organized in time order, moving from 1862 to 1866 to 1911.

31. A. As a fable, the passage is designed to teach a lesson: here, to stay unified.

32. E. The father is concerned that his sons stay united, as the symbol of the strength of the bundle of sticks shows.

33. C. That the young men can't break the bundle but can break each individual stick shows that united we stand, divided we fall. Only by sticking together can the sons have the greatest possible strength.

34. B. This is a straight recall question: you can find every choice in the passage except B. With these types of questions, skim the passage to find each choice. Check them off as you find them.

35. B. From the details *the shark is considered an evolutionary success story* and *through scavenging and predation, the 250 species of sharks perform a valuable service in maintaining the ecological balance of the oceans,* you can infer that the author admires sharks. There is no support for any of the other answer choices.

36. A. Details about the Congressional Medal of Honor are presented in time order. For example: *The medal was first awarded by the Army on March 25, 1863, and then by the Navy on April 3, 1863.*

37. E. Given the description of the award (for *actions that are above and beyond the call of duty in combat against an armed enemy*) and the rewards that come with it, you can infer that the Congressional Medal of Honor is very prestigious. This directly contradicts choices A and B. There's no proof in the passage for choice C; the detail *recipients of the medal receive $400 per month for life* shows that choice D cannot be true.

38. C. Use process of elimination to figure out that PAs can do all of the following except treat major illnesses and wounds.

39. D. This passage is developed through examples. The writer gives a long list of duties the PAs can perform.

40. A. You can infer that the duties of PAs are determined by the supervising physician and by state law. Use the following sentences: *(PAs) provide health care services under the supervision of physicians. . . . PAs <u>may be</u> the primary health care providers in rural or inner-city clinics, <u>where a physician is present</u> for a day or two a week. PAs also may make house calls or go to hospitals and nursing homes to check on patients and <u>report back to the physician.</u>*

Skills Spread

Skill Type	Item Numbers
Literal understanding	1, 5, 6, 9, 11, 16, 18, 19, 21, 25, 26, 27, 28, 30, 34, 36, 38, 39,
Inferential and critical understanding	2, 3, 4, 7, 8, 10, 12, 13, 14, 15, 17, 20, 22, 23, 24, 29, 31, 32, 33, 35, 37, 40

WRITING PRACTICE TEST 2

Answer sheet

1 Ⓐ Ⓑ Ⓒ Ⓓ Ⓔ
2 Ⓐ Ⓑ Ⓒ Ⓓ Ⓔ
3 Ⓐ Ⓑ Ⓒ Ⓓ Ⓔ
4 Ⓐ Ⓑ Ⓒ Ⓓ Ⓔ
5 Ⓐ Ⓑ Ⓒ Ⓓ Ⓔ
6 Ⓐ Ⓑ Ⓒ Ⓓ Ⓔ
7 Ⓐ Ⓑ Ⓒ Ⓓ Ⓔ

8 Ⓐ Ⓑ Ⓒ Ⓓ Ⓔ
9 Ⓐ Ⓑ Ⓒ Ⓓ Ⓔ
10 Ⓐ Ⓑ Ⓒ Ⓓ Ⓔ
11 Ⓐ Ⓑ Ⓒ Ⓓ Ⓔ
12 Ⓐ Ⓑ Ⓒ Ⓓ Ⓔ
13 Ⓐ Ⓑ Ⓒ Ⓓ Ⓔ
14 Ⓐ Ⓑ Ⓒ Ⓓ Ⓔ

15 Ⓐ Ⓑ Ⓒ Ⓓ Ⓔ
16 Ⓐ Ⓑ Ⓒ Ⓓ Ⓔ
17 Ⓐ Ⓑ Ⓒ Ⓓ Ⓔ
18 Ⓐ Ⓑ Ⓒ Ⓓ Ⓔ
19 Ⓐ Ⓑ Ⓒ Ⓓ Ⓔ
20 Ⓐ Ⓑ Ⓒ Ⓓ Ⓔ
21 Ⓐ Ⓑ Ⓒ Ⓓ Ⓔ

22 Ⓐ Ⓑ Ⓒ Ⓓ Ⓔ
23 Ⓐ Ⓑ Ⓒ Ⓓ Ⓔ
24 Ⓐ Ⓑ Ⓒ Ⓓ Ⓔ
25 Ⓐ Ⓑ Ⓒ Ⓓ Ⓔ
26 Ⓐ Ⓑ Ⓒ Ⓓ Ⓔ
27 Ⓐ Ⓑ Ⓒ Ⓓ Ⓔ
28 Ⓐ Ⓑ Ⓒ Ⓓ Ⓔ

29 Ⓐ Ⓑ Ⓒ Ⓓ Ⓔ
30 Ⓐ Ⓑ Ⓒ Ⓓ Ⓔ
31 Ⓐ Ⓑ Ⓒ Ⓓ Ⓔ
32 Ⓐ Ⓑ Ⓒ Ⓓ Ⓔ
33 Ⓐ Ⓑ Ⓒ Ⓓ Ⓔ
34 Ⓐ Ⓑ Ⓒ Ⓓ Ⓔ
35 Ⓐ Ⓑ Ⓒ Ⓓ Ⓔ

36 Ⓐ Ⓑ Ⓒ Ⓓ Ⓔ
37 Ⓐ Ⓑ Ⓒ Ⓓ Ⓔ
38 Ⓐ Ⓑ Ⓒ Ⓓ Ⓔ

WRITING PRACTICE TEST 2

SECTION 1: MULTIPLE-CHOICE QUESTIONS

38 questions, 30 minutes

Directions: The following sentences require you to identify errors in grammar, usage, punctuation, and capitalization. Not every sentence has an error, and no sentence will have more than one error. Every sentence error, if there is one, is underlined and lettered. If the sentence does have an error, select the one underlined part that must be changed to make the sentence correct and blacken the corresponding circle on your answer sheet. If the sentence does not have an error, blacken circle E. Elements of the sentence that are not underlined are not to be changed.

Part A
21 questions

suggested time: 10 minutes

1. Everyone always wants <u>his or her achievements</u> at work to be
   A
   <u>rewarded by management</u> in the form of raises, promotions, and other tangible signs of
   B
   appreciation, the ability to get along with others is <u>often as important to</u> success as
   C   D
   accomplishment itself. <u>No error.</u>
   E

2. <u>Rosie O'Donnell,</u> a stand-up comedian <u>and who has</u> written a book of jokes for
   A   B
   children, is now <u>making a name for herself</u> as a crusader for <u>adoption rights</u>.
   C   D
   <u>No error.</u>
   E

3. Chez Raddish is a <u>superb and inexpensive</u> restaurant <u>where fine food</u> <u>is served</u>
   A   B   C
   by waiters and waitresses <u>in appetizing forms</u>. <u>No error.</u>
   D   E

4. "Rarely has one individual, <u>espousing</u> so difficult a philosophy, <u>served as a</u>
   A   B
   <u>catalyst</u> for so much significant social change. There are few people <u>of who</u> it can be
   C
   said that <u>their lives changed the world.</u>" <u>No error.</u>
   D   E

5. The speaker <u>didn't say nothing</u> that the audience had not already <u>heard; as a</u>
            A   B
<u>result,</u> the <u>audience quickly</u> lost interest in his speech and <u>began to talk</u> among
                        C   D
themselves. <u>No error.</u>
                    E

6. <u>The Word workshop trains employees</u> about maximizing skills <u>to improve</u>
                        A   B
employees' <u>productivity, the Internet</u> training teaches <u>employees how to use</u>
                        C   D
<u>the Internet</u> for product searches and e-mail to worldwide subscribers. <u>No error.</u>
                                                                                    E

7. <u>The recipe was complex</u> but <u>the effort is worth it</u> because chicken and
            A   B
biscuits <u>made this way</u> <u>tastes more deliciously</u>. <u>No error.</u>
                    C   D   E

8. According to the schedule posted on <u>the teams bulletin board,</u> <u>there are</u> three
                                                    A   B
exhibitions before the season officially begins but only <u>one after the playoffs</u>
                                                                    C
had been completed <u>by the entire league</u>. <u>No error.</u>
                            D   E

9. Every day, Katie Couric interviews <u>many politicians</u> on the news, and some
                                                A
of them <u>seemed flabbergasted</u> by <u>her probing questions</u>, the correct answers to which
                    B   C
sometimes reveal attempts <u>to recast political missteps</u> in a more favorable light.
                                        D
<u>No error.</u>
    E

10. The real estate broker <u>promised to notify</u> my <u>partner and I</u> as soon as the
                                    A   B
<u>house was put up for sale</u> so <u>we could make</u> any necessary repairs to the structure.
                C   D
<u>No error.</u>
    E

11. <u>Either the witness or the defendant was</u> lying<u>; but</u> the <u>judge was unable</u> to
                        A   B   C
determine <u>which</u> of the two men was committing perjury. <u>No error.</u>
                D   E

12. A close friend of the family, the patient was referred to a psychologist
<u>   </u>   <u>   </u>
     A   B
<u>with several emotional problems</u> to <u>receive counseling</u>. <u>No error.</u>
              C   D   E

13. The cat <u>lays down</u> <u>near the fireplace</u> every afternoon to take a <u>nap, but</u> the dog
              A   B   C
never lets the cat rest <u>undisturbed</u>. <u>No error.</u>
                              D   E

14. In many parts of the country <u>(especially in the summer)</u>, traffic <u>grinding</u> to a
                                              A   B
standstill as <u>everyone fumbles</u> with the sun visor and <u>squints</u> into their
                    C   D
windshield. <u>No error.</u>
                  E

15. <u>Trapped</u> in an open field when a <u>sudden, fierce</u> storm came out of <u>nowhere they</u>
        A   B   C
were terrified <u>for their lives</u>. <u>No error.</u>
                    D   E

16. The average student <u>who</u> is burdened with large <u>college loans, car payments, and</u>
                          A   B
other bills is <u>frequent</u> hard-pressed for <u>immediate cash</u> for leisure-time
                    C   D
activities. <u>No error.</u>
                  E

17. The new parents<u> exhausted after staying awake with their baby for three straight</u>
                                                  A
<u>days</u> <u>realized</u> they had to get some sleep<u>;</u> therefore, they <u>hired</u> a babysitter.
    B   C   D
<u>No error.</u>
      E

18. The telephone <u>ringed</u> <u>,</u> <u>but</u> it was a <u>wrong number</u>. <u>No error.</u>
                      A   B C   D   E

19. <u>Even though a lightning bolt lasting a fraction of a second</u>, <u>it has</u> enough
                                  A   B
power<u>—30 million volts—</u>to light up <u>all of Miami</u>. <u>No error.</u>
              C   D   E

20. <u>Confirming</u> our <u>lengthy</u> conversation<u>, have</u> arranged <u>for the shipment</u> will be
          A   B   C   D
ordered in a week. <u>No error.</u>
                          E

21. The prominent lawyer won more awards than <u>anyone else</u> at the ceremony, which
                                                        A

surprised <u>her she</u> had long <u>taken on</u> unpopular cases <u>and defendants</u>. <u>No error.</u>
              B   C   D   E

Part B
17 questions

suggested time: 20 minutes

Directions: Choose the best version of the underlined portion of each sentence. Choice A is the same as the underlined portion of the original sentence. If you think that the original sentence is better than any of the suggested revisions, choose A. Otherwise, choose the revision you think is best. Answers and explanations follow the questions.

22. A new language can come into being as a <u>pidgin, a pidgin is</u> a makeshift jargon containing words of various languages and little in the way of grammar.

(A) pidgin, a pidgin
(B) pidgin a pidgin
(C) pidgin,
(D) pidgin, because it is
(E) pidgin and it is a

23. Because I am interested in nutrition, I am glad that Luis gave <u>my sister and I</u> a year's subscription to a health and fitness magazine.

(A) my sister and I
(B) me and my sister
(C) I and my sister
(D) we
(E) my sister and me

24. For this reason, very few people suspected the players <u>had been bought, the very next</u> day sports-writer Hugh Fullerton made a suggestion that something was not legitimate.

(A) had been bought, the very next
(B) have been bought, the very next
(C) had been boughted, the very next
(D) had been bought the very next
(E) had been bought; the very next

25. Our ancestors had to plant and <u>were cultivating</u> their own foods, but since we can just drive to the local supermarket or restaurant and pick what we want, we often eat too much.

(A) were cultivating
(B) to cultivate
(C) cultivating

(D) cultivated

(E) had been cultivating

26. <u>Being that</u> the iceberg ruptured 5 of the 16 watertight compartments, the ship sunk into the icy waters of the North Atlantic.

    (A) Being that
    (B) Being
    (C) If
    (D) Because
    (E) Yet

27. <u>Rushing up the stairs of the museum, the tomb of the Egyptian king was seen,</u> in all its awe-inspiring majesty.

    (A) Rushing up the stairs of the museum, the tomb of the Egyptian king was seen
    (B) Rushing up the stairs of the museum, the tomb of the Egyptian king was seen by us
    (C) The tomb of the Egyptian king was seen rushing up the stairs of the museum
    (D) As we rushed up the stairs of the museum, we saw the tomb of the Egyptian king
    (E) Rushing up the stairs of the museum, the tomb of the Egyptian king had been seen

28. When Europeans first settled in the New World in the seventeenth and eighteenth centuries <u>brought their culinary heritage and their recipes with them.</u>

    (A) brought their culinary heritage and their recipes with them
    (B) they brought their culinary heritage and their recipes with them
    (C) their culinary heritage and their recipes with them were brought
    (D) they having brought their culinary heritage and their recipes with them
    (E) their culinary heritage and their recipes with them they brought with them

29. A system of education should be judged by the caliber of students it turns <u>out in</u> summary, quality is preferable to quantity.

    (A) out in
    (B) out; in
    (C) out, in
    (D) out
    (E) in

30. <u>Everyone at the meetings speak</u> well of them and their good works in the community.

    (A) Everyone at the meetings speak
    (B) Everyone at the meetings speaked
    (C) Everyone at the meetings speaking
    (D) Everyones at the meetings speak
    (E) Everyone at the meetings speaks

31. <u>Due to the fact that</u> the textbook delivery has been delayed, we'll start the semester with the unit on public speaking.

    (A) Due to the fact that

    (B) As a result of the fact that

    (C) Since

    (D) In which case

    (E) As a direct consequence of the situation that

32. The expertise with which the flight attendant soothed the passengers' muttered concerns and calmed their outright panic at the sudden acceleration <u>show</u> her compassion and skill.

    (A) show

    (B) shows

    (C) showed

    (D) showing

    (E) was showing

33. If you are not feeling <u>good, you should lie</u> down.

    (A) good, you should lie

    (B) good, you should lay

    (C) good, you should lies

    (D) well, you should lay

    (E) well, you should lie

34. <u>That there</u> is the book we read for the science project.

    (A) That there

    (B) That

    (C) This here

    (D) That their

    (E) That they're

35. My teacher <u>doesn't</u> care much for contemporary music.

    (A) doesn't

    (B) don't

    (C) kind of don't

    (D) sort of don't

    (E) can't help but not

36. Science writers paraphrase a <u>scientists' explanations</u> before incorporating them in an article to make sure they understand the topic and can explain it clearly.

(A) scientists' explanations
(B) scientists explanation's
(C) scientists explanations'
(D) scientist's explanations
(E) scientist's explanation's

37. <u>Each of the students contribute</u> to the fund-raising drive in school.

(A) Each of the students contribute
(B) Each of the students contributing
(C) Each of the students having contributed
(D) Each of the students were contribute
(E) Each of the students contributes

38. The film was completely devoid of any plot or character <u>development it</u> was merely a montage of striking images.

(A) development it
(B) development; it
(C) development, it
(D) development
(E) development. it

STOP. This is the end of Section 1: Multiple-Choice Questions.

SECTION 2: ESSAY

30 minutes

Directions: Write an essay on the following topic. You will not receive any credit for writing on a topic other than the one given here. Plan your essay carefully and be sure to include specific examples and details that illustrate your point. Write your essay on your own sheets of paper. (On the real Praxis PPST test, paper for writing your essay will be provided.)

You will not receive credit if you write on any other topic. For your response to be scored, you must write in English. You cannot write in a foreign language.

Read the opinion stated:

High school students should be encouraged to work at least 20 hours a week.

In an essay, agree or disagree with this statement. But be sure to support your opinion with specific examples from reading, your experiences, your observations, or the media.
The space below is for your notes.

WRITING PRACTICE TEST 2: ANSWERS

SECTION 1: MULTIPLE-CHOICE

Part A

1. C. This is a sentence question. As written, the sentence is a run-on because the two clauses are incorrectly joined: a comma is not sufficient between two independent clauses (two complete sentences.) Here are two ways to correct the sentence.

- *Everyone always wants his or her achievements at work to be rewarded by management in the form of raises, promotions, and other tangible signs of appreciation, but the ability to get along with others is often as important to success as accomplishment itself.* –or-

- *Everyone always wants his or her achievements at work to be rewarded by management in the form of raises, promotions, and other tangible signs of appreciation; however, the ability to get along with others is often as important to success as accomplishment itself.*

2. B. There is no reason to add the word "and" to the sentence here.

3. D. This is a misplaced modifier. As written, the sentence states that the waiters and waitress are in appetizing forms. The sentence should read: *Chez Raddish is a superb and inexpensive restaurant where fine food is served in appetizing forms by waiters and waitresses.*

4. C. This question tests case: Use the objective case (*whom*) as the object of the preposition *of.*

5. A. This is a double negative. The correct form is *didn't say anything* or *said nothing.*

6. A. This is a run-on, two sentences run together without the correct punctuation. There are several ways that you can correct this sentence; here are two different correct versions:

- *The Word workshop trains employees about maximizing skills to improve employees' productivity, while the Internet . . .*

- *The Word workshop trains employees about maximizing skills to improve employees' productivity; the Internet . . .*

7. D. Use an adjective after a linking verb, not an adverb. The correct form is *tastes more delicious.*

8. A. Use an apostrophe to show ownership. The correct form is *team's.*

9. B. Don't switch tenses in midsentence. Since the sentence begins in the present (*interviews*), it should continue in the present (*seems*).

10. B. The real estate agent is doing the action and *my partner and me* are receiving the action, so use the objective case.

11. B.   This is a question on sentence structure. There is no reason to use a semi-colon with the coordinating conjunction *but*, since they fulfill the same function here. Place a comma before the coordinating conjunction.

12. C.   This is a misplaced modifier. The correct sentence should read: A *close friend of the family, the patient with several emotional problems, was referred to a psychologist to receive counseling.*

13. A.   Use the verb *lie* to mean "to be in a horizontal position, to repose." The correct word in this sentence is *lies*.

14. B.   This is a fragment because the verb is in the wrong form. The correct sentence reads: *In many parts of the country (especially in the summer), traffic grinds to a standstill . . .*

15. C.   Use a comma after an introductory phrase.

16. C.   Use an adverb to modify (describe) an adjective. The adverb here is *frequently*; the adjective is *hard-pressed*.

17. A.   Set off nonessential information with commas. Here, the nonessential phrase is *exhausted after staying awake with their baby for three straight days.*

18. A.   *Ring* has an irregular past participle, *rung*.

19. A   This is a sentence error. The sentence is not complete because the verb *lasting* is in the wrong form. The verb should be *lasts*.

20. C.   This is a dangling modifier. According to the sentence, the shipment—not the speaker—confirmed the conversation. One possible revision is: *Confirming our lengthy conversation, I have arranged for the shipment to be ordered in a week.*

21. B.   This is a run-on, two sentences incorrectly joined. Here is one correct revision: *The prominent lawyer won more awards than anyone else at the ceremony, which surprised her because she had . . .*

Part B

22. C.   This is a question on wordiness. Generally, choose the most concise construction. All the other variations given here are unnecessarily wordy.

23. E.   This is a question on pronoun case, the form the pronoun takes to show whether it is being used as a subject, as an object, or to show possession. Here, *Luis* is the subject (doing the action); my *sister and me* is the object (receiving the action). Choice B is incorrect because you always put yourself last. Thus, the phrase is *written my sister and me*, not *me and my sister*. Choice D is wrong because it is the nominative (subject) case rather than the object case, which would be us.

24. E.   This is a question sentence structure. As written, the sentence is a run-on. Removing the comma (choice D), does not correct the error. Changing the tense (choice B) doesn't correct the error and introduces an error in agreement. Choice C introduces a new error as well, as "boughted" is not a word.

25. B.   This is a question on parallel structure. Make the infinitive (base form of the verb) *to cultivate* parallel with the infinitive *to plant*.

26. D. This is a question on usage. *Being that* is considered substandard usage, so use *because* or *since* instead.

27. D. This is a dangling participle. Only choice D corrects the error.

28. B. As written, this sentence is a fragment, as it is missing the subject in the independent clause (the second part of the sentence.) Choice C has the necessary grammatical elements, but it is in the passive voice, which is not as concise and vigorous as the active voice. Choices D and E are awkward and wordy.

29. B. This is a run-on, two incorrectly joined sentences. Only choice B corrects the error.

30. E. This is a question on agreement. The singular pronoun *everyone* requires the singular verb *speaks*. Ignore the intervening prepositional phrase at the meetings.

31. C. The phrase *due to the fact that* is unnecessarily wordy. Use *since* instead.

32. C. This is a question on verb tense. Use the past tense (*showed*) to match the past tense in the first clause (*soothed*).

33. E. This is a usage question. *Good* is an adjective. Never use it after an action verb. Use the adverb *well* instead. *Lie,* which means "to be in a horizontal position, to recline," is correct as used here.

34. B. *That there* and *this here* are considered substandard usage. Use *that* or *there* alone. Choices D and E are incorrect because they not only maintain the substandard usage but also spell there wrong.

35. A. The sentence is correct as written.

36. D. The explanations belong to one scientist, so the correct possessive form is *scientist's.* Do not confuse possession (ownership) with plural (adding an *s* or changing the spelling of the noun). Thus, there is no reason to add an apostrophe to *explanations.*

37. E. This is a question on agreement. The singular pronoun *each* requires the singular verb *contributes.* Ignore the intervening prepositional phrase *of the students*. Choice C creates a fragment, an incomplete sentence.

38. B. This is a run-on, two incorrectly joined sentences. Only choice B corrects this error. For choice E to be correct, it must be capitalized.

Skills Spread

Specific Content Area	Item Numbers
Grammar and usage	4, 7, 8, 9, 10, 16, 20, 23, 26, 27, 30, 32, 33, 37
Sentence structure	1, 3, 6, 11, 12,14,19, 21, 24, 25, 28, 29, 38
Mechanics (punctuation, capitalization)	2, 5, 13, 15, 17, 18, 22, 31, 34, 35, 36
Diction (word choice	
Essay	1

SECTION 2: ESSAY

The following model essay would receive a 6, the highest score, for its specific details, organization, and style (appropriate word choice, sentence structure, and consistent facility in use of language). It is an especially intelligent and insightful response.

Society has a tendency to try to fit teenagers into a single mold, as if what is beneficial for one student will be equally beneficial for all her peers. Trying to create an environment in which high school students do not spend all of their time outside of class in front of the television is a laudable goal. Insisting that all high school students should work a minimum of 20 hours a week to ensure this is a heavy-handed solution at best. While high schoolers should be encouraged to fill some of their time productively, the activities they engage in should be chosen to fit the individual.

Some students would indeed benefit from experience in the workplace, even if it is only in a "McJob." The lowliest position in the grocery store still demands timeliness, professionalism, and hard work. Many teenagers benefit from learning such values. The added responsibility of managing their earnings wisely increases the opportunities for learning real-life skills, even in the most humble of positions.

However, these lessons may also be learned elsewhere. Working in the stage crew, running for student government, performing in an orchestra, playing a sport, participating in scouting, or any of the other numerous extracurricular activities available offer similar lessons for those self-motivated enough to join. Taking a role among their peers can inspire leadership and organization qualities that are rarely tapped in lower level jobs.

Furthermore, many college-bound high school students do not have time to hold a 20-hour-a-week job. For a student taking advanced classes, schoolwork does not end after classes are over. Coming home, they face hours of homework every night. Forcing these students to spend the time they need for their studies flipping burgers may lower their grades, which will have a far greater effect on their futures than any part-time job might.

Finally, society also must recognize that not all of teenagers' time need be spent doing "constructive" activities. High school is the last breath of childhood. Students should still have some free time to spend on social activities like dating and hanging out with their friends. They are not yet full adults and should not be forced into the full responsibilities of adults. In short, high school students should still have time in their busy schedules for fun.

High school students should indeed have something to do with their time after school that will help prepare them for later life. However, imposing a single set of activities on everyone cannot be a solution. There must be room for individuals to find their own niches. And while it is important to have some structure in their lives, filling up all available time leaves the students no time to be what they actually are—kids.

MATHEMATICS PRACTICE TEST 2

Answer sheet

1 Ⓐ Ⓑ Ⓒ Ⓓ Ⓔ
2 Ⓐ Ⓑ Ⓒ Ⓓ Ⓔ
3 Ⓐ Ⓑ Ⓒ Ⓓ Ⓔ
4 Ⓐ Ⓑ Ⓒ Ⓓ Ⓔ
5 Ⓐ Ⓑ Ⓒ Ⓓ Ⓔ
6 Ⓐ Ⓑ Ⓒ Ⓓ Ⓔ
7 Ⓐ Ⓑ Ⓒ Ⓓ Ⓔ

8 Ⓐ Ⓑ Ⓒ Ⓓ Ⓔ
9 Ⓐ Ⓑ Ⓒ Ⓓ Ⓔ
10 Ⓐ Ⓑ Ⓒ Ⓓ Ⓔ
11 Ⓐ Ⓑ Ⓒ Ⓓ Ⓔ
12 Ⓐ Ⓑ Ⓒ Ⓓ Ⓔ
13 Ⓐ Ⓑ Ⓒ Ⓓ Ⓔ
14 Ⓐ Ⓑ Ⓒ Ⓓ Ⓔ

15 Ⓐ Ⓑ Ⓒ Ⓓ Ⓔ
16 Ⓐ Ⓑ Ⓒ Ⓓ Ⓔ
17 Ⓐ Ⓑ Ⓒ Ⓓ Ⓔ
18 Ⓐ Ⓑ Ⓒ Ⓓ Ⓔ
19 Ⓐ Ⓑ Ⓒ Ⓓ Ⓔ
20 Ⓐ Ⓑ Ⓒ Ⓓ Ⓔ
21 Ⓐ Ⓑ Ⓒ Ⓓ Ⓔ

22 Ⓐ Ⓑ Ⓒ Ⓓ Ⓔ
23 Ⓐ Ⓑ Ⓒ Ⓓ Ⓔ
24 Ⓐ Ⓑ Ⓒ Ⓓ Ⓔ
25 Ⓐ Ⓑ Ⓒ Ⓓ Ⓔ
26 Ⓐ Ⓑ Ⓒ Ⓓ Ⓔ
27 Ⓐ Ⓑ Ⓒ Ⓓ Ⓔ
28 Ⓐ Ⓑ Ⓒ Ⓓ Ⓔ

29 Ⓐ Ⓑ Ⓒ Ⓓ Ⓔ
30 Ⓐ Ⓑ Ⓒ Ⓓ Ⓔ
31 Ⓐ Ⓑ Ⓒ Ⓓ Ⓔ
32 Ⓐ Ⓑ Ⓒ Ⓓ Ⓔ
33 Ⓐ Ⓑ Ⓒ Ⓓ Ⓔ
34 Ⓐ Ⓑ Ⓒ Ⓓ Ⓔ
35 Ⓐ Ⓑ Ⓒ Ⓓ Ⓔ

36 Ⓐ Ⓑ Ⓒ Ⓓ Ⓔ
37 Ⓐ Ⓑ Ⓒ Ⓓ Ⓔ
38 Ⓐ Ⓑ Ⓒ Ⓓ Ⓔ
39 Ⓐ Ⓑ Ⓒ Ⓓ Ⓔ
40 Ⓐ Ⓑ Ⓒ Ⓓ Ⓔ

MATHEMATICS PRACTICE TEST 2

40 questions, 60 minutes

Directions: Select the best choice for each item and mark the answer on your answer sheet.

1. Which answer is closest to $1,865 \times 6,285$?

(A) 6,000,000   (B) 7,000,000   (C) 10,000,000

(D) 12,000,000   (E) 14,000,000

2. Which of these fractions is the least?

(A) $^3/_4$ (B) $^9/_7$ (C) $^{23}/_{17}$

(D) $^2/_5$ (E) $^{10}/_6$

3. If $A = 3r - 2$, and $r = 4$, then $A =$

(A) 1   (B) 12   (C) 10

(D) 6   (E) 18

4. If you roll 2 six-sided dice, what is the probability that the combined total shown will be 7?

(A) $^1/_6$ (B) $^7/_{36}$ (C) $^1/_{12}$

(D) $^3/_{36}$ (E) 0

5. Your electric bill for June was \$25, but your electric bill for July was \$28.50. Assuming you used the same amount of power both months, what is the percent increase in the cost of electricity?

(A) 12.3 percent
(B) 14.0 percent
(C) 25.0 percent
(D) 87.7 percent
(E) 114.0 percent

6. Which of these problems have the same numerical answer?
I. If a box holds 12 apples, how many boxes do you need to hold 40 apples?
II. If 12 people share the \$40 cost of a gift evenly, how much does each pay?
III. If I need 12 cups of flour to make one batch of waffles, how many full batches can I make with 40 cups of flour?

(A) I and II   (B) I and III   (C) II and III

(D) I, II, and III   (E) None of the above

7. If the probability of picking a chocolate chip cookie from a bag of mixed cookies is 0.40, then if you randomly picked 40 cookies out of the bag, about how many would be chocolate chip?

(A) 4   (B) 12   (C) 16

(D) 24   (E) 40

8. Number of comic books owned:

> **Jimmy** ☺ ☺ ☺ ☺
> **Billy** ☺ ☺
> **Steve** ☺ ☺ ☺ ☺ ☺ ☺

Each ☺ represents 6 comic books.
How many comics does Jimmy own?

(A) 4   (B) 6   (C) 12

(D) 20   (E) 24

9. If $x \div 4 = y$, what is $x \div 2$?

(A) y (B) $y \div 2$ (C) $y \div 4$

(D) $2y$ (E) $4y$

10. Which answer is closest to 0.0005×25?

(A) 125

(B) 1.25

(C) 0.125

(D) 0.0125

(E) 0.000125

11. How many square feet of carpet would you need to carpet the room pictured here?

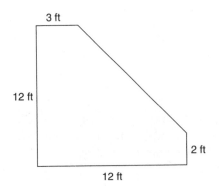

(A) 144   (B) 90   (C) 45

(D) 115   (E) 99

12. Which formula describes the relationship between X and Y shown in the table?

X	Y
2	6
6	14
13	28
17	36
22	46

(A) $Y = 2X + 1$
(B) $Y = 2(X + 1)$
(C) $Y = 3X - 4$
(D) $Y = 3X$
(E) $Y = X + 4$

13. To convert millimeters to meters, you should

(A) multiply by 10
(B) divide by 100
(C) multiply by 100
(D) multiply by 1,000
(E) divide by 1,000

14. If I have four red socks, four black socks, and seven white socks in my drawer, and I pick one at random, what is the probability I'll pick a black sock?

(A) $\frac{1}{3}$ (B) $\frac{4}{15}$ (C) $\frac{1}{5}$
(D) $\frac{7}{15}$ (E) $\frac{11}{15}$

15. According to the graph, which employee made twice as many sales as Ed?

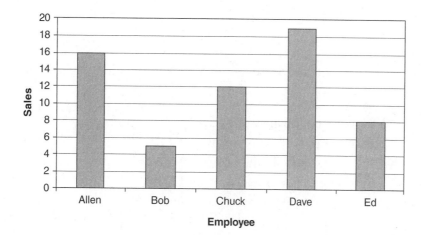

(A) Allen   (B) Bob   (C) Chuck
(D) Dave   (E) None of the above

16. Which decimal is the least?

(A) 0.00121
(B) 0.000753
(C) 0.0299
(D) 0.00654
(E) 0.000913

17. In a box of chocolates, 8 are milk chocolate and 12 are dark chocolate. What percentage are milk chocolate?

(A) 8 percent
(B) 20 percent
(C) 30 percent
(D) 40 percent
(E) 50 percent

18. On the dial shown here, the arrow most likely indicates:

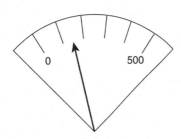

(A) 1.5
(B) 150
(C) 2.5
(E) 50
(D) 250

19. If there are 12 inches in a foot, and 5,280 feet in a mile, how would you find the number of inches in 5 miles?

(A) Divide 5 by 12, then divide the answer by 5,280
(B) Divide 5 by 12, then multiply the answer by 5,280
(C) Multiply 5 by 5,280, then multiply the answer by 12
(D) Multiply 5 by 5,280, then divide the answer by 12
(E) None of the above

20. Which point on the graph is located at (3,4)?

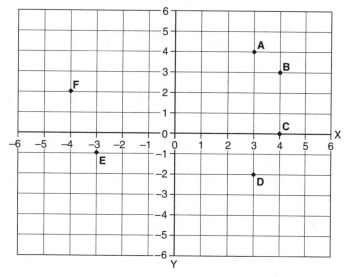

(A) A   (C) C   (E) F
(B) B   (D) D

21. "Some perfect squares are less than 100." According to this statement, which of the following statements is true?

(A) 100 is a perfect square.
(B) All perfect squares are less than 100.
(C) All numbers less than 100 are perfect squares.
(D) Some perfect squares are greater than 100.
(E) No perfect squares are greater than 100.

22. Jose left New York with a full tank of gas. He drove to Baltimore and then refilled his tank. The tank took 9.8 gallons of gas. Joe looked at the map and saw that he had gone approximately 230 miles. What is a good estimate of his miles per gallon?

(A) 20   (B) 23   (C) 25
(D) 25.6   (E) 28.75

23. Using the data from the previous problem, if Jose wanted to drive another 345 miles, about how much gas would he need?

(A) 10 gallons   (B) 14 gallons   (C) 15 gallons
(D) 20 gallons   (E) 34.5 gallons

24. My car is more efficient than Jose's; I get 32 miles to the gallon. I want to travel the 230 miles from New York to Baltimore. About how many gallons of gas do I need?

(A) 6   (B) 8   (C) 10
(D) 15   (E) 23

25. On the dial shown, the arrow most likely indicates:

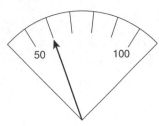

(A) 55   (C) 65   (E) 90

(B) 60   (D) 75

26. A wall is 11 feet high and 16 feet long. There is a window set into the wall that is 4 feet high and 4 feet wide. If 1 quart of paint covers 20 square feet, how many quarts of paint are needed to cover the wall?

(A) 0.8   (C) 8.8   (E) 20

(B) 8   (D) 9.6

27. If $A = 5x + 5$, and $A = 35$, then $x =$

(A) 6   (C) 35   (E) 200

(B) 5   (D) 10

28. The following chart tracks the number of meetings a company has scheduled at five different times. At which time are the 39 meetings scheduled?

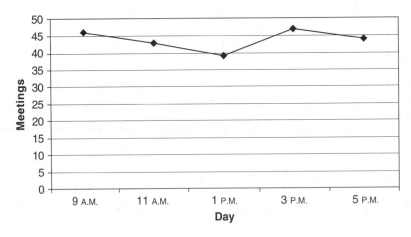

(A) 9 A.M.   (C) 1 P.M.   (E) 5 P.M.

(B) 11 A.M.   (D) 3 P.M.

29. Which of the following numbers is three-quarters of 10,000?

(A) 3,000   (B) $10,000 \times 3 \div 4$ (C) $\dfrac{3}{4,000}$

(D) $\dfrac{10,000}{3}$ (E) $10,000 \div 0.75$

30. Using the ruler shown, approximately how long is the line?

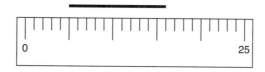

(A) 16   (B) 11   (C) 5
(D) 10¹/₅   (E) 2¹/₅

31. A large group of your friends takes you out to a restaurant for a birthday dinner. When the bill comes, the tax on it is $24.96. If you know the tax rate is 8.75 percent, approximately how much should they leave as an 18 percent tip?

(A) $25.00   (B) $40.00   (C) $45.00
(D) $50.00   (E) $87.50

32. If the scale on a dollhouse is 1 inch to 2.5 feet and a coat rack is 5.5 feet high, how high would you make a dollhouse-scale coat rack?

(A) 0.45 inch
(B) 2.2 inches
(C) 13.75 inches
(D) 1.15 feet
(E) 2.2 feet

33. In a class of 20 students, 6 received As this term. What percentage of the students received As this term?

(A) 14 percent
(B) 20 percent
(C) 25 percent
(D) 30 percent
(E) 43 percent

34. I went cross-country skiing in a straight line 3 miles from my home, then made a 90° right turn and skied straight for another 4 miles. If I wanted to ski straight home from here, how far would I have to go?

(A) 3 miles   (B) 4 miles   (C) 5 miles
(D) 6 miles   (E) 7 miles

35. How many square inches of wrapping paper are needed to exactly cover a cylinder-shaped box that is 12 inches tall and has a 3 inch radius?

(A) 12π (B) 90π (C) 108π
(D) 18π (E) 72π

36. Five salespeople earned the following commissions. Whose was the greatest?

(A) 5 percent of $100
(B) 5 percent of $200
(C) 10 percent of $200
(D) 5 percent of $150
(E) 10 percent of $150

37. Which number falls between $\frac{1}{2}$ and $\frac{4}{5}$?

(A) $\frac{2}{3}$ (B) 0.97   (C) 37%
(D) $\frac{3}{15}$ (E) 0.444

38. Which pairs of decimals and fractions are equivalent?
     I. 0.25, $\frac{1}{4}$ II. 0.45, $\frac{7}{17}$ III. 0.2, $\frac{2}{5}$

(A) I only
(B) III only
(C) I and III
(D) I and II
(E) I, II, and III

39. 550,000 is how many times 5.5?

(A) 100   (B) 1,000   (C) 10,000
(D) 100,000   (E) 1,000,000

40. On a scale drawing of a room, 1 inch = 6 feet. The drawing of the room is 3.5 inches wide. How wide is the actual room?

(A) 1.75 feet
(B) 6 feet
(C) 21 feet
(D) 30 feet
(E) 252 feet

STOP. This is the end of Mathematics Practice Test 2.

MATHEMATICS PRACTICE TEST 2: ANSWERS

1. D. Estimate by rounding to the nearest thousand. $2,000 \times 6,000 = 12,000,000$.

2. D. Choices B, C, and E are all greater than 1. Cross multiply to show $^3/_4 > ^2/_5$.

3. C. $(3 \times 4) - 2 = 10$.

4. A. Six combinations that add up to 7, out of 36 possible combinations.

5. B. $28.5 - 25 = 3.5, 3.5 \div 25 = 0.14$.

6. E. This is a remainder interpretation problem. I is 4 boxes; II is $3.33; III is 3 batches.

7. C. 0.4×40.

8. E. Each ☺ $= 6$, and there are 4 of them. $6 \times 4 = 24$.

9. D. $x = 4y$, so $x \div 2 = 2y$.

10. D. Multiply, then count spaces past the decimal point. $0.0005 \times 25 = 0.0125$.

11. E. This is an area problem. The room is a 12×12 square, minus a 9 ($12 - 3$) by 10 ($12 - 2$) triangle. $(12 \times 12) - (^1/_2 \times 9 \times 10) = 99$.

12. B. Trial and error. Try all of the pairs in each equation and find which one works for all of them.

13. E. 1 meter $= 1,000$ millimeters.

14. B. 4 choices out of a possible 15 ($4 + 4 + 7$).

15. A. Ed made 8; Allen made 16.

16. B. Find the number with the most leading zeros, then compare the first nonzero place if two are tied.

17. D. As a fraction, $^8/_{20}$. Convert fractions to decimals by dividing: $^8/_{20} = 0.4. 0.4 = 40$ percent.

18. B. There are 5 hashes between 0 and 500, so each of the hashes is 100 units. The arrow is about $1^1/_2$ hashes away from 0, and $1.5 \times 100 = 150$.

19. C. Multiply 5 miles times 5,280 feet/mile, then multiply the answer by 12 inches/foot.

20. A. (3,4) means 3 over and 4 up.

21. D. If some perfect squares are less than 100, then some are greater than 100, and some numbers less than 100 are not perfect squares. You don't know anything about 100 itself.

22. B.   He bought almost 10 gallons of gas: $230 \div 10 = 23$.

23. C.   345 is half again as much as 230. He'd need about 15 gallons of gas, half again as much (or divide 345 by 23).

24. B.   Estimate: $230 \div 30 = 23 \div 3 = 7.7$.

25. B.   There are 5 hashes between 50 and 100, so each of the hashes is 10 units. The arrow is about 1 hash away from 50, and $50 + 10 = 60$.

26. B.   The wall is 176 square feet minus 16 square feet of window. To cover 160 square feet at 20 square feet per quart of paint, you will need $160 \div 20 = 8$ quarts of paint.

27. A. $35 = 5x + 5$, so subtract from both sides to get $30 = 5x$, then divide both sides to get $6 = x$.

28. C.   The point for 1 P.M. is 39 on the chart.

29. B. $(10,000 \times 3) \div 4$.

30. B.   There are 25 hashes between 0 and 25, so each of the long hashes is 5 units, and each of the small hashes is 1 unit. The line begins at the 5 hash and ends at 16, and $16 - 5 = 11$.

31. D.   Estimate. $25 is about 9 percent of the bill, so 18 percent of the bill would be twice as much.

32. B.   Use equivalent fractions: $\dfrac{1}{2.5} = \dfrac{x}{5.5}$, so $2.5x = 5.5$, and $x = 2.2$.

33. D.   As a fraction, $^6/_{20}$. Convert fractions to decimals by dividing: $^6/_{20} = 0.3$. $0.3 = 30$ percent.

34. C.   Drawing a picture might be helpful. I have walked the two legs of a right triangle, so use the Pythagorean theorem. $3^2 + 4^2 = 5^2$.

35. B.   This is a surface area problem: $SA = 2\pi r(h + r)$. $SA = 2\pi \times 3(12 + 3) = 90\pi$.

36. C.   Multiply to find each commission; $20 is greatest.

37. A.   The number must fall between 0.5 and 0.8, or 50 percent and 80 percent.

38. A. $0.45 = ^9/_{20}$ and $0.2 = ^1/_5$. Change fractions to decimals by dividing.

39. D. $5.5 \times 100,000 = 550,000$.

40. C.   Use equivalent fractions: $^1/_6 = \dfrac{3.5}{x}$, so $x = 21$.

READING PRACTICE TEST 3

Answer sheet

1 Ⓐ Ⓑ Ⓒ Ⓓ Ⓔ
2 Ⓐ Ⓑ Ⓒ Ⓓ Ⓔ
3 Ⓐ Ⓑ Ⓒ Ⓓ Ⓔ
4 Ⓐ Ⓑ Ⓒ Ⓓ Ⓔ
5 Ⓐ Ⓑ Ⓒ Ⓓ Ⓔ
6 Ⓐ Ⓑ Ⓒ Ⓓ Ⓔ
7 Ⓐ Ⓑ Ⓒ Ⓓ Ⓔ

8 Ⓐ Ⓑ Ⓒ Ⓓ Ⓔ
9 Ⓐ Ⓑ Ⓒ Ⓓ Ⓔ
10 Ⓐ Ⓑ Ⓒ Ⓓ Ⓔ
11 Ⓐ Ⓑ Ⓒ Ⓓ Ⓔ
12 Ⓐ Ⓑ Ⓒ Ⓓ Ⓔ
13 Ⓐ Ⓑ Ⓒ Ⓓ Ⓔ
14 Ⓐ Ⓑ Ⓒ Ⓓ Ⓔ

15 Ⓐ Ⓑ Ⓒ Ⓓ Ⓔ
16 Ⓐ Ⓑ Ⓒ Ⓓ Ⓔ
17 Ⓐ Ⓑ Ⓒ Ⓓ Ⓔ
18 Ⓐ Ⓑ Ⓒ Ⓓ Ⓔ
19 Ⓐ Ⓑ Ⓒ Ⓓ Ⓔ
20 Ⓐ Ⓑ Ⓒ Ⓓ Ⓔ
21 Ⓐ Ⓑ Ⓒ Ⓓ Ⓔ

22 Ⓐ Ⓑ Ⓒ Ⓓ Ⓔ
23 Ⓐ Ⓑ Ⓒ Ⓓ Ⓔ
24 Ⓐ Ⓑ Ⓒ Ⓓ Ⓔ
25 Ⓐ Ⓑ Ⓒ Ⓓ Ⓔ
26 Ⓐ Ⓑ Ⓒ Ⓓ Ⓔ
27 Ⓐ Ⓑ Ⓒ Ⓓ Ⓔ
28 Ⓐ Ⓑ Ⓒ Ⓓ Ⓔ

29 Ⓐ Ⓑ Ⓒ Ⓓ Ⓔ
30 Ⓐ Ⓑ Ⓒ Ⓓ Ⓔ
31 Ⓐ Ⓑ Ⓒ Ⓓ Ⓔ
32 Ⓐ Ⓑ Ⓒ Ⓓ Ⓔ
33 Ⓐ Ⓑ Ⓒ Ⓓ Ⓔ
34 Ⓐ Ⓑ Ⓒ Ⓓ Ⓔ
35 Ⓐ Ⓑ Ⓒ Ⓓ Ⓔ

36 Ⓐ Ⓑ Ⓒ Ⓓ Ⓔ
37 Ⓐ Ⓑ Ⓒ Ⓓ Ⓔ
38 Ⓐ Ⓑ Ⓒ Ⓓ Ⓔ
39 Ⓐ Ⓑ Ⓒ Ⓓ Ⓔ
40 Ⓐ Ⓑ Ⓒ Ⓓ Ⓔ

READING PRACTICE TEST 3

40 questions, 60 minutes

Directions: Each of the following passages is followed by questions. Answer the questions based on what is directly stated or suggested in each passage. Indicate your answers by filling in the corresponding circle on your answer sheet.

Questions 1–2

> Dogs, like humans, are highly social animals. This similarity in their overall behavioral pattern accounts for their trainability and playfulness. It also explains their ability to fit into human households and social situations. Dogs live and work with humans so well that they have earned the nickname "man's best friend."

1. Which of the following best describes the organization of the passage?

(A) The writer uses chronological order.

(B) The writer uses cause and effect.

(C) The writer makes an assertion and backs it up with specific details.

(D) The writer introduces a current debate and then presents both sides.

(E) The writer begins with a summary of the research and then proposes the thesis.

2. Which is the most logical conclusion that you can draw from this passage?

(A) The writer, most likely a dog owner, does not feel the same affection toward other animals commonly kept as pets.

(B) The writer feels that dogs are invaluable as service animals, especially for those people who are visually impaired.

(C) Dogs' sociability is a result of their long history of helping people; after all, dogs were the first animals to be domesticated.

(D) Dogs are indeed our best friends because they help us accomplish work on farms and protect our homes.

(E) Most dogs are usually easily trained because they are comfortable with people.

Questions 3–6

> In the fifth century, Germanic tribes, most notably the Suevi and the Visigoths, invaded the Iberian peninsula, set up kingdoms, and became assimilated in the Roman culture of the peninsula. An Islamic invasion took place in 711. Many of the ousted nobles took refuge in the unconquered north Asturian highlands. From there
> (5) they aimed to reconquer their lands from the Moors. In 868, Count Vimare Peres

reconquered and governed the region between the Minho and Douro rivers. The county became known as *Portucale* (i.e., Portugal), due to its most important city, Portucale (today's Oporto).

(10) While a dependency of the Kingdom of Leon, Portugal occasionally gained de facto during weaker Leonese government, but it lost its autonomy in 1071 due to one of these attempts, ending the rule of the counts of the House of Vímara Peres. Twenty years later, Count Henry from Burgundy was appointed Count of Portugal as a reward for military services to Alfonso VI of León, and given the task of expanding the terri-tory southwards. The county's territory corresponded to what is now northern Portugal,

(15) with its capital in Guimares.

3. The word *autonomy* in line 11 most nearly means

(A) freedom
(B) monarchy
(C) fame
(D) tourists
(E) culture

4. The next paragraph of this essay will most likely

(A) compare and contrast Portugal and its closest neighbor, Spain.
(B) argue that Portugal's greatness is a direct result of its strong leadership.
(C) describe the effect of Portugal's tumultuous history on its current state.
(D) explain what happened in Portugal in subsequent years.
(E) trace Portugal's principal exports and explain its economic success.

5. This excerpt would most likely be published in a

(A) college history textbook
(B) web page for a general audience
(C) scholarly article for history professors
(D) trade publication for genealogists
(E) popular travel magazine

6. Based on the information in this passage, Portugal's early history is best described as

(A) linear
(B) free
(C) peaceful
(D) continually oppressive
(E) tumultuous

Questions 7–8

The successful investigation and prosecution of crimes requires, in most cases, the collection, preservation, and forensic analysis of evidence, which can be crucial to demonstrations of guilt or innocence. Analyses of physical evidence ranging from blood and other biological materials to explosives, drugs, and firearms are con-

(5) ducted by the laboratory, which also serves as a continual source of new scientific techniques. Laboratory examiners provide expert witness testimony in court cases regarding the results of forensic examinations, and specially trained teams and support personnel assist domestic and international law enforcement agencies in large-scale investigations and disasters.

7. The laboratory does all the following EXCEPT

(A) decide who is innocent and guilty in the commission of a crime
(B) gather different kinds of clues that will be used by the courts to adjudicate the case
(C) examine information that has been gathered, including biological evidence
(D) develop new and advanced ways of testing evidence to determine its validity
(E) appear in court to testify about their scientific findings and share their expertise

8. Which of the following is an unstated assumption the author of this passage would MOST likely make?

(A) All crimes can be successfully investigated and prosecuted because the laboratory is so proficient in sifting evidence.
(B) It is more difficult to analyze blood and other biological matter than to investigate explosives, drugs, and firearms.
(C) The laboratory is a crucial link in the chain of command that investigates a crime; indeed, it can sometimes make or break a case.
(D) The laboratory's job has gotten much more challenging today, given the realities of modern life and the sophistication of modern criminals.
(E) The laboratory is the preeminent such facility in the world, given its wide ranging services and superbly trained, expert technicians.

Questions 9–12

What constitutes an American? Not color nor race nor religion. Not the pedigree of his family nor the place of his birth. Not the coincidence of his citizenship. Not his social status nor his bank account. Not his trade nor his profession. An American is one who loves justice and believes in the dignity of man. An American is one who will fight for

(5) his freedom and that of his neighbor. An American is one who will sacrifice property, ease, and security in order that he and his children may retain the rights of free men. An American is one in whose heart is engraved the immortal second sentence of the Declaration of Independence.

Americans have always known how to fight for their rights and their way of life.

(10) Americans are not afraid to fight. They fight joyously in a just cause. We Americans

know that freedom, like peace, is indivisible. We cannot retain our liberty if three-fourths of the world is enslaved. Brutality, injustice, and slavery, if practiced as dictators would have them, universally and systematically, in the long run would destroy us as surely as a fire raging in our nearby neighbor's house would burn ours if we didn't help to put out his.

9. This passage is primarily concerned with

   (A) striking down unfair immigration policies and border patrols
   (B) persuading people to support a war through an appeal to patriotism
   (C) defining the qualities that differentiate Americans from outsiders
   (D) rousing support for an expensive municipal fire department
   (E) gaining support for a substantial and unexpected tax increase

10. Which is the best synonym for *indivisible* as it is used in line 11?

   (A) essential
   (B) undividable
   (C) not visible
   (D) guaranteed
   (E) universal

11. The short sentences, parallel structure, and organization suggest that this document was originally an excerpt from a

   (A) general-audience web page
   (B) nineteenth-century novel
   (C) scholarly text
   (D) speech
   (E) private journal entry

12. The author would be MOST likely to agree with which of the following statements about Americans?

   (A) Americans are different from Europeans because Americans have no regard for social rank.
   (B) You can always identify an American simply by looking at his or her passport.
   (C) Americans are a complex race, not easily defined by traditional benchmarks.
   (D) All Americans should know the Declaration of Independence and Constitution by heart.
   (E) Americans have an obligation to help protect the freedom of others around the world.

Questions 13–16

A king whose only son was fond of martial exercises had a dream in which he was warned that his son would be killed by a lion. Afraid the dream should prove true, the king built for his son a pleasant palace and adorned its walls for his amusement with murals of all kinds of life-sized animals, among which was the picture of a lion.

(5)   When the young prince saw this, his grief at being thus confined burst out afresh, and, standing near the picture of the lion, he said: "O you most detestable of animals! Through a lying dream of my father's, which he saw in his sleep, I am shut up on your account in this palace: what shall I now do to you?"

With these words, he stretched out his hands toward a thorn-tree, meaning to cut a
(10) stick from its branches so that he might beat the lion's visage. But one of the tree's prickles pierced his finger and caused great pain and inflammation, so that the young prince fell down in a fainting fit. A violent fever suddenly set in, from which he died not many days later.

13. This story is best described as

(A) a fable because it has a moral and teaches a lesson
(B) a myth because it concerns animals and death
(C) a biography because it traces the life of a famous person
(D) a fairy tale because it involves fantasy and magic
(E) a short story because it has a plot, setting, and characters

14. The word *martial* in line 1 most nearly means

(A) hunting
(B) manly
(C) military
(D) dangerous
(E) outdoor

15. It can be inferred from the passage that

(A) the king has a deep-seated fear of animals, especially wild ones
(B) the king believes that he can control fate
(C) the king is very old and worried about the succession
(D) all the king's other children have died tragic deaths
(E) the prince has previously run into dangerous trouble

16. The theme of this selection is best stated as:

(A) People should always heed their dreams because the unconscious is a powerful force.
(B) Even if they are already all grown-up, children should listen to their parents because parents know best.
(C) Wild animals are truly dangerous and must be confined correctly.
(D) You can change reality and the future if you are brave, resourceful, and powerful.
(E) It is better to bear our troubles bravely than to try to escape them.

Question 17

China, one of the earliest centers of human civilization, was also one of the few to invent writing independently. The other civilizations are ancient Mesopotamia (Sumerians), India, the Mayan civilization, and ancient Egypt. The ancient Chinese script is still used today by the Chinese, Japanese, Koreans, and Vietnamese.

17. It can be inferred from the passage that

(A) modern Chinese, Japanese, Koreans, and Vietnamese cultures are all remarkably similar
(B) contemporary Chinese writing is very difficult, which is why few people have mastered it
(C) ancient Chinese culture left a rich heritage of literature and the arts that far surpasses the European tradition
(D) the ancient Chinese people enjoyed a literate and advanced culture
(E) in ancient days, only educated people could read and write

Questions 18–21

The habit of reading is one of the greatest resources of mankind; and we enjoy reading books that belong to us much more than if they are borrowed. A borrowed book is like a guest in the house; it must be treated with punctiliousness, with a certain considerate formality. You must see that it sustains no damage; it must not suffer
(5) while under your roof. You cannot leave it carelessly, you cannot mark it, you cannot turn down the pages, you cannot use it familiarly. And then, some day, although this is seldom done, you really ought to return it.

But your own books belong to you; you treat them with that affectionate intimacy that annihilates formality. Books are for use, not for show; you should own no
(10) book that you are afraid to mark up, or afraid to place on the table, wide open and face down. A good reason for marking favorite passages in books is that this practice enables you to remember more easily the significant sayings, to refer to them quickly, and then in later years, it is like visiting a forest where you once blazed a trail. You have the pleasure of going over the old ground, and recalling both the intellectual
(15) scenery and your own earlier self.

Everyone should begin collecting a private library in youth; the instinct of private property, which is fundamental in human beings, can here be cultivated with every advantage and no evils. One should have one's own bookshelves, which should not have doors, glass windows, or keys; they should be free and accessible to the hand as well as
(20) to the eye. The best of mural decorations is books; they are more varied in color and appearance than any wallpaper, they are more attractive in design, and they have the prime advantage of being separate personalities, so that if you sit alone in the room in the firelight, you are surrounded with intimate friends. The knowledge that they are there in plain view is both stimulating and refreshing. You do not have to read them all. Most of
(25) my indoor life is spent in a room containing 6,000 books; and I have a stock answer to the invariable question that comes from strangers. "Have you read all of these books?"

"Some of them twice." This reply is both true and unexpected.

18. The author feels that we enjoy reading our own books more than borrowed books for all of the following reasons EXCEPT

(A) if you own a book, you can have a conversation with it and record your thoughts in the margin

(B) you have to be too careful with borrowed books to make sure that they don't get damaged

(C) owning a book is a more personal experience than borrowing a book because the owned book becomes an extension of yourself

(D) borrowing a book is inconvenient because people always want their books back before you have finished reading them

(E) you have to maintain a distance from a borrowed book, which is not the case with a book you own

19. The author would MOST likely agree that

(A) people should own their own homes or apartments

(B) books should never be defaced with writing of any sort

(C) people spend too much time reading; they should get outdoors more

(D) it is more important to know one book well than to have read many books

(E) books are preferable to people because you can learn more from books

20. Which is the best definition of *punctiliousness* as it is used in line 4?

(A) great care

(B) attention to time

(C) strict attention to minute details

(D) sophistication

(E) admiration and respect

21. You can infer that the author would support all of the following EXCEPT

(A) literacy programs

(B) writing classes

(C) public libraries

(D) inexpensive paperback books

(E) online book stores

Questions 22–23

In particle physics, quarks are one of the two basic constituents of matter. (The other Standard Model fermions are the leptons.) Antiparticles of quarks are called antiquarks. Quarks are the only fundamental particles that interact through all four of the fundamental forces. An important property of quarks is called confinement, which states that indi-
(5) vidual quarks are not seen because they are always confined inside subatomic particles

called hadrons (e.g., protons and neutrons). (An exception is the top quark, which decays so quickly that it does not hadronize, and can therefore be observed more directly via its decay products.) Confinement began as an experimental observation, and is expected to follow from the modern theory of strong interactions, called quantum
(10) chromodynamics (QCD).

22. What is the relationship between hadrons and quarks?

    (A) "Hadron" and "quark" are basically two words for the same subatomic force.
    (B) Hadrons are a special type of nuclear experiment called "quantum chromodynamics."
    (C) A quark is the material that is left over when a hadron decays through its half-life.
    (D) A hadron is the force that decays quickly; as a result, quarks are invisible to the naked eye.
    (E) Quarks are inside hadrons, subatomic particles.

23. Which is the best title for this passage?

    (A) The Dangers of Nuclear Physics
    (B) Nuclear Physics Today
    (C) A Startling Discovery
    (D) Invisible to the Naked Eye
    (E) Quarks

Questions 24–26

How do you get plants to grow on Mars? Step one: relieve their anxiety. Anxiety in people can be a positive thing because it helps initiate signals that get you ready to act. However, while an occasional bit of anxiety can save your life, constant anxiety causes great harm. The hormones that put your body on high alert also damage your brain,
(5) your immune system, and other systems if they constantly flood through your body.

Plants don't get anxious in the same way that humans do, but they do suffer from stress, and they deal with it in much the same way. They produce a chemical signal—superoxide (O_2)—that puts the rest of the plant on high alert. Superoxide, however, is toxic; an excess amount of it harms the plant. This could be a problem for plants on Mars.
(10) Humans will likely visit and explore Mars in the decades ahead. Inevitably, they'll want to take plants with them because plants provide food, oxygen, companionship, and a patch of green far from home. On Mars, plants would have to tolerate conditions that usually cause them a great deal of stress—severe cold, drought, low air pressure, and unfamiliar soils—but plant physiologists and microbiologists believe they can develop
(15) plants that can live in these conditions. Stress management is key: oddly, there are already Earth creatures that thrive in Mars-like conditions. They're not plants, though. They're some of Earth's earliest life forms—ancient microbes that live at the bottom of the ocean and deep within Arctic ice. Scientists hope to produce Mars-friendly plants by borrowing genes from these extreme-loving microbes, and the first genes they're taking
(20) are those that will strengthen the plants' ability to deal with stress. The goal, of course, is not to develop plants that can merely survive Martian conditions. To be truly useful, the plants will need to thrive: to produce crops, to recycle wastes, and so on.

24. How are plants and people the same?

(A) They both experience physiological stress and react to it in similar ways.
(B) They will both one day not only live on Mars but also flourish there.
(C) They can both adapt to severe cold, drought, low air pressure, and unfamiliar soils.
(D) They will both be able to adapt to stress as a result of advanced genetic engineering.
(E) They both produce superoxide, but in slightly differing quantities.

25. Which is the best definition of *toxic* as it is used in line 10?

(A) exotic
(B) extraterrestrial
(C) harmful
(D) unnatural
(E) problematic

26. The main idea of this passage is BEST stated as

(A) Experiencing some stress is beneficial for people because it helps them react appropriately to danger.
(B) If humans are to survive, they must colonize other planets: Mars is the likely choice because it is closest to Earth.
(C) Scientists are working on developing plants that can adapt to the stress of life on Mars.
(D) Mars has a cruel environment, characterized by severe cold, drought, low air pressure, and lack of plants.
(E) Very old microbes that live at the bottom of the sea present the best possibility of adapting to life on Mars.

Question 27

Sikhism, the ninth-largest organized religion in the world, began in sixteenth century Northern India with the teachings of Nanak. Adherents of Sikhism, known as Sikhs, number over 23 million and are spread across the world, although most Sikhs live in the state of Punjab; prior to partition, millions of Sikhs resided in what is now the Punjab province of
(5) Pakistan. Sikhs believe in one God and advocate the pursuit of salvation through disciplined, personal meditation. The followers of Sikhism are ordained to follow the teachings of the 10 Sikh Gurus, or enlightened leaders, as well as the holy scripture which includes the selected works of many authors from diverse socioeconomic and religious backgrounds.

27. In order to validate the author's claim that most Sikhs live in the state of Punjab, it would be helpful to know which of the following?

(A) exactly where Punjab is located in the world
(B) why the Sikhs moved from the Punjab province of Pakistan
(C) statistics for the distribution of Sikhs throughout the world
(D) more detailed information about the origin of the religion
(E) how the religion of Sikhism affects daily life for its adherents

Questions 28–30

Located on the rugged coast of Maine, Acadia National Park encompasses over 47,000 acres of granite mountains, woodlands, lakes, ponds, and ocean shoreline. Such diverse habitats create striking scenery and make the park a heaven for wildlife and plants. Entwined with the natural diversity of Acadia is the story of people: Native peoples, explorers from far-off

(5) lands, European settlers, European and American tourists have all gloried in its beauty. Affluent people at the turn of the century flocked to the area; these early conservationists had much to do with preserving the landscape we know today.

28. All of the following are associated with Acadia National Park EXCEPT

(A) original settlers
(B) land builders and developers
(C) visitors from the continent
(D) immigrants
(E) wealthy, powerful people

29. The word *diverse* in line 3 most nearly means

(A) varied
(B) beautiful
(C) natural
(D) unusual
(E) protected

30. Based on the details in the passage, you can make the generalization that the passage reveals the author's

(A) mild support for using tax revenues to buoy up deteriorating national parks
(B) enthusiastic belief in the benefits of camping, hiking, and other outdoor activities
(C) belief that Maine's Acadia National Park is the jewel in the national park system
(D) distrust of wealthy people, especially those who expose the conservationist credo
(E) admiration for Acadia National Park and its rich, varied history

Questions 31–33

Education is the instruction of the intellect in the laws of nature, under which I include not only things and their forces, but men and their ways; and the fashioning of their affections and of the will into an earnest and living desire to move in harmony with these laws. That man, I think, has had a liberal education who has been so trained in his

(5) youth that his body is the ready servant of his will, and does with ease and pleasure all the work that, as a mechanism, it is capable of; whose intellect is a clear, cold, logic engine, to be turned to any kind of work, to spin the gossamers as well as to forge the anchors of the mind; whose mind is stored with the great and fundamental truths of

nature and the laws of her operations; one whose passions are trained to come to heel
(10) by a vigorous will, the servant of a tender conscience; one who has learned to love all
beauty, whether of nature or of art, to hate all vileness, and to respect others as himself.
   Instead of rearing an oversensitive hot-house plant that must be fragile in the extreme,
strive to rear a sturdy plant that can hold its own amid the storms. The child should spend
as much of its life as possible in the open air, and in the warm months live out-of-doors.
(15) City children should be taken to the seashore or country to spend several months every
summer. Together with outdoor sports, gymnastics adapted to the age of the child should
be begun early and continued throughout life. Good muscular development is attended
with good digestion and a well-balanced nervous system.

31. You can infer from the passage that a thorough liberal education includes all the following
EXCEPT

(A) training in various athletics, sports, and physical exercises
(B) instruction in the rules of logic, likely through formal debating
(C) the ability to speak, read, and write a foreign language like a native speaker
(D) a complete grounding in fine art appreciation, including paintings
(E) mastery of good manners and deportment

32. Which of the following would the author MOST likely support?

(A) community greenhouses to raise rare orchids
(B) animal parks to shelter endangered species
(C) lessons in gourmet cooking for children
(D) subsidized outdoor summer camps for children
(E) educational television, especially shows involving puppets

33. Who or what are the plants in the last paragraphs?

(A) children
(B) ill-equipped parents
(C) skilled teachers
(D) overpaid nannies
(E) weeds

Questions 34–35

   Matthew Alexander Henson was an American explorer who accompanied Robert Peary
on his explorations to the North Pole in 1909. Due to his race and his status as Peary's
paid assistant, Henson was denied credit for his accomplishments at the time. In 1937,
when Peary was 70 years old, this error was finally rectified. That year, the explorers made
(5) him an honorary member. In 1946, the Navy awarded him a medal.

34. Which of the following best describes the organization of this passage?

    (A) A controversial theory is proposed, dissected, and then convincingly defended.
    (B) A series of interrelated events in Henson's life are arranged in chronological order.
    (C) An important topic is summarized, analyzed, and then evaluated.
    (D) A problematic issue is discussed and a partial solution suggested.
    (E) A criticism is explained, evaluated, and then completely resolved.

35. The best synonym for the word *rectified* in line 5 is

    (A) recognized
    (B) corrected
    (C) publicized
    (D) shared
    (E) acknowledged

Questions 36–39

In *The Language Instinct*, Steven Pinker argues that humans are born with an innate capacity for language. Pinker sets out to disabuse the reader of a number of common ideas about language; for example, that children must be taught to use it, that most people's grammar is poor, that the quality of language is steadily declining, that language has a heavy influence
(5) on a person's possible range of thoughts (the Sapir-Whorf hypothesis), and that animals have been taught language. Each of these claims, he argues, is false. Instead, Pinker sees language as an ability unique to humans, produced by evolution to solve the specific problem of communication among social hunter-gatherers. He compares language to other species' specialized adaptations such as spiders' web-weaving or beavers' dam-building
(10) behavior, calling all three "instincts," by which he means that it is not a human invention in the sense that metalworking and writing are. While only some human cultures possess these technologies, all cultures possess language itself.

   As further evidence for the universality of language, Pinker notes that children spontaneously invent a consistent grammatical speech (a creole) even if they grow up
(15) among a mixed-culture population speaking an informal trade pidgin with no consistent rules. Deaf babies "babble" with their hands as others normally do with voice, and spontaneously invent sign languages with true grammar rather than a crude pointing system. Speech also develops in the absence of formal instruction or active attempts by parents to correct children's grammar. These signs suggest that rather than being a human
(20) invention, language is an innate human ability.

36. Which of the following is an unstated assumption made by the author of this passage?

    (A) Everyone recognizes that English is the easiest language and will soon be the universal language.
    (B) Language is really the only way that we have to express ourselves.
    (C) Language is linked to our general reasoning ability, a mark of advanced intelligence.
    (D) People who are systematically taught to speak have better language skills than those who have not been instructed.
    (E) Steven Pinker is a recognized authority on language and thus his theories deserve serious consideration.

37. Pinker argues that all of the following ideas about language acquisition are false EXCEPT

(A) that only humans have language, which they developed as a favorable adaptation
(B) that apes have learned to recognize signs and thus communicate with human language
(C) that babies learn language through a conscious process taught by their parents or caretakers
(D) that the average person doesn't have a clear understanding of the structure of language
(E) that people spoke and wrote with greater skill and mastery in the past than now.

38. The author's purpose is MOST likely to

(A) convince readers that language is universal
(B) describe the different ways that language can manifest itself.
(C) explain Pinker's theories to a general audience
(D) show the overarching importance of language in daily discourse
(E) compare and contrast different theories of language acquisition.

39. The best antonym for the word *innate* (line 2) is

(A) undeveloped
(B) serious
(C) inborn
(D) acquired
(E) infinite

Question 40

Fire has many modern uses. In its broadest sense, fire is used by nearly every human being on earth in a controlled setting every day: for instance, owners of internal combustion vehicles use fire every time they drive and thermal power stations provide electricity for a large percentage of humanity. Fire is also used more directly; many nomadic
(5) people still use fire for cooking.

40. The writer believes that fire

(A) is beneficial but frequently abused by careless people
(B) is a valuable tool today as it was in the past
(C) is without doubt the most crucial tool available to humankind
(D) is useful to contemporary people but not prehistoric ones
(E) must be used with extreme care, especially by nomads

STOP. This is the end of Reading Practice Test 3.

READING PRACTICE TEST 3: ANSWERS

1. C. The writer makes an assertion—"Dogs, like humans, are highly social animals"—and supports it with specific examples.

2. E. When you draw a conclusion, you use details from a passage and what you already know to make an unstated assumption. Since the passage emphasizes that dogs are social, you can logically conclude that they are easily trained. You know this from your own experience as well. None of the other statements can be concluded from the information provided here. For instance, you cannot conclude that the writer owns a dog because there is no indication of that at all. Further, you cannot conclude that dogs were the first animals to be domesticated (although that is true), because that information is not provided in the passage.

3. A. *Autonomy* means self-rule or independence. The closest choice is freedom. You can figure this out from the contrast context clue "*but* it lost its autonomy in 1071 due to one of these attempts, ending the rule of the counts of the House of Vímara Peres." You can also use structural analysis, as the prefix *auto-* means "self."

4. D. Since the details in the passage are arranged in chronological order, it seems most logical that this order will continue. Further, since the passage traces Portugal's history, we can most logically expect to read what happened in Portugal in subsequent years.

5. B. The article traces the history of Portugal for a general readership. It is not technical or scholarly enough to appeal to college students (choice A), history professors (choice C), or genealogists (choice D). Travelers (choice E) who want this much information would read a travel book on Portugal, not a magazine.

6. E. Portugal had a tumultuous past, marked by invaders, shifting rulers, and periods of independence interspersed with periods of domination. Choice A—linear—is meaningless: all time is linear by its very nature. Portugal did gain its independence during the weaker Leonese government, but it lost its freedom in 1071, so you can eliminate choices B, C, and D.

7. A. The laboratory does not have the power to decide who is innocent and guilty in the commission of a crime: that power is reserved solely for the courts, as guaranteed by the U.S. Constitution. Every other detail can be found in the passage. This is a literal recall question, so to find the correct answer, go back to the passage and try to match each choice to the information you find there.

8. C. The process of elimination technique works well here. While the author does indeed show a bias toward the laboratory, choices A and E are too great a stretch, given the evidence in the passage. You can also eliminate choice A because it contains the absolute word "all." Beware of choices that contain absolute words such as *all, none, always, never* because they usually indicate that a choice isn't correct. Few things are *always* or *never*, black and white. There is no proof for choice B: *It is more difficult to analyze blood and other biological matter than to investigate explosives, drugs, and firearms.* The same is true of choice D—*The laboratory's job has gotten much more challenging today, given the realities of modern life and the sophistication of modern criminals.* Even though this may be true, you can't prove it based on the evidence here. Thus, only choice C can be inferred from the examples and author's positive tone.

9. B.   You can conclude that this passage is primarily concerned with persuading people to support a major war through an appeal to patriotism from the following details: "An American is one who will fight for his freedom and that of his neighbor," "An American is one who will sacrifice property, ease, and security in order that he and his children may retain the rights of free men," and "Americans are not afraid to fight. They fight joyously in a just cause. We Americans know that freedom, like peace, is indivisible."

10. B.   *Indivisible* means "cannot be divided." None of the other choices has this meaning.

11. D.   Effective speeches are usually characterized by short sentences, parallel structure, and clear-cut organization. Short sentences make the ideas easy to understand. Parallel structure gives writing and speech a musical, rhythmic flow. Clear-cut organization makes it easy to follow the speaker's ideas. Eliminate choice A because a general audience web page would not necessarily have any of these features. Eliminate choice B because this passage is clearly not fiction. Likewise, choice C is illogical because a scholarly text would have long sentences, not short ones. Choice E is also unlikely the tone of this document as it is exactly the opposite of what we would encounter in a private journal entry.

12. E.   The author would be MOST likely to agree that Americans have an obligation to help protect the freedom of others around the world. You can infer this from the following detail in the text: "[Americans]... They fight joyously in a just cause. We Americans know that freedom, like peace, is indivisible. We cannot retain our liberty if three-fourths of the world is enslaved. Brutality, injustice, and slavery, if practiced as dictators would have them, universally and systematically, in the long run would destroy us as surely as a fire raging in our nearby neighbor's house would burn ours if we didn't help to put out his."

13. A.   This story is best described as a fable because it has a moral and teaches a lesson. Choice E is correct but too general: all fables are short stories by definition, but fables are a subset of stories. Choice B is incorrect because myths are origin stories that concern gods and goddesses; choice C is incorrect because the characters are never named. Choice D is incorrect because it doesn't take the story's moral into account.

14. C.   The word *martial* most nearly means "military." The word comes from Mars, the god of war.

15. B.   You can infer from the information in the passage that the king believes that he can control fate. You can figure this out because the king believes that locking up his son will protect him. The king's effort fails, but that does not negate the king's belief that it will succeed.

16. E.   The theme of this story is best stated as: *It is better to bear our troubles bravely than to try to escape them.* Choice D is the exact opposite; choice C is off the topic because the prince does not die from an animal attack. Choice A is wrong because it is too general. Recall the need to avoid absolute words such as *always.* Choice B is incorrect because the prince did listen to his father and stay in the palace, but it did not alter his fate.

17. D.   Because they invented writing independent of all other civilizations, you can draw the conclusion that the ancient Chinese had a literate and advanced culture. Choices B, C, and E may be correct, but you cannot infer any of them from the passage. Likewise, just because they share aspects of the written alphabet, you cannot make the leap that modern Chinese, Japanese, Koreans, and Vietnamese cultures are all remarkably similar. This eliminates choice A.

18. D. The author does say that you must return borrowed books, but not before you have finished them. All the other choices are listed in the passage.

19. A. Remember that when you make an inference, you combine textual proof with what you already know to "read between the lines" and find unstated information. There are two details in this passage that you can use to make this inference. First, in the beginning of the essay, the author argues that people should own books because then they can make the books an extension of their own personality. People can write in the books or turn down a page, for instance. Second, the author says: "Everyone should begin collecting a private library in youth; *the instinct of private property, which is fundamental in human beings*, can here be cultivated with every advantage and no evils." From these two clues, you can infer that the author would most likely agree that people should own their own homes or apartments because then they can make the space their own. There is no support for any of the other inferences.

20. C. You can figure out that *punctiliousness* means "strict attention to minute details" because the author follows the term with a list of strict details that you must follow when you borrow someone else's book.

21. B. The entire passage describes the joy of owning books, so the author would likely support virtually any program that teaches people to read and gets books into the hands of people. Only choice B does not do this because the author does not propose that people learn to write their own books.

22. E. Don't be misled by the jargon and technical words: this is actually a relatively simple question that merely requires close reading. You can find the answer in the following sentence: *An important property of quarks is called confinement, which states that individual quarks are not seen because they are always confined inside subatomic particles called hadrons (e.g., protons and neutrons).*

23. E. This is a main idea question, as effective titles serve two purposes: express the main idea and get the reader's attention. Start by identifying the topic sentence because it states the main idea. In an expository passage (a passage that explains), the topic sentence is usually the first sentence, as is the case here: *In particle physics, quarks are one of the two basic constituents of matter.* This tells you that the main idea of the passage is quarks. Choices A and C have nothing to do with the passage, choice B is far too broad, and choice D is too narrow.

24. A. Both plants and humans experience physiological stress and react to it in similar ways. You can find the answer in this sentence: "Plants don't get anxious in the same way that humans do, but they do suffer from stress, and they deal with it in much the same way." You cannot assume that choice B—*They will both one day not only live on Mars but also flourish there*—is true, and certainly not based on the information in the passage. The same is true of choice C: *They can both adapt to severe cold, drought, low air pressure, and unfamiliar soils.* There is no mention of genetic engineering, so choice D is wrong. Humans do not produce superoxide, so choice E is wrong.

25. C. You can infer the answer from this context clue: "Superoxide, however, is toxic; too much of it will end up harming the plant." The key word is *harming*.

26. C. Only choice C summarizes the author's thesis: How scientists are trying to develop plants that can survive the stress of Mars' harsh environment. Remember that the main idea is the overarching thesis, the author's primary point. Details are small pieces of information that support the main idea. Choices A, D, and E are details, not the main idea. Choice B is off the topic.

27. C. The term "most" is vague; to validate it, readers would have to know statistics for the distribution of Sikhs throughout the world. The other information is not germane to the topic.

28. B. Since Acadia is a national park, the land cannot be used for homes or businesses. It is protected by federal law. In addition, all the other people provided as choices are included in the passage.

29. A. *Diverse* means "varied," which you can infer from the context clue "granite mountains, woodlands, lakes, ponds, and ocean shoreline."

30. E. Based on the details in the passage, you can generalize that the passage reveals the author's admiration for Acadia National Park and its rich, varied history. Choices A, B, and D are off the topic and twist details the passage contains. Choice C overstates the author's tone.

31. C. The passage states that a thorough liberal education includes all the following EXCEPT the ability to speak, read, and write a foreign language. You can infer that students should receive training in various athletics, sports, and exercises (choice A) from the following detail: "*That man, I think, has had a liberal education who has been so trained in his youth that his body is the ready servant of his will.*" You can infer choice B, instruction in the rules of formal debating, from this detail: "*whose intellect is a clear, cold, logic engine.*" Choice D, a complete grounding in art appreciation, comes from "*one who has learned to love all beauty, whether of nature or of art.*" You can find choice E, good manners and deportment, from "*respect others as himself.*"

32. D. The author would most likely support summer camps, which you can infer from the following two details: *That man, I think, has had a liberal education who has been so trained in his youth that his body is the ready servant of his will . . .* and *one who has learned to love all beauty, whether of nature or of art.* There is no support for any of the other choices.

33. A. The plants in the last paragraph are a metaphor for children: the author compares effete children to "oversensitive hot-house plant[s]" and healthy children to "sturdy plant[s]." The storms are the vicissitudes of life.

34. B. The details in the passage are related in chronological (time) order. The passage begins in 1909 with Henson and Peary's famous trip to the North Pole, then progresses to 1937, when Peary received the honor due to him. The passage ends 9 years later, in 1946, when the Navy awarded Henson a medal. To determine whether or not a passage is written in chronological order, look for dates and time-order words (*first, second, third, next, then, finally*, and so on).

35. B. To *rectify* something is to correct it. You can infer this from the fact that the explorers made Henson an honorary member. This recognition helped correct the earlier error of not giving Henson recognition for his accomplishments.

36. E. The author assumes that readers know that Steven Pinker is a recognized authority on language and thus his theories deserve serious consideration. The author assumes that we have heard of Pinker and his work. Choice A is wrong because nowhere does the author suggest that any one language is better than any other. Choice B is incorrect because we can also express ourselves through nonverbal means such as gestures, body language, and facial expressions. Choice C is wrong because it contradicts his thesis: if language is innate, it cannot be the mark of advanced intelligence. The same is true of choice D: innate language does not have to be taught.

37. A. Pinker argues that only humans have language, which they developed as a favorable adaptation. You can find this detail in the following sentence: *Instead, Pinker sees language as an ability unique to humans, produced by evolution to solve the specific problem of communication among social hunter-gatherers.*

38. C. The distinction between what the author is proving and what Pinker believes is crucial: Pinker believes that language is universal (choice A) but the author is explaining Pinker's theories (choice C) rather than proving them. The decision whether or not to believe Pinker's hypothesis is left to the reader.

39. D. *Innate* means "inborn." Thus, the best antonym is "acquired."

40. B. The writer believes that fire is a valuable tool today as it was in the past, which you can infer from the list of fire's uses. Choice C overstates the case; choices A and E are off the topic. Choice D shows a basic misunderstanding of the passage.

Skill Spread

Skill Type	Item Numbers
Literal understanding	1, 7, 8, 10, 14, 18, 20, 22, 24, 26, 27, 28, 34, 36 37, 38, 39, 40
Inferential and critical understanding	2, 3, 4, 5, 6, 9, 11, 12, 13, 15, 16, 17, 19, 21, 23, 25, 29, 30, 31, 32, 33, 35

WRITING PRACTICE TEST 3

Answer sheet

1 Ⓐ Ⓑ Ⓒ Ⓓ Ⓔ
2 Ⓐ Ⓑ Ⓒ Ⓓ Ⓔ
3 Ⓐ Ⓑ Ⓒ Ⓓ Ⓔ
4 Ⓐ Ⓑ Ⓒ Ⓓ Ⓔ
5 Ⓐ Ⓑ Ⓒ Ⓓ Ⓔ
6 Ⓐ Ⓑ Ⓒ Ⓓ Ⓔ
7 Ⓐ Ⓑ Ⓒ Ⓓ Ⓔ

8 Ⓐ Ⓑ Ⓒ Ⓓ Ⓔ
9 Ⓐ Ⓑ Ⓒ Ⓓ Ⓔ
10 Ⓐ Ⓑ Ⓒ Ⓓ Ⓔ
11 Ⓐ Ⓑ Ⓒ Ⓓ Ⓔ
12 Ⓐ Ⓑ Ⓒ Ⓓ Ⓔ
13 Ⓐ Ⓑ Ⓒ Ⓓ Ⓔ
14 Ⓐ Ⓑ Ⓒ Ⓓ Ⓔ

15 Ⓐ Ⓑ Ⓒ Ⓓ Ⓔ
16 Ⓐ Ⓑ Ⓒ Ⓓ Ⓔ
17 Ⓐ Ⓑ Ⓒ Ⓓ Ⓔ
18 Ⓐ Ⓑ Ⓒ Ⓓ Ⓔ
19 Ⓐ Ⓑ Ⓒ Ⓓ Ⓔ
20 Ⓐ Ⓑ Ⓒ Ⓓ Ⓔ
21 Ⓐ Ⓑ Ⓒ Ⓓ Ⓔ

22 Ⓐ Ⓑ Ⓒ Ⓓ Ⓔ
23 Ⓐ Ⓑ Ⓒ Ⓓ Ⓔ
24 Ⓐ Ⓑ Ⓒ Ⓓ Ⓔ
25 Ⓐ Ⓑ Ⓒ Ⓓ Ⓔ
26 Ⓐ Ⓑ Ⓒ Ⓓ Ⓔ
27 Ⓐ Ⓑ Ⓒ Ⓓ Ⓔ
28 Ⓐ Ⓑ Ⓒ Ⓓ Ⓔ

29 Ⓐ Ⓑ Ⓒ Ⓓ Ⓔ
30 Ⓐ Ⓑ Ⓒ Ⓓ Ⓔ
31 Ⓐ Ⓑ Ⓒ Ⓓ Ⓔ
32 Ⓐ Ⓑ Ⓒ Ⓓ Ⓔ
33 Ⓐ Ⓑ Ⓒ Ⓓ Ⓔ
34 Ⓐ Ⓑ Ⓒ Ⓓ Ⓔ
35 Ⓐ Ⓑ Ⓒ Ⓓ Ⓔ

36 Ⓐ Ⓑ Ⓒ Ⓓ Ⓔ
37 Ⓐ Ⓑ Ⓒ Ⓓ Ⓔ
38 Ⓐ Ⓑ Ⓒ Ⓓ Ⓔ

WRITING PRACTICE TEST 3

SECTION 1: MULTIPLE-CHOICE QUESTIONS

38 questions, 30 minutes

Directions: The following sentences require you to identify errors in grammar, usage, punctuation, and capitalization. Not every sentence has an error, and no sentence will have more than one error. Every sentence error, if there is one, is underlined and lettered. If the sentence does have an error, select the one underlined part that must be changed to make the sentence correct and blacken the corresponding circle on your answer sheet. If the sentence does not have an error, blacken circle E. Elements of the sentence that are not underlined are not to be changed.

Part A
21 questions

suggested time: 10 minutes

1. The woman with all the dogs walk down the street; she stopped to chat with
          A   B   C
    friends and neighbors along the way. No error.
          D   E

2. Although they were sophisticated and wealthy, the guests at the fancy banquet
                                                   A
    nonetheless surreptitiously set aside the pieces of meat for the dog that had been
                     B   C   D
    left on their plate. No error.
          E

3. After much consideration, the food critics decided that cod is a good fish, salmon
          A   B
    is even better, but lobster and shrimp are the most best of all. No error.
          C   D   E

4. My mother asked, "Please take the zip drive out of your father's computer and
                  A   B   C
    repair it." No error.
          D   E

5. Ricardo became interested in computer science, as a result, he decided to take a
                A   B   C
    summer school class in programming. No error.
          D   E

6. Tony's new puppy Spot <u>broke</u> his <u>mothers new vase</u> by jumping on the
                                    A   B

    <u>table, but</u> the puppy <u>was so endearing</u> that everyone just laughed. <u>No error.</u>
        C   D   E

7. The captain did not want to desert the sinking <u>ship but</u> once he <u>knew</u> his
                                                  A   B

    <u>passengers were safe</u> and the weather had <u>stabilized, he felt</u> secure enough to
          C   D

    leave. <u>No error.</u>
           E

8. <u>Cybil's speech</u> contained at least three clichés<u>:</u> <u>"A watched pot never boils,"</u>
       A   B   C

    "Look before you lea<u>p," and</u> "The early bird gets the worm." <u>No error.</u>
                        D   E

9. To get to the <u>Country Inn</u> where <u>you're staying this weekend,</u> drive six blocks
                       A   B

    <u>north</u> and then take the principal road <u>Main Street</u> five more blocks. <u>No error.</u>
       C   D   E

10. When you decide to take advantage of a <u>sale, the</u> line at the store entrance is
                                                     A

    <u>usually quite</u> <u>long, so</u> <u>one</u> should try to get around this crowd problem by
        B   C   D

    arriving at the store early. <u>No error.</u>
                               E

11. <u>The painter is so talented</u> that the art critic <u>decided</u> his pictures <u>belongs</u> in a
                A   B   C

    museum, such as the <u>Metropolitan Museum of Art in New York City.</u> <u>No error.</u>
                                              D   E

12. <u>My Grandmother</u> and most of the travelers to <u>famous sites</u> such as the <u>Pyramids at</u>
            A   B   C

    <u>Giza in Egypt and the Lascaux Caves in France</u> <u>were</u> amateur historians, not professional
                                              D

    archeologists. <u>No error.</u>
                E

13. For the <u>twins' birthday,</u> a hot-fudge sundae <u>with bananas</u> and chopped walnuts
                  A   B

    <u>was served</u> to each guest, <u>dripping with chocolate sauce.</u> <u>No error.</u>
       C   D   E

14. Between you and I, the garage sale across the street has much higher prices than
          A   B
the one on Main Street, but the latter does have a better selection. No error.
                   C   D   E

15. Rushing to finish the paper, Bob's printer broke, so he failed to meet the
           A   B   C D
deadline. No error.
         E

16. The press noted repeatedly that the jury consisted solely of people who had
                A   B
completed at least one year of education beyond high school, whose annual income
                                                                                  C
exceeded $60,000, and who had lived in the Miami area for at least 10 years. No error.
                                    D   E

17. All workers need a record of accomplishments when it comes time for their
          A   B
annual review be sure to keep a detailed list of your job responsibilities. No error.
             C   D   E

18. My cousins on my mother's side—Nick, Margo, and Ted—are nineteen, seventeen,
                       A   B   C
and fifteen, respectfully. No error.
               D   E

19. Ms. Berger described to Martha and I her plans for the new luxury spa
                                  A   B   C
in the revitalized downtown area. No error.
       D   E

20. The company's quarterly meetings consisted of reviewing the previous meeting's
                  A   B   C
minutes, hearing a financial report, and the president's plans for future expansion.
                                                             D
No error.
   E

21. Us girls cleaned the neighbor's yard as part of our student council community
    A   B   C   D
service. No error.
       E

Part B
17 Questions

suggested time: 20 minutes

Directions: Choose the best version of the underlined portion of each sentence. Choice A is the same as the underlined portion of the original sentence. If you think that the original sentence is better than any of the suggested revisions, choose A. Otherwise, choose the revision you think is best. Answers and explanations follow the questions.

22. The study of spiders is known as <u>arachnology those</u> who study spiders are arachnologists.

    (A) arachnology those
    (B) arachnology, and those
    (C) Arachnology those
    (D) arachnology, but those
    (E) arachnology, because those

23. Nicknamed "The Wizard of Menlo Park," <u>Thomas Edison being one</u> of the first inventors to apply the principles of mass production to the process of invention.

    (A) Thomas Edison being one
    (B) Thomas Edison be one
    (C) Thomas Edison was one
    (D) Thomas Edison one
    (E) Thomas Edison are one

24. Nearly half of all Americans attend at least 1 year of <u>college, but American</u> universities award many degrees for professional training that might be more efficiently and affordably accomplished on-the-job.

    (A) college, but American
    (B) college, American
    (C) college; American
    (D) college or American
    (E) college, if American

25. Mars has half the radius of the Earth and only one-tenth the <u>mass, but it's surface</u> area is only slightly less than the total area of Earth's dry land.

    (A) mass, but it's surface
    (B) mass, but its' surface
    (C) mass but its surface
    (D) mass, but its surface
    (E) mass; but it's surface

26. Films are produced by recording actual people and objects with cameras, or <u>you can create them</u> using animation techniques and/or special effects.

   (A) you can create them using
   (B) one can create them using
   (C) being created all of them by using
   (D) having created them using
   (E) by creating them using

27. According to legend, the Teddy Bear was created during a bear-hunting trip in Mississippi in <u>1902 President</u> Teddy Roosevelt refused to kill an old, injured bear.

   (A) 1902 President
   (B) 1902, President
   (C) 1902, when President
   (D) 1902; and President
   (E) 1902 because at that moment in historical time, President

28. <u>Walking back from the village, my wallet was lost.</u>

   (A) Walking back from the village, my wallet was lost.
   (B) As I was walking back from the village, I lost my wallet.
   (C) As I was walking back from the village, my wallet was misplaced.
   (D) My wallet was lost by me as I was walking back from the village.
   (E) The wallet was lost by me as I walked back from the village.

29. Despite the growth of flora in a rain forest, <u>the actual quality of the soil is quite poor.</u>

   (A) the actual quality of the soil is quite poor.
   (B) the actual quality of the soil is quiet poor.
   (C) the actual quality of the soil are quiet poor.
   (D) the actually quality of the soil is quite poorly.
   (E) the actual quality and quantity of the soil all around the region is quiet poor.

30. This way is <u>more quicker</u> than the other way, and there can be no doubt about that!

   (A) more quicker
   (B) more quickest
   (C) quicker
   (D) most quicker
   (E) most quickest

31. <u>Despite the fact that she was feeling a bit under the weather and not quite up to speed,</u> Harriet decided to go to her education class anyway.

(A) Despite the fact that she was feeling a bit under the weather and not quite up to speed,
(B) Despite the fact that she was feeling a bit under the weather,
(C) Despite the fact that she was feeling not quite up to speed,
(D) Although she was ill,
(E) Despite the fact that she was feeling ill and not quite up to speed,

32. My brother-in-law Jacques has a hot temper so he was real <u>careful</u> not to insult anyone at the party.

(A) real careful
(B) real carefully
(C) really carefully
(D) real carefuller
(E) really careful

33. Contrary to a common misconception, <u>DNA is not a single molecule; rather, it is</u> organized as two complementary strands, head-to-toe, with the hydrogen bonds between them.

(A) DNA is not a single molecule; rather, it is
(B) DNA is not a single molecule rather it is
(C) DNA is not a single molecule, rather, it is
(D) DNA is not a single molecule, rather its'
(E) DNA is not a single molecule rather it's

34. The book discusses how to build a profitable stock portfolio and <u>saving for college tuition expenses.</u>

(A) saving for college tuition expenses.
(B) one saving for college tuition expenses.
(C) how to save for college tuition expenses.
(D) people saving for college tuition expenses.
(E) putting aside sufficient savings for college tuition expenses.

35. In addition to clothing and other <u>handicrafts is</u> also used for items like parachutes, bicycle tires, comforter filling, and gunpowder bags.

(A) handicrafts is
(B) handicrafts, silk is
(C) handicrafts, it is
(D) handicrafts, is
(E) handicrafts; is

36. My mother's apple pie is without doubt the <u>worse tasting dessert</u>, even with ice cream on it.

 (A) worse tasting dessert
 (B) worse tasting desert
 (C) most worst tasting dessert
 (D) worst tasting dessert
 (E) worser tasting dessert

37. The car had <u>hardly no</u> systematic care, so it was falling apart and had actually become a hazard to drive.

 (A) hardly no
 (B) barely no
 (C) scarcely no
 (D) not quite no
 (E) hardly any

38. The first aid class being given at the local high school will concentrate either on water safety issues or <u>how to administer CPR.</u>

 (A) how to administer CPR.
 (B) on CPR.
 (C) methods of administering CPR.
 (D) being able to know how to administer CPR to people who are in respiratory distress.
 (E) ways to administer CPR.

STOP. This is the end of Section 1: Multiple-Choice Questions.

SECTION 2: ESSAY

30 minutes

Directions: Write an essay on the following topic. You will not receive any credit for writing on a topic other than the one given here. Plan your essay carefully and be sure to include specific examples and details that illustrate your point. Write your essay on your own sheets of paper. (On the real Praxis PPST test, paper for writing your essay will be provided.)

You will not receive credit if you write on any other topic. For your response to be scored, you must write in English. You cannot write in a foreign language.

Read the opinion stated below:

> "Criminals are born, not made. People who commit crimes have inherited faulty genes that predispose them to a life of crime, much as a person inherits the genes for blue eyes or curly hair."

In an essay, agree or disagree with this statement. But be sure to support your opinion with specific examples from reading, your experiences, your observations, or the media. The space below is for your notes.

WRITING PRACTICE TEST 3: ANSWERS

SECTION 1: MULTIPLE-CHOICE

Part A

1. B. This sentence has faulty subject-verb agreement. The subject and verb must agree in number: both must be singular or both must be plural. The verb agrees with the subject, not with a noun or pronoun in the phrase. Don't be misled by a phrase that comes between the subject and the verb. In this sentence, the subject is the *woman*, which is singular. Thus, it takes the singular verb *walks*, not the plural verb *walk*. Ignore the intervening prepositional phrase *with all the dogs*.

2. D. This is a misplaced modifier. Modifiers are words and phrases that describe. To make your intended meaning clear, place a modifier as close as possible to what it describes. The modifier in this sentence is *that had been left on their plate*. As the sentence reads, the dog—not the meat—had been left on their plate. The sentence should read: *Although they were sophisticated and wealthy, the guests at the fancy banquet nonetheless surreptitiously set aside the pieces of meat that had been left on their plates for the dog.*

3. D. This is a faulty comparison. Use the comparative form (*more* or *-er*) to compare two things. Use the superlative form (*most* or *-est*) to compare three or more things. NEVER use "more" or "most" with *-er* or *-est*; you get one or the other. The sentence should read: *After much consideration, the food critics decided that cod is a good fish, salmon are even better, but lobster and shrimp are the best of all.*

4. D. This is a faulty pronoun reference. Always make sure that the pronoun has a clear antecedent, the word to which it refers. Here, the pronoun "it" could refer to the zip drive or the computer. In these instances, use the noun instead of the pronoun to avoid confusion.

5. B. This is a run-on sentence, two complete sentences (independent clauses) run together or incorrectly joined. Two sentences can be joined with a coordinating conjunction (*for, and, nor, but, or, yet, so*) or with a semi-colon. They can be divided into two sentences by using a period, too. In this instance, correct the sentence by using a semi-colon in place of the comma. Or, you can create two sentences by using a period in place of the comma.

6. B. Use an apostrophe with a noun (NEVER with a pronoun) to show ownership. The new vase belongs to the mother, so the phrase should read *mother's new vase*.

7. A. Use a comma before a coordinating conjunction (*but*) that joins two complete sentences.

8. E. This sentence does not have an error. It is correct as written.

9. A. This is an error in capitalization. There is no reason to capitalize "country inn" because it is not a proper noun, or the title of anything.

10. D. This is a shift in pronoun person. The sentence starts with the pronoun *you* and then shifts to the pronoun *one*. Stay with the same pronoun throughout a sentence.

11. C. This is an error in subject-verb agreement. The plural verb *pictures* requires the plural verb *belong*, not the singular verb *belongs*.

12. A. This is an error in capitalization. Capitalize titles showing family relations when the title is used with the person's name. Exception: Do not capitalize the title when it comes after a possessive noun or pronoun, as is the case here.

13. D. This is a misplaced modifier. As you read earlier, modifiers are words and phrases that describe. Place a modifier as close as possible to what it describes to make your meaning clear. The modifier in this sentence is *dripping with chocolate sauce*. As the sentence reads, the twins—not the hot-fudge sundae—was served dripping with chocolate sauce. The sentence should read: *For the twins' birthday, a hot-fudge sundae with bananas and chopped walnuts dripping with chocolate sauce was served to each guest.*

14. A. Both pronouns are objects of the preposition *between* and so should be in the objective case: *Between you and me.*

15. A. This is a dangling participle. A present participle is a verb ending in *-ing* ; it is called *dangling* when the subject of the *-ing* verb and the subject of the sentence do not agree. In the sentence given, the subject is Bob's printer, but the printer isn't doing the rushing. You can correct the sentence this way: *While Bob was rushing to finish the paper, his printer broke,* . . . . One way to tell whether the participle is dangling is to put the phrase with the participle directly after the subject of the sentence and see if it sounds logical. In this instance, *Bob's printer, rushing to finish the paper, broke, so he failed to meet the deadline* sounds illogical so you know that it is incorrect.

16. E. The sentence is correct as written.

17. C. This is a run-on sentence, two complete sentences (independent clauses) run together or incorrectly joined. Two sentences can be joined with a coordinating conjunction (*for, and, nor, but, or, yet, so*) or a semi-colon. Correct this sentence by placing a semi-colon after *review*. Or, create two sentences by using a period after *review* and capitalizing B in *Be*.

18. D. This is a usage error. *Respectfully* means "with respect or full of respect" ("The reporters listened respectfully to the senator's request.") *Respectively* means "each in the order given." This is the word needed to complete the meaning of the sentence in this example.

19. A. This is an error in pronoun case. *Ms. Berger* is the subject because she is doing the action. Therefore, *Martha and me* are the objects, requiring the pronoun in the objective case, *me*.

20. D. This is faulty parallel structure. Parallel structure means using the same pattern of words to show that two or more ideas have the same level of importance. This can happen at the word, phrase, or clause level. The correct sentence should read: *The company's quarterly meetings consisted of reviewing the previous meeting's minutes, hearing a financial report, and evaluating the president's plans for future expansion.* The clauses <u>reviewing</u> the previous meeting's minutes, <u>hearing</u> a financial report, and <u>evaluating</u> the president's plans for future expansion are now all parallel.

21. A. This is an error in pronoun case. Use the subject case "We" because we are doing the action. Read the sentence without the noun to hear the error: *We cleaned* sounds correct; *Us cleaned* sounds awkward.

Part B

22. B. This is a run-on sentence, so-called because two sentences are run together. Two independent clauses (two complete sentences) can be joined with a coordinating conjunction (*for, and, nor, but, or, yet, so*) or a semi-colon. Of the choices offered here, only B correctly and logically joins the two sentences.

23. C. The phrase *being that* is considered substandard usage. In its place, use the correct past tense of the verb "to be," *was*.

24. A. This sentence is correct as written. Choice C is correct, but choice A is more logical. Thus, it is better writing.

25. D. *It's* is a contraction for the words "it is," but the sentence requires the possessive pronoun *its*. Study the following chart to help you distinguish between contractions and possessive pronouns:

Contractions	Possessive Pronouns
it's	its
you're	your
they're	their
who's	whose

Also, use a comma before a coordinating conjunction (*for, and, nor, but, or, yet, so*) that links two sentences. This eliminates choice C.

26. E. This is a faulty parallel structure. Parallel structure means using the same pattern of words to show that two or more ideas have the same level of importance. This can happen at the word, phrase, or clause level. The correct sentence should read: *Films are produced by recording actual people and objects with cameras, or by creating them using animation techniques, and/or special effects.* The words *recording* and *creating* create parallel phrases.

27. C. This is a run-on sentence, so-called because two sentences are run together. Two independent clauses (two complete sentences) can be joined with a coordinating conjunction (*for, and, nor, but, or, yet, so*) or a semi-colon. Or, one of the sentences can be made into a dependent clause by using a subordinating conjunction (such as *when, although, because, since*). Choice C does just that:

> *According to legend, the Teddy Bear was created during a bear-hunting trip in Mississippi in 1902,*
>> independent clause

> *when President Teddy Roosevelt refused to kill an old, injured bear.*
>> dependent clause

Notice the subordinating conjunction "when" in the second part of the sentence. It starts the dependent clause.

28. B. This is a dangling participle. A present participle is a verb ending in *-ing;* it is called "dangling" when the subject of the *-ing* verb and the subject of the sentence do not agree. In this sentence, the subject is *my wallet,* but the wallet is not doing the walking. The correct sentence should read: *As I was walking back from the village, I lost my wallet.* Choice C is incorrect because it changes the meaning. Choices D and E create passive constructions. In the passive voice, the action is done to the subject. The active voice, where the subject does the action, is more direct and concise. Thus, it is better writing.

29. A. This sentence is correct as written.

30. C. In the comparative case, you compare two people, places, or things. Use *-er* or *more* to create the comparison—never both.

31. D. This sentence is wordy. The phrase *despite the fact that* is much better stated as the simple *although.*

32. E. Use an adverb to modify (describe) a verb, adjective, or other adverb. Use an adjective to modify nouns and pronouns. The word *careful* is an adverb, so you need an adverb to modify it. *Real* is an adjective, and *really* is an adverb. Hint: Many adverbs are formed by adding *-ly* to an adjective.

33. A. This sentence is correct as written.

34. C. This is a faulty parallel structure. Parallel structure means using the same pattern of words to show that two or more ideas have the same level of importance. This can happen at the word, phrase, or clause level. The correct sentence should read: *The book discusses how to build a profitable stock portfolio and how to save for college tuition expenses.* The phrases "how to" are parallel. Choice E is very wordy, so it can be eliminated right away.

35. B. This sentence is a fragment because it is missing the subject. Ask yourself: "What is also used for items like parachutes, bicycle tires, comforter filling, and gunpowder bags?" Only choice B provides a clear subject. Choice C has a subject—the pronoun *it*—but we don't know what it refers to.

36. D. This is a faulty comparison. With regular adjectives and adverbs, use the comparative form (*more* or *-er*) to compare two things. The words *good* and *bad* are irregular, however. Study this chart:

Positive	Comparative	Superlative
good bad	better worse	best worst

The sentence should read: *My mother's apple pie is without doubt the worst tasting dessert . . .*

37. E. This is a double negative: the words *hardly* and *no* are both negative. Use a single negative word to convey negation. Only choice E is a single negative word.

38. B. This is faulty parallel structure. Parallel structure means using the same pattern of words to show that two or more ideas have the same level of importance. This can happen at the word, phrase, or clause level. The correct sentence should read: *The first aid class being given at the local high school will concentrate either on water safety issues or on CPR.*

Skills Spread

Specific Content Area	Item Numbers
Grammar and usage	1, 3, 4, 10, 11, 13, 14, 18, 19, 21, 30, 32, 36
Sentence structure	2, 5, 15, 17, 20, 22, 26, 27, 28, 29, 33, 34, 35 , 38
Mechanics (punctuation, capitalization)	
Diction (word choice)	6, 7, 8, 9, 12, 16, 23, 24, 25, 31, 37
Essay	1

SECTION 2: ESSAY

The following model essay would receive a 6, the highest score, for its specific details, organization, and style (appropriate word choice, sentence structure, and consistent facility in use of language). It is an especially intelligent and insightful response.

Criminality: Nature or Nurture?

As far back as recorded time, we've struggled to find out why people commit crimes. What would make a seemingly "normal" person—someone just like you or me—suddenly veer off the track of civilized behavior? Some people believe that criminal genes are inherited; others, that criminal behavior is learned. While genetics may indeed play a role in antisocial actions, the environment plays a far more critical role in the formation of a criminal.

Cesare Lombroso, an Italian anthropologist in the late nineteenth century, was one of the first to propose that criminality was inherited. Clearly influenced by the prejudices of his time, Lombroso argued that criminality was essentially a reversion to a less-evolved state and thus could clearly be observed in individuals possessing primitive physical attributes such as large jaws, high cheekbones, long arms, and insensitivity to pain. Today we laugh at such nonsense, recognizing that Jay Leno's lantern jaw doesn't predispose him to life in the Big House any more than Cher's high cheekbones signal a vacation at the government's expense. But theories such as this die hard. Today, some scientists argue that low levels of the neurotransmitter serotonin result in poor self-control and high impulsivity. The science has clearly become more sophisticated, but whether or not it's any less preposterous is open to debate. Every day it seems like the *New York Times* is running an article informing us that low levels of serotonin are responsible for migraines, shyness, anxiety, pessimism, and obsessive-compulsive disorder. About the only thing we can be sure of in all this media hype about genes is that your behavior affects the way people react to you.

When you find out that people are anxious or pessimistic or engage in repetitive behaviors, you're less likely to reach out to them. We reject those who are different and may require a bit more effort on our part. Our rejection is more powerful than any genetic factors. If it is true that low levels of serotonin cause impulsive behavior, society reinforces this through harsh and punitive discipline. Suspending little Johnny from school for a week because he hit little Billy teaches Johnny only that a free vacation is just one black eye away. We haven't taught Johnny to deal with and channel his anger and aggression, only that he's disposable like a used tissue. If a group of children decides to ignore little Sally because she's too bashful to speak up, Sally may decide to make her actions speak louder than her words. After all, even negative reinforcement provides some attention.

The jury is still out on the issue of genes causing criminality, but the jury has long returned its verdict on environment: we have the power to help others. The key issue is your political stance and support of others. Lombroso's arguments were used to support the eugenics movement in the United States. This led to the forced sterilization of over 20,000 prisoners in the early twentieth century. But we have power to change things for the better. We can support treatment and social programs that encourage literacy, lift kids from poverty, and teach adults to be responsible parents. We can support social programs that reduce drug dependency and treat chronic illnesses, too.

MATHEMATICS PRACTICE TEST 3

Answer sheet

1 Ⓐ Ⓑ Ⓒ Ⓓ Ⓔ
2 Ⓐ Ⓑ Ⓒ Ⓓ Ⓔ
3 Ⓐ Ⓑ Ⓒ Ⓓ Ⓔ
4 Ⓐ Ⓑ Ⓒ Ⓓ Ⓔ
5 Ⓐ Ⓑ Ⓒ Ⓓ Ⓔ
6 Ⓐ Ⓑ Ⓒ Ⓓ Ⓔ
7 Ⓐ Ⓑ Ⓒ Ⓓ Ⓔ

8 Ⓐ Ⓑ Ⓒ Ⓓ Ⓔ
9 Ⓐ Ⓑ Ⓒ Ⓓ Ⓔ
10 Ⓐ Ⓑ Ⓒ Ⓓ Ⓔ
11 Ⓐ Ⓑ Ⓒ Ⓓ Ⓔ
12 Ⓐ Ⓑ Ⓒ Ⓓ Ⓔ
13 Ⓐ Ⓑ Ⓒ Ⓓ Ⓔ
14 Ⓐ Ⓑ Ⓒ Ⓓ Ⓔ

15 Ⓐ Ⓑ Ⓒ Ⓓ Ⓔ
16 Ⓐ Ⓑ Ⓒ Ⓓ Ⓔ
17 Ⓐ Ⓑ Ⓒ Ⓓ Ⓔ
18 Ⓐ Ⓑ Ⓒ Ⓓ Ⓔ
19 Ⓐ Ⓑ Ⓒ Ⓓ Ⓔ
20 Ⓐ Ⓑ Ⓒ Ⓓ Ⓔ
21 Ⓐ Ⓑ Ⓒ Ⓓ Ⓔ

22 Ⓐ Ⓑ Ⓒ Ⓓ Ⓔ
23 Ⓐ Ⓑ Ⓒ Ⓓ Ⓔ
24 Ⓐ Ⓑ Ⓒ Ⓓ Ⓔ
25 Ⓐ Ⓑ Ⓒ Ⓓ Ⓔ
26 Ⓐ Ⓑ Ⓒ Ⓓ Ⓔ
27 Ⓐ Ⓑ Ⓒ Ⓓ Ⓔ
28 Ⓐ Ⓑ Ⓒ Ⓓ Ⓔ

29 Ⓐ Ⓑ Ⓒ Ⓓ Ⓔ
30 Ⓐ Ⓑ Ⓒ Ⓓ Ⓔ
31 Ⓐ Ⓑ Ⓒ Ⓓ Ⓔ
32 Ⓐ Ⓑ Ⓒ Ⓓ Ⓔ
33 Ⓐ Ⓑ Ⓒ Ⓓ Ⓔ
34 Ⓐ Ⓑ Ⓒ Ⓓ Ⓔ
35 Ⓐ Ⓑ Ⓒ Ⓓ Ⓔ

36 Ⓐ Ⓑ Ⓒ Ⓓ Ⓔ
37 Ⓐ Ⓑ Ⓒ Ⓓ Ⓔ
38 Ⓐ Ⓑ Ⓒ Ⓓ Ⓔ
39 Ⓐ Ⓑ Ⓒ Ⓓ Ⓔ
40 Ⓐ Ⓑ Ⓒ Ⓓ Ⓔ

MATHEMATICS PRACTICE TEST 3

40 questions, 60 minutes

Directions: Select the best choice for each item and mark the answer on your answer sheet.

1. How many obtuse angles are in a right triangle?

(A) 0
(B) 1
(C) 2
(D) 3
(E) Cannot be answered from the information given

2. Which pairs of decimals and fractions are equivalent?
I. 0.125, ⅛   II. 0.25, ⅜   III. 0.6, ⅗

(A) I only
(B) II only
(C) I and II
(D) II and III
(E) I, II, and III

3. If $\frac{x}{3} + 6 = 12$, then $x =$

(A) 2   (B) 6   (C) 10
(D) 12   (E) 18

4. If the scale on a model is 1 inch: 10 feet and a house is 2.5 inches tall, how tall would the actual house be?

(A) 0.25 feet   (B) 2.5 feet   (C) 10 feet
(D) 25 feet   (E) 250 feet

5. If 1 liter of water takes up 1,000 cubic centimeters of volume, then how much water will fit in a cubic container that is 20 centimeters on each side?

(A) 1 liter   (B) 0.2 liter   (C) 0.4 liter
(D) 0.8 liter   (E) 8 liters

6. What is 23,450,000,000 expressed in scientific notation?

(A) 23.45×10^9 (B) 23.45×10^{10} (C) 2.345×10^9
(D) 2.345×10^{10} (E) -2.345×10^{-10}

7. Myra is making up her new diet plan. If her breakdown of calories is shown on the following chart, approximately what percentage of them come from fat?

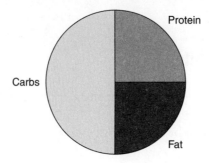

(A) 4 percent
(B) 10 percent
(C) 25 percent
(D) 50 percent
(E) 100 percent

8. "All dice have six sides, and all cubes have six sides." Which of the following statements is true according to the statement above?

(A) All dice are cubes.
(B) Some dice are cubes.
(C) No dice are cubes.
(D) Things with four sides are not cubes.
(E) Anything with six sides must be a die or a cube.

9. Which of the following is true?

(A) $\frac{9}{7} < 1.1$ (B) $\frac{5}{4} = 1.25$ (C) $\frac{7}{14} = 0.14$

(D) $\frac{5}{6} > 1$ (E) $\frac{1}{10} > 0.1$

10. Which of the following fractions is not equivalent to the other four?

(A) $\frac{1}{3}$ (B) $\frac{9}{27}$ (C) $\frac{1}{9}$ (D) $\frac{6}{18}$ (E) $\frac{4}{12}$

11. If I need one-third of a pound of beef to feed one hungry teenager, how many pounds do I need to feed 12 hungry teenagers?

(A) ⅓ (B) 1 (C) 3
(D) 4 (E) 12

12. Which answer is closest to 20,997 ÷ 7,134?

(A) 1 (B) 3 (C) 300
(D) 700 (E) 1200

13. If I roll two fair dice, what percentage of the time will I roll the same number on both?

(A) 0.16 percent
(B) 6.0 percent
(C) 10.0 percent
(D) 16.7 percent
(E) 166.7 percent

14. Using 3.14 for π, what is the area of a circle with a diameter of 10 inches?

(A) 31.4   (B) 78.5   (C) 157
(D) 246.5   (E) 314

15. If $12x - 9 = 3y$, and $y = 5$, then $x =$

(A) 2   (B) 3   (C) 9
(D) 15   (E) 24

16. What is the surface area of a cube that is 7 inches per side?

(A) 49 square inches
(B) 294 square inches
(C) 294 cubic inches
(D) 343 square inches
(E) 343 cubic inches

17. The length of the hypotenuse of a right triangle is 10 inches and one of the legs is 6 inches long. How long is the other leg?

(A) 4 inches
(B) 6 inches
(C) 8 inches
(D) 10 inches
(E) 11.7 inches

18. To convert yards to inches, you should

(A) divide by 12
(B) multiply by 12
(C) divide by 36
(D) multiply by 36
(E) divide by 3

19. For the set $(1, 5, 5, 9, 10, 12)$, 5 is the

    (A) mean
    (B) median
    (C) mode
    (C) range
    (E) none of the above

20. If you have the choice of three kinds of pasta and five sauces, how many different dishes can you make using one type of pasta and one sauce?

    (A) 3   (B) 5   (C) 8
    (D) 15   (E) 120

21. If I flip a fair coin 10 times, and it comes up heads each time, what is the probability it will come up heads on the eleventh flip?

    (A) 0   (B) $\frac{1}{10}$ (C) $\frac{9}{10}$
    (D) $\frac{99}{100}$ (E) $\frac{1}{2}$

22. Five waitresses received the following tips. Whose was the greatest?

    (A) 10 percent of $100
    (B) 10 percent of $200
    (C) 15 percent of $200
    (D) 20 percent of $125
    (E) 15 percent of $150

23. Which point on the graph is located at $(3, -2)$?

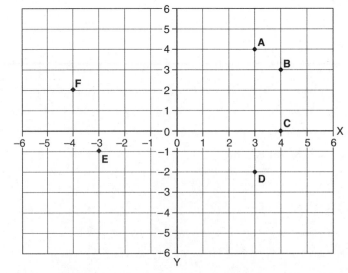

    (A) A   (B) B   (C) C
    (D) D   (E) F

24. If the probability of picking a king from a deck of cards is ⅓, then if you randomly picked 26 cards out of the deck, about how many would be kings?

(A) 0   (B) 1   (C) 2
(D) 13   (E) 26

25. To convert centimeters to kilometers, you should

(A) divide by 100
(B) multiply by 100
(C) divide by 100,000
(D) multiply by 100,000
(E) multiply by 1,000,000

26. If $2x + 4 = 9x - 10$, then $x =$

(A) 2   (B) 6   (C) 10
(D) 12   (E) 18

27. The chart above shows the amount of profit a company earns for a given number of employees and computers. If the company has 40 employees, how many computers should it buy in order to have the greatest profit?

	Employees				
	10	**20**	**30**	**40**	**50**
1	30	32	34	36	38
2	25	60	62	64	66
3	20	55	90	92	94
4	15	50	85	120	122
5	10	45	80	115	150
6	5	40	75	110	145

(Computers, rows 1–6)

(A) 1   (B) 2   (C) 3
(D) 4   (E) 5

28. Which decimal is least?

(A) 0.0112
(B) 0.0985
(C) 0.006445
(D) 0.008211
(E) 0.00715

29. Which of these numbers is 3,457,746 NOT evenly divisible by?

(A) 2   (B) 3   (C) 4
(D) 6   (E) 9

30. What is 6.72×10^{-4} in standard notation?

(A) 6,720
(B) 67,200
(C) 0.00672
(D) 0.000672
(E) 0.0000672

31. Which formula describes the relationship between X and Y shown below?

X	Y
2	2
6	4
14	8
18	10
22	12

(A) $Y = X$
(B) $Y = 3X - 2X$
(C) $Y = 2X - 2$
(D) $Y = \dfrac{X}{2} + 1$
(E) $Y = 2X + 2$

32. Which of the following is $\sqrt{2}$?

(A) A real number
(B) A rational number
(C) An integer
(D) A counting number
(E) An imaginary number

33. Which of these fractions is the greatest?

(A) $\dfrac{2}{3}$ (B) $\dfrac{2}{11}$ (C) $\dfrac{12}{18}$ (D) $\dfrac{6}{100}$ (E) $\dfrac{4}{5}$

34. Number of Papers Written

Smith	☺ ☺ ☺
Jones	☺ ☺ ☺ ☺
Brown	☺ ☺

Each ☺ represents 4 papers.
How many papers have Smith and Jones written in total?

(A) 4   (B) 7   (C) 9
(D) 16   (E) 28

35. After a meal, three friends have the check split evenly among them. Each person's bill comes to $23.33. If they each leave a 15 percent tip, what does the total tip come out to?

(A) $3.50

(B) $10.50

(C) $15.00

(D) $31.50

(E) $70.00

36. Which of the following is the best estimate of 395,673 × 996?

(A) 400,000

(B) 4,000,000

(C) 400,000,000

(D) 4,000,000,000

(E) 400,000,000,000

37. If a > b and b > c, which of the following is FALSE?

(A) a > c

(B) c < b

(C) b < a

(D) b = b

(E) c > a

38. $4\frac{2}{8} = \frac{x}{12}$. Solve for x.

(A) 3

(B) 9

(C) 27

(D) 51

(E) 408

39. What is the probability of flipping a fair coin three times and having it come up heads all three times?

(A) ½

(B) ¼

(C) ⅛

(D) ¹⁄₁₆

(E) ¹⁄₆₄

40. What is the mean of the following set: 1, 1, 5, 5, 7, 14, 23?

(A) 1

(B) 5

(C) 7

(D) 8

(E) 22

STOP. This is the end of Mathematics Practice Test 3.

MATHEMATICS PRACTICE TEST 3: ANSWERS

1. A. An obtuse angle is greater than 90°. The angles in a triangle must add up to 180°. If a right triangle has one right angle (which equals 90°), then the other two angles must be less than 90° each so that they can add up to 180°.

2. B. $\frac{1}{8} = 0.125, \frac{3}{9} = 0.\overline{3}$. Change fractions to decimals by dividing.

3. E. $\frac{x}{3} + 6 = 12$, subtract 6 from both sides so $\frac{x}{3} = 6$, then multiply both sides by 3, $x = 18$.

4. D. Use equivalent fractions. $\frac{1}{10} = \frac{2.5}{x}, x = 25$.

5. E. The volume of a cube is the length of any side raised to the third power. $20^3 = 8,000$. Then set up equivalent fractions: $\frac{1}{1000} = \frac{x}{8000}, x = 8$.

6. D. $2.345 \times 10^{10} = 23,450,000,000$, and proper scientific notation uses a number between 1 and 10.

7. C. The chart shows approximately one-quarter of the calories from fat. ¼ = 25 percent.

8. D. You know that all dice have six sides, and all cubes have six sides. You don't know how many, if any, dice are also cubes. You also don't know how many other six-sided objects exist besides dice and cubes, or how they overlap. All you can determine is that if all cubes have six sides, then something that does not have six sides cannot be a cube.

9. B. $\frac{5}{4} = 1\frac{1}{4} = 1.25$.

10. C. $\frac{1}{3} = \frac{4}{12} = \frac{6}{18} = \frac{9}{27}$.

11. D. $\frac{1}{3} \times 12 = \frac{12}{3} = \frac{4}{1}$.

12. B. Round to the nearest thousand: $21,000 \div 7,000 = 3$.

13. D. $\frac{6}{36} = \frac{1}{6} = 0.167 = 16.7$ percent.

14. B. Area of a circle $= \pi r^2$. $r = \frac{1}{2}d$, so $r = 5$ inches. $3.14 \times 5^2 = 78.5$.

15. A. $12x - 9 = 3(5)$, add 9 to both sides so $12x = 24$, then divide both sides by 12, $x = 2$.

16. B. Each side is a square, and the area is $7 \times 7 = 49$ square inches. 49×6 sides $= 294$ square inches. Cubic inches would be used to measure the volume of the cube.

17. C. Use the Pythagorean theorem. $6^2 + b^2 = 10^2 => 36 + b^2 = 100 => b^2 = 64 => b = 8$.

18. D. 1 yard = 3 feet = 36 inches.

19. C.   The mode is the number that appears most often in the set.

20. D.   This is a combination problem. $3 \times 5 = 15$.

21. E   Each flip is an independent event. The probability that the coin will come up heads is still $\frac{1}{2}$ each time.

22. C.   Multiply to find each tip. $30 is greatest.

23. D. $(3, -2)$ means 3 over and 2 down.

24. C. $\frac{1}{13} \times 26 = 2$.

25. C.   100,000 centimeters = 1 kilometer.

26. A. $2x + 4 = 9x - 10$, subtract $2x$ from both sides so $4 = 7x - 10$, add 10 to both sides so $14 = 7x$, then divide both sides by 7, $x = 2$.

27. D.   Four computers give a profit of 120, which is higher than any of the other possibilities.

28. C.   Find the number with the most leading zeroes, then compare the first nonzero place if two are tied.

29. C.   3,457,746 is evenly divisible (can be divided without a reminder) by 2, 3, 6, and 9.

30. D. 10^{-4} means you should move the decimal point four places to the left.

31. D.   Trial and error. Try all of the pairs in each equation and find which one works for all of them.

32. A. $\sqrt{2}$ is irrational, which means it is not a rational number, an integer, or a counting number; but it is real, not imaginary.

33. E.   You can cross multiply to show ⅘ is greater than each of the others.

34. E.   Each ☺ = 4, and there are 7 of them. $7 \times 4 = 28$.

35. B. $(23.33 \times 0.15) \times 3 = 10.50$.

36. C. $395,673 \times 996$ rounds to $400,000 \times 1,000 = 400,000,000$.

37. E. $a > c$, so c cannot be greater than a.

38. D.   First change the mixed numbers into improper fractions, then cross multiply: $\frac{34}{8} = \frac{x}{12}$, $408 = 8x$, $x = 51$.

39. C. $\frac{1}{2} \times \frac{1}{2} \times \frac{1}{2} = \frac{1}{8}$.

40. D. $\frac{1 + 1 + 5 + 5 + 7 + 14 + 23}{7} = \frac{56}{7} = 8$.